William B. Ruger Chair of National Security Economics Papers

Number 3
Defense Strategy and Forces: Setting Future Directions

Proceedings
A Workshop Sponsored by the
William B. Ruger Chair of National Security Economics
Newport, Rhode Island
13–15 November 2007

Richmond M. Lloyd, editor
William B. Ruger Chair of National Security Economics

Naval War College
Newport, Rhode Island

The Naval War College expresses appreciation to the Naval War College Foundation, through the generosity of the William B. Ruger Chair of National Security Economics, in the preparation and presentation of this workshop.

The views expressed in the William B. Ruger Chair of National Security Economics Papers are those of the authors and do not necessarily reflect the opinions of the Naval War College or the Department of the Navy.

Correspondence concerning the Ruger Papers may be addressed to Richmond M. Lloyd, William B. Ruger Chair of National Security Economics, Naval War College, 686 Cushing Road, Newport, RI 02841-1207; by telephone at 401.841.3669; or by e-mail at richmond.lloyd@nwc.navy.mil. Our website is http://www.nwc .navy.mil/academics/courses/nsdm/rugerpapers.aspx.

ISBN 978-1-884733-51-2

Printed in the United States of America

Contents

Introduction

Workshop Focus

The purpose of this workshop is to provide a collegial forum for a small and select group of defense strategists and force planners to formulate and recommend strategic and force choices for the future.

Workshop Background

The nation is in the sixth year of war since 9/11. The FY 2008 Defense budget request of $481.4 billion and the Global War on Terror request of $141.7 billion, if approved, will represent the tenth year of robust growth in defense spending since its low point in the late 1990s. Even given these resource levels, the Department of Defense faces significant strategic and force choices as it attempts to deal with today's realities and prepare for future challenges. Today's realities include the war on terrorism; stability and reconstruction operations in Iraq and Afghanistan; significant OPTEMPO, PERSTEMPO, readiness, and quality of life issues; and the costs of resetting and recapitalizing the forces, among others. Future challenges include the attention given to irregular, catastrophic, and disruptive, as well as traditional, challenges; new operational concepts; force structure and end strength choices; active and reserve component realignments; R&D, modernization, and procurement bow waves; the reorientation of U.S. global defense posture; and joint and interagency unity of effort.

This workshop addresses security challenges and strategy; defense resources and risks; land, maritime, air, space, and special operations forces; and joint interagency efforts. The primary focus is on strategic and force choices for the future.

Workshop Venue and Format

A total of thirty-seven individuals participated in this by-invitation-only workshop held at the Naval War College in Newport, Rhode Island. The college and its staff provide a professional environment to facilitate small group workshops in exploring their specific issues.

Panelists prepared and presented their papers (approximately three to four thousand words) on topics of their choice within the subject areas of their respective panels. Following a presentation of each panelist's paper, all participants engaged in extensive discussion of the papers and of the focus of the panel. All discussions were conducted under a nonattribution policy.

All papers (some longer versions have been included) and summaries of working-group discussions (prepared by each panel moderator) are included in this monograph. The monograph is being widely distributed within the national security community and the general public. The monograph is also available electronically at http://www.nwc.navy.mil/academics/courses/nsdm/rugerpapers.aspx.

William B. Ruger Chair of National Security Economics

The Ruger Chair was established to support research and study on the interrelationships between economics and security. A fundamental premise is that without security it is difficult to have economic prosperity and without prosperity it is difficult to have security.

The intent of this Ruger Chair–sponsored workshop is to support individual research, publication, and a continuing dialogue on matters important to national security economics. It is hoped that research done for this workshop will provide participants with the building blocks for further research and publication.

Agenda

Defense Strategy and Forces:
Setting Future Directions

A Workshop Sponsored by
William B. Ruger Chair of National Security Economics
Naval War College, Newport, Rhode Island
13–15 November 2007

Tuesday, 13 November 2007

1840   Depart Hotel

1900   Welcome Dinner, Officers' Club, Naval Station Newport

Wednesday, 14 November 2007

0740   Depart Hotel

0800   Welcome Continental Breakfast, Decision Support Center

0835   Opening Remarks

> *Rear Admiral Jacob L. Shuford, U.S. Navy, President,*
> *U.S. Naval War College*

0845   Panel I: Security Challenges and Strategy

> *Dr. Robert J. Art, Christian A. Herter Professor of*
> *International Relations, Brandeis University*
>
> *Dr. Ashton B. Carter, Preventive Defense Project, Kennedy*
> *School of Government, Harvard University*
>
> *Moderator: Dr. Bradford A. Lee, Philip A. Crowl Chair in*
> *Comparative Strategy, U.S. Naval War College*

1015   Break

1030   Panel II: Defense Resources and Risks

> *Dr. J. Michael Gilmore, Assistant Director for National*
> *Security, Congressional Budget Office*
>
> *Dr. Cindy Williams, Principal Research Scientist, Security*
> *Studies Program, Massachusetts Institute of Technology*
>
> *Moderator: Professor Thomas C. Hone, Joint Military*
> *Operations Department, U.S. Naval War College*

1200   Lunch, RADM Joseph Strasser Dining Room

1330   Panel III: Land Forces

> *Colonel H. R. McMaster, U.S. Army, Senior Research Associate, International Institute for Strategic Studies*
>
> *Mr. David A. Shlapak, Senior Analyst, RAND Corporation*
>
> *Moderator: Dr. Mackubin Thomas Owens, Associate Dean of Academics for Electives and Directed Research, and Professor, National Security Decision Making Department, U.S. Naval War College*

1500   Break

1515   Panel IV: Maritime Forces

> *Dr. Geoffrey Till, Professor of Maritime Studies, Defence Studies Department, King's College London*
>
> *Mr. Robert O. Work, Vice President for Strategic Studies at the Center for Strategic and Budgetary Assessments*
>
> *Mr. Ronald O'Rourke, Naval Analyst, Congressional Research Service of the Library of Congress*
>
> *Moderator: Dr. Thomas R. Fedyszyn, Security, Strategy, and Forces Course Director, National Security Decision Making Department, U.S. Naval War College*

1645   Adjourn

1650   Return to Hotel

1845   Depart Hotel

1900   Dinner, La Forge Casino Restaurant

Thursday, 15 November 2007

0740   Depart Hotel

0800   Continental Breakfast, Decision Support Center

0845   Panel V: Air and Space Forces

> *Lieutenant General David A. Deptula, U.S. Air Force, Deputy Chief of Staff for Intelligence, Surveillance, and Reconnaissance, Headquarters, U.S. Air Force*
>
> *Mr. Barry D. Watts, Senior Analyst at Center for Strategic and Budgetary Assessments*

Mr. Dean Cheng, Research Fellow, Center for Naval Analyses Corporation

Moderator: Professsor Roger H. Ducey, Associate Professor, National Security Decision Making Department, U.S. Naval War College

1015 Break

1030 Panel VI: Joint Special Operations Forces

Dr. Richard Shultz, Professor of International Politics, Director, International Security Studies Program, The Fletcher School, Tufts University

Dr. David C. Tucker, Associate Professor, Department of Defense Analysis, Naval Postgraduate School

Moderator: Commander Thomas C. Sass, U.S. Navy, Professor of Joint Military Operations, U.S. Naval War College

1200 Lunch, RADM Joseph Strasser Dining Room

1315 Panel VII: Joint Interagency

Ms. Michèle A. Flournoy, President and Cofounder, Center for a New American Security

Ms. Donna L. Hopkins, Plans and Policy Team Lead in the Office of Plans, Policy, and Analysis, Bureau of Political-Military Affairs, Department of State

Captain Kevin C. Hutcheson, U.S. Navy, Deputy Director for Interagency Integration, J9 Interagency Partnering Directorate, U.S. Southern Command

Moderator: Ms. Deborah A. Bolton, State Department Advisor to President, U.S. Naval War College

1445 Concluding Remarks

Dr. Richmond Lloyd, William B. Ruger Chair of National Security Economics, U.S. Naval War College

1500 Adjourn

1515 Depart to Airport

Participants:

Vice Admiral K. K. Nayyar, Indian Navy (Retired), Chairman, National Maritime Foundation, India

Professor Gwyn Prins, Director, LSE MacKinder Centre, The London School of Economics and Political Science, United Kingdom

Rear Admiral Bill Burke, U.S. Navy, Director, Assessment Division, OPNAV N81

Rear Admiral Frank C. Pandolfe, U.S. Navy, Commander, Carrier Strike Group Two

Mr. Richard Diamond, Strategic Assessments, Raytheon Integrated Defense Systems

Mr. Charles B. Dixon, Senior Managing Consultant, Strategy and Change, IBM Global Business Services

Dr. R. Robinson Harris, Director, Advanced Concepts, Lockheed Martin

Mr. Adam B. Siegel, Senior Analyst, Northrop Grumman Analysis Center

Dr. Peter Dombrowski, Chairman, Strategic Research Department, U.S. Naval War College

Dr. Timothy D. Hoyt, Professor of Strategy and Policy, U.S. Naval War College

Dr. Derek S. Reveron, Associate Professor, National Security Decision Making Department, U.S. Naval War College

Professor Sean Sullivan, Workshop Administrative Assistant and Assistant Professor, National Security Decision Making Department, U.S. Naval War College

Opening Remarks

Rear Admiral Jacob L. Shuford, USN
President, Naval War College

Welcome! We need to start moving! I have to tell you I'm happy this morning to see that some of you did not take me literally last evening when I said during the course of our lively dinner conversations that "we had resolved all of the issues that were up for discussion," and relieved that you in fact recognize that we have *not* exhausted all of those things that we need to deal with over the course of the two-day workshop! Thanks, and to those of you that weren't able to join us yesterday evening, welcome to the Naval War College and to Newport. Welcome to the third William B. Ruger Workshop. We call it a "workshop" because, as you can see,

this is not a conference. It's not an auditorium full of folks that are auditing the discussion and taking notes and going off in some corner somewhere. This is designed to be a very aggressive, forward-leaning discussion to continue to make sure the edge you leave with is sharper than the one you brought. That's the great benefit of off-the-record, unfettered, expert discussion from diverse, authoritative, and informed perspectives. That's what we think we are doing here. If the earlier two conferences or workshops are any indication of things to come, this is going to produce a lot of good discussion and some very, very valuable insights. It will move things.

It has been a very rewarding year since then-CNO [chief of naval operations] Admiral Mike Mullen challenged the Navy to develop a new maritime strategy—one "of and for its time." This new strategy was rolled out in October at the International Seapower Symposium here in Newport. It is important to note that the effort was informed by last year's Ruger Workshop, where we focused on national security issues in terms of economics and maritime strategy. It was fairly narrowly focused, but we were aware that you cannot talk about a maritime strategy, or really any strategy, without the orientation of a grand strategy.

As the Navy continued its deliberations on what we need most to do with our own forces as a function of our national policy—our grand strategy—there were a number of conversations that went on among me and many others (some of you here today) that recognized we have not yet arrived at a clear consensus regarding U.S. grand strategy. Those conversations have evolved—through the tri-service "Cooperative Strategy for the 21st Century"—to provide a basis for this Ruger Workshop.

Most, if not all, of you have had an opportunity to read this new maritime strategy. You note, I am sure, the prominence given to the relationship among maritime capability and capacity, sustaining a robust peace, and global prosperity. It articulates a powerful logic and explicitly elevates war prevention to a position alongside the war-winning function of the Navy.

I believe the new strategy to be compelling in its fundamental logic, which, therefore, cannot be ignored as we continue to evolve this nation's grand strategy and our notion of how military—and particularly naval—forces must be structured and employed to provide the greatest utility in the geostrategic landscapes we currently survey.

We have built some intellectual momentum that I hope this workshop will help maintain. Thanks for your willingness to participate and for spending time with us here in Newport.

A few notes on the process and analysis behind the work here at the Naval War College. It has been a very different kind of strategy development process. In the words of Paul Bracken, "it represents a break with recent U.S. strategic thinking in that it did not start with the answer." I am not saying that we started with a completely blank sheet of paper, but we did free ourselves of preexisting biases on desired fleet size or shape. In fact, we all but banned any discussion of ships, submarines, and aircraft, focusing instead on the relationship between grand strategy and sea power.

By maintaining that discipline throughout the project, I think we achieved one of then-CNO Mullen's going-in goals: to elevate the discussion to create a broader definition of sea power. By doing so, the maritime services worked together to produce the "front-end piece" that so many decision makers have been wanting for a number of years. I believe this new maritime strategy gives us the overarching logic of how sea power serves the interests of the Republic, and I anticipate that it will be an influential document for years to come.

Part of its influence will be due to the way we went about crafting it—openly and collaboratively. Instead of sticking a couple of bright commanders in a cipher-locked room and not letting them out until they produced a classified strategy, we laid all our cards on the table from the outset and invited everyone, including as many foreign navies as we could link up with, to give us their ideas. Thus the strategy the service chiefs presented in October to maritime leaders from around the world (from ninety-eight countries—the largest convocation of top naval leadership in history) has a genuine joint, interagency, and international pedigree, with solid intellectual underpinnings. Thus my expectation that it will be robust and durable.

Despite the strategy's strong pedigree, I don't think anyone would consider it a finished product in the sense that we can now put it in a drawer and go on to other things. Quite the contrary: it will take a lot more tending before we reap the harvest from this effort. If history is any guide, a number of years will unroll before the implications of the new strategy are completely understood. It took several decades for us to sort out the program and resource implications of War Plan Orange, and the 1980s Maritime Strategy was still being refined and interpreted when the Soviet Union fell. So I think we will be discussing, analyzing, arguing, and gaming the new strategy for years to come. It is my expectation that this workshop, convened here today, will, in the tradition established since the inaugural Ruger conference in 2005, serve to focus academic and policy-making genius on those issues that cry out most urgently for understanding and action.

It is only proper, therefore, that we have invited you, very distinguished and highly respected national security experts, to take stock of what we have accomplished, and then to further weigh the propositions of our new strategy and its implications for national policy and force choices for the future.

We expect the product from this effort in the form of a widely distributed monograph to have significant impact as we as a nation examine and debate our way ahead in achieving security and prosperity. Thank you for investing yourselves in this endeavor.

Panel I

Security Challenges and Strategy

Dr. Robert J. Art
Christian A. Herter Professor of International Relations, Brandeis University

Dr. Ashton B. Carter
Preventive Defense Project, Kennedy School of Government, Harvard University

Moderator:
Dr. Bradford A. Lee
Philip A. Crowl Chair in Comparative Strategy, U.S. Naval War College

America's Grand Strategy after Bush

Dr. Robert J. Art
Christian A. Herter Professor of
International Relations
Brandeis University

Introduction

The United States today stands at the pinnacle of its power when measured in terms of its capabilities vis-à-vis other states. It is the mightiest state in the world militarily. It has the world's largest single national economy, which is three times larger than that of its nearest national competitor (Japan) when measured in nominal dollars, and somewhere between 20 percent and 100 percent larger than China's when measured in purchasing power parity.[1] It is the world's most economically competitive economy, and it continues to exert a cultural influence globally that no other state can match.[2] Yet, while its hard power assets remain unrivaled and its cultural appeal remains extensive, its political appeal, if not influence, is significantly diminished from where it was in the decade after the cold war's end; its image as a positive force in world politics is at low ebb; and the legitimacy of its international actions in the eyes of other states has reached its lowest point since the end of World War II.[3]

Why is the gap so large between America's hard power assets and cultural appeal, on the one hand, and its legitimacy, image, and general standing in the eyes of others, on the other? Has the country been pursuing the wrong interests, or has it been pursuing the right interests but in the wrong way? Does its grand strategy need major adjustment and if so, in what ways? To answer these questions, I first lay out U.S. interests in the current era; then I set forth the grand strategies available to it, together with the one I believe best suited to realizing these interests; and finally, I highlight a key task for the next administration, whatever its political complexion.

America's National Interests

The United States has six fundamental national interests in the current era. They are, first, to protect the homeland from attack; second, to keep a deep peace among the Eurasian great powers; third, to preserve assured access to stable supplies of oil; fourth, to preserve an open international economic order; fifth, to spread democracy and the rule of law, protect human rights, and prevent mass murders in civil wars; and sixth, to avert severe climate change.[4]

The first goal requires that the United States prevent the spread of weapons of mass destruction (WMD), especially nuclear and biological, to more states and keep such weapons out of the hands of terrorists. The second requires that the United States retain its two central alliances at either end of Eurasia—the NATO alliance and the United States–Japan alliance. The third requires that the United States act in ways that prevent any state, from within the region or from without, acquiring hegemony over Persian Gulf oil supplies. The fourth requires that the United States maintain its commitment to international economic openness and use its military power in ways that preserve global stability. The fifth requires that the United States help foster political liberalization and the rule of law within states and promote economic development that helps create the large middle classes upon which stable democracies depend, as well as acting in concert with other states to stop or prevent mass murder in ethnic and civil wars that has already begun or is highly likely to occur. The sixth requires that the United States and the world first cut and then stabilize the emissions of CO_2 and its equivalents into the atmosphere at levels that avoid severe climate change.

Why Are These Goals in America's Interests to Pursue?

When it comes to homeland security, the United States faces no state-centered threat of attack, either conventional or nuclear. No state, except the United States, is capable of launching transoceanic conventional attacks; consequently, there is no conventional threat to the U.S. homeland. Similarly, the United States need not fear nuclear attack from hostile states because deterrence works between nuclear-armed state actors. In the hands of states, nuclear weapons are weapons par excellence of defense. The only serious threat to the American homeland comes from terrorist groups, like al Qaeda, that would use weapons of mass destruction—either for blackmail or attack—if they had them. Avoiding grand terror attacks against the U.S. homeland necessitates, in turn, doing two things: limiting nuclear and biological spread to state actors, and locking down better than has been done to date fissile material in the hands of states. The reason for the latter is obvious: terrorist theft of fissile material enables terrorists to bypass the most difficult step in acquiring nuclear weapons. The reason for the former should also be clear: the more states that have nuclear weapons, the greater are the chances that fissile material can fall into the hands of nonstate actors, especially when we consider some of the likely candidates for state acquisition of nuclear weapons. Whereas terrorist acquisition of nuclear weapons is the near-term threat of greatest severity to the United States, the biological threat will probably be the more serious in the medium to longer term because of the continuing advances in modern biology, and it is harder to control the spread of biological weapons than nuclear ones.

A deep peace among the Eurasian great powers means that none of them seriously contemplate war with others in order to resolve their inevitable political conflicts. Keeping the peace deep among these powers has many advantages for the United States. It preserves economic openness (wars lead to economic closure), it avoids intense security competitions (these can encourage nuclear and biological spread), and it averts big Eurasian great power wars (they have traditionally dragged in the United States). Keeping the peace deep in western Eurasia is easy because of the current and foreseeable state of relations among the European great powers. This task is more difficult in eastern Eurasia because of the rivalry between a Japan used to being number one in the area and a rising China that no longer cedes that position to Japan, but it is by no means impossible. There are many things the United States can do to help keep the Eurasian great power peace deep, but one clearly stands out: preserve its two central alliances in Eurasia—NATO in Europe and the United

States–Japan alliance in East Asia. These two alliances reassure America's allies, help deter war, dampen down political conflicts, generally help to maintain stable great power relations, give the United States fairly reliable allies, and provide bases from which to exert global influence.

Preserving assured access to stable oil supplies is necessary as long as the United States and the rest of the world remain so dependent on oil to run their economies. Because it contains two-thirds of the world's proven reserves of oil and at least one-third of its proven natural gas supplies, the Persian Gulf area must, of necessity, remain of vital interest to the United States, even though it obtains only about 16 percent of its oil imports from the Gulf. The world oil market is highly integrated; big disruptions in one area affect supply and price globally. Because Gulf oil currently supplies about 40 percent of the oil consumed globally every day, and is projected to supply even a greater percentage a decade or two from now, the United States must prevent any power—external or internal to the region—from disrupting the flow of oil out of the Gulf. The 2003 Gulf War eradicated the Iraqi threat to the stable flow of Gulf oil; Iran is now beginning to take Iraq's place.

The fourth interest may not be as important as the first three, but it is, nonetheless, highly important to the United States. An open international economic order benefits a country as efficient and competitive as the United States because such an order translates into more exports and overseas investment, and cheaper imports and consumer goods, than would otherwise be the case. An open international economic order facilitates economic growth in other states (the record shows that those developing states whose economies are more open to the international economy grow faster than those whose economies are more closed to it), and economic growth, in turn, helps generate the middle classes upon which are built stable and mature democracies. Finally, to the extent that states believe they can prosper through trade, not war, international openness can be a force for peace among states.

The fifth interest of the United States—to promote the spread of democracy and to prevent mass murder in ethnic and civil wars—is a combination, respectively, of self-interest and moral duty. By fostering political liberalization, the rule of law, economic development, and the generation of large middle classes in the developing world, the United States will help create societies that are more likely to be democratic, rich, satisfied, respectful of human rights, and more peaceful than if these societies remain poor, nondemocratic, and more conflict prone, both internally and externally. A world in which democracy is spreading is clearly preferable on hard-headed grounds for the United States than one in which democracy is in retreat.

The injunction to prevent or stop mass murder is a moral imperative for the United States. Clearly, it cannot intervene in every civil war in the world; neither the United States nor the international community has either the political will or the resources to do this. But in cooperation with other states, the United States, out of moral conscience, can and should act to stop the worst civil wars—those that experience or that are likely to experience the mass murder of noncombatants.[5] Such interventions not only save lives; they can, if done properly, which requires a considerable investment of resources and a prolonged international presence in the affected states, rescue failing or failed states from capture by extremist groups that may provide shelter to terrorists, and perhaps even help promote the spread of democracy.

The sixth interest of the United States—to cut CO_2 emissions so as to avert severe climate change—is either highly important or vital, depending on the severity of climate change. Because it is rich and technologically advanced, the United States, under moderate warming scenarios (2 to 3 degrees centigrade), will be less hard hit by global warming than the poorer states in that it will be better able to adapt than they. Even if it suffers less, however, the United States will still suffer. All sections of the country will be affected, although unevenly; the costs of adaptation will be large; and public-sector budgets will be under severe strain.[6] Even worse is eventually in store for the United States if the Greenland ice sheet continues to contract because that will lead to a significant rise in sea level measured in meters, which, in turn, will directly affect the 53 percent of Americans living in coastal regions.[7] Finally, should global warming continue, there is the distinct possibility that the earth could be kicked into a new climatic state that could have catastrophic consequences for human life. Past evidence concerning large climate changes suggests this could occur over decades, not centuries.

Over the next 50 years, as a consequence of the previous 150 years of CO_2 emissions by the rich, industrialized states, the earth's average temperature will inevitably rise, and hence climate change will occur. The only questions now are how large the temperature increase will be and how extensively the climate will change. Both depend critically on what actions are taken over the next decade or so. Thus, because of the potentially large costs to the United States, and especially because of the risk of triggering a dramatic change to a new and more adverse climatic state for human life, arresting the rise in global temperature and averting severe climate change are clearly in America's interest, and U.S. action is all the more imperative because other states, notably China, are unlikely to take serious steps to limit their CO_2 emissions unless the United States does also.[8]

Available Grand Strategies

If these are America's overarching interests in the current era, what realistic grand strategies are there to protect them? I count four: "muscular Wilsonianism," which is the neoconservative strategy of the first George W. Bush administration; offshore balancing, which is the preferred position of those who call for a wholesale withdrawal of the United States from military involvement in global affairs; a policy of restraint, advocated by Barry Posen of MIT; and selective engagement, which I have advocated. The first two are at opposite ends of a continuum running from extensive military involvement abroad at one end (muscular Wilsonianism) to little or no such involvement at the other (offshore balancing). The strategies of restraint and selective engagement are somewhere in the middle of these two extremes, with selective engagement more activist than restraint.

The central elements of muscular Wilsonianism are these: preventive war against rogue states on the cusp of acquiring weapons of mass destruction; the spread of democracy through force of arms; a belief that states bandwagon, not balance, in the face of the ruthless exercise of superior power; and a strong dose of unilateralism and the downplaying of multilateral institutions, especially the United Nations. This was the policy of George W. Bush in his first term, and all four of these elements combined to produce an aggressive, in-your-face grand strategy.

Not surprisingly, the world pushed back. America's image abroad is in shambles, and its legitimacy, as noted above, is at low ebb. Democratic spread in Iraq is proceeding badly, and America's European allies have refused to help the United States in Iraq and have not fully met their commitments in Afghanistan. In general, the United States is suffering from the "Lippmann gap": its commitments exceed the resources available to meet them. The policy of waving the big stick backfired and instead of bringing Iran and North Korea to heel, it pushed both to accelerate their nuclear programs, engaging in "asymmetric balancing" against the United States. Whatever success has been achieved with North Korea in Bush's second term is due to the fact that the Bush administration changed tack and offered carrots as well as sticks to North Korea, thereby returning basically to the Clinton administration approach.

Muscular Wilsonianism is not a viable policy in an era when there is no overarching threat to unite states, when the United States needs the cooperation of other states against terrorism, when nationalism remains a strong force in international politics, and when America's economic and military dominance over others will inevitably decline in the years ahead as other centers of power arise. The strategy will only backfire against the United States if pursued in the future, as it has during the first Bush administration. The fact that the Bush administration itself backed away from the strategy during the second term speaks volumes about its viability.

Offshore balancing is at the other extreme of the continuum. Its central elements are an end to America's alliances abroad; the return of American troops to the United States; a willingness to use force abroad in the sparest way—primarily to prevent a regional hegemon from arising in Eurasia, rescue Americans in trouble, and maintain freedom of the seas; a belief that local balances of power will form after the recession of American power and that these balances will protect, or at least not harm, U.S. regional interests; and a conviction that the projection of military power abroad is not required to protect America's political and economic interests, except for the three specific cases noted above. Under an offshore balancing strategy, the United States will decide when to use force, where to use force, with whom to use force, and against whom to use force. It will not be bound in peacetime by any standing military commitments because it will have none. Offshore balancing is best described as the policy of the "completely free hand."[9]

This is not a strategy well suited to protect America's interests in the current and foreseeable era. It removes the United States as a key buffer and stabilizer in Eurasia, especially in northeast Asia and the Persian Gulf. It will abet, not retard, nuclear spread as states, again especially in northeast Asia and the Persian Gulf, find that they have to fend for themselves because they will no longer be under the U.S. nuclear umbrella. It forgoes the opportunity to help shape regions along lines conducive to U.S. political and economic interests. It does little if anything to assure the free flow of oil out of the Persian Gulf, and it belies the empirical fact that markets only operate well if they are embedded in a political framework that is partially supported by force. An offshore balancing strategy is a reactive, not a shaping, strategy, and it will put the United States at the mercy of international events, rather than allowing it to help shape them.

The third grand strategy—the strategy of restraint—is advocated by Barry Posen.[10] Its thrust is to scale down what the United States does internationally with its military forces and to be smarter in the use of its political instruments. Its central elements are a belief that since the end of the cold war the United States has tried to do too much—not only trying to control international events, but also to transform societies, both of which are beyond American power; a prescription, therefore, that the United States should be less ambitious in its goals, working to shape rather than control international events and working indirectly rather than directly to spread democracy by concentrating on those practices that help foster democracy, such as the rule of law and a free press; a rebalancing of America's alliances, which means removing all American troops from Europe over a decade, and getting Japan to do more, although Posen is not specific as to what the latter means; a lowering of America's profile in the Arab world by getting rid of permanent and semipermanent bases on Arab soil, and instead relying on U.S. power projection capabilities; a counterterrorism strategy that relies heavily on other states' local security forces; and an eschewing of preventive war in favor of containment and deterrence of hostile states armed with nuclear weapons.

There is much to commend in this strategy, but several of its features will harm, not help, America's interests as defined above. Its call for withdrawing all U.S. troops from Europe is not wise because an effective NATO alliance is more likely with some U.S. military presence on the continent than with none, and because Europe still serves a useful logistical function for deployments in central Asia and the Middle East. A complete withdrawal from an onshore presence in the Persian Gulf is not wise either, given the rise of Iranian power, and flies in the face of several of the Gulf sheikhdoms that want the United States there. Moreover, while the U.S. Navy is central in maintaining the free flow of oil through the Persian Gulf, nonetheless, its task is much easier if supplemented by land-based air, which requires onshore bases. The strategy's call for a rebalancing of the United States–Japan alliance is unclear in its content and misses the fact that much has happened in that regard already.[11] The strategy of restraint makes more sense for the United States under current and foreseeable circumstances than either muscular Wilsonianism or offshore balancing, but not as much sense as selective engagement.

As I have defined it, selective engagement is a shaping strategy.[12] Its central elements are the retention of America's key alliances in Europe (NATO), East Asia (United States–Japan alliance), and the Persian Gulf (Kuwait, Saudi Arabia, and the smaller Gulf sheikhdoms); the retention of a forward defense posture—that is, the basing of American troops in these three regions for deterrence, reassurance, and, when necessary, war-waging purposes; the continued extension of the American nuclear umbrella to key allies of the United States so as to discourage further nuclear proliferation among them; the selective use of U.S. military power for intervention in humanitarian crises according to clear-cut criteria;[13] the avoidance of excessive ambition and excessive unilateralism; the need to take allies' interests into account when formulating policies, which means compromising, not simply consulting; the necessity for American leadership if collective-action failures are to be avoided; a counterterrorism policy that does not allow the campaign against terrorism to hijack America's grand strategy, but that also does not allow policies in other areas to undermine the counterterrorism strategy; a political-military posture that emphasizes containment and deterrence toward hostile, nuclear-armed states, on the one hand, and preemption and prevention against terrorists, on the other; and finally, a posture that is shaping, not merely reactive.

For reasons laid out at length elsewhere, I believe this strategy best protects America's interests in the current and foreseeable international environment.[14] If properly implemented, selective engagement is superior to its above three competitors. It is more likely to avoid backlash and balancing against America's use of military power, or at least minimize those two, than muscular Wilsonianism because it eschews excessive unilateralism and ambition, and because it takes into account the interests of key regional allies in framing policy. It avoids the Lippmann gap by the judicious use of American military power. It better preserves America's key alliances and their stabilizing roles in Europe, East Asia, and the Persian Gulf through maintenance of a forward presence than does the strategy of restraint. It assures the free flow of Persian Gulf oil through an onshore and offshore military presence there better than either the strategy of restraint or offshore balancing. It helps to preserve an open international economic order by providing a stable political-military framework within which the international economy operates, something offshore balancing does not provide. It advances the spread of democracy through the generation of wealth and the expansion of middle classes that an open international economic order facilitates. Finally, even if indirectly, it can help combat climate change by making the world more stable, and hence better able to muster the resources necessary to deal with climate change, than if the world were more conflictual than is now the case.

For all these reasons, selective engagement should be the preferred grand strategy of the four.

Restoring Legitimacy

Let us return to the questions posed at the outset of this essay. What has gone wrong with America's foreign policy since 2001? Why is the country's international standing so low? Has the United States been pursuing the wrong interests, or has it been pursuing the right interests but in the wrong way?

It is hard to argue that the six national interests set out above are not to America's advantage to pursue. Imagining the converse shows why: doing nothing to stop WMD terrorist attacks, permitting intense arms racing and crises among the Eurasian great powers, ignoring the security of oil supplies, allowing economic closure to occur, permitting the rollback of democracy, doing nothing to avert severe climate change. Clearly, then, it cannot be that the interests the United States has pursued (or should be pursuing in the case of climate change) are misplaced. The explanation lies elsewhere.

Two factors explain the precipitous decline in America's global standing over the last seven years. First is America's overwhelming power, especially military power; second is the foolish manner in which the Bush administration has wielded it. It is the arrogant, unilateralist way that the Bush administration has used America's overweening power that has proved a deadly combination to America's global standing.[15] The reasons why are clear.

Great concentrations of power have always caused concern in world politics. There is an inevitable amount of resentment, fear, and wariness that a powerful state engenders in others just by being so powerful, no matter how benign that state may be, and the more powerful the state, the greater the concern, resentment, fear, and wariness. Enemies of powerful states fear that they are the object at which the great power is directed; allies worry that the powerful state will either drag them into situations from which they prefer to remain aloof, or will bring in train effects that will redound adversely against them. The United States today is the world's only superpower (the condition called unipolarity), and, as a consequence, it engenders concern in enemies and allies alike.

Paradoxically, the more powerful a state is, the greater the care it has to take in how it utilizes its power. It has to be especially mindful of how its actions affect others and how they look to others. By its foolish approach, the Bush administration enhanced and magnified the inevitable worries that America's unipolar condition engenders in others. What was an emerging concern in the last years of the Clinton administration became a torrent in the Bush administration. Bush made an underlying problem much, much worse than it needed to be.

The single most important thing the next administration must do for U.S. foreign policy is to rectify this situation by restoring America's legitimacy. Right now, the United States looks to too much of the rest of the world like a malign hegemon. The task for the next administration is a tough one: to make the United States look like a benign hegemon, while at the same time advancing America's national interests by employing the considerable power that the nation wields in world politics.

Structure is not destiny. America's unipolar position does not condemn it to being hated and distrusted by the rest of the world, even though a certain amount of fear and envy will be there. After all, the United States was as powerful, if not more powerful, under Clinton than under Bush (because China was not as strong and the European Union not as cohesive when Clinton was president), but the image of the United States was much more positive. Agency has a role to play here: good policies can make a difference. No great power can wholly remove the concerns that others have about its power, but these concerns can be mitigated through proper policies. The place to begin is to avoid excessive ambition and excessive unilateralism, which are the all-too-natural impulses of a state as powerful as the United States is today.[16] If properly conceived and executed, the strategy of selective engagement can reverse the damage that Bush has inflicted on America's grand strategy and global image.

Notes

1. These comparisons are based on 2006 figures in trillions of dollars. Nominal and purchasing power parity (PPP) figures, respectively, are United States, $13,228 and

$12,939; Japan, $4,421 and $4,069; China, $2,530 and $10,581. See International Monetary Fund (IMF), *World Economic Outlook* (Washington, DC: 2007), available at http://www.imf.org/external/pubs/ft/weo/faq.htm. Using IMF figures puts the U.S. GDP 20 percent larger than China's; using new World Bank calculations for China's GDP in 2005 PPP figures puts the U.S. GDP about 100 percent (twice as large) as China's GDP, because new World Bank calculations put China's output at roughly 40 percent less than the bank's previous estimates. See Keith Bradsher, "A Revisionist Tale: Why a Poor China Seems Richer," *New York Times*, 21 December 2007, p. C1. For geopolitical comparisons and weight in the global economy, as Richard Cooper argues, nominal dollars are superior to PPP dollars. (See Richard N. Cooper, *Chinese Economic and Budgetary Prospects*, testimony before the US-China Economic and Security Review Commission, 7 December 2001, available at http://www.uscc.gov/textonly/transcriptstx/tescpr.htm.)

2. World Economic Forum, *Global Competitiveness Report, 2007–2008* (Palgrave Macmillan, 2007), available at http://www.weforum.org/en/initiatives/Global%20Competitiveness%20Report/index. In the report's words: "The United States confirms its position as the most competitive economy in the world."

3. For example, in January 2007, a BBC World Service poll taken in twenty-five countries found that one in two citizens felt the United States was playing a "mainly negative" role in the world. See World Public Opinion.Org, "World View of US Role Goes from Bad to Worse," http://www.worldpublicopinion.org/incl/printable_version.php?pnt=306.

4. For fuller analysis, see Robert J. Art, *A Grand Strategy for America* (Ithaca: Cornell University Press, 2003), chap. 2.

5. By mass murder, I mean the deliberate killing of more than fifty thousand noncombatants within a 5-year period. By this criterion, 20 to 25 percent of civil wars since 1945 have experienced mass murder. This definition of mass murder comes from Benjamin Valentino's *Final Solutions: Mass Killing and Genocide in the 20th Century* (Ithaca: Cornell University Press, 2004), pp. 10–16; the 20–25 percent figure for civil wars comes from Art, *A Grand Strategy for America*, pp. 151–152.

6. For details, see *The US Economic Impacts of Climate Change and the Costs of Inaction: A Review and Assessment by the Center for Integrative Environmental Research (CIER) at the University of Maryland* (CIER, October 2007), executive summary, available at http://www.cier.umd.edu/climateadaptation/index.html.

7. The percentage of Americans living in coastal areas comes from Art, *A Grand Strategy for America*, p. 74. According to the Intergovernmental Panel on Climate Change, gaps in current scientific understanding about sea-level rise do not permit a clear upper limit for the rise. Current models do not predict significant melting of the Antarctic ice sheet. See Intergovernmental Panel on Climate Change, *Climate Change 2007: Synthesis Report; Summary for Policymakers*, Intergovernmental Panel on Climate Change Fourth Assessment Report (16 November 2007), pp. 8 and 13, available at http://www.ipcc.ch/pdf/assessment-report/ar4/syr/ar4_syr_spm.pdf.

8. For a comprehensive analysis of how the United States can reduce CO_2 emissions, see Jon Creyts et al., *Reducing U.S. Greenhouse Gas Emissions: How Much at What Cost?* (McKinsey and Company, December 2007), available at http://mckinsey.com/clientservice/ccsi/greenhousegas.asp.

9. The best proponent of this strategy is Christopher Layne. See Christopher Layne, *The Peace of Illusions: American Grand Strategy from 1940 to the Present* (Ithaca: Cornell University Press, 2006), chap. 8.

10. See Barry R. Posen, "The Case for Restraint," *American Interest*, (November/December 2007), pp. 7–17; and Barry R. Posen, "Restraining Order," *American Interest* (January/February 2008), pp. 1–4. The latter is Posen's reply to commentators on his November/December article.

11. See, for example, Richard Samuels, *Security Japan: Tokyo's Grand Strategy and the Future of East Asia* (Ithaca: Cornell University Press, 2007), chaps. 6 and 7.

12. Art, *A Grand Strategy for America*, chap. 4 and, for a nutshell description, pp. 223–226.

13. Ibid., pp. 146–157.

14. Ibid., chaps. 3 and 6.

15. The precipitous decline in America's standing begins with the Bush administration and was especially steep with the onset of the 2003 Iraq War. See Stephen M. Walt, *Taming American Power: The Global Response to U.S. Primacy* (New York: W.W. Norton, 2006), p. 97 and more generally chap. 2, for documentation on the precipitous decline in U.S. legitimacy and an analysis of the reasons for it.

16. As I wrote in 2003: "It is all too tempting for the United States, like every powerful state of the past, to believe that it can impose its will on others; succeed where others before have failed; make rules for others but violate the rules itself; ignore the counsel of others because it is so easy to go its own way; and ride roughshod over others' interests to serve its own. These temptations must be resisted because they would lead to certain ruin." Art, *A Grand Strategy for America*, p. 234.

Defense Management Challenges in the Post-Bush Era

Dr. Ashton B. Carter
Preventive Defense Project
Kennedy School of Government
Harvard University

Defense leaders in the coming decade will inherit three categories of daunting challenges.

The first category, of course, includes ongoing operations in Iraq, Afghanistan, and the Balkans, and against Islamist extremism, none of which are going to end entirely anytime soon. To these must be added the threats from North Korea's and Iran's runaway nuclear programs, which have burgeoned in the first decade of the twenty-first century. And then there will be the still-unpredictable but near-certain crises that will arise in Africa, the Middle East, or elsewhere.

Second, these immediate challenges will need to be met against the sad necessity to restore or "reset" some of the traditional sources of American influence and effectiveness in the world. The project to restore the U.S. position to its rightful place will take years, but a new administration will need to begin it immediately. We will need to reset our global leadership by repairing alliances and security partnerships that in some cases have become badly frayed. We will need to reset our reputation, in the eyes of much of the world, for thoughtful deliberation in how we choose our strategic intentions and—even more worryingly—our reputation for simple competence in executing them. Both of these have been called into question in connection with Iraq. We will need to reset civil-military relations, which have become strained in the minds of many, most especially military leaders both senior and junior. In some quarters we will even need to restore our honor, which has been seen to be compromised by excesses such as Abu Ghraib, Guantánamo, and waterboarding. These are huge challenges, and it will take time to meet them. But I'm confident that we will.

But a third category of challenges for the next administration's national security leadership, less discussed but equally demanding, concerns the management of investment in the future—budgets, programs, and the strategy-resources match, or mismatch. This third category is the topic of my remarks today.

The strategy-resources mismatch is of concern because of several factors that will impinge upon the defense program, quickly and severely, early in the term of the next president:

- A likely leveling of the Defense top line. The American people will certainly not be demanding a "peace dividend," because they will realize there is no peace at hand. But neither is there likely to be a continuation of the rapid upward trend that has put DoD total obligational authority (TOA) 60 percent higher today (even excluding supplemental funding) than on 9/11.

- The very real possibility that supplemental funding (now a third of Defense spending) will be cut faster than the actual commitment in Iraq can be safely curtailed. This will mean that activities and some new and innovative programs now funded in the supplementals will be forced to compete with the program of record for survival.

- The related possibility that ground-force reset costs will be higher than currently forecasted.

- A bow wave resulting from a failure to take account of cost growth in weapons systems and defense services, meaning that the actual expenditures needed to fund the forces programmed will probably exceed those budgeted by a wide margin.

- The inexorable encroachment of health care and other personnel and current operating costs on the portion of the Pentagon's budget that invests in future forces—procurement and research, development, test, and evaluation (RDT&E).

- The government's uncertain overall fiscal position, especially in the event of a downturn in the economy—its willingness to tax, borrow, or make cuts elsewhere to fund DoD's needs.

- Growing evidence of the need to improve acquisition practices, program management, and system engineering skills in both government and the defense industry.

Added to these Defense Department issues are wider issues of national security capability and management, where our edge in marshaling all elements of national power is not nearly as sharp as that of our military prowess. An edge of excellence outside of Defense must be created to match the edge our military forces possess. Among the challenges, which will be addressed by Michèle Flournoy later in this workshop, are:

- The continuing need to build a better capacity to protect America and its friends from violent extremism and terrorism, which requires investment outside of the Defense Department as well as within it: in intelligence, law enforcement, homeland security, foreign assistance, and diplomacy.

- The crippling inadequacy of the non-Defense instruments of crisis intervention: civil reconstruction, political stabilization, and interagency coordination and command.

- Frayed alliances and security partnerships and a palpable diminution in U.S. moral authority and ability to persuade, as revealed in extensive and consistent worldwide polling data as well as lack of success in building new coalitions and maintaining long-standing alliances.

- Lack of willingness or capacity in many countries, including important allies, to share the burden with the United States by augmenting and complementing our own efforts.

It is against this background that we must consider defense strategy for the future, which is the guide to investment.

The future is uncertain to be sure. But while there might be talk about "known unknowns" and "unknown unknowns," five future requirements are in fact pretty well known. They provide a sturdy basis for realistic planning and programming for Defense. The U.S. national security establishment, including especially DoD, will need to be able, in parallel, to (1) conduct irregular stability operations in difficult politico-military circumstances; (2) combat violent extremists, including radical Islamist terrorists; (3) hedge against an unlikely but possible downturn in U.S.-China relations; (4) prevent and protect against weapons of mass destruction (WMD) threats; and (5) continue to overmatch possible adversaries on the conventional battlefield.

Each of these missions requires investment in future defense forces. Each requires, in fact, very different types of investment. Since it is not easy to imagine a future world in which the need for any one of these five missions would disappear entirely, the Pentagon leadership in the post-Bush era must find a way to do them all, spreading available resources over them in a thoughtful investment portfolio.

It is also difficult to imagine having enough forces and dollars to do everything possible to accomplish each of the five missions in the portfolio. There will accordingly be some risk inherent in any investment plan to accomplish this multitasking strategy. The investment plan for Defense must therefore do what planners call "accept risk," and it must allocate that risk within each of the five mission areas and among the different mission areas.

In recent years, the long-established processes in DoD to manage risk and set budgets have been undermined. The Defense budget has increased by more than half since 9/11 in inflation-adjusted dollars, while huge supplementals have been added for Iraq. The result has been good in one way—adequate funding for Defense—but in other ways has been corrosive of the processes and discipline that ensure that strategy and budgets align.

The task of Defense leaders in the post-Bush era will be to explain the portfolio strategy and to win the support of Congress and the American people for the needed investments. The remarks that follow describe the principles that should guide Defense investments in the coming years for each of the five mission areas in the portfolio.

Conducting Irregular Stability Operations in Difficult Politico-military Circumstances

Projected ongoing operations in Iraq (while probably diminishing), Afghanistan, and the Balkans and possible future operations in many locations (the Horn of Africa and Darfur among them) all point in different ways to this broad requirement for Defense in the future. This complex of missions comprises stability operations, postconflict reconstruction, peacekeeping, counterinsurgency, and other related types of mission. There are important distinctions among these concepts, and they need to be applied differently to each situation. But they result in a common Defense requirement—relatively large multipurpose ground forces capable of operating among civilian populations with strong self-protection and minimal harm to friendly civilians. Outside of Defense, this mission requires better U.S. civilian capabilities and interagency coordination, and outside of the U.S. government it requires international burden sharing.

Much as America would like to leave the field of irregular warfare behind and return to an era of traditional military-versus-military warfare, almost two decades of post–cold war experience show that this complex of missions is here to stay. Defense must invest to keep and build its edge in irregular warfare. This will require a Defense investment effort to:

- Maintain and slightly enlarge the sizes of the Army and Marine Corps, while changing their shapes to emphasize the military specialties that are currently in high demand but low supply.

- Continue to evolve the mission of the Army and Marine reserves from strategic backup for World War III to adding value to active-duty ground forces in this mission area—selectively and, for the citizen-soldiers involved, predictably.

- Launch a comprehensive program of innovation in the technology and tactics of self-protection for U.S. forces compelled to operate with restraint in the midst of civilian populations containing hostile elements, frequently in congested urban settings. Threats such as improvised explosive devices (IEDs), explosively formed projectiles (EFPs), mortars, rocket-propelled grenades (RPGs), and shoulder-fired antiair missiles are relatively minor factors in conventional force-on-force warfare on the open battlefield, but they can be a major factor in irregular warfare.

- Create a larger capability within Defense for training foreign security forces.

- Enlist the help of allies and partners. There is no reason that the United States should bear the entire burden of irregular warfare operations where they are needed for international security.

- Rebalance national security investment to build civilian capabilities, as noted above.

Combating Violent Extremists, Including Radical Islamist Terrorists

No one can say how long it will take to defeat or contain radical Islamist extremists bent on terrorism. But there are reasons to believe that combating terrorism will be an enduring feature of the national security landscape long after what the Bush administration calls the "Long War" against Islamist extremism is over. The fact is that the destructive power available to even small groups of extremists is growing with the advance of technology. At the same time, society is growing more interdependent and connected and thus more vulnerable to terror—physically and psychologically. These two fundamental trends are visible as far into the future as any of us can see. Whatever the lifetime of Islamist extremism, therefore, it will long remain the business of national security authorities to counter these trends arising from other groups and movements.

But for future investment, this mission points in a largely different direction from stability operations.[1] Within DoD, it emphasizes the capability to respond to catastrophic events at home and abroad—for example, a terrorist nuclear detonation—with troops, logistics, and command and control. It also emphasizes special forces. Outside of DoD, it stresses law enforcement, intelligence, homeland security, foreign assistance, and diplomacy.

Hedging against an Unlikely but Possible Downturn in United States–China Relations

China is undergoing a transformation unprecedented in history in both scale and scope. United States–China relations are overall positive and the two nations have developed a mutual dependency that would make unbridled antagonism or armed conflict a disaster for both. But historical experience suggests that the question remains: will China be friend or foe of the United States twenty or thirty years hence? This question is sometimes wrongly posed as a matter of Chinese leaders' "true intentions." But the fact is that no one, including the current Chinese leaders themselves, knows where destiny will take China as a military power. That will be determined by the attitudes of China's younger generation, the policies of its future leaders, its internal development and stability, and the possibility of unforeseen crises with the United States—for example, over Taiwan. There is no convincing way for Chinese leaders to persuade Americans of their peaceful "intentions" decades in the future. China's future intentions are not a *secret* they are keeping from us; they are a *mystery* unknown to all.

In this strategic circumstance, the United States has no choice but to have a two-pronged policy.[2] The most important prong is to *engage* China to encourage it to become a "responsible stakeholder" in the international community. But a second prong is to *hedge* against a downside scenario of competitive or aggressive behavior by China. Successive U.S. administrations have struggled to sustain public support for the needed two-pronged policy—a policy that at first glance can seem self-contradictory. But there is no reason for our policy to *be* self-contradictory. Determination to engage should not get in the way of prudent hedging, but so also excessive hedging should not create a self-fulfilling prophecy whereby treating China as an enemy contributes to making it an enemy. And since today's Chinese military leaders also cannot know where destiny will carry the relationship, it follows that they, too, probably have a two-pronged strategy. The Chinese will be preparing militarily for the downside scenario, and their hedging will look to the United States like the leading indicator of the very competitive behavior against which the United States is hedging. And so hedging can beget more hedging in a dangerous spiral. Hedging is contagious. The China hedge in our strategy must therefore be a prudent hedge.

For Defense, the China hedge creates an investment requirement very different than either irregular warfare or combating violent extremism does. The China hedge emphasizes advanced maritime and aerospace forces. It also emphasizes focused investments to frustrate Chinese efforts in counterair, countercarrier, counterspace, and counterinformation capabilities. China's military leaders seek these capabilities in the hope of finding some way of puncturing the U.S.

military's decisive dominance in a crisis or confrontation—for example, in the Taiwan Strait. These Chinese efforts are quite clear—reflected, for example, in the test of an antisatellite interceptor in January 2007. U.S. investments in a prudent hedge should focus on showing China that its efforts will not succeed in shifting the balance.

Preventing and Protecting against WMD Threats

Weapons of mass destruction, meaning mostly nuclear weapons and biological weapons (chemical and radiological weapons' effects being much less dangerous and correspondingly more manageable), in the hands of hostile state or nonstate actors can jeopardize the way of life, if not the survival, of the United States. These weapons are therefore the highest-priority threat to national security. Overall U.S. government efforts must include prevention of the spread of dangerous weapons, protection from them if they do spread, deterrence to discourage their use, and response to minimize damage if they are used.

Prevention is especially important for nuclear weapons, since they require unique materials (highly enriched uranium and plutonium) that can only be made with difficulty. Once these materials are obtained by governments or terrorists, however, the barriers to fabricating and delivering a weapon are much lower. The grave setbacks in prevention suffered by U.S. policy in recent years—allowing North Korea to obtain a nuclear arsenal and failing to slow Iran's nuclear program—have made the nuclear threat today greater than it was just a few years ago. To these disastrous developments must be added instability in nuclear-armed Pakistan and the incomplete security of Russia's nuclear materials.

DoD plays a role in all phases of protection against WMD attack. But once again, it cannot accomplish the entire counter-WMD mission, which requires the contribution of other parts of government. And once again also, the investments DoD needs to make to play its role in this mission are different from those it needs to make for other missions. In the post-Bush era, the Department of Defense will need to take the following steps to make the department's contribution to protection from WMD:

- Fund and support the expansion (in scope and geographic application) of Cooperative Threat Reduction ("Nunn-Lugar") prevention programs.

- Examine and be prepared to expand the role and funding of the Defense Threat Reduction Agency (DTRA) to serve as a DoD and government-wide center of excellence for countering WMD threats.

- Fund the development and acquisition of a robust suite of nonnuclear counters to the threat or use of WMD against U.S. territory, forces, and allies. While the president will always have nuclear retaliation as a possible U.S. response to WMD use, no president would wish that to be his or her only option. Nonnuclear alternatives include passive defenses like protective suits and vaccines; active defenses, including missile defenses; and counterforce, including nonnuclear strategic strike.

- Formulate realistic responses to a situation in which terrorists obtain a nuclear weapon or detonate one, including holding responsible, as appropriate, the government from which the terrorists obtained the weapon or fissile materials and stepping up to DoD's inevitable lead role in response and cleanup.[3]

- Review military requirements for the number of accountable deployed and reserve strategic nuclear weapons and tactical nuclear weapons to determine their role in deterrence and reassurance in east Asia, the Middle East, and Europe.

Continuing to Overmatch Possible Adversaries on the Conventional Battlefield

For much of the post–cold war period, the single mission that had the most influence on the size of U.S. forces, and thus the Defense budget, was the requirement to be able to conduct two major regional wars simultaneously. The two wars that planners had in mind were against Kim Jong Il's North Korea and Saddam Hussein's Iraq. The reason to have enough forces to win both wars simultaneously was that if the U.S. military was entirely consumed by fighting North Korea, for example, Saddam Hussein might be emboldened to choose that moment to launch his own war. The two-simultaneous-war construct resulted in an analytically derived number of units of ground, air, and naval forces required in the scenarios and thus in the Defense budget. In reality the two-war requirement never exactly matched available budgets, and the construct was continually amended by both the Clinton and Bush Defense leadership (by conceiving the two wars as overlapping but not strictly simultaneous and by ignoring or trimming the need for postwar occupation and stabilization). But it nevertheless had a powerful influence on where DoD spent its money.

Each of the two wars underpinning Defense planning through the first post–cold war decade has changed dramatically. On the Korean peninsula, South Korea's ground forces have strengthened and North Korea's have weakened, to the point where a large infusion of U.S. ground forces to halt and reverse a North Korean invasion is not needed—naval and air forces and information systems would comprise the distinctive and decisive U.S. contribution to defeating North Korea's armed forces. The unfortunate aftermath of the invasion of Iraq makes clear that planning for territorial wars should take into account the needs for ground forces in the postconflict period for stability. But in a war on the Korean peninsula, South Korea would probably insist that its ground troops be the mainstay of order in the North during the reunification process. The U.S. role in a war on the Korean peninsula would therefore be to contribute airpower, naval power, and information to the combat phase. The capabilities needed to do this have much in common with those needed for the China hedge.

The second of the two major conventional wars of the 1990s planning construct—Saddam Hussein's Iraq—is gone. Its replacement might seem to be Iran. But Iran is more likely to challenge the United States with tactics other than territorial invasion: irregular warfare and terrorism through Hezbollah and certain Palestinian factions, selective efforts to puncture U.S. overall dominance (e.g., concealment and deception against U.S. attack from the air, jamming of GPS), and nuclear weapons aboard long-range missiles. The military counter to Iran therefore looks more like the previous four missions—respectively, irregular warfare, countering violent extremists, hedging against China, and countering WMD—than like traditional conventional force-on-force warfare.

In view of these fundamental changes in the threats motivating the traditional two-war construct, there is a need for a new construct in this mission area to size it in the context of DoD's overall force and budget planning and investment. As a global power with global interests and unique responsibilities, the United States must maintain the capability to defeat aggression in more than one theater at a time. But the new two-war strategy cannot be based any longer on two particular wars of a conventional sort but on the widest range of possible plausible scenarios.

Conclusion

Given that Defense must be prepared to accomplish all five missions and that resources will be limited, it is essential to devise the smartest and most parsimonious approach to accomplishing each of them. It is also important that everything we buy make a vital contribution to at least one of these missions.

Even under the best of circumstances, the U.S. Department of Defense in the post-Bush era will inherit a Defense program that has not been aligned with the budget; a strategy not matched to resources; a need to restore and reset American influence and effectiveness on the world stage; and threats in Iraq, Afghanistan, North Korea, and Iran that have not been managed or resolved. This daunting inheritance can and will be overcome, but it will take years of strong leadership.

Notes

1. Ashton B. Carter, "The Architecture of Government in the Face of Terrorism," *International Security* 26, no. 3 (Winter 2001/02), pp. 5–23, available at http://www.belfercenter.org/files/carter_winter_01_02.pdf.

2. Ashton B. Carter and William J. Perry, "China on the March," *National Interest*, no. 88 (March–April 2007), pp. 16–22, available at http://www.belfercenter.org/files/carterperry_nationalinterest_marapr2007.pdf.

3. Ashton B. Carter and William J. Perry, "The Day After," *Washington Quarterly* 30, no. 4 (Autumn 2007), pp. 19–32, available at http://www.belfercenter.org/publication/17435/day_after.html?breadcrumb=%2Fproject%2F2%2Fpreventive_defense_project.

Panel I: Security Challenges and Strategy

Summary of Discussion

Dr. Bradford A. Lee
Philip A. Crowl Chair in Comparative Strategy
U.S. Naval War College

The purpose of the first panel at the 2007 Ruger Conference was to provide a broad overview of the major issues of the international environment that impinge on American national security and an array of suggestions of how policy makers might best deal with those challenges. The first presentation, by Professor Robert Art of Brandeis University, reflected his expertise as a distinguished scholar of international relations. After identifying the half-dozen most important American interests in the world and calibrating a realistic grand-strategy middle ground between the extremes of neo-isolationist variants of "offshore balancing" and recent manifestations of "muscular Wilsonianism," Professor Art highlighted the crucial tasks of restoring American legitimacy in the eyes of the international community, thinking harder about the global jihadist threat, and building on a foundation of common interest shared by the United States and the People's Republic of China. The second presentation, by Professor Ashton Carter of Harvard University, added the judicious perspective of an experienced policy maker in the Department of Defense. After noting the continuing importance of ongoing problems with Iran and North Korea, and in Iraq and Sudan, and after reinforcing Professor Art's point about the importance of restoring American influence, partnerships, and honor in the world, Professor Carter focused on investment choices facing the Pentagon in a future where fiscal constraints are likely to become much tighter and where costs of DoD systems and services are likely to continue to balloon. He discussed the high-priority need for investment in the missions of dealing with violent extremists and other irregular forces, hedging against a deterioration in U.S.-PRC relations and maintaining potent conventional military capabilities, and—not least—trying to prevent the use of nuclear and biological weapons in the American homeland and preparing to deal with the catastrophic consequences of such a horrific eventuality.

The presentations opened the way for a flood of comments from other participants in the conference that threatened to burst the bounds of the carefully organized schedule. One major area of discussion had to do with the need to "rebalance" and perhaps "restructure" the executive branch of the U.S. government in order better to handle the challenges to American national security that Professors Art and Carter had highlighted. There was widespread agreement that government departments other than the Defense Department needed more capacity, more competence, and more money. In particular, greater budgetary resources should flow to the State Department, though there was some doubt expressed that, in the absence of a sophisticated strategic-planning arm, professional diplomats would make efficient and effective use of more money. The need for more capacity and more funding for economic-development projects, with a reinvigorated U.S. Agency for International Development, was also noted. But, while acknowledging the current importance of stability and reconstruction operations, one participant expressed the hope that the United States would not establish a new institution along the lines of the old British colonial service. To think that the United States "should go out and rebuild every failed state," was, in the participant's opinion, "just nuts." Another participant reminded the conference of the "growing pains" of the Department of Homeland Defense. "It's a disaster," as the participant pungently put the point. Reform of that new institution was an urgent matter.

Along with such discussion of institutional reform and resource reallocation, there emerged a powerful line of argument about a talent gap in DoD, DoS, and the intelligence agencies. The national security community desperately needs more officials and officers with foreign-language competence, cultural knowledge, and nation-building skill sets relevant to the struggle against jihadists and other extremist, irregular challenges. Whether or not an infusion of such talent into intelligence agencies would prevent repetition in the future of recent "intelligence failures" was a matter of some debate. A participant noted a talent gap in an area that has been less a matter of intense public debate: defense acquisition. The participant saw deficiencies, for example, in systems engineering expertise within the Defense Department and among Defense contractors. There was a link between deficiencies in the acquisition process and the ballyhoo of "transformation." Transformation had proved to be rich in rhetoric and poor in results. Partly that was because, in the participant's opinion, Donald Rumsfeld as secretary of defense had missed good opportunities to turn rhetoric into reality. But also worth consideration is how mounting unit costs of putatively transformational systems had led to less money being available for projects waiting in the queue.

The conference participants juggled their queries and comments between problems inside the American government, on one hand, and problems in the international environment, on the other hand. The issue of access to energy, especially in the troubled Persian Gulf, was prominent in the discussion. One provocative comment was that the United States should seek to extricate itself from "the oil protection racket" and step up on a significant scale its investment in alternative energy technologies and sources. That triggered a wide-ranging discussion about the prospective costs and benefits to the nation of investing in renewable sources of energy, ethanol, nuclear power plants, and the like. One participant noted that whereas maintaining access to overseas oil for the economically advanced countries of the world entails naval power, secure sea lines of communications, and attention to geostrategic choke points, access to coal on their own territories for countries such as China poses no such issues. In addition, while the cost of extracting oil from oil reservoirs is rising dramatically, the cost of extracting coal from mines is not. Thus, the participant foresaw ever-more-massive use of coal, especially by China and India, as their economies grow apace. No doubt there would be progress in cleaner use of coal, but nonetheless coal would mean even worse environmental pollution in China. Indeed, in the participant's view, Chinese environmental problems might even lead to a serious popular challenge to the stability of the Chinese Communist regime. This image of a future in which coal loomed large drew a passionate retort from a participant concerned about the impact on global warming. Heavy use of coal as well as oil would only make the problem of global warming more acute.

Another issue on which the conference opened up a long-term perspective on the future was demography. A participant played a catalytic role in the demographic discussion by noting that such major powers as Russia and Japan face "demographic collapse." Another participant pointed out that demography was "the one really predictable aspect of the future," but it might be added that the impact of demographic trends on American national security is by no means easy to predict. China is aging, too—"faster than it's getting rich"—but what might that portend for its behavior toward the United States? Two areas are not aging: the Middle East and Africa. An excess of young men in those areas spells instability as far as the eye can see.

Even without the invocation of such demographic trends, one topic that cannot go unmentioned in a discussion of "security challenges and strategy" is the conflict against jihadists. A participant expressed the hope that American diplomacy might help resolve the knotty problems of Palestine and Kashmir. That success in turn might give the United States greater moral stature in the Muslim world, to the disadvantage of those Islamist firebrands who seek to mobilize new recruits by preaching about the malevolence of American policy. Another participant cautioned that the nature of "jihad, fundamentalism, and terrorism . . . has nothing to do with Palestine" and "nothing to do with Kashmir" (which in turn should not be grouped with Palestine). Instead it is part of "a great civil war . . . in this great region of Islam" between "puritans who want to take back the Islamic world to the seventh century" and "sensible people who want to align the religion with the times." Americans cannot resolve this civil war by offering extremists diplomatic concessions on particular issues. For the most part, "it is better to leave that civil war to the adherents of Islam than try to impose your values on them."

As the time for a scheduled midmorning break approached, another participant jumped into the discussion to say that while loath to interpose "between angry and anxious people and their coffee," the participant wanted to remind American experts on national security issues not to get so caught up in management problems that they lose sight of the more important moral challenges facing the United States in a world where many people have become disillusioned with American shortcomings. That reminder sounded the end to the first period of discussion at the 2007 Ruger Conference on a powerful note.

Panel II

Defense Resources and Risks

Dr. J. Michael Gilmore
Assistant Director for National Security, Congressional Budget Office

Dr. Cindy Williams
Principal Research Scientist, Security Studies Program, Massachusetts
Institute of Technology

Moderator:
Professor Thomas C. Hone
Joint Military Operations Department, U.S. Naval War College

Federal Budget Trends and the Outlook for the Defense Program

Dr. J. Michael Gilmore
Assistant Director for National Security
Congressional Budget Office

During the latter part of the cold war, defense spending peaked at $473 billion during the Reagan administration (see figure 1); subsequently it declined, reaching a low point of $319 billion in 1997. Defense spending has since rebounded, reaching $620 billion in 2007—including $169 billion for operations associated with the war on terrorism, mostly for the wars in Iraq and Afghanistan. The president's request for fiscal year 2008 is $481 billion for the "base" defense budget, with $189 billion currently anticipated in emergency supplemental funding, mostly for operations in Iraq and Afghanistan. Thus total defense spending in 2008 will be about $670 billion. The FYDP anticipates defense spending totaling $497 billion in 2013—including no funding for operations in Iraq and Afghanistan—a 3.5 percent real increase relative to the 2008 "base" request.

In the Congressional Budget Office's (CBO's) projection of the Defense Department's (DoD's) current plans, the demand for defense resources averages about $520 billion annually (in 2008 dollars) from 2014 to 2025, or about 8 percent more than the total obligational authority (TOA) for defense—excluding emergency supplemental appropriations—requested by the administration for 2008 (see figure 1).[1] The request for 2008 is, in turn, about 4 percent greater than the administration had anticipated it would be last year, due primarily to the decision to increase the size of the Army and Marine Corps.

Considering potential unbudgeted costs increases the projected long-term demand for defense funding to an annual average of about $617 billion through 2025, or 28 percent more than the administration's 2008 figure. CBO's analysis of unbudgeted costs included several possibilities: that the costs of weapon systems now under development would exceed early estimates, as they have in the past (about $24 billion in annual unbudgeted costs); that real increases in military pay will continue and medical costs might rise more rapidly than DoD has assumed (about $18 billion in annual unbudgeted costs); and that DoD would continue to conduct contingency military operations overseas as part of the war on terrorism, albeit at reduced levels—about 70,000 personnel versus over 200,000 personnel currently—relative to current operations in Iraq and Afghanistan (about $53 billion in annual unbudgeted costs).

Operations and Support (O&S)

Funding for O&S composes 60 percent of the base budget. The 2008 FYDP envisions that spending for O&S activities—running units, maintaining equipment, and providing pay and benefits—will grow from $283 billion in 2008 (excluding supplemental appropriations) to $310 billion in 2013 (see figure 2).

(Those estimates translate into an average annual rate of real growth of 1.8 percent during the five-year period.) CBO projects that, over the longer term, carrying out current plans would push O&S spending to $366 billion in 2025 (again, starting from 2008, a 1.5 percent pace of annual real growth); if potential unbudgeted costs are included, that figure would rise to $422 billion (see figure 2). The $106 billion of emergency supplemental O&S funding in 2008 composes about 56 percent of the $189 billion total supplemental request.

Figure 1
Past and Projected Spending for Defense*

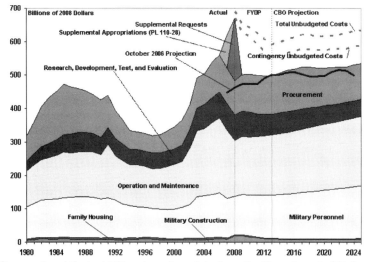

Source: Congressional Budget Office, based on data from the Department of Defense.

In comparison with last year's FYDP, DoD's current plans show an average increase in total O&S spending of 6 percent. That increase is largely the result of planned growth in the number of Army and Marine Corps personnel. Over the 2007 to 2013 period, the 2008 FYDP shows a cumulative end-strength increase of 65,000 active duty Army personnel and nearly 28,000 active duty Marine Corps personnel. (The Army and Marine Corps will have end strengths of 547,400 and 207,482, respectively, by 2013.) Last year's FYDP did not indicate any significant changes in Army or Marine Corps end strength.

In CBO's projection, most of the growth projected for O&S spending, if unbudgeted costs are excluded, will stem from personnel-related increases, such as rising real wages and increasing costs for medical benefits. If the medical and operating forces categories were excluded, increases in military and civilian pay would account for the entire growth of costs in CBO's projections (excluding unbudgeted costs). DoD plans to raise pay for military personnel at a nominal rate of 3.0 percent in 2008 and 3.4 percent each year from 2009 to 2013.[2] After that, CBO's projections incorporate the assumption that pay for military personnel will rise at the same rate as the employment cost index (ECI) for wages and salaries (a measure of compensation in the civilian economy).

---

*(Note: All funding displayed in this paper is in constant fiscal year 2008 dollars.)

For civilian employees, DoD plans to increase pay at a nominal rate of 3.0 percent in 2008 and 2.3 percent each year from 2009 to 2013. In recent decades, civilian and military personnel have usually received equivalent percentage pay increases.[3] Consequently, CBO projects that civilian pay will also rise after 2013 at the same rate as the ECI.[4] If all of those increases occurred, military and civilian pay would grow in real terms by 33 percent and 26 percent, respectively, between 2007 and 2025—because wages (as measured by the ECI) are projected to grow more rapidly than prices (as measured by the GDP deflator).[5]

Figure 2
Past and Projected Spending for Defense Operations and Support

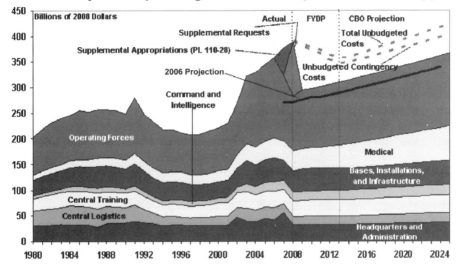

Source: Congressional Budget Office, based on data from the Department of Defense.

In the 2008 FYDP, DoD projects real growth in medical spending of $6.8 billion between 2008 and 2013, from $38.6 billion to $45.3 billion. CBO estimates that, under current plans, DoD's medical spending will grow to $68.3 billion by 2025, for a real increase of $29.7 billion, or 77 percent, compared with the 2008 amount. CBO estimates that medical spending will account for more than one-third of the growth projected for O&S spending between 2008 and 2025.

Overall Investment

Investment—which pays for developing, testing, and buying weapon systems and other equipment—peaked at $204 billion in 1985 and reached a low point of $99 billion in 1996 (see figure 3). The administration requested $162 billion for investment in 2007 in the "base" budget; total investment funding in 2007 reached about $200 billion including emergency supplemental requests. The administration has requested $177 billion for investment in the "base" budget in 2008, as well as another $71 billion—almost all for procurement—in emergency supplemental funding. The 2008 FYDP envisions that over the 2008–2013 period, investment spending will remain relatively constant, averaging about $181 billion annually. Carrying out current plans over the long term would cause investment spending—excluding unbudgeted costs—to peak at $185 billion in 2015, CBO projects, and average about $172 billion annually.

Figure 3

Past and Projected Spending for Defense Investment

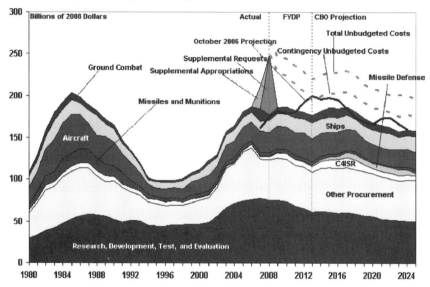

Source: Congressional Budget Office, based on data from the Department of Defense.

Unlike its previous projections for DoD investment spending, CBO's current projection indicates that a substantial rise in funding will not be needed relative to current levels to execute DoD's current investment plans over the long term. CBO projects that unbudgeted costs—including costs to repair, replace, and upgrade equipment used in contingency operations—could cause defense spending to peak in 2015 at $227 billion.[6] In that case funding for investment over the 2014–2025 period would average $208 billion annually, about 20 percent more than in the case excluding unbudgeted costs.

In both the FYDP's and CBO's projections, funding for research, development, and testing (RDT&E) activities declines steadily, falling from $75 billion in 2008 to $50 billion in 2025. This decline occurs because over the projection period programs now in development complete that phase and enter procurement. Although DoD's plans have consistently incorporated declines in RDT&E spending consistent with CBO's projection, those declines are often not realized due to schedule slippage, cost increases, and new ideas for research and development activities.

In CBO's projection, defense procurement—about two-thirds of total investment—averages $116 billion a year over the period from 2014 to 2025 (see figure 4). This amount is 13 percent greater than the president's FY 2008 request of $102 billion excluding supplemental appropriations, but two-thirds of the roughly $170 billion in total procurement including supplemental appropriations. (Thus, in 2008, supplemental appropriations will compose about 40 percent of total procurement.)

Given current plans, CBO estimates that steady-state levels of procurement for all systems—the annual purchases needed to keep planned fleets from aging, which are based on the sizes of those fleets divided by their lifetimes— would cost between $128 billion and $164 billion, depending upon the age at which systems will be retired (see figure 4). (This estimate assumes no growth in weapon system costs.) Thus, average procurement over the long term will be below the steady-state range, and the planned program will not sustain all of DoD's systems within age bounds that the department would consider acceptable. However, the majority of the supplemental procurement funding that has been (and is likely to be) appropriated has been used to upgrade existing weapons and procure new weapons for the Army. This means that much of the Army's equipment is likely to be relatively new once operations in Iraq decline substantially or end.

Figure 4
Past and Projected Spending for Defense Procurement

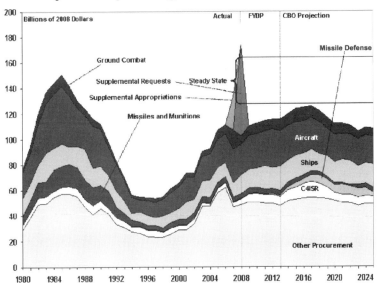

Source: Congressional Budget Office, based on data from the Department of Defense.

Navy and Marine Corps Investment

Under the DoD's current plans, investment resources for the Department of the Navy (which includes the Marine Corps) would rise from $56 billion in 2008 to a peak of about $62 billion in 2014 and then decline to $39 billion by 2025, CBO projects. Between 2014 and 2025, Navy investment would average $50 billion a year. If program costs grew as they have in the past, however, the department's investment spending could peak at $70 billion in 2016 and then fall back to about $47 billion by 2025—averaging $59 billion a year over the 2014–2025 period (see figure 5). Funding contingency operations could further increase long-term demands for Navy investment.

Figure 5
Past and Projected Spending for Investment by the
Department of the Navy

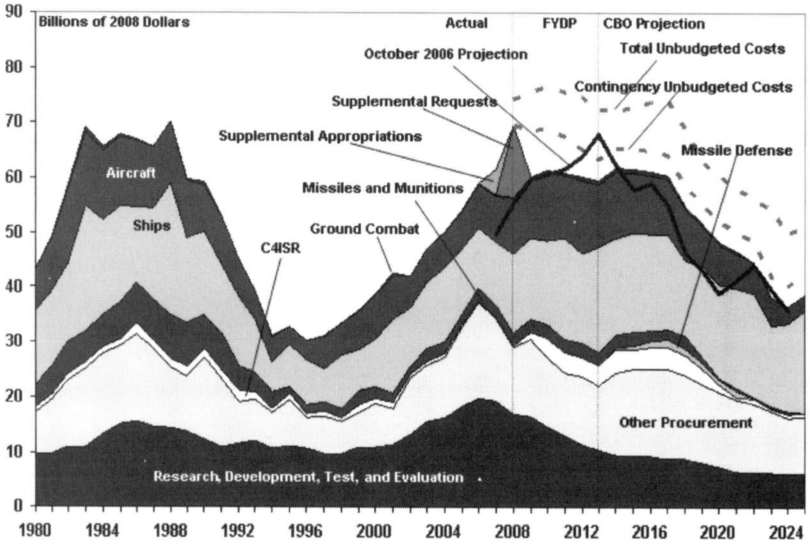

Source: Congressional Budget Office, based on data from the Department of Defense.

Projections of the Navy's resource demands are driven largely by the procurement of battle force ships. CBO based its assumptions about ship procurement on the Navy's new plan for building a fleet of 313 ships, compared with 278 today.[7] Based on the profile provided in the Navy's shipbuilding plan, CBO estimates that the Navy would need to spend $17 billion a year between 2007 and 2025 to increase its fleet to about 313 ships, or $21 billion a year through 2025 if historical trends in cost growth continued. The planned increase in the Navy's fleet is reflected primarily in the surface combatant force, as a result of the Navy's plans to purchase large numbers of littoral combat ships (LCSs).

The Marine Corps's plans for equipment bought through its procurement account also changed substantially between the 2007 FYDP and the 2008 FYDP. In particular, plans to purchase the new expeditionary fighting vehicle, which replaces the amphibious assault vehicle, were reduced by nearly half and would begin in 2010 rather than in 2007. CBO projects that carrying out current Marine Corps plans would require substantial resources: an average of about $540 million a year, without cost growth—or twice the average amount that this category of procurement has received for the past two decades.

The major change since CBO's prior projection of the Navy's plans has been the cost growth in the LCS program. That growth resulted in a restructuring of the Navy's plans to acquire those ships in the short term. The Navy originally planned to buy two LCSs in 2007, three in 2008, and six per year in 2009 to 2011. In order to pay for a doubling in the cost of the first two ships, the Navy canceled the 2007 ships and reduced the purchases in 2008 to two and in 2009 to three.[8] In total, the Navy's current procurement plan for surface combatants would cost an average of $6.1 billion a year between 2008 and 2025—or $8.7 billion annually, CBO estimates, if historical cost growth is considered. CBO's estimates indicate that the Navy's overall plans for shipbuilding would cost about 30 percent more than the Navy now projects, including $4.8 billion for lead DDG-1000 vice the cost of $3.1 billion currently estimated by the Navy (see figure 6). If the Navy is able to carry out its plans, the average age of ships in the fleet would increase gradually from about 17 years in 2008 to about 20 years in 2025.

Figure 6
Procurement of Battle Force Ships

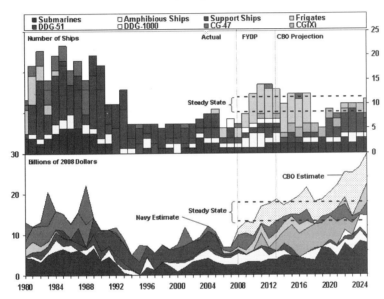

Source: Congressional Budget Office, based on data from the Department of Defense.

To put the Navy's plan in perspective, consider that from 1981 to 1988, 147 ships were procured at an average cost per ship of $870 million and an average annual cost of $16 billion. From 1993 to 2000, 54 ships were procured at an average cost per ship of $1 billion; average annual cost of $7 billion. From 2001 to 2008, 54 ships are to be procured at an average cost per ship of $1.4 billion; average annual cost of $9.5 billion. And, from 2009 to 2016, 95 ships are planned to be procured at an average cost per ship of $1.1 billion ($1.4 billion, CBO estimates); average annual cost of $13 billion ($17 billion, CBO estimates). Thus, relative to the most recent eight-year period, the Navy plans over the next comparable period to increase ship purchases by 76 percent and ship construction funding by 37 percent. However, CBO estimates that those increased purchases will require a 79 percent increase in funding.

Air Force Investment

Under the administration's current plans, funding for RDT&E and for procurement of Air Force systems would total roughly $61 billion in 2008 and then rise to a fairly steady level of about $64 billion per year from 2009 through 2013. CBO projects that continuing those plans beyond the FYDP period would require similar average investment funding—about $68 billion per year—from 2014 through 2025. Year-to-year funding would remain stable over the projection, with a low of about $62 billion in 2014 and a high just over $73 billion in 2024 (see figure 7). If the costs of developing and purchasing Air Force systems grew beyond the service's current estimates to the same extent that they have in the past, carrying out the administration's current plans for that time period would require an additional $6 billion per year between 2014 and 2025. Funding contingency operations could further increase long-term demands for Air Force investment.

Figure 7
Past and Projected Air Force Spending for Investment

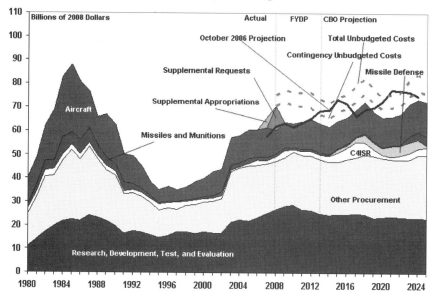

Source: Congressional Budget Office, based on data from the Department of Defense.

The administration's 2008 budget request for Air Force investment is about $1.5 billion lower than the level anticipated in the previous year's FYDP. Much of that decrease results from cancellation of the E-10 surveillance aircraft and delays in procurement of the KC-X replacement for the KC-135 airborne tanker. Nonetheless, average investment spending for the period spanning 2009 through 2011, years included in both the 2007 FYDP and 2008 FYDP, increased by about $1 billion per year.

For 2014 through 2025, CBO's current projections of spending for Air Force investment are significantly lower than its previous projection for every year except 2018. Average investment spending over that period would be about $7.5 billion per year below CBO's previous projection. Much of that decrease was due to changes in three major programs:

- A decrease in peak production rates for the F-35A Joint Strike Fighter (JSF) from 110 per year to 80 per year

- Cancellation of the E-10 surveillance and tracking aircraft decreasing projected funding for C4ISR by about $12 billion over the projection

- A decrease in the capability of the long-range strike aircraft the Air Force hopes to field around 2018.

Based on the 2008 FYDP, CBO projects that the number of purchases of tactical aircraft will be below the steady-state range through 2025 (see figure 8). The 2008 FYDP has reduced future purchases of the JSF from 110 per year to the rate of 80 per year (displayed in the figure) and has extended the program seven years to 2034.

Through 2025, CBO projects that the program in the 2008 FYDP buys 175 F-22s at $210 million per plane and 1,089 JSFs at $80 million per plane. During 1981 to 1988, 1,661 aircraft were purchased for a total cost of $54 billion—an overall average unit cost of $32 million. During 1993 to 2000, 86 aircraft were purchased for a total cost of $5 billion—an overall average unit cost of $58 million. During 2001 to 2008, 170 aircraft will be purchased for a total cost of $34 billion—an overall average unit cost of $198 million.

These plans will cause the average age of Air Force fighters to increase through 2016, reaching more than 24 years. Thereafter, deliveries of JSFs will cause the average age to decline to 19 years by 2025.

Figure 8
Procurement of Air Force Fighter and Attack Aircraft

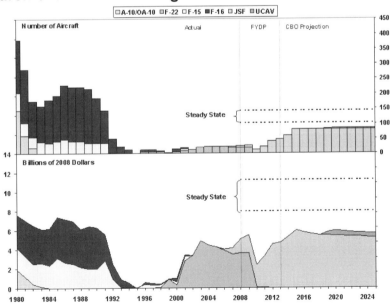

Source: Congressional Budget Office, based on data from the Department of Defense.

Army Investment

In 2007, the Army's investment budget included about $26 billion provided through emergency supplemental appropriations to pay for the costs of repairing and replacing equipment worn out and lost in operations in Iraq and Afghanistan, to upgrade equipment, and to buy new equipment, including equipment for the Army National Guard. In 2008, the president's requests for emergency supplemental appropriations anticipate about $33 billion in funding for Army investment. If the Congress enacts those requests, funding provided through supplemental appropriations will compose 49 percent of total Army investment in 2008; they composed 46 percent of Army investment in 2007 (see figure 9).[9]

Excluding emergency supplemental appropriations, relative to the 2007 FYDP total investment resources allocated to the Department of the Army in the 2008 FYDP increased for the 2008–2011 period common to both plans. Average annual investment spending would increase from $30 billion to $35 billion, and more funds would be devoted to procurement between 2008 and 2011—$103 billion in the 2008 FYDP, as compared with $85 billion in the 2007 FYDP for the same period. Those increases are attributable primarily to additional funds provided to purchase equipment—mostly trucks—for the units that the Army intends to add to its forces. Those funds, totaling $15 billion from 2008 to 2013, are included in the Army's "Grow the Force Initiative."

Figure 9
Past and Projected Spending for Investment by the Department of the Army

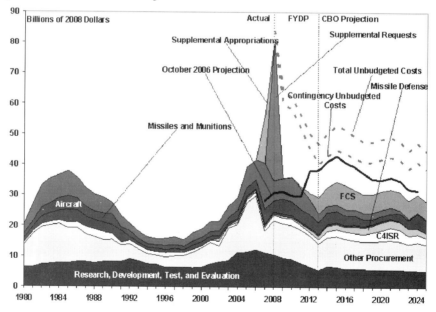

Source: Congressional Budget Office, based on data from the Department of Defense.

Compared to CBO's projection from October 2006, investment spending under the 2008 president's budget would be lower in the last two years of the six-year period covered by the 2008–2013 FYDP that is now subject to fiscal controls within DoD. Funding is also lower beyond 2013. The early decline results in part from the Army's decision to delay the start of procurement of the Future Combat Systems (FCS), which will replace current ground combat equipment, and from cuts in spending on minor programs and missile defense. The later decline results primarily from the decision to reduce procurement of the Future Combat Systems (FCS).

FCS will now be purchased at the rate of one brigade-set per year. At that rate, it will require 31 years to purchase enough FCS equipment for the active Army's 19 heavy brigades and the National Guard's 6 heavy brigades, as well as to equip up to six prepositioned and other equipment sets.

Some measure the affordability of the defense program using the share of the gross domestic product (GDP) that it composes. Others argue that the defense "topline" ought to be set as a certain percentage of GDP. Defense spending reached 9.5 percent of GDP during the Vietnam War and declined thereafter as a share of the economy until the end of the Carter administration. It rebounded to reach about 6 percent of GDP during the Reagan administration but subsequently resumed a decline lasting throughout most of the Clinton administration (see figure 10).

Figure 10
Past and Projected Defense Spending as a Share of Gross Domestic Product

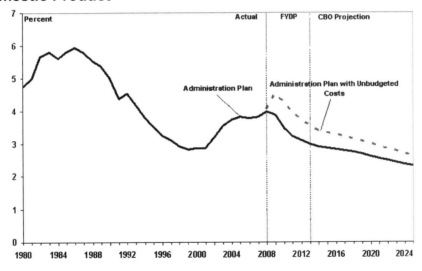

Source: Congressional Budget Office.

Operations in Iraq and Afghanistan have caused defense spending to reach about 4 percent of GDP recently. CBO projects that if current defense plans remain unchanged and the economy continues to grow, defense spending will compose a steadily declining share of GDP over the long term, reaching somewhat more than 2.5 percent of GDP by 2025. Of course, the economy has grown throughout the historical period shown on the chart and, under CBO's projections, would continue to grow. GDP is currently more than $13 trillion; it was $2.7 trillion in 1980.

CBO's projections indicate deficits averaging about $131 billion annually through fiscal year 2011 (see figure 11). As a percentage of annual GDP, those deficits are within recent historical experience. CBO's projections by law assume no changes to current policies and enacted legislation. (In particular, they assume that tax reductions enacted in 2001 and 2003 expire in 2010 and that no changes are made to the Alternative Minimum Tax (AMT).) The expiration of tax reductions would cause annual surpluses averaging about 1 percent of GDP to accrue during the period spanning 2011 through 2017.

Figure 11
Total Revenues and Outlays as a Percentage of Gross Domestic Product

(percentage of gross domestic product)

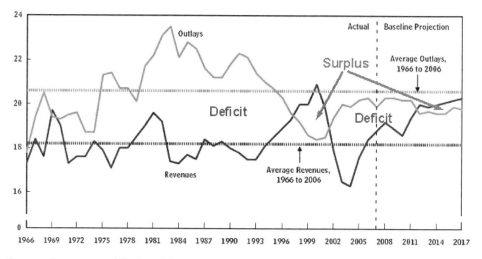

Source: Congressional Budget Office.

Over the long run, the retirement of the baby-boom generation portends a significant, long-lasting shift in the age profile of the U.S. population, which will alter the balance between the working-age and retirement-age components of that population. The share of people age 65 or older is projected to grow from 12 percent in 2000 to 19 percent by 2030, while the working-age population is expected to fall from 59 percent to 56 percent. As a result, the Social Security trustees project that the number of workers per Social Security beneficiary will decline over the next three decades: from about 3.3 now to 2.2 in 2030. Unless immigration or fertility rates change substantially, that figure will continue to decrease slowly after 2030. The interaction of that growth in the retired population with the current structure of the program leads CBO to project that the cost of Social Security benefits will rise from 4.2 percent of GDP now to 5.9 percent in 2030 (see figure 12).

Figure 12
Past and Projected Spending for Social Security

(percentage of gross domestic product)

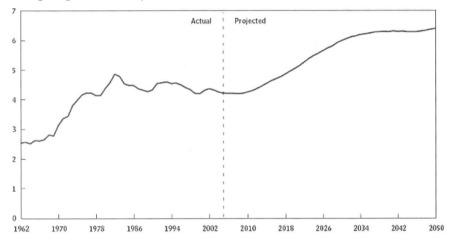

Source: Congressional Budget Office.

CBO's analysis of long-term budget trends published in December 2005 considers a number of scenarios for future federal spending, including scenarios that differ in their assumptions about the health care cost differential (see figure 13). The scenario displayed in the top panel of figure 14 assumes a cost differential of 2.5 percentage points, roughly consistent with overall average experience since 1970. The scenario displayed in the bottom panel of the figure assumes a cost growth differential of 1 percentage point, consistent with the assumptions used by the Medicare trustees. Each scenario assumes that federal revenues are constrained to 18 percent of GDP, their average share since 1966. (This would be roughly consistent with extending the tax reductions beyond 2011 and indexing the AMT for inflation.)

In the 2.5-percentage-point scenario, federal spending doubles relative to its current 20 percent share of GDP by around 2040 (see figure 14). In the 1-percentage-point scenario, that doubling would be delayed until shortly after 2050. Although increasing costs for Social Security are a component, the largest contributor to those increases is growth in health care costs. Federal deficits under both scenarios would be unprecedented (see figure 15 and figure 16).

For the past 50 years, federal outlays have averaged about 20 percent of GDP—about 2.4 percentage points above the average for the 1950s. In 2006, those outlays totaled $2.7 trillion (and GDP was 13.1 trillion).

The composition of that spending has changed significantly. Spending for mandatory entitlement programs has increased from less than one-third of total federal spending in 1962 to more than one-half in recent years. Most of that growth has been concentrated in Social Security, Medicare, and Medicaid (see figure 17). Together, those programs now account for about 41 percent of federal outlays, compared with 2 percent in 1950 (before the health programs were created), and 25 percent in 1975.

Figure 13
Total Federal Spending for Medicare and Medicaid under Different Assumptions about the Health Cost Growth Differential

(percentage of gross domestic product)

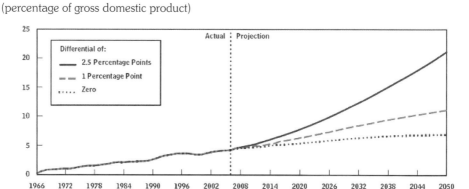

Source: Congressional Budget Office.

Note: The health cost growth differential refers to the number of percentage points by which the growth of annual health care spending per beneficiary is assumed to exceed the nominal growth of gross domestic product per capita, after an adjustment for the growth and aging of the Medicare and Medicaid populations.

Figure 14
Total Federal Spending and Revenues under Long-Term Budget Scenarios

(percentage of gross domestic product)

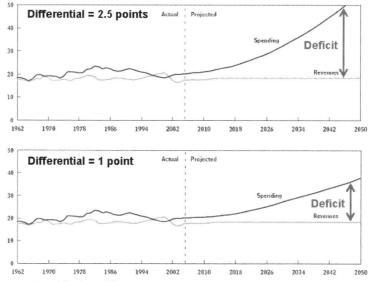

Source: Congressional Budget Office.

Figure 15
Federal Debt Held by the Public under Long-Term Budget Scenarios

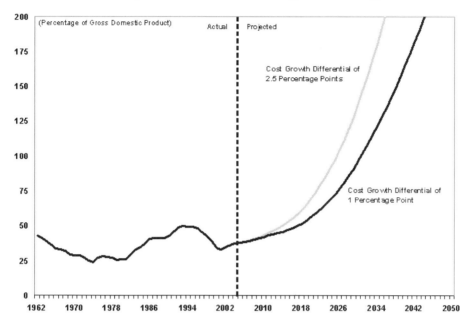

Source: Congressional Budget Office.

Figure 16
Federal Debt Held by the Public, 1790 to 2004

(percentage of gross domestic product)

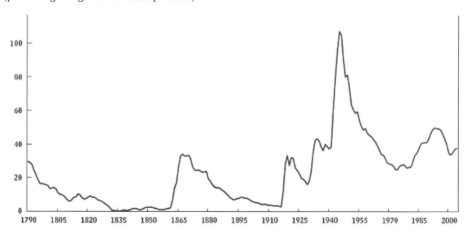

Source: Congressional Budget Office.

The share of the budget associated with discretionary spending—appropriations that must be enacted annually by the Congress—has been declining steadily. The share of discretionary spending that defense comprises has also declined—defense now constitutes about one-half of discretionary spending, compared with 73 percent in 1962. If current policies remain unchanged, spending for Social Security, Medicare, and Medicaid will compose 20 percent of GDP by around 2034, as much as all federal spending composes today.

Figure 17
Categories of Federal Spending as a Percentage of Gross Domestic Product

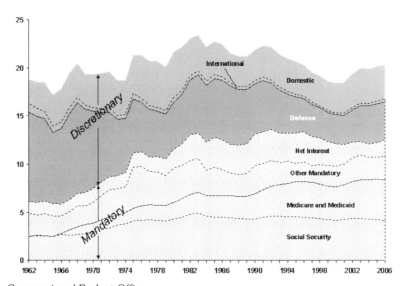

Source: Congressional Budget Office.

Notes

1. All FYDP funding is calculated as total obligational authority. The bulk of that funding is budget authority, which is the authority provided by the Congress to incur financial obligations; however, TOA also includes funding derived from receipts, trust funds, and interfund transactions, minus other amounts, such as accrual payments for military retirement. In most years, the difference between TOA and budget authority in subfunction 051 of the federal budget (which funds the Department of Defense) is about $2 billion or less.

2. Memorandum from John P. Roth, Deputy Comptroller, Department of Defense, to the Secretaries of the Military Departments and others, "Inflation Guidance—Fiscal Year (FY) 2008/2009 President's Budget," 18 January 2007.

3. Civilian personnel received the same percentage pay raise as military personnel in 26 of the past 32 years (1975 to 2007).

4. In calculating unbudgeted O&S costs, CBO increased civilian pay raises to achieve parity with military pay raises during the FYDP period (2008 to 2013).

5. The ECI grew more rapidly than the GDP deflator (an index of overall prices) in each year of the period 1981 through 2007, and CBO projects that the pattern will continue between 2008 and 2025. Over the latter period, growth of the ECI will exceed growth of the GDP deflator by an average of 1.5 percentage points per year, CBO projects.

6. Supplemental funding displayed in figure 8 for 2007 excludes amounts provided under Title IX of the regular defense appropriation, Public Law 109–289; it includes amounts appropriated under Public Law 110–28.

7. Department of the Navy, *A Report to Congress on Annual Long-Range Plans for the Construction of Naval Vessels, Fiscal Year 2008* (February 2007).

8. The Navy also planned to buy one LCS in 2005 and three in 2006, designated LCS 1-4. However, LCS-3 was canceled by the Navy in the spring of 2007 as a result of the cost overruns. The House and Senate Appropriations and Armed Services committees have proposed reducing the purchase of LCSs even further, with the Senate Appropriators proposing to eliminate the funding for LCS-4. The Navy has now also canceled LCS-4 because of growth in its cost.

9. Supplemental funding displayed in figure 9 for 2007 excludes amounts provided under Title IX of the regular defense appropriation, Public Law 109–289; it includes amounts appropriated under Public Law 110–28.

The Other Resources: The People Factor in Future Defense Strategy

Dr. Cindy Williams
Principal Research Scientist
Security Studies Program
Massachusetts Institute of Technology

A review of the foreign policy statements of the front-runners in the U.S. presidential race reveals a high degree of consensus among Democratic and Republican elites regarding threats and interests and the outlines of U.S. grand strategy for the future. Both sides generally agree that the prospect of nuclear weapons falling into the hands of terrorists is among the gravest dangers the United States faces; that failed states, weak states, and ungoverned areas are easy marks for terrorist groups looking for a home, and thus an important threat to U.S. security; that extending to other countries the American ideals of freedom and the rule of law is an important goal; and that the United States should do what it can to prevent internal conflicts in other countries or, if they cannot be prevented, to help bring them to an early end. Democrats and Republicans also generally agree that sustaining U.S. primacy in the world is crucial to achieving the other aims of foreign policy.

Neither Republicans nor Democrats envision further cuts beyond the self-imposed reductions already under way in the Navy and Air Force. Nevertheless, elites of both parties emphasize the importance of so-called irregular warfare, including counterterrorism, counterinsurgency, stabilization, and reconstruction. Such operations require sizable ground forces and capable special operations forces. Among the front-runners, John Edwards stands alone in questioning the need for adding 92,000 troops to the Army and Marine Corps.

The strategies will be costly in financial terms. They also pose substantial costs and risks on the other side of the resource equation: people. Yet ongoing operations in Iraq have caused and revealed limitations on that side of the equation that need to be recognized. This paper examines some current problems and the limitations they may impose on future missions and strategic aims.

Military Personnel Costs Are Rising Rapidly

The cost of military personnel is high and rising. Already the Navy and Air Force have cut their forces by tens of thousands of troops in an effort to offset the rising cost per troop and preserve as much money as possible for equipment and upkeep. Absent steady, sizable increases in Defense budgets, these rising costs will constrain the Department of Defense's (DoD's) choices about future force structure, modernization, and readiness.

In recent years, the costs of pay and benefits for military personnel have grown dramatically as pay, housing allowances, and retiree benefits have expanded. The Government Accountability Office (GAO) estimates that the total cost to taxpayers of military pay and benefits, including veterans' benefits, rose by 28 percent in real terms between 2000 and 2004.[1] DoD estimates that the average cost to taxpayers per active-duty service member is $138,000 (FY 2005 dollars).[2]

The cost per service member will continue to rise in the future. On 1 January 2008, all service members will receive a 3.5 percent pay raise. The raise is 0.5 percentage points higher than DoD requested and, like military across-the-board raises since 2000, higher than wage inflation in the private sector.

Health care costs for military personnel, their families, and retirees will also continue to grow. The military's health care system faces the same sources of cost growth that affect the civilian sector. Military health care costs are rising even more rapidly than those in the private sector, however, both because Congress has greatly expanded the benefits for retirees in recent years and because the fees charged to retirees are so low that large numbers of those who can are choosing the DoD system in preference to civilian alternatives they would have chosen in previous years. The upshot is that absent changes in policy, health care costs will rise from 8 percent of the DoD budget today to 12 percent by 2015.

The planned expansion of the ground forces will also push personnel costs higher. The Congressional Budget Office (CBO) estimates that adding 92,000 troops will cost $108 billion over the period from 2007 to 2013.[3]

Expanding the Army Will Be a Challenge

The Army is the largest of the four services, and its goals for expansion are the most ambitious. Current plans are to expand the active-duty force by 65,000 troops, relative to the permanent end strength authorized for FY 2004. This means an increase of 28,000 troops relative to the level actually in the Army as of 31 August 2007 (see table 1).

Table 1
Army Active-Duty End Strength

(thousands)

2004		2005		2006		2007		2010
Authorized	Actual	Authorized	Actual	Authorized	Actual	Authorized	Actual	Planned
482	500	502	493	512	505	512	519[a]	547

Sources: CBO, *Recruiting, Retention, and Future Levels of Military Personnel* (October 2006), p. 2; DoD Personnel Statistics Web site (http://siadapp.dmdc.osd.mil/personnel/MILITARY/ms1.pdf), as of 12 November 2007.

Note: a) End strength not available; figure is as of 31 August 2007.

Expanding the Army as planned will require sustained effort and more money. A numerical simulation by the Congressional Budget Office found that even expanding the active-duty force to 524,000 by 2010 would require recruiting levels and continuation rates that are higher than the Army has been able to sustain at any time during the past two decades.[4] Getting to 547,000 troops will require even more recruits and better retention. To achieve the planned expansion, the Army will need to increase recruiting and retention bonuses, add recruiters, and expand advertising.

To boost retention in recent years, the Army has encouraged soldiers to reenlist a year before they would normally be permitted to do so. This policy may make it more difficult to achieve retention goals in future years, because those who intend to stay in service may already have made the choice to do so.[5]

The planned expansion of U.S. ground forces may be sufficient for continuing operations in Iraq and Afghanistan at 2006 (presurge) levels. It is not sufficient to sustain additional deployments or deployments larger than about 170,000 ground troops using active-duty forces. A steady diet of stability and reconstruction operations around the world would require even larger additions.

At the end of the cold war, the U.S. active-duty Army numbered some 660,000 troops.[6] The nation's population of eighteen-year-olds is growing, and by 2010 there will be about 15 percent more eighteen-year-old males than there were in 1988. Thus a return to cold war troop levels—an expansion of 140,000 troops above the level of August 2007—hardly seems impossible.

Yet for young people, expectations of what Army service will mean have changed dramatically since the cold war. From the inception of the all-volunteer force (AVF) in 1973, the Army of the cold war was a garrison army. Most soldiers served within the United States or Europe. For most rotations overseas, soldiers were accompanied by their families.

In contrast, even in a cold war–sized Army, the soldier of the future envisioned by both Left and Right should expect at least one deployment during a 4-year term of service. Sustaining the needed levels of recruitment and retention under such conditions may require substantially greater resources.

The Army's Quality Advantage Is Eroding

An infusion of recruiters and money for bonuses and advertising in recent years has helped the services to meet (or nearly meet) their annual numerical goals for active-duty enlisted recruiting, retention, and force size. To achieve its quantity goals, however, the Army has traded substantial quality.

The war in Iraq has taken a pronounced toll on the quality of Army enlistees. The Department of Defense reports the quality of its enlisted recruits using three measures: the fraction of recruits who hold high school diplomas; the fraction who score above the median on the DoD's entrance test of cognitive aptitude, called the Armed Forces Qualification Test (AFQT); and the fraction who score below the 30th percentile on the AFQT. Experience shows that recruits who graduated from high school are more likely to complete their initial service contracts. Those who score above the median on the AFQT are easier to train and perform better at military tasks.[7]

The DoD benchmark standard calls for at least 90 percent of new troops to be high school graduates, at least 60 percent to score above the median on the AFQT, and no more than 4 percent to score below the 30th percentile on the AFQT (see table 2). Meeting these benchmarks has been a hallmark of the AVF. Until recently, the Army has enjoyed a significant quality advantage in both education and cognitive aptitude over the civilian population. Today, however, the educational advantage has disappeared, and the advantage in cognitive aptitude has narrowed significantly. The Army is losing the quality edge that for two decades has distinguished the AVF from what could be expected from a draft force.

Table 2
Quality of Active-Duty Army Enlisted Recruits

	Percentage		
	High school diploma graduates	AFQT	
		Above median	Below 30th percentile
FY 2000	91	65	2
FY 2003	92	73	0
FY 2007	79	61	4
Benchmark	90	60	4
Eighteen- to twenty-four-year-old civilians	79	50	30

Sources: Web site of Under Secretary of Defense (Personnel and Readiness), http://www
.defenselink.mil/prhome/docs/page.html; Department of Defense, "DoD News Briefing with
Under Secretary Chu from the Pentagon," news transcript, 10 October 2007.

Between 1984 and 2004, the fraction of entering enlisted soldiers who were high school diploma graduates never fell below 90 percent.[8] In FY 2007, only 79 percent were high school diploma graduates. This share is consistent with the high school graduation rate for eighteen- to twenty-four-year-olds in the civilian population.

In 2007, 4 percent of Army enlistees—the maximum number allowed under the law—scored in the bottom 30 percent of the AFQT. Only about 60 percent scored above the median, putting the all-volunteer Army closer to the lower level of the civilian population in terms of cognitive aptitude than it has been in more than two decades.

Army recruits are getting to look more like the rest of America in another way: they are older. The tough recruiting environment of the Iraq war pushed the Army to raise the maximum age at which one can enter the force. In January 2006, the Army raised the maximum age of enlistment from thirty-five years to forty years. In June 2006, the maximum age was raised to forty-two. Nearly 2 percent of Army recruits in 2006 were more than thirty-five years old.

The quality problem among Army enlistees is exacerbated by the Army's decision to allow almost every recruit to complete basic training and enter service. As late as the spring of 2006, 18 percent of Army recruits washed out of boot camp. By the end of FY 2007, boot camp attrition was only 7 percent.[9]

Thus, even the weakest members of an already weak class of recruits were passed forward into advanced training and on to operational units.

Recruiting and retention generally respond to changes in the economy. A booming economy and low unemployment make it harder to recruit people and keep them in service, because good jobs in the private sector are plentiful. In contrast, a recession can make things easier. Recruiting and retention are also likely to improve if the war in Iraq ends, or even if troop levels in Iraq decline dramatically.

Unfortunately, however, outside opportunities will be the most plentiful for the soldiers with the most to offer. The lower-quality troops who entered in recent years may find fewer reasons to leave of their own accord. Yet if too many of the higher-quality troops leave when outside opportunities arise, it may be difficult in future years for the Army to restore a suitable level of quality to the cohorts that entered in recent years, without reducing the numbers below the levels it needs in those cohorts. The Army's quality problem could persist for years or even decades, and is likely to hamper Army effectiveness in the missions of the future.

Black Participation Is Declining

African Americans have been a mainstay of the all-volunteer Army since its inception. Black soldiers made up 18 percent of the Army active-duty enlisted force when the draft ended in 1973, and black participation rose to a high of 33 percent in 1981. As of 2001, blacks still made up 29 percent of active-duty enlisted soldiers and 22 percent of new Army recruits. Since then, however, the representation of blacks among new enlistees has plummeted, to just 14 percent in 2005 and 15 percent in 2006—about the same as the share of blacks in the population of eighteen- to twenty-four-year-olds (see table 3).

Black interest in serving in the military also declined between 2001 and 2006 (refer to table 3). In the DoD's 2006 survey of youth propensity, only 9 percent of black young people said that they would definitely or probably serve in the military. Of course, many young people who say they will not join the military ultimately do enlist. Nevertheless, the drop in propensity to serve among black youth does not bode well for black participation in the Army of the future.

Table 3
Black Participation and Interest in the Army

(percent)

	FY 2001	FY 2006
Black share of Army recruits	22	15
Black share of eighteen- to twenty-four-year-old civilians	14	14
Propensity of black youth to serve in military	16	9

Source: Barbara A. Bicksler and Lisa G. Nolan, "Recruiting an All-Volunteer Force: The Need for Sustained Investment in Recruiting Resources" (Arlington, VA: Strategic Analysis, September 2006), p. 8.

The erosion in black interest and participation may not be permanent. Public-opinion surveys indicate that blacks are more likely to oppose the war in Iraq than whites, and they hold a lower opinion of President Bush's performance in office. It is possible that a new administration or the end of the Iraq war will bring them back. In the meantime, however, the bond between the Army and an important source of soldiers has weakened.

The Size and Quality of the Army Officer Corps Are in Jeopardy

The Army today is short about 2,700 captains, majors, and lieutenant colonels.[10] That shortage is likely to persist at a level of about 3,000—or 6 percent of the required total number of officers—until at least 2013. The shortage stems from a combination of factors, including the Army's decision after the cold war to retain existing officers in preference to bringing in new ones, recent difficulties in attracting as many new officers as it wants, and the ongoing expansion and restructuring of Army units.[11]

To improve the situation, the Army has raised its annual targets for bringing freshmen into the Reserve Officer Training Corps (ROTC) at civilian colleges and universities. But it takes four years for a student to advance through ROTC and be commissioned as a second lieutenant. It takes another three years (even under today's accelerated promotion cycles) for the newly minted officer to become a captain, and nine to eleven years of service to make major. Thus it will take seven to fifteen years for the added ROTC freshmen to grow into additional captains or majors.

The numerical shortage of officers is only the tip of the iceberg. Much more problematic for the Army is a hollowing out of quality in the middle and upper ranks that will haunt the service for decades.

During the mid- to late 1990s, young Army officers left service at higher-than-usual rates. To compensate for the loss of captains, the Army initially raised the number of fresh lieutenants brought in each year, reduced the length of time individuals would serve as lieutenants before being promoted to captain, and increased the fraction of lieutenants promoted to captain.[12]

In recent years, company-grade (lieutenant and captain) attrition improved through 2003, but then worsened again, reaching its historical average of 8.5 percent in 2007. To compensate for the earlier and current shortfalls, the Army has increased the promotion rate for every rank from captain to colonel (see table 4).

Because of their hierarchical structures, the services typically cannot add high-quality service members at senior ranks. Instead they sustain quality by bringing in more people than they will ultimately need at the lowest ranks and selecting only the more suitable ones for promotion. Normally the chance of being selected for promotion from lieutenant to captain is 95 percent, while the chance of being promoted from major to lieutenant colonel is only 70 percent.

In 2005, however, fully 98 percent of lieutenants were promoted to captain, and 89 percent of majors were promoted to lieutenant colonel. Those promoted to lieutenant colonel may remain in the force for another decade or more. Thus, the 19 percent of them who under normal circumstances would have ended their careers as majors will continue for a long time as supervisors and mentors of lieutenants, captains, and majors who serve in subordinate positions.[13] The lowered quality in the Army officer corps could persist for decades.

An equally disturbing trend is the recent low retention rate of Army West Point graduates. The Army is experiencing the highest dropout rate for West Point graduates in 25 years. Nearly half of the Military Academy's class of 2001 left active duty during 2006, the year in which they completed their service obligation. The normal 5-year departure rate is between 10 percent and 30 percent.[14]

Table 4
Army Promotion Opportunity

(percent)

Promotion to	Goal	2001	2005
Captain	95	99	98
Major	80	83	98
Lieutenant Colonel	70	76	89
Colonel	50	56	60

Source: Charles A. Henning, "Army Officer Shortages: Background and Issues for Congress" (CRS Report for Congress, 5 July 2006), p. 9.

The Army relies heavily on its West Point graduates for leadership. Today's top Army leaders were the academy graduates of thirty years ago. The high West Pointer attrition rate bodes poorly for the Army leadership of the future. Unfortunately, it may also be a signal of fundamental leadership problems already caused by the current officer shortages and the problematic promotion rates.

The Allies Will Not Fill the Gap

One way the United States could compensate for limited ground forces is to ask allies to commit more troops to the missions of the future. Unfortunately, allied forces are likely to be even more constrained than those of the United States in both quantity and quality.

Some observers hope that African or Arab League nations will provide ground forces to UN missions or to peacekeeping and nation-building operations in which they have a stake. While those countries may be able to muster sizable numbers of troops, however, the quality of their offerings in recent years has been lacking. It would be a mistake to count on such forces to carry the brunt of complex operations like the ones in Iraq or Afghanistan.

Israel has high-quality forces, but teaming with them for operations in the Middle East would be fraught with political concerns. The forces of several European countries are suitable in terms of quality, but about half of Europe's militaries are going through difficult transitions from conscription to all-volunteer forces.[15] Europe's NATO forces were stretched thin even for their limited contributions to operations in Iraq and Afghanistan. They are far from being able to deliver the NATO Response Force of sixty thousand deployable troops as promised at the NATO Prague Summit in 2002.[16]

Civilian Agencies Are Not Staffed for Stability and Reconstruction Operations

Pursuing the foreign policy aims espoused by the front-runners of both political parties will require cadres of territorial administrators to help run governments; build financial and governmental institutions; turn the electricity on; keep water flowing; and set up and monitor elections in weak, failing, and failed states around the globe. Today's State Department is generally populated not by such individuals but by diplomats. Other federal agencies do include people with such skills, but those individuals often lack the international outlook and cultural understanding that will be needed of future administrators.

Building the cadre that would be needed is likely to take decades. In the meantime, the U.S. military, and especially the Army, will likely bear the brunt of this effort.

Notes

1. GAO-05-799, *DoD Needs to Improve the Transparency and Reassess the Reasonableness, Appropriateness, Affordability, and Sustainability of Its Military Compensation System* (Washington, DC: GAO, 19 July 2005).

2. Department of Defense unpublished estimate, cited in Congressional Budget Office, *Evaluating Military Compensation* (Washington, DC: CBO, June 2007), p. 5.

3. Congressional Budget Office, "Estimated Cost of the Administration's Proposal to Increase the Army's and the Marine Corps's Personnel Levels" (Washington, DC: CBO, 16 April 2007), p. 1.

4. Congressional Budget Office, *Recruiting, Retention, and Future Levels of Military Personnel* (October 2006), pp. 30–31. Continuation rate is the proportion of soldiers who remain in the Army for a given period of time, independent of the expiration dates of their contracts.

5. Ibid., p. 11.

6. Office of the Under Secretary of Defense (Personnel and Readiness), *Population Representation in the Military Services* (2005), Table D-11, available at https://humrro03 .securesites.net/poprep/poprep05/contents/contents.html.

7. Bernard D. Rostker and Curtis L. Gilroy, "The Transition to an All-Volunteer Force: The U.S. Experience," in *Service to Country: Personnel Policy and the Transformation of Western Militaries*, ed. Curtis L. Gilroy and Cindy Williams (Cambridge, MA: MIT Press, 2006), pp. 244–245.

8. Web site of Office of the Under Secretary of Defense (Personnel and Readiness), http:// www.defenselink.mil/prhome/docs/page.html (accessed 12 November 2007).

9. Department of Defense, "DoD News Briefing with Under Secretary Chu from the Pentagon," news transcript, 10 October 2007.

10. Charles A. Henning, "Army Officer Shortages: Background and Issues for Congress," CRS Report for Congress (CRS, 5 July 2006), p. 3.

11. Ibid., pp. 3–4.

12. Mark R. Lewis, "Army Transformation, the Exodus, and the Cycle of Decay" (Washington, DC: Institute for Defense Analyses, 2003).

13. Under normal circumstances, officers who are not promoted to lieutenant colonel by the time they complete 20 years in service are required to retire.

14. Bryan Bender, "West Point Grads Exit Service at High Rate; War's Redeployments Thought a Major Factor," *Boston Globe*, 11 April 2007.

15. Cindy Williams, "Introduction," in *Service to Country: Personnel Policy and the Transformation of Western Militaries*, ed. Curtis L. Gilroy and Cindy Williams (Cambridge, MA: MIT Press, 2006), pp. 1–34.

16. The Prague Summit agreed to an initial operational capability for the NRF by October 2004 and full operational capability by October 2006. See NATO Web site (http://www.arrc.nato.int/brochure/nrf.htm [accessed 12 November 2007]).

Panel II: Defense Resources and Risks
Summary of Discussion

Professor Thomas C. Hone
Joint Military Operations Department
U.S. Naval War College

Two issues came to the fore quickly as the papers were presented. The first issue was whether current levels of defense spending would continue long enough to sustain the planned forces. The second issue was whether the future force—especially the Army—would both have the quality of the volunteer force that stormed through Iraq in 2003 and be large enough to satisfy the needs of the combatant commanders in this era of "the long war."

As regards the first issue, Dr. Michael Gilmore's paper assessing the implications of budget projections was clear: the projected program would not sustain the planned forces. As Dr. Gilmore argued, realistic projections of defense spending beyond the current Future Years Defense Program (FYDP) show a mismatch between likely spending and actual needs. Efforts by the military services to overcome this mismatch by reducing their investment levels in research and development (RDT&E) will not work because all the services need to recapitalize—as well as modernize—significant elements of their forces.

Moreover, though the Social Security Trust Fund will probably be able to meet the surge in demand posed by the aging "baby boomers" without drastic changes in the benefit structure, the Medicare and Medicaid programs will probably take significantly more of the nation's gross domestic product (GDP) in the future. That is, the real long-term challenge to sustaining existing defense spending levels is not the projected future end of supplemental appropriations for the conflicts in Iraq and Afghanistan but the steadily growing costs of government-subsidized medical care.

In the discussion triggered by Dr. Gilmore's presentation, it was generally agreed that trying to peg defense spending to some fixed percentage of the GDP was considered a poor substitute for sensibly and rigorously assessing defense requirements. At the same time, those attending the workshop acknowledged that the political leaders of the nation would need to face the challenge of balancing strategic possibilities against budgetary realities and that they might agree to use "percent of GDP" as a defense budget goal.

The second issue consumed much of the discussion time. According to research conducted by Dr. Cindy Williams, the Army is in danger of serious long-term decline because of changes in both the Army's recruiting pool and its officer promotion policies. Moreover, the current policy of enlarging the Army will not offset the decline in the quality of Army recruits and the tendency of young Army officers to leave the Army after their first two tours of duty.

The two major issues were clearly related. For example, personnel costs for all the services have been rising as the services have boosted reenlistment bonuses and as the increase in the cost of medical care generally has also pushed up the cost of medical care for active and retired military personnel. The workshop participants briefly considered returning to conscription as a means of providing the Army with adequate numbers of quality soldiers, but rejected that option because conscripts would have to serve for four to six years to be of any use in conflicts such as those in Iraq and Afghanistan, and no one felt that there was public support for conscripting young citizens for such an extended period of time. While no one wanted to accept a situation where future strategy would be dictated primarily by resource constraints, all the workshop participants realized that such constraints would affect both strategy and operations in the future.

One proposed potential solution to the Army's lack of recruits was the use of waivers for age, lack of a high school diploma, minor teenage misdemeanors, and excess body weight. Though waivers in principle are not such a bad idea, the wholesale use of them to bolster numbers in the short term would hurt the Army over the long run unless the Army chose to let "waivered" recruits go if they didn't turn out to be qualified soldiers. Similarly, promoting large percentages of midcareer officers into the upper ranks (from major to lieutenant colonel and from lieutenant colonel to colonel) might help in the short term but might also rob the Army of a talented pool from which to select its future generals.

No one knew for sure just why so many younger West Point graduates were deciding to leave the Army as captains. However, interviews with departing officers indicated that they and their families were exhausted by extended and frequent deployments to combat zones. The Army has changed its posture dramatically since Desert Storm in 1991. Then, the Army was a garrison force that rarely deployed away from its bases. Now, however, the Army has become a forward-deployed force. It is being "transformed" deliberately and by events in Iraq and Afghanistan into a *routinely deployable* force that will spend much of its time on operations (whether conventional combat or peacekeeping) away from its bases in the United States and Europe. Many potential recruits and many young officers understand this dramatic change in the rhythm of Army life, and many appear not to want to serve in such a force.

The discussion kept returning to a key question: Would the problems associated with long and/or frequent force deployments negatively constrain U.S. strategy? Clearly, capability may not determine policy (or strategy), but it certainly affects it. Would the United States have the ability to conduct two simultaneous campaigns like those in Iraq or Afghanistan in the future? Will the U.S. government avoid future Iraqs? What about picking up troops from allies and coalition partners? Could allied and partner contributions make up for a shortage of U.S. land forces?

No one had firm answers to these questions because the answers had to depend on the circumstances. For example, when the Army completes its transformation plans, it should have forty-eight brigades that are both mobile and equipped with the new Future Combat System. But the projections of the Congressional Budget Office now show the Army not completing that plan in full until about 2035—but the average age of the Army's existing armored vehicles will rise steadily after 2010, creating a mismatch between what systems are needed and when those systems will be available.

Finally, it was suggested that the United States needs to place more emphasis on those forces—mainly air and sea forces—that give it a military "edge" over possible adversaries.

Panel III

Land Forces

Colonel H. R. McMaster
U.S. Army, Senior Research Associate, International Institute for Strategic Studies

David A. Shlapak
Senior Analyst, RAND Corporation

Moderator:
Dr. Mackubin Thomas Owens
Associate Dean of Academics for Electives and Directed Research, and Professor, National Security Decision Making Department, U.S. Naval War College

Learning from Contemporary Conflicts to Prepare for Future War

Colonel H. R. McMaster
U.S. Army
Senior Research Associate
International Institute for Strategic Studies

War is the final auditor of military institutions. In theory, contemporary conflicts such as those in Afghanistan and Iraq provide opportunities for military innovation because of a high sense of urgency and opportunity for feedback based on actual experience.[1] Analysis of the present combined with an understanding of history should permit a grounded projection into the near future and allow defense officials to meet what Sir Michael Howard identified as the challenge to: "steer between the danger of repeating the errors of the past because he is ignorant that they have been made, and the danger of remaining bound by theories deduced from past history although changes in conditions have rendered these theories obsolete."[2] To steer between those dangers we should endeavor to improve dramatically the quality of our thinking about war. We should study recent and ongoing conflicts to identify implications for joint operational concepts, officer education, and the organization, training, and equipping of our forces. Understanding the continuities as well as the changes in the character of armed conflict will help us make wise decisions about force structure and develop relevant joint force capabilities.

Such an effort might begin with an explicit rejection of fantastical ideas concerning the nature of future conflict, ideas that gained wide acceptance in the 1990s and that recent and ongoing experiences have thoroughly discredited. Flushed with the ease of the military victory over Saddam's military forces in the 1991 Persian Gulf War and aware of the rapid advance of communications, information, and precision munitions technologies, many observers argued that U.S. competitive advantages in these technologies had brought about a "revolution in military affairs," or RMA. Many argued that if these technologies were pursued aggressively, military forces could "skip a generation" of conflict and achieve "full-spectrum dominance" over potential adversaries well into the future. It was assumed that, based on the military technological advantages the United States already enjoyed, there would be "no peer competitor" of U.S. military forces until at least 2020. These confident predictions were based on the fundamental assumption that, in the near future, U.S. forces could count on "dominant battlespace knowledge." Joint and service concepts based on this assumption, such as Rapid Decisive Operations, Shock and Awe, Halt Phase, Network Centric Operations and various permutations of Effects Based Operations, proliferated. The most enthusiastic proponents of these concepts argued that U.S. technological advances would "lock out" potential adversaries from the "market" of future conflict. Ultimately, these ideas became subsumed within an amorphous movement termed "defense transformation."[3]

One might think that experiences in Afghanistan and Iraq have administered a corrective to these overconfident predictions. Our track record in learning from even our most proximate experiences, however, is not good. Even before the conflicts in Afghanistan and Iraq, faith in the orthodoxy of defense transformation grew despite experiences that revealed fundamental flaws and false assumptions.[4] RMA advocates "validated" new operational concepts in joint experiments that used attrition-based computer simulations against mirror-imaged future adversaries. These concepts separated war from its political, cultural, and psychological context; military campaigns in these simulations were largely reduced to targeting exercises. Influential organizations within the U.S. military, such as the Army's battle labs and Joint Forces Command J9, focused on how U.S. forces might prefer to fight and then assumed that preference was relevant to the problem of future war. The rejection of the flawed concepts of the 1990s and the associated belief that technological advantage would give U.S. forces the ability to achieve "full spectrum dominance" is overdue.

Today, the United States and our coalition partners are engaged in conflicts in Afghanistan and Iraq that advocates of defense transformation never considered—protracted counterinsurgency and state-building efforts that require population security, security-sector reform, reconstruction and economic development, development of governmental capacity, and establishment of the rule of law. The disconnect between the true nature of these conflicts and prewar visions of future war helps explain the lack of planning for the aftermath of both invasions as well as why it took so long to adapt to the shifting character of the conflicts after initial military operations removed the Taliban and Baathist regimes from power. The wide disparity between prewar military thought and the reality of those conflicts also helps explain why the overextension and strain on U.S. land forces was described as a temporary "spike," why senior military and defense officials resisted reinforcing forces that were clearly overtasked, and why leaders repeatedly denied the need to expand the size of the Army and Marine Corps despite the strain on these forces.[5]

Hubris is an ancient Greek term defined as extreme pride that leads to overconfidence and often results in misfortune. In Greek tragedies, the hero vainly attempts to transcend human limits and often ignores warnings that portend a disastrous fate. The momentum behind defense transformation was based on the belief that technological advantages would permit U.S. forces to transcend war's natural limits, including its political, psychological, cultural, and human dimensions. We now have an opportunity to study ongoing and recent conflicts and ground concepts for future war in an understanding of battle and counterinsurgency at the tactical level, as well as how military operations should support policy goals and objectives. Our experiences in Afghanistan and Iraq as well as Israel's experience in 2006 in Lebanon provide strong warnings that we should abandon the orthodoxy of defense transformation and make appropriate adjustments to force structure and force development.

Policy and Strategy Must Determine Force Structure

We must base force development on how U.S. forces will be employed to protect vital national interests against current and emerging threats. Nineteenth-century

Prussian philosopher of war Carl von Clausewitz observed that "war should never be thought of as something autonomous but always as an instrument of policy." He argued that "the first, the supreme, the most far reaching act of judgment that the statesman and commander have to make is to establish the kind of war on which they are embarking, neither mistaking it for, nor trying to turn it into something that is alien to its nature. This is the first of all strategic questions and the most comprehensive."[6]

During the decade prior to the terrorist attacks against the United States in September 2001, rather than thinking clearly about emerging dangers to national security and viewing threats in the context of history and contemporary conflict, thinking about defense was driven by a "capabilities-based" approach that disconnected war from policy and strategy. Unrealistic expectations concerning the ability to "lift the fog of war" through the application of surveillance and information technology elevated a military capability to the level of strategy. Bad habits developed in peacetime carried over into wartime as military operations were not clearly subordinated to comprehensive plans that aimed to achieve policy goals and objectives. Disconnects between military operations and policy complicated U.S. efforts in Afghanistan and Iraq.[7]

In the 1990s, defense analysis founded on a "capabilities-based" approach reinforced shallow thinking about war. Proponents of capabilities-based analysis argued that:

> the United States cannot know with confidence what nation, combination of nations, or non-state actors will pose threats to vital U.S. interests or those of our allies and friends decades from now. . . . A capabilities-based paradigm—one that focuses more on how an adversary might fight than on whom the adversary might be and where a war might occur—broadens the strategic perspective.[8]

In practice, capabilities-based analysis was narrow and focused on how the United States would like to fight and then assumed that the preference was relevant. In joint force war games during the 1990s, defeat of mirror-imaged enemy forces using U.S. technological capabilities was viewed as an end in and of itself. Operational concepts acknowledged ambiguity in the strategic environment but assumed U.S. technological advantages would allow the military to solve complex strategic problems through the precise application of military force. The elevation of tactical capabilities to the level of strategy skipped the operational level of war that "links the tactical employment of forces to national and military and strategic objectives" through the integration of "ends, conditions, ways, and means."[9]

The principal lesson of the wars in Afghanistan, Iraq, and southern Lebanon might be that military campaigns must be subordinate to strategic plans that integrate political, military, diplomatic, economic, and informational efforts.[10] Because war is an extension of politics, it is illogical to acknowledge an uncertain, unpredictable strategic environment, yet believe in assured results in military operations.[11] The political determinants of war rarely exhibit homogeneity or constancy; political uncertainty carries over into military strategy and operations. War's conduct and outcome depend in large measure on subjective factors such as the will of the people, the wisdom of political objectives, and consistency between those objectives and military strategy. Other factors, such as cultural, tribal, and political identities increase complexity and influence the course of events. Strategy, therefore, must be grounded in social and cultural realities, oriented on achieving clearly defined objectives, and call for the application of resources adequate to achieve those objectives as well as cope with unanticipated conditions and enemy actions.

As Michèle Flournoy argues in the essay in this volume, the U.S. government must develop improved interdepartmental capabilities for planning and executing complex operations, including state-building and counterinsurgency operations.[12] Military operations disconnected from a sound and comprehensive strategy are unlikely to succeed even if the stakes are low and the objectives modest. Military planning must emphasize operational design that begins with a comprehensive understanding of the environment and the enemy. Joint forces must be designed not only to defeat organized and identifiable enemy forces, but also to impose security and undertake the wide range of activities necessary to achieve political objectives. Until other departments within the U.S. government expand deployable capabilities in the areas of establishing local governance and rule of law, developing police forces, improving basic services, building institutional capacity, and setting conditions for economic growth and development, the U.S. military will continue to bear responsibility for those missions. In short, U.S. forces must be capable of conducting complex operations that support policy goals and objectives in the current and anticipated strategic environments.

Counterterrorism Demands a Broad Range of Capabilities

As Richard Schultz and Robert Art point out, protecting vital interests against transnational terrorist organizations will remain a top national defense priority.[13] While experts have been correct to emphasize terrorist organizations' use of improved communications, especially the Internet, as well as their access to increased destructive capacity, terrorist organizations still find it difficult to operate effectively in the absence of an ungoverned safe haven or support base, or without sponsorship or tacit support from nation-states or communities within nation-states.[14] As counterterrorism efforts improve, networked movements like al Qaeda become less effective as they are forced to operate in a more dispersed and compartmentalized manner. It is for this reason that al Qaeda continues to emphasize control of real estate. Indeed, Ayman al Zawahiri and others within al Qaeda's leadership repeatedly emphasize the importance of controlling geographic space, whether it is in the Federally Administered Tribal Areas of Pakistan, in Somalia, or a particular region within Iraq. Considering the terrorist threat as merely a law enforcement, homeland defense, and intelligence problem not only fails to address the long-term causes of terrorism but also overlooks terrorist organizations' immediate sources of strength and support, such as freedom of movement and the ability to plan, organize, and prepare for operations in a safe location.

As Iran engages in proxy wars through terrorist and insurgent groups in Lebanon, Gaza, Iraq, and Afghanistan, it seems clear that the United States must retain its ability to defend its interests against both networked transnational terrorist organizations and nation-states that sponsor those organizations. Indeed, one might argue that the greatest danger to international security lies at the intersection between hostile states and terrorist organizations. It is for this reason that the U.S. Joint Force must retain and expand upon its ability to deter, coerce, or defeat nations that threaten U.S. vital interests or attack those vital interests through proxies.

While maintaining our conventional capability, our joint force must also improve its ability to take on a wide range of missions including interdiction of terrorist movement and support; raids against leadership and support bases; and counterinsurgency, peace support, and state-building operations in places like Afghanistan, Iraq, and other areas that terrorists would like to use as bases of operation. Military forces will also continue to play a vital role in working with friendly governments to develop professional and legitimate security forces capable of defeating terrorist organizations and securing their populations. An examination of recent and ongoing conflicts should be the basis for determining what capabilities are needed to conduct this broad range of operations.[15]

Conventional Conflict Requires Balanced Joint Forces Capable of Fighting Under Conditions of Uncertainty

The realities of campaigns in which the United States and coalition partners have been engaged since 2001, as well as Israel's experience in southern Lebanon in 2006, contrast starkly with pre-2001 predictions about the character of future conventional combat.[16] As Sir Michael Howard observed, no matter how clearly one thinks, it is impossible to predict precisely the character of future conflict. The key, however, is to not be so far off the mark that it becomes impossible to adjust once challenges to security or the conditions of conflict are revealed.[17] Prior to the wars in Afghanistan and Iraq, our assumptions about the nature of future war were widely off the mark. One might argue that if defense transformation had run its course prior to 2001, the United States would have been in a very difficult position without the "legacy" forces that the 2001 Quadrennial Defense Review (QDR) assumed would no longer be relevant. As Dr. Stephen Biddle and others observed, initial military operations in Afghanistan and Iraq revealed increased capabilities of special forces, information and surveillance technology, and precision munitions, but also betrayed more continuities than breaks with previous conflicts.[18]

In Afghanistan and Iraq, surveillance and information technologies failed to deliver the promised "dominant battlespace knowledge" as enemy forces employed traditional countermeasures to coalition technological capabilities, such as dispersion, concealment, deception, and intermingling with civilian populations. While long-range surveillance and precision strike capabilities were essential to the success of both campaigns, an overreliance on these capabilities not only complicated the transition from major combat operations, but also limited the effectiveness of our forces during major combat operations. In Afghanistan, at Tora Bora for example, surveillance of the difficult terrain could not compensate for a lack of ground forces to cover exfiltration routes. After a

16-day battle, many al Qaeda forces, probably including Osama bin Laden, escaped across the Pakistan border.[19]

A close examination of Operation Anaconda in Afghanistan in March 2002 might have administered a corrective to flawed thinking that influenced Army force design as well as coalition planning efforts in Iraq in 2003 and Israeli planning for operations in Lebanon against Hezbollah in 2006. When U.S. intelligence detected a concentration of Taliban forces in the Shah-i-Kot valley, commanders deliberately planned an attack that would include two American infantry battalions reinforced with Afghan and other allied troops. Intelligence preparation for the operation spanned two weeks. U.S. forces focused every available surveillance and target acquisition capability, including satellite imagery, unmanned aerial vehicles, and communications and signal intelligence assets, on a 10- by 10-kilometer box that defined the battleground. Every landing zone for the aerial insertions received extensive unmanned aerial vehicle overflights. Enemy countermeasures to sensors, however, were effective, and the fight during Operation Anaconda was characterized by a very high degree of uncertainty. On March 2, infantry air assaulted almost directly on top of undetected enemy positions. Soldiers came under immediate fire from small arms, mortars, rocket-propelled grenades, and machine guns as their helicopters landed. Battalion and brigade command posts were pinned down; commanders fought alongside their men. Attack helicopters responding to provide direct fire support were hit and rendered inoperable. The planned second lift of soldiers had to be canceled. Some units were immobilized by enemy fire during the first night of the battle and through the next day; they, including many of the wounded, could not be extracted until the following night. The unit had deployed with no artillery under the assumption that surveillance combined with precision fires from the air would be adequate. Even the most precise bombs proved ineffective, however, against small, elusive groups of enemy infantry; soldiers relied on small mortars. As the fight developed over the next 10 days, it became apparent that over half of the enemy positions and at least 350 al Qaeda fighters had gone undetected. The enemy's reaction to the attack was also unexpected. American commanders had expected al Qaeda forces to withdraw upon contact with the superior allied force rather than defend as they did from fortified positions. A combination of small-unit skill, soldier initiative, and determined leadership permitted American forces to shake off the effects of tactical surprise, defeat al Qaeda attacks on the landing zones, and then mount an offensive.[20]

Approximately one year after Operation Anaconda, conventional "legacy" Army organizations designed to fight under uncertain conditions again proved critical during the attack into Baghdad; some of those organizations have since been eliminated or redesigned, based, in part, on the assumption that future tactical and operational environments will be marked by a high degree of certainty.[21] The commander of the U.S. Army's 5th Corps recalled that, contrary to the assumption that future forces would "develop the situation out of contact," every mission during the attack to Baghdad was a "movement to contact," meaning that units had to fight for intelligence and consistently encountered restrictive terrain or enemy forces about which they had received no advance warning.[22] At points in the campaign, even large Iraqi units were able to achieve surprise. For example, during Third Infantry Division's crossing of the Euphrates River, an Iraqi armored brigade counterattacked, undetected in a failed attempt to regain control of crossing sites along the river.[23] Although the divisional cavalry squadron of the Third Infantry Division (a unit designed to fight for information, protect against surprise, and ease the forward movement of follow-on forces) proved invaluable during the attack toward Baghdad, that formation and all others like it have since been eliminated from Army organization in favor of small, lightly armed recon squadrons designed to use mainly aerial and ground sensors to develop situational awareness out of contact. Uncertainty dominated in the rear as well as at the front. Fedayeen Saddam forces that intermingled with the population surprised coalition forces with attacks on supply convoys. The Second Light Cavalry Regiment, a unit designed to conduct security operations across wide areas, was flown from Fort Polk to protect the supply routes; the unit has since been reorganized into a Stryker infantry brigade, due, in part, to the assumption that future enemies will be unable to avoid detection in the same manner as the Fedayeen Saddam.

The major offensive operation that quickly toppled the Hussein regime in Iraq clearly demonstrated the possibilities associated with new technology as well as the effects that improved speed, knowledge, and precision can have in the context of a large-scale offensive operation. However, the initial phases of Operation Iraqi Freedom (OIF) also demonstrated important continuities in warfare that lie beyond the reach of technology. It seems an inescapable conclusion that unconventional forces will continue to evade detection from even the most advanced surveillance capabilities. Moreover, what commanders needed to know most about enemy forces, such as the degree of competence and motivation among them, lay completely outside the reach of technology. Coalition forces in Iraq faced a wide range of enemy forces, including Republican Guard forces, regular Army units, paramilitary forces, and unconventional militias. All exhibited varying degrees of commitment and skill that could be evaluated only after they were engaged in close battle.

The experience of the conflict in Lebanon in 2006 parallels experiences during Operation Anaconda and the offensive phase of Operation Iraqi Freedom. Prior to the 2006 war against Hezbollah, Israeli strategic thought and defense decision-making was infected with some of the worst strains of RMA-related thinking. In a November 2002 article, former U.S. deputy assistant secretary of defense Elizabeth Sherwood-Randall and former Israeli deputy national security adviser Ariel Levite argued that a high degree of discrimination and control was now possible in war because of a "knowledge base that will enable aiming attacks at high-leverage targets, while avoiding irrelevant, politically sensitive, incorrectly identified, or illegitimate sites." The authors suggested that future military operations would emphasize "stand-off firepower over physical movement, software over hardware, and extensive deployment of light infantry as well as special forces over armored or mechanized forces."[24] Sherwood-Randall and Levite called for "capabilities and options for the highly discriminate, calibrated, and nuanced application of conventional military power" to affect the "cost/benefit calculations" of the enemy. With improvements in "intelligence and other situational awareness tools," war would be dominated by the application of "cutting-edge air power."[25] It is difficult to imagine a description of armed conflict that contrasts more starkly with Israel's experience in Lebanon four years later.

The former chief of the Israeli Air Force observed that the Israeli Defense Force (IDF) fixation with new technologies was "addictive and obscured thinking" in connection with the 2006 war against Hezbollah.[26] Consistent with what Sherwood-Randall and Levite proposed, Israeli war plans envisioned a heavy reliance on surveillance and precision strike capabilities and assumed that ground operations would be limited to small skirmishes. Prior to the war, only a small number of Israeli special forces received training geared to operations in southern Lebanon, under the assumption that these small teams could rely on joint fires to accomplish military objectives. Since late 2002, the IDF had reduced armored units, cut back on conscript military service, truncated reserve duty, and abridged training. In 2006, severe training deficiencies were evident when units were mobilized; armored units were in short supply.[27] The U.S. military was on a path similar to the IDF prior to 9-11 as the Department of Defense considered a dramatic reduction in the size of the Army, and especially armored forces, based on the assumption that technology could substitute for legacy forces and weapon systems. Light forces were assumed to have the same capability as combined arms formations because armor protection and firepower could be traded off for improved "knowledge" and access to joint fires.

Experiences in Lebanon, Iraq, and Afghanistan highlighted the enduring uncertainty of combat and the need for balanced air, ground, and maritime forces that can both project power from a distance and conduct operations on the ground to close with and defeat the enemy and secure critical terrain. Yet some observers continue to portray the impressive performance of new technologies and airpower during major combat operations in Afghanistan and Iraq as decisive and consistent with the prewar belief that these capabilities had revolutionized the nature of armed conflict.[28] It seems as if the direction set for force development in the 2001 Quadrennial Defense Review (QDR) has not been altered significantly despite experiences that expose fatal flaws in the assumptions that underpinned that document.

According to the 2001 Quadrennial Defense Review, the purpose of defense transformation was "to maintain or improve U.S. Military pre-eminence" through "the evolution and deployment of combat capabilities that provide revolutionary or asymmetric advantages to US Forces." The QDR stated that transformation efforts will have succeeded when "we divest ourselves of legacy forces and they move off the stage and resources move into new concepts, capabilities and organizations that maximize our warfighting effectiveness and the combat potential of our men and women in uniform." However, it was legacy forces working in combination with improved communications, surveillance, information, and precision strike capabilities that were required in the first major conflicts of the twenty-first century. It was also those legacy forces that were in particularly high demand and short supply during the major combat operations phases as well as during the transition to and conduct of stability and counterinsurgency operations.

It seems obvious that we must develop new joint and service operational concepts or idealized visions of future war that are consistent with what recent and ongoing conflicts have revealed as the enduring uncertainty and complexity of war. We must make these concepts "fighting-centric" rather than "knowledge-centric." Rather than "capabilities-based," these concepts ought to be based on real and emerging threats, informed by recent combat experience, and connected to scenarios that direct military force toward the achievement of policy goals and objectives. We must then design and build balanced forces that are capable of conducting operations consistent with the concepts we develop.

As we administer a corrective to our thinking about the nature and requirements of armed conflict, we should not view force design as a zero-sum game between the services. While we have to recognize that capabilities previously regarded as the answer to the problem of future war are not a substitute for balanced joint forces, they are vitally important. Indeed, without dominance at sea or supremacy in the air, U.S. ground forces would be extremely vulnerable to enemy action, assuming that they could even deploy to an area of operation. Improvements in communications, surveillance, and precision strike technologies do permit a higher level of situational understanding, especially in connection with the disposition of friendly forces. Additionally, U.S. air and naval strike capabilities make it difficult for enemy ground forces to concentrate, except in very complex terrain or urban areas. Vulnerability to our strike capabilities compels enemy forces to disperse and makes them vulnerable to concentrated efforts on the ground.[29] Additionally, the ability of small U.S. forces to bring overwhelming firepower to bear upon contact with the enemy permits our own forces to operate dispersed across wide areas with confidence. Indeed, the psychological benefit associated with ground forces' knowledge that they face no threat from the air and that air and naval forces are prepared to come to their assistance with precise fires at a moment's notice underwrites bold action and is an advantage that should not be taken for granted.

However, recent conventional combat experience also suggests that we should reject the notion that lightness, ease of deployment, and reduced logistical infrastructure are virtues in and of themselves. Indeed, what a force is expected to achieve once it is deployed is a far more important consideration than how quickly it can be moved and how easily it can be sustained. As we endeavor to expand and improve ground force capability for current operations and future contingencies, we must increase airlift and sealift capabilities while maintaining air supremacy and dominance at sea.

Counterinsurgency and Stability Operations Require Joint Forces Capable of Securing the Population

Already committed to two counterinsurgency campaigns, the United States is likely to become engaged in future conflicts against armed groups that employ tactics and strategies similar to those we are facing in Afghanistan and Iraq. As Rupert Smith observed, "frequently we can see that our opponents are deliberately operating below the threshold of the utility of our weapons and organizations as we would wish to use them."[30] Additionally, consistent with previous counterinsurgency experiences, operations in Afghanistan and Iraq have revealed that the key battleground is the population. As the counterinsurgency manual states, "the cornerstone of any COIN effort is establishing security for the civilian populace."[31]

In both Afghanistan and Iraq, some commanders and defense officials were slow to recognize the nature of those conflicts, in part, because those conflicts were incompatible with prewar idealized concepts for military operations. Initial emphasis in both conflicts was on an attrition approach to the complex problem of growing insurgencies against our forces and nascent Afghan and Iraqi governments and security forces. Mainly using technical intelligence and surveillance capabilities, U.S. forces attempted to defeat networked enemy organizations through attacking leadership and reducing critical capabilities. This approach appeared as a counterinsurgency version of "nodal analysis" that viewed the enemy as a complex system that could be collapsed if the right nodes were destroyed.[32] What one might call a raiding approach to counterinsurgency, combined with the rapid generation of Iraqi security forces, seemed to promise rapid results and compensate for coalition troop strength insufficient to secure the population. Similar to defense transformation thinking of the 1990s, however, this approach elevated an important capability to the level of strategy without full consideration of the causes of violence, the sources of enemy strength, enemy strategy, or likely enemy reactions or initiatives.

It seemed as if resources were dictating the strategy rather than the other way around. As indigenous security forces came under increased enemy pressure and insurgent groups replaced leaders who were killed or captured, commanders who had the means to do so moved off large bases and conducted area security operations to protect the population, isolate the insurgents from sources of support, foster political and economic development, build security forces, and help establish the rule of law. However, because of an unwillingness to commit additional forces to secure the population in critical areas, many commanders were only able to continue raiding operations to disrupt the enemy. Meanwhile, insurgent forces were able to coerce the population, retain freedom of movement, establish safe operating bases in areas beyond coalition reach, incite sectarian conflict, and deny coalition and Iraqi forces the ability to establish the degree of security necessary for economic and political development. A lack of troop strength also compelled dispersed coalition forces to move continuously along routes that they were unable to secure, which, one might argue, was the principal cause of large numbers of casualties due to roadside bombs. In 2007, a reinforced security effort in Iraq achieved positive results, but it remains to be seen whether those reinforcements will be sustained in sufficient strength and duration to prevent a resurgence of violence before Iraqi security forces gain sufficient strength and political developments reduce fundamental causes of violence.

Experiences in Afghanistan and Iraq reveal that population security must be the focus of military forces in counterinsurgency operations; technology can assist greatly in that effort, but it cannot substitute for the employment of land forces in sufficient strength to accomplish the broad range of tasks necessary to achieve sustainable security. In weak or collapsed states such as Afghanistan or Iraq, indigenous forces will not have the capability to provide security on their own. Security sector reform and the building of capable and professional security forces take time. While defense transformation theory and doctrinal development in the 1990s emphasized speed, knowledge, and precision, recent combat experience has revealed the need to sustain military operations to shape political outcomes consistent with vital interests, as well as the need for military forces to possess critical skill sets relevant to state-building and the development of security forces. Joint forces must be capable of accomplishing complex mission sets such as those in Afghanistan and Iraq and have the staying power to complete those missions.

The publication of the U.S. Army and Marine Corps counterinsurgency manual, the development of the *Irregular Warfare Joint Operating Concept*, the acknowledgment in the 2006 QDR that U.S. military missions would include counterinsurgency and stability operations, and a November 2005 Department of Defense directive that identifies stability operations as "a core U.S. military mission . . . comparable to combat operations" all indicate a positive shift in thinking about future conflict.[33] Additionally, the decision in January of 2007 to expand the Army and Marine Corps will help relieve pressure on those services and begin to address the imbalance in joint forces that recent combat experience has revealed. However, the same flawed assumptions that complicated U.S. efforts in Iraq and Afghanistan and undermined the IDF's performance in Lebanon are threatening once again to corrupt U.S. force development with promises that improved technology will make future wars conform to the idealized vision of armed conflict that drove the defense transformation movement at the turn of the century.

Obstacles Undermine Our Ability to Learn from Recent and Ongoing Conflicts

Despite what appear to be clear lessons from recent and ongoing conflicts in Lebanon, Iraq, and Afghanistan, we should not assume that the U.S. Defense establishment will make the adjustments necessary to meet future challenges to national security. Historian Williamson Murray concluded that the familiar contention that military institutions fail in war because they focus too closely on the last war was incorrect. In the often-cited case of German military triumph and French defeat in 1940, for example, the Germans benefited from a detailed study of World War I to determine what really happened and identify implications for future war. Meanwhile, the French studied their last war only superficially and used selective observations to justify existing organizations and doctrinal trends. The French avoided meaningful debate and designed war games and exercises to ensure results that reinforced flawed assumptions. Historian Eugenia Kiesling observed that "hard truths were blurred both by optimistic language and by refusal to ask questions whose answers might have proved unsettling."[34] Because flawed assumptions escaped exposure, French military doctrine and institutional culture developed in a way that was incongruous with the conditions of war in 1940. When the Germans invaded, the French, who had assumed they would be able to conduct "methodical battle," maintain communications, prevent surprise, and control operations very closely, were paralyzed and unable to contend with the actual conditions of war.[35] Similarities with the orthodoxy of defense transformation are difficult to overlook. Recent conflicts represent an opportunity to repair the intellectual foundation for defense modernization and adjust force development, but parochial agendas and narrow perspectives threaten to impede the effort to do so.

While it might seem obvious to some that the joint force should focus on improving its ability to conduct counterterrorism, conventional, counterinsurgency, and stability operations similar to those experienced since 2001, others continue to cling to theories that recent experiences should have discredited thoroughly. One argument used to defy reality is that current operations either are derived from flawed policy or are unimportant to U.S. vital interests. For example, U.S. Air Force Major General Charles Dunlap argued recently that the Iraq war is an aberration—an ill-advised "hearts and minds campaign." He went on to suggest that America should eschew conflicts like those in Afghanistan, Iraq, and Lebanon in favor off what he called "scenarios" that call for the destruction of an adversary's "capacity to project power." In Dunlap's construct, war could once again be made simple, fast, inexpensive, and efficient by divorcing military operations from policy or limiting the application of military force to targets capable of "projecting power." Dunlap argued that, in future, "air strikes to demolish enemy capabilities complemented by short-term, air assisted raids and high-tech Air Force surveillance" would be needed, not what he described as "colossal, boots on the ground efforts." Divorced from its political context and limited to armed competition against mirror-imaged adversaries, the problem of future war could be solved by America's "asymmetric advantages."[36] The argument has appeal, in part, because it defines war as we might like it to be.

Additionally, those who advocate for a return to the thinking of the 1990s assert that U.S. airpower and the delivery of "effects" from long range (e.g., bombing) are more "culturally compatible," because these capabilities represent America's "asymmetrical advantage."[37] In an essay in this volume, Air Force Lieutenant General David Deptula argues that increased investment in asymmetric capabilities would permit U.S. forces to "project power without projecting mass."[38] While it is clear that air, space, and cyber systems deliver valuable speed and flexibility, it is unclear how those systems alone deliver sufficient capability to overcome countermeasures, defeat determined adversaries, or achieve political objectives. It is also unclear how ceding control of populations and contested areas and relying mainly on "power projection" capabilities would advance U.S. interests in either Afghanistan or Iraq.

Another argument used to advocate adherence to the orthodoxy of the RMA despite experience to the contrary is that remotely delivered effects hold promise for making war less risky, less costly, and even more humane. Dunlap and Deptula, for example, observe that U.S. ground forces are targeted in Iraq and Afghanistan, and then use that observation to advocate for an increased emphasis on airpower and a decreased emphasis on land forces in future conflict. They seem to attribute combat in Iraq and Afghanistan to the mere presence of U.S. forces rather than the possibility that these forces pose a threat to enemy organizations and enemy designs hostile to U.S. political goals. Deptula argues, for example, that "adversaries have a limited opportunity to contest our presence when we are delivering effects from outside their reach, and often operating outside their awareness." Dunlap and Deptula neglect the political, human, psychological, and cultural dimensions of conflict. They also fail to consider the enemy's ability to react and adopt countermeasures that complicate our ability to deliver relevant effects from outside their awareness. One wonders what kind of remotely delivered capability might secure people from terrorists living in their midst, reconstitute a police force, or interdict concealed vehicle bombs aimed at crowded marketplaces. Dunlap and Deptula imply that one way to compensate for fewer ground forces is more bombing. They suggest that the United States reexamine the degree to which it will accept "collateral damage." They do not explain how bombing suspected targets without the ability to secure the population or discriminate effectively between combatants and noncombatants would support U.S. objectives in Iraq, Afghanistan, or any potential conflict.[39]

Finally Deptula, Dunlap, and others argue that future war will be fundamentally different and suggest that looking at the global economy is more revealing about the nature of future war than ongoing conflicts. For example, Deptula states that "the profound effects of globalization and the information revolution are mirrored, if not magnified in the realm of conflict—where they have recast the nature of our adversaries, redefined the fabric and scope of the battlespace, and reinvented the tools and techniques used to conduct warfare." While Deptula presents no evidence to support his statement, recent experience seems to confirm Clausewitz's observation that "war is a special activity, different and separate from any other pursued by man."[40]

The assumption that future war will lie mainly in the realm of certainty has obscured differences between business and war and fosters the belief that the influence of information technology on business and the economy is directly transferable to war. Prior to the wars in Afghanistan and Iraq, the RMA movement was driven in large measure by the belief that business, finance, and economic analogies are more relevant to understanding future war than war itself. That belief was reinforced by computer simulations that failed to replicate the conditions of war. Faulty analogies and flawed experiments were mutually reinforcing; the experiments promoted the assumption of near-certainty in war and that assumption made war appear comparable to business practices and the economy. The belief that technology can "lift the fog of war" was often combined with business analogies to argue for the efficient and carefully controlled conduct of war. [41] However, as the experiences in Afghanistan, Iraq, and Lebanon have revealed, the continuous interaction with the enemy in war, and uncertainties associated with those interactions, are fundamentally different from business interactions with either markets or competitors. Moreover, efficiency in war means barely winning, and barely winning in war is an ugly proposition. In war one seeks to overwhelm the enemy such that he is unable to take effective action; the business principle of maximum payoff for minimum investment does not apply. Business relies on projections to gauge demand, control production, and manage supply chains, but business practices such as centralization of logistical assets and concepts such as just-in-time delivery, velocity management, and supply chain management are potentially disastrous if applied to the military without consideration of war's unique difficulties.[42] In general, the complexity and uncertainty of war require decentralization and a certain degree of redundancy, concepts that cut against business's emphasis on control and efficiency. The beliefs that technology has made war more certain and permitted war to be waged efficiently betray linear thinking and a failure to consider the continuous interaction with the enemy.[43] This misunderstanding is consequential because military forces designed for business model efficiency rather than effectiveness in war will evidence organizational deficiencies that only become apparent when they confront the uncertainty of combat.

Recent experiences indicate that wars cannot be waged efficiently and highlight the dangers of linear thinking. In both Afghanistan and Iraq, the United States planned troop reductions based on the assumption of linear progression toward stability. As a result, units shifted areas of operation to compensate for troop shortages and unit deployments were accelerated as it became clear that "off ramp" plans were unrealistic. Planners endeavored to commit just enough force to achieve objectives in Afghanistan and Iraq, as well as do just enough to establish security and help nascent governments and security forces assume responsibility for those conflicts. Manifestations of this minimalist approach based on linear thinking and the assumption that war can be waged efficiently included an overestimation of indigenous forces' capabilities and an underestimation of the enemy. Moreover, a short-term approach to long-term problems generated multiple short-term plans that sometimes confused activity with progress.

Rejecting the assertion that future war will be fundamentally different from recent and ongoing conflicts is necessary to protect future commanders from what could become a tendency toward risk aversion and over-control. A belief that technology will deliver information superiority in future war threatens to have a stultifying effect on high-level command. Assuming information superiority might lead some to conclude that making near-perfect decisions based on near-perfect intelligence is the essence of command. As Martin van Creveld warned in *Command in War*, "communications and information processing technology merely constitutes one part of the general environment in which command operates. To allow that part to dictate the structure and functioning of command systems, as is sometimes done, is not merely to become the slave of technology, but also to lose sight of what command is all about."[44] Commanders must be capable of conceptual thought and be able to communicate a vision of how the force will achieve its objectives. Their concepts of operation must harmonize the efforts of disparate entities and direct the force in a way that permits initiative at lower levels while achieving synergy.

America's potential adversaries have detected flaws in U.S. strategic thinking and are determined to capitalize on U.S. overconfidence in technology. A study by two People's Liberation Army officers of the American vision of future conflict observed:

> They believe that as long as the Edisons of today do not sink into sleep, the gate to victory will always be open to Americans. Self-confidence such as this has

made them forget one simple fact—it is not so much that war follows the fixed racecourse of rivalry of technology and weaponry, as it is a game field with continually changing direction and many irregular factors. . . . It appears that Americans, however, do not pay attention to this.[45]

Potential adversaries are developing technological countermeasures to attack components of emerging capabilities. Recent examples include the Chinese demonstration of an antisatellite capability and cyber attacks that demonstrate the vulnerability of information systems. It seems likely that future adversaries will develop countermeasures that pose a significant threat to U.S. surveillance, information, communications, and precision strike capabilities and the network on which those capabilities depend.[46]

Anticipated countermeasures to U.S. capabilities, the nature of recent and ongoing conflicts, and the fundamental flaws in the arguments of those who favor a return to the RMA orthodoxy militate for the development of balanced joint forces. Joint forces must be capable of operating against determined enemies that will attempt to evade and attack our technological advantages. Arguments to the contrary based on narrow or parochial perspectives ought to be rejected. As Charles Callwell observed in his book *Small Wars* at the beginning of the twentieth century, "theory cannot be accepted as conclusive when practice points the other way."[47]

Theory continues to triumph over practice, however, due in large measure to informal relationships between defense contractors, the Department of Defense, Congress, and think tanks; those relationships often cloud judgment, and much of the defense analysis conducted is either convoluted or tainted by conflicts of interest. Military and civilian defense professionals must not surrender intellectual responsibilities to contractors and think tanks, some of whom built client bases on marketing or lending legitimacy to flawed concepts. Conflicts of interest present obstacles to unbiased experimentation. For example, J9 of Joint Forces Command has responsibility both for developing and testing future war concepts.[48] Studies commissioned by the Department of Defense continue to validate concepts using dubious systems analysis and contrived simulations of war. For example, in 2004, after actual combat in Iraq and Afghanistan had revealed valuable lessons in connection with the enduring uncertainty of war, the Acquisition and Policy Center of RAND's National Defense Research Institute (a federally funded research center sponsored by the Office of the Secretary of Defense) responded to a request from the Assistant Secretary of Defense for Networks and Information Integration for a "mathematical framework that can facilitate the development of alternative measures of performance and associated metrics that assess the information quality and team collaboration on shared situational awareness" and "link the improvements in C4ISR [Command, Control, Communications, Computers, Intelligence, Surveillance, and Reconnaissance] to their effects on combat outcomes." The RAND report, authored by analysts who were also part of the Information Superiority Metrics Working Group at DoD, described a "methodology—including metrics, formulas for generating metrics, and transfer functions for generating dependencies between metrics—for measuring the quality of information and its influence on the degree of shared situational awareness."[49] The technical yet ambiguous language in the RAND report is typical of much of the analysis that drives force development. The stark contrast between actual experience and the results of tests and experiments argues for a critical examination of joint and Defense experimentation.

Implications for Land Forces

The U.S. Army, despite having fought for six years under conditions that run counter to the orthodoxy of defense transformation, is still finding it difficult to break away from years of wrongheaded thinking. A recent Association of the United States Army pamphlet, for example, portrays the Army transformation efforts of the late 1990s as completely consistent with the experiences in Iraq and Afghanistan. The Army brigade organization, designed using mainly computer simulations to validate a smaller, lighter, more efficient organization that could "see first, understand first, act first, and finish decisively," has not undergone any significant revision. That so-called doctrine of firsts, based on the assumption of dominant knowledge in future war, has gone largely unchallenged.[50] Indeed, the doctrine of firsts, despite being continually exposed as unrealistic by recent and ongoing combat experience, continues to provide the primary conceptual justification for the Army's modular BCT organization and large acquisition programs such as the Future Combat System.[51]

The belief in the RMA and its related assumptions such as the doctrine of firsts have had a profound effect on Army doctrine and organization. In particular, many Army combat organizations have been designed based on the assumption that "information superiority" over an adversary can substitute for reconnaissance forces, organic firepower, armor protection, engineer units, and other capabilities. Displacement of real fighting capability by anticipated "dominant knowledge" was a key driver of the Army's division redesign in the late 1990s, as well as the current BCT design. Recent combat experience has had no discernible effect on BCT organization, due in large measure to a continued fixation on futuristic experiments in constructive simulations even as U.S. forces are at war. Indeed, as U.S. forces were engaged in Operation Anaconda, analysts at RAND were "validating" the Army future force in computer simulations based on the assumption that ground forces would be able to detect and destroy all enemy from a great distance. Because of that assumed capability, it was no longer necessary to fight for information, engage in close battle, or conduct security operations over wide areas. The Army's new reconnaissance doctrine, for example, makes it clear that the

> BCT reconnaissance squadrons are not designed, equipped, or intended to be employed as a robust direct combat force. Although they possess sufficient armament and firepower for self-defense, they were not overendowed with weapons systems and armor protection for a distinct reason. . . . When reconnaissance units engage in direct combat missions, reconnaissance ceases. When reconnaissance ceases, the potential for achieving and capitalizing upon information dominance is degraded.[52]

Flaws in Army doctrine persist despite experience that points in the opposite direction; flawed doctrine is having a negative effect on Army organization.

Forces equipped only for self-defense under the assumption that information superiority will protect them are certain to suffer a high number of casualties when they engage in actual combat with inadequate firepower, protection, and all-arms capabilities. Indeed, significant deficiencies in the BCT design are obvious to those who have served in combat, yet no comprehensive review has been conducted and Army force development efforts are still based on the fundamental assumption that information superiority and precision long-range munitions permit efficiencies in force design.

The flaws in Army doctrine and force development are potentially fatal. It is obvious that in war, the enemy takes part in decisions that determine when, where, and how forces will fight. If a force optimized for operations under conditions of information superiority loses communications, it could become isolated and unable to access remote fires. Even if such a force is able to prevent tactical surprises, operations are certain to be slow and deliberate, because any degree of ambiguity will necessitate a reallocation of sensors and an analysis effort to avoid risks associated with encountering the enemy unexpectedly. Moreover, if leaders are not conditioned to cope with uncertainty, they are likely to wait for orders when they confront chaotic circumstances. While much of the transformation literature stresses speed, adaptability, and initiative, the force's inability to overmatch the enemy in a close fight will predispose leaders toward waiting for information rather than taking resolute action in uncertain conditions. Indeed, they will have to act cautiously to ensure their force's survival. Ironically, a force that was supposed to be fast and agile will operate ponderously.

Conclusion

We might recognize, as recent and ongoing combat experience indicates, that the factors that preserve uncertainty in war are mainly land-based. This is fundamentally because people live on land and land is where political, social, and cultural factors interact with complex geography to generate profound uncertainty. Also, as C. Kenneth Allard observed, the numbers of "targets" on land are far greater than on sea or in the air. He noted further that "many of these potential targets resist that characterization by becoming extremely adept at using terrain, vegetation, and similar features of an environment that is far more "cluttered" and "dirty" than either the sea or aerospace—and therefore much less susceptible to electronic or other forms of penetration." Operations on land, he observed, provide challenges "for which technology at best provides only incomplete answers."[53]

Learning from real experience could help reverse the trend toward designing imbalanced or vulnerable forces dependent on centralized resources and unable to overmatch the enemy in close combat. Joint and Army doctrine based on theories that recent and ongoing experiences have discredited must be discarded. The disparity between the doctrinal foundation for Army forces and experiences in Afghanistan, Iraq, and Lebanon demand a thorough review of Army organization. Instead of creating more of the same BCT organizations as the Army grows in strength, the Army should conduct a comprehensive review of the BCT design and eliminate deficiencies based on a flawed vision of the nature of conflict. Army programs based on unsound visions of war such as the FCS program should also be reviewed after rejecting the "doctrine of firsts" and acknowledging that future war will remain firmly in the realm of uncertainty.

New doctrine based on logical projections into the near future and grounded in a thorough study of recent and ongoing experience should provide the conceptual foundation for joint and service force design. Forces ought to be designed explicitly to fight under conditions of uncertainty and with degraded capabilities based on enemy countermeasures. In general, flatter, less hierarchical, and more autonomous organizations are more capable of operating in uncertain environments than hierarchical organizations. Forces must also be designed for effectiveness rather than efficiency. While a higher degree of joint integration is desirable, the concept of joint interdependence is interpreted as the ability to achieve economies by eliminating redundancies.[54] Organizing units to operate in uncertain environments, however, will entail tolerating a higher degree of redundancy; autonomous organizations must be capable of not only employing but also controlling the full range of capabilities.[55] If lower-level commanders have to rely on higher-level commands for assets and capabilities, it is not clear if those assets will be made available or if the capabilities will be responsive under all conditions.

The following additional actions might be undertaken to ensure that U.S. forces are developed in such a way that they are relevant to the problem of future conflict and are capable of achieving military outcomes consistent with U.S. vital interests.

- Discard obviously flawed idealized visions of future war and the assumptions that underpin them.

- Declare that the "revolution" in sensor, communication, information, and precision engagement technologies has occurred. Study these advances in the context of recent conflicts and integrate what is available (or what will become available shortly); explicitly abandon the idea of "skipping a generation" of technology.

- Pay attention to countermeasures; anticipate them by hardening networks and creating redundant capabilities, but also understand that U.S. forces must have the capability to continue fighting if networks are degraded.

- Go back to the drawing board on selected Joint Concepts, Joint and Service Doctrine, and Army Training and Doctrine Command pamphlets meant to direct force development. Inform new concepts and revised doctrine with a thorough study of recent and ongoing conflicts and an examination of what those conflicts reveal about the possibilities and limitations of emerging technology. Give senior officers with recent combat experience oversight of doctrinal and concept development.

- Eliminate the practice of contracting out the intellectual responsibilities of military professionals, civil servants, and civilian defense leaders. Eliminate conflicts of interest; defense contractors should not be producing and testing operational concepts that can later be used to justify the purchase of their systems or products.

- Declare a moratorium on joint and service experimentation until these programs can be audited and evaluated.

- Educate officers to think broadly about the problem of future conflict; develop additional opportunities for graduate-level education in relevant disciplines at the best programs.

- Continue to pursue joint integration and look for economies and synergies between the services, but abandon the concept of joint interdependence and accept necessary redundancies to ensure that forces are designed for effectiveness rather than efficiency and in recognition of the unique demands of combat in each of the media of air, space, sea, and land.

- Discard the notion that lightness is a virtue in itself. Design forces for what they are to accomplish in wartime and then build sufficient logistical and lift capacity to sustain and transport that force.

Notes

1. Stephen Rosen, *Winning the Next War: Innovation and the Modern Military* (New York: Cornell University Press, 1994), pp. 109–110.

2. Michael Howard, "The Use and Abuse of Military History," in Michael Howard, ed., *The Causes of War and Other Essays* (Cambridge, MA: Harvard University Press, 1983), p. 195.

3. According to the 2001 Quadrennial Defense Review (QDR), the purpose of defense transformation was "to maintain or improve US Military pre-eminence" through "the evolution and deployment of combat capabilities that provide revolutionary or asymmetric advantages to US Forces." The QDR stated that current transformation efforts would have succeeded when "we divest ourselves of legacy forces and they move off the stage and resources move into new concepts, capabilities and organizations that maximize our warfighting effectiveness and the combat potential of our men and women in uniform." Successful transformation would allow the United States to "dominate future military competitions." For a discussion of Defense Transformation, see H. R. McMaster, "Crack in the Foundation: Defense Transformation and the Underlying Assumption of Dominant Knowledge in Future War," U.S. Army War College Center for Strategic Leadership, Nov. 2003. Available at http://www.carlisle.army.mil/usacsl/Publications/S03-03.pdf.

4. The American experience in Somalia between December 1992 and early 1994 might have exposed the folly of assuming dominant battlespace knowledge. Technological sources of intelligence were of little value in Somalia. Commanders relied on human intelligence as the primary source of information. Strategic and operational uncertainties were amplified at the tactical level. Soldiers and Marines operated in a populous, congested urban area in which almost everyone was armed; it was difficult to distinguish between friendly forces, neutrals, and those opposed to the humanitarian effort. For Marines and soldiers, the complex social, political, and geographical environment blurred distinctions between peacekeeping operations and combat operations. The inherent uncertainties of the Somalia operation were revealed and amplified on 3 October 1993, as U.S. Army Rangers began what they thought would be a mission of short duration to apprehend two of General Aidid's principal deputies. The interactions that occurred between Somali militia and the Rangers defied situational understanding. NATO's Kosovo experience in 1999 also demonstrated that the causes of uncertainty in the conduct of war

lie mainly outside technology's reach: war's political nature, its human dimension, its complexity, and interaction with the enemy. NATO enjoyed air supremacy and faced antiquated air defenses. The Serbs had no ability to disrupt NATO communications or information systems. Near-certainty combined with long-range precision fires was supposed to vitiate the need for ground forces and make possible a fast, low-cost, low-casualty war. The campaign was supposed to last five days; it lasted eleven weeks and ended after 40,000 aircraft sorties and the threat of a ground invasion. The way in which the war was conducted increased the suffering of both Kosovar Albanians and Serbian civilians and made air power much less effective than it would have been if it had been employed as part of air-land operations. NATO achieved dominance of the air, but that achievement did not translate into dominance on the ground. The absence of a ground force to compel the Serbs to desist from their campaign of terror and to render ineffective the countermeasures taken against air forces allowed Serbia to terrorize the ethnic Albanians and work to turn world public opinion against NATO. The problems experienced during Operation Allied Force were not failures of air power; they were failures based on unrealistic expectations that elevated a military capability to the level of strategy. Once the effects of Operation Allied Force were combined with other elements, such as increased diplomatic pressure (especially from Russia), a Kosovo Liberation Army offensive, and the threat of a NATO ground offensive, NATO succeeded and Milosevic acquiesced.

5. See, for example, Secretary of Defense Donald Rumsfeld's FY2005 budget testimony delivered on 4 February 2004. He stated that "the increased demand on the force we are experiencing today is likely a 'spike,' driven by the deployment of nearly 115,000 troops in Iraq. We hope and anticipate that that spike will be temporary. We do not expect to have 115,000 troops permanently deployed in any one campaign." Available at http://findarticles.com/p/articles/mi_m0PAH/is_2004_Feb_4 . His comment might have inspired a question: If forces are not designed for the "spike" of wartime, what are they designed for?

6. Carl von Clausewitz, *On War*, ed. and trans. Michael Howard and Peter Paret (Princeton, NJ: Princeton University Press, 1976), pp. 88–89.

7. This self-delusion has not been limited to the United States. Many of the difficulties that Israel experienced in southern Lebanon in the summer of 2006, for example, can be traced to conceptual flaws similar to those that corrupted U.S. thinking about conflict.

8. Department of Defense, Annual Report to the President and the Congress, 2002, pp. 19–20. Available at http://www.dod.mil/execsec/adr2002/pdf_files/chap2.pdf.

9. On this point, see Antulio J. Echevarria, *Toward an American Way of War* (Carlisle, PA: Strategic Studies Institute, March 2004), available at http://www.strategicstudiesinstitute.army.mil. The definition of the operational level of war is taken from the definition of operational art in Joint Publication 3.0, *Joint Operations*, 17 September 2006, pp. xiii, xx. Available at http://www.dtic.mil/doctrine.

10. Similar to coalition plans for Iraq that failed to anticipate the collapse of the Iraqi state, the demands of post-conflict stability operations, or the growth of an insurgency, Israeli plans did not subordinate military operations to political goals and objectives or fully consider likely enemy reactions. As a result, the IDF encountered unanticipated military difficulties and performed poorly on the critical battleground of perception.

11. The idea of "war as an extension of politics" included far more than the connection between military strategy and national policy. Clausewitz was particularly sensitive to the emotions and social forces unleashed by the French Revolution. For an analysis of Clausewitz's views of *Politik* and war, see Antulio J. Echevarria II, "War, Politics, and the RMA—The Legacy of Clausewitz," *Joint Force Quarterly*, Winter 1995–1996, pp. 76–80.

12. Michèle A. Flournoy, "Navigating Treacherous Shoals: Establishing a Robust Interagency Process for National Security Strategy, Planning, and Budgeting," pp. 271–279 in this monograph.

13. Dr. Richard Shultz, "The Evolving International Security Environment of the 21st Century: Armed Groups and Irregular Warfare," pp. 241–259 in this monograph; and Dr. Robert J. Art, "America's Grand Strategy after Bush," pp. 13–22 in this monograph.
    Schultz identifies al Qaeda, Hezbollah, and the Global Salafi-Jihad Movement as groups that pose a "direct strategic threat" to the United States.

14. For a detailed study of critical ungoverned territories, see Angel Rabosa, Steven Boraz, et al., *Ungoverned Territories: Understanding and Reducing Terrorism Risks*, (Santa Monica, CA: RAND Corporation, 2007). Available at http://www.rand.org/pubs/ monographs/2007/RAND_MG561.pdf.

15. This examination should also include recent unconventional operations in the Philippines and Somalia.

16. Perhaps with this in mind, Secretary of Defense Robert Gates recently observed, "We have seen in Iraq that once war is unleashed, it becomes unpredictable." David Cloud and Mark Mazzetti, "Senate Panel Approves Defense Nominee," *New York Times*, 5 December 2006. Available at http://www.nytimes.com/2006/12/05/washington/ 06gatescnd.html.

17. Howard, "The Use and Abuse of Military History," pp. 194–195.

18. See Stephen Biddle, "Afghanistan and the Future of Warfare: Implications for Army and Defense Policy," Strategic Studies Institute, Carlisle Barracks, PA, November 2002, esp. pp. 1–3. On Iraq, see Stephen Biddle et al., "Iraq and the Future of Warfare: Implications for Army and Defense Policy," August 2003, U.S. Army War College, available at http://www .globalsecurity.org/military/library/congress/2003_hr/03-10-21warcollege.pdf. A senior officer on the U.S. Army staff initially suppressed the Iraq briefing and the paper on which it is based.

19. See Philip Smucker, *Al Qaeda's Great Escape: The Military and the Media on Terror's Trail* (Washington: Potomac Books, 2004), pp. 139–142.

20. On Operation Anaconda, see Biddle, "Afghanistan and the Future of Warfare: Implications for Army and Defense Policy." See also Sean Naylor, "Operation Anaconda," paper delivered at the MIT Security Studies Program, 22 March 2006, available at http://web.mit.edu/ssp/seminars/ wed_archives_06spring/naylor.htm.

21. "Units of Action will be able to see first, understand first, act first, and finish decisively on the tactical battleground. This leap-ahead operational capability, enabled by advanced technologies, is a completely new paradigm of how tactical units will fight and win. . . . " Department of the Army, Training and Doctrine Command, TRADOC Pamphlet 525-3-90, "Objective Force Maneuver Units of Action," 1 November 2002.

22. On the assumption that forces would be able to develop situations out of contact, see ibid. Interview with GEN William Wallace, available at http://www.pbs.org/wgbh/pages/ frontline/shows/invasion/interviews/wallace.html.

23. See interview with LTC Ernest Marcone, available at http://www.pbs.org/wgbh/pages/ frontline/shows/invasion/interviews/marcone.html#gap.

24. Ariel E. Levite and Elizabeth Sherwood-Randall, "The Case for Discriminate Force," *Survival* 44, no. 4 (Winter 2002–2003), pp. 81–98.

25. Ibid.

26. The Air Force conducted a comprehensive review of the operation and recommended organizational and procedural adjustments to make better use of surveillance and strike assets and improve air and ground force integration. The report did not conclude that the operation exposed limits in surveillance and strike capabilities. See United States Air Force, *Operation Anaconda: An Air Power Perspective* (Washington: U.S. Air Force, 2005). Available at http://www.af.mil/library/posture/Anaconda_Unclassified.pdf.

27. Ephraim Inbar, "How Israel Bungled the Second Lebanon War," *Middle East Quarterly* 14, no. 3 (Summer 2007), available at http://www.meforum.org/article/1686. See also David Makovsky and Jeffrey White, "Lessons and Implications of the Israel-Hizballah War: A Preliminary Assessment," Washington Institute for Near East Policy, Policy Focus

#60, October 2006, available at http://www.washingtoninstitute.org/pubPDFs/PolicyFocus60.pdf.

28. Early interpretations of operations in Afghanistan suggested the possibility of applying the "Afghan Model" of U.S-provided air and sea-based firepower combined with indigenous forces to future conflicts, including the coalition offensive in Iraq. For a list of articles and statements concerning the "Afghan Model," see Biddle, "Afghanistan and the Future of Warfare: Implications for Army and Defense Policy," pp. 1–3. These arguments persist. See, for example, LtGen David A. Deptula, "Air and Space Power Going Forward: Lead Turning the Future," pp. 189–198 in this monograph.

29. For one perspective on how technology has influenced the relative roles of air and ground forces, see David Johnson, *Learning Large Lessons: The Evolving Roles of Ground Power and Air Power in the Post–Cold War Era*, available at http://www.rand.org/pubs/monographs/MG405-1/.

30. Rupert Smith, "Thinking About the Utility of Force in War Amongst the People," in *On New Wars*, ed. John Andreas Olsen (Oslo, Norway: Oslo Files on Defense and Security, 2007), p. 37.

31. FM 3–34, Counterinsurgency (Washington, DC: U.S. Government Printing Office, December 2006), p. 1-23. Available at http://www.fas.org/irp/doddir/army/fmi3-07-22.pdf.

32. See, for example, John A. Warden III, "Employing Air Power in the Twenty-first Century," in *The Future of Air Power in the Aftermath of the Gulf War*, ed. Richard H. Shultz, Jr., and Robert L. Pfaltzgraff, Jr. (Maxwell AFB, AL: Air University Press, July 1992).

33. Department of Defense Directive 3000.05, "Military Support for Stability, Security, Transition, and Reconstruction (SSTR) Operations," 28 November 2005, available at http://www.dtic.mil/whs/directives/corres/pdf/300005p.pdf.

34. Eugenia C. Kiesling, *Arming Against Hitler: France and the Limits of Military Planning* (Lawrence, KS: University Press of Kansas, 1996), pp. 136–143, 175–181. Quotation is from p. 180.

35. Robert Doughty, *The Breaking Point: Sedan and the Fall of France, 1940* (Hamden, CT: Archon Books, 1990), esp. pp. 27–32.

36. Major General Charles Dunlap, "America's Asymmetric Advantage," *Armed Forces Journal*, available at http://www.armedforcesjournal.com/2006/09/2009013. One might also make the observation that 160,000 U.S. troops in Iraq does not represent a "colossal" commitment by historical standards.

37. Ibid. Deptula, "Air and Space Power Going Forward."

38. Deptula, "Air and Space Power Going Forward." In January 2003, LtGen Deptula suggested the following: "I want to see a set of integrated physical and cognitive effects models that could help this nation achieve its national security objectives without the adversary even knowing that he's been influenced." MajGen David Deptula, USAF, "A Dialogue on Analyzing Effects Based Operations (EBO)," an interview by Dr. Jacqueline Henningsen, Director, Air Force Studies & Analyses Agency, http://www.mors.org/publications/phalanx/mar02/Lead2.htm (3 January 2003).

39. Dunlap, "America's Asymmetric Advantage." Deptula, "Air and Space Power Going Forward."

40. Clausewitz, *On War*, p. 187.

41. In the late 1990s, network-centric warfare formalized analogies between war and business. In a 1998 book that advanced the concept, David Alberts, John Gartska, and Frederick Stein indicated that network-centric warfare depended on a high-performance information grid that "translates information into combat power by effectively linking knowledgeable entities in the battlespace." David Gompert and Irving Lachow, "Transforming U.S. Forces: Lessons from the Wider Revolution," RAND Issue Paper, 15 November 2002, p. 2, available at http://www.rand.org/publications. In an article that appeared in the Naval Institute's *Proceedings* during that same year, the late VADM Cebrowski and Mr. Gartska asserted that, "Network centric operations deliver to the US military the same powerful dynamics as they produced in American business. At the strategic level the critical element

for both is a detailed understanding of the appropriate competitive space—all elements of the battlespace and battletime." Arthur K. Cebrowski and John J. Gartska, "Network Centric Warfare: Its Origin and Future," *Proceedings*, January 1998, p. 32. Other examples included a direct application of Metcalf's Law—the idea that as the number of nodes in a network increases linearly, the effectiveness of that network "increases exponentially as the square number of nodes in the network." Based on that "law," the network promised to deliver a "superior information position." The authors argued that the military and business shared interest in gaining access to an "information grid." As a "sensor grid" generates "competitive space awareness" for business, it would generate "battlespace awareness" for the military. As network-centric businesses use "transaction grids" to translate high levels of awareness into specific actions such as shipping orders, increasing production, and ordering parts, the network-centric military would use "engagement grids" to target and strike enemy assets. Alberts, Gartska, and Stein, *Network Centric Warfare*, pp. 25–26.

42. The human and psychological dimensions of war often make projecting demand for needs such as fire support or logistical supplies impossible to make with any degree of specificity. Consider, for example, an attack during which an enemy who was expected to offer stiff resistance collapses suddenly. If the means to exploit that transitory advantage, such as fuel, are not immediately at hand, forces may miss a fleeting opportunity. Unanticipated enemy actions, such as the interdiction of air or ground supply lines, and weather, such as sandstorms that limit air and ground resupply operations, militate for decentralization of assets even if such an organization seems inefficient in peacetime.

43. Prior to experiences in Afghanistan and Iraq, many believed that a systems approach to war based on "operational net assessment (ONA)" would produce "a comprehensive system-of-systems understanding of the enemy and the environment." Operations could thereby achieve a high degree of speed as well as precision in operational effects. ONA would permit commanders to understand even second and third-order effects, and military operations (essentially precision attacks against enemy "nodes") would deliver progress linearly and rapidly toward victory. The enemy would be unable to respond effectively and would fall victim to "cumulative and cascading effects." It is assumed that because of near-perfect intelligence and knowledge of the enemy's reactions, actions necessary to achieve desired effects can be calculated with a great deal of precision and the application of force, therefore, can become very efficient and controlled. Under the concept of distributed operations, for example, it is assumed that commanders will have enough "knowledge" to "give distributed combat groups enough combat power to accomplish the required ends and survive the encounter." U.S. Joint Forces Command, Notes from Distributed Operations Workshop 3–4, December 2002. Concept developers identified "knowledge" as the critical enabler of distributed operations and also identified the risks associated with conducting distributed operations without information superiority.

44. Martin van Creveld, *Command in War* (Cambridge, MA: Harvard University Press, 1985), p. 275.

45. Qiao Liang and Wang Xiangsui, *Unrestricted Warfare*, trans. FBIS (Beijing: People's Liberation Army Literature and Arts Publishing House, February 1999), pp. 215, 221.

46. Historically, countermeasures have limited the effects of all "dominant" weapons on the battlefield. A cursory examination of twentieth-century conventional weapons development reveals technological interactions that limited the effects of new technology. On land, the machine gun seemed decisive until the introduction of mobile protected firepower; the tank seemed decisive until the introduction of tank-killing systems. In the air, the development of radar limited the effectiveness of the bomber. The submarine may have dominated the seas were it not for the invention of sonar, and battleships controlled the ocean's surface until the advent of naval aviation. Although Nazi Germany's strategic communications seemed invulnerable, the Allies had access to transmissions after capturing an Enigma machine and breaking the codes. Advocates of decisive weapons or technological capabilities have a history of ignoring countermeasures. Today, potential adversaries are closely monitoring American military operations and defense transformation initiatives to develop countermeasures to U.S. capabilities. As Secretary of

Defense Donald Rumsfeld observed, "No nation relies more on space for its national security than the United States. Yet elements of the U.S. space architecture—ground stations, launch assets and satellites in orbit—are threatened by capabilities that are increasingly available." For Secretary Rumsfeld's comments, see Molly Peterson, "Defense Chief Outlines Challenges of Information Warfare," *Government Executive Magazine*, 16 August 2002, available at http://www.govexec.com. For countermeasures under development that threaten American communications and "network-centric" capabilities, see Michael O'Hanlon, *Technological Change and the Future of Warfare* (Washington, DC: Brookings, 2000), pp. 58–61, 195–196. The Chinese are pursuing electromagnetic pulse weapons and other countermeasures. Mark A. Stokes, "Chinese Ballistic Missile Forces in the Age of Global Missile Defense: Challenges and Responses," in *China's Growing Military Power: Perspectives on Security, Ballistic Missiles, and Conventional Capabilities*, ed. Andrew Scobell and Larry Wortzel (Carlisle Barracks, PA: Strategic Studies Institute, 2002), pp. 135–136. See also Susan Pushka, "Rough But Ready Force Projection: An Assessment of Recent PLA Training," in the same volume, pp. 240–241. See also essays in Steven Lambakis, James Kiras, and Kristin Kolet, eds., *Understanding "Asymmetric" Threats to the United States* (Washington, DC: National Institute for Public Policy, 2002). Marie Squeo, "US Military's GPS Reliance Makes a Cheap, Easy Target," *Wall Street Journal*, 24 September 2002. Similarly, LtGen Deptula highlights the dangers of countermeasures to U.S. space-based systems. Deptula, "Air and Space Power Going Forward."

47. Charles E. Callwell, *Small Wars* (London: Greenhill Books, 1990), p. 270.

48. Government Accounting Office, "Military Transformation: Actions Needed to Better Manage DoD's Joint Experimentation Program," August 2002, pp. 5–6. That conflict of interest appears similar to accounting firms such as Arthur Anderson having management consulting and auditing responsibilities.

49. Walter Perry, David Signori, and John Boon, "Exploring Information Superiority: A Methodology for Measuring the Quality of Information and Its Impact on Shared Awareness," 2004, available at http://www.rand.org/pubs/monograph_reports/MR1467/MR1467.pdf.

50. Mark Rocke and David Fitchitt, "Establishing Strategic Vectors: Charting a Path for Army Transformation," Association of the United States Army, April 2007, available at http://www.ausa.org/pdfdocs/special/may07.pdf.

51. It is assumed that "multispectral sensors" will permit the FCS-equipped brigades to "see first, understand first, act first, and finish decisively." See Program Manager FCS, "FCS Whitepaper," 11 April 2006, p. 4, available at http://www.army.mil/fcs/whitepaper.

52. FM 3-20.96, Cavalry Squadron (RSTA), September 2006, pp. 1–9, 1–10.

53. C. Kenneth Allard, "Information Warfare: The Burden of History and the Risk of Hubris," in *The Information Revolution and National Security: Dimensions and Directions*, ed. Stuart J. D. Schwartzstein (Washington, DC: Center for Strategic and International Studies, 1996).

54. Joint interdependence was based, in part, on the assumption that war on land was similar to war at sea and in the air. Recent experience has revealed, however, that technologies that permit naval and air forces to dominate the fluid media in which they operate do not have a similar effect on land. By the late 1990s, important efforts to enhance joint interoperability began to describe the air, ground, and sea environments as a "singular" or "unified" battlespace. While encouraging a holistic view and recognizing the need for improved integration of air, sea, and land operations were positive developments, those terms and the more recent term joint interdependence obscured critical differences.

55. Diversification of capabilities and the formation of smaller, autonomous units are consistent with general methods for coping with uncertainty and complexity. See F. David Peat, *From Certainty to Uncertainty: The Story of Science and Ideas in the Twentieth Century* (Washington, DC: Joseph Henry Press, 2002), esp. pp. 143–144.

Adapting U.S. Land Forces to Meet Future Demands[1]

David A. Shlapak
Senior Analyst, RAND Corporation

Profound as the effects of the terrorist attacks on New York City and Washington, DC, were and will continue to be, they are but one dimension of a global security environment that is undergoing multiple, wrenching changes. Indeed, if the period between 1990 and 2001 can be called the "post–Cold War world," it may be apropos to term the current period the "post post–Cold War world." This paper aims to do two things: illuminate some aspects of the complex and potentially dangerous nature of this new era and suggest how U.S. military forces—particularly land forces—might need to change to adapt to its demands.[2]

Not One but Five "Long Wars"

The Department of Defense's (DoD's) 2006 *Quadrennial Defense Review Report* characterizes the wars in Afghanistan and Iraq as elements of a "long war" against "the enemies of freedom."[3] While one may quarrel with the specifics of how the report portrays this struggle, it is undoubtedly accurate in at least one respect: the offensive that the United States and its partners have undertaken against al Qaeda and its ilk has indeed been protracted. It has already lasted six years—longer than the U.S. Civil War or the nation's involvement in the two world wars combined—and victory, however defined, does not seem near. In violent Islamic extremism, the United States appears to find itself confronting an enduring challenge to its security and interests.[4]

However, the "long war" against terrorism is not the only substantial security problem confronting the United States. The United States in fact presently faces five such lasting challenges. While none of the other four entail ongoing violence, three feature some risk of conflict and all impose difficult and divergent demands on American military posture; it is therefore only slightly hyperbolic to refer to them as "five long wars." The list consists of

- Containing violent Islamic extremism (the Quadrennial Defense Review's [QDR's] "long war")

- Dealing with nuclear-armed regional powers like North Korea and possibly others in the future

- Managing an emerging security competition in Asia, especially countering the growing power of a rising China

- Coping with a Russia that is increasingly both authoritarian and assertive

- Managing this complex set of challenges while the foundations of the network of U.S. alliances and partnerships are undergoing tectonic, historic shifts.

These enduring problems will be the defining characteristic of a new era in U.S. national security.[5] This new world is one from the vantage of which the 1990s appear a golden age of unrivaled U.S. power.

In the interest of (relative) brevity, we will eschew a description of each of the "long wars" and instead focus on two of their principal implications for force planning. These are:

- The wars in Afghanistan and Iraq are not the right models for the future of the "war on terror."

- Future major combat operations (MCOs) will likely be much more challenging than the "standard-issue" scenarios that dominated planning for conventional forces for the past fifteen years.

Containing Violent Islamic Extremism: The Future of the "War on Terror"

This first "long war" needs little or no introduction, as conflicts associated with it in Afghanistan and, especially, Iraq have been and remain at the forefront of both public attention and DoD planning.[6] These large-scale invasion, occupation, and security and stabilization operations (SASOs), however, should not be seen as the template for the future of the "war on terror." The experience in Iraq has almost certainly reduced American willingness to undertake similar ventures in the future, and it is difficult to identify serious candidate targets for the next "regime change" that would or could be undertaken by the United States acting largely alone.[7] Indeed, one lesson of these two campaigns is not simply that the United States generally *should* not undertake operations of such scope, complexity, and length on its own but the hard-earned recognition that it *cannot*.

Instead, our analysis suggests that containing or defeating violent Islamic extremism can best be achieved by an approach that focuses strategically on close cooperation with and support of friendly and allied governments, and operationally on small but sustained missions aimed at helping those governments "maintain relentless pressure" on terrorists and insurgents.[8] These missions, which could range in scope from a single mobile education training team (METT) to larger security-assistance efforts, will more closely resemble undertakings such as supporting counterinsurgency in El Salvador, the Georgia Train and Equip Program, and the *Balikatan* series of exercises with the Philippines than they will the wars in Iraq and Afghanistan.

While any individual operation is likely to be fairly small, the aggregate demand could be sizable. Up to thirty or more train, equip, advise, and assist (TEAA) missions might need to be undertaken simultaneously to achieve the desired effects against transnational terrorist organizations.[9] To succeed, the joint force will need to develop and maintain a large pool of personnel with appropriate language skills and cultural knowledge, experience in the applicable countries and regions, and intensive training in the right military and civil-operations skills, and who are provided with ample intelligence, information, security, and support personnel and resources. Even absent another contingency of the magnitude of Iraq or Afghanistan, these requirements for people and capabilities—people and capabilities that do not appear to exist in the right kinds or numbers in the force today—will not be easy to fill.[10]

"Not Your Father's MCO": The Challenges of Future Major Conflict Scenarios

For most of the period since the fall of the Berlin wall and the collapse of the Soviet Union, official planning for U.S. general-purpose forces has centered on meeting the requirements levied by two "big war" scenarios, referred to variously as "major theater wars," "major regional contingencies" (MRCs), or MCOs, and generally associated with defeating a North Korean invasion of South Korea and beating back an Iraqi attack on Kuwait and Saudi Arabia. These scenarios had much in common:

- They pitted U.S. and coalition forces against an opponent who was qualitatively vastly inferior.

- The adversary had a large army but minimal air or naval capabilities.

- The fight was about defeating a mass invasion across a land border.

- Nuclear weapons figured little or not at all in the adversary's strategy.

In the near to midterm, none of America's three most likely MCO opponents match all the above characteristics, and one matches none.[11]

That one is China, whose growing military power is amply documented, as is Beijing's emphasis on fielding "antiaccess" capabilities intended to complicate a U.S. military response to an attack on Taiwan.[12] China is developing the ability to contest U.S. control of the seas, air, and space; its burgeoning arsenal of conventional ballistic and cruise missiles threatens not just targets on Taiwan but United States power-projection bases in the region; and its ability to strike targets throughout Eurasia and North America with nuclear weapons poses escalatory risks not seen since the end of the Cold War.[13]

North Korea's nuclear test in October 2006 shook more than the real estate surrounding the detonation site in Gilju. While the Six-Party Talks appear to have made progress in reining in at least some aspects of Pyongyang's identified nuclear program, concerns remain. How many weapons has Kim Jong-Il already produced and stashed away? Even a few could prove disastrous to the United States and its allies in the event a confrontation with North Korea turned violent.[14] Does the North have hidden nuclear infrastructure that can continue to operate? Given the histories and ultimate failures of previous deals with Pyongyang, including the 1994 "Agreed Framework," how long will the new agreement hold? Of course, the threat of an attack southward remains, although the balance of conventional forces has shifted in South Korea's favor, and North Korea retains the ability to lash out, using artillery, conventional ballistic missiles, and special forces, against its neighbor.[15]

The third potential adversary, Iran, has the feeblest conventional military forces of the trio, although the acquisition of the nuclear weapons that Tehran apparently seeks could do much to offset its weakness. Although, unlike North Korea and China, Iran lacks a specific territorial bone to pick with a U.S. friend or ally, the Iranian regime is definitely hostile toward the United States. It has a track record of both supporting international terrorism and endeavoring to subvert Gulf Arab states, and is striving to field a military more capable of threatening its neighbors (albeit more via coercion than invasion), most of whom are U.S. friends or clients.

A conflict with any of these actors could present the U.S. military with one or more very stressing challenges not associated with the old-line MCO scenarios against which its forces are tuned:

- Nuclear weapons in the hands of actors who may, in crisis or conflict, prove difficult to deter

- Land-attack ballistic and cruise missiles

- Advanced air defenses

- Airborne and space-based sensors

- Antiship cruise missiles (ASCMs), quiet attack submarines, and advanced naval mines

- Unconventional warfare and terrorism

- Counterspace and counter-ISR capabilities.

If we find this broad-brush depiction of future demand plausible—that the "war on terror" after Iraq will entail multiple, low-key engagements rather than large-scale operations, and future MCOs will not primarily entail facing down massive but crude armies across land borders—what kinds of implications might there be for U.S. forces?

Shaping U.S. Forces for the Post–Post–Cold War World

The "two war" sizing criterion for U.S. forces remains important, if only because the United States, as a power with global interests and alliances, cannot risk being put in a situation where it is seen as having fired the last shot in its magazine. However, the composition of the forces needed to prosecute those wars, as well as the allocation of responsibilities within a new "steady state" involving numerous deployments to disparate places to combat Islamic extremism and instability, may be substantially different from what currently prevails. The impacts of these changes are different for air and maritime forces on the one hand, and land forces on the other.[16]

U.S. air and naval forces should be focused on and sized to the demands of two new MCO cases. All three plausible MCO scenarios discussed above call for responses of a speed, scale, and kind for which air and naval assets are well suited: gaining freedom of operation, rapidly engaging and destroying a wide array of fixed and mobile targets, and so forth. There are no obvious roles for sizable U.S. ground maneuver forces in a China-Taiwan fight—unless one imagines a full-scale U.S. attempt to liberate Taiwan after first failing to defend it—or against an Iran that is unlikely to attempt a large-scale land invasion of its neighbors.[17] South Korea's large army is prepared to defend its territory and would certainly carry the lion's share of the burden for any occupation of the former North Korea; this assessment is reflected in the ongoing withdrawal of about one-third of U.S. troops from Korea, the repositioning of the remainder to locations further from the demilitarized zone, and the impending change of command within the alliance from American control to South Korean leadership.[18]

This does not mean that the U.S. Air Force and Navy would be excused from participating in the eponymous "long war" against Islamic extremism; air, space, and maritime intelligence-collection and surveillance capabilities, for example, will be engaged globally and for the long term in that campaign, and from time to time the USAF and Navy will be called upon in their combat roles. However,

> [t]he Army and Marine Corps, along with much of the special operations community, must play the leading roles in countering terrorist and insurgent groups abroad and in helping to stabilize nations trying to emerge from authoritarian forms of governance. The key to long-term success in these operations is to foster the emergence of competent security forces within host countries so that governments that share the U.S. interest in suppressing terrorism and insurgency can do so increasingly on their own. The host-country forces that accomplish these missions will be primarily ground forces and will, perforce, be trained and assisted by other ground forces.[19]

These added responsibilities—and, to remind, up to thirty-plus simultaneous TEAA and stability missions, of varied sizes and durations, may be called for—mean that the Army and Marine Corps should be relieved of the requirement to prepare maneuver forces to wage the second of two concurrent or overlapping MCOs. Substantial U.S. ground forces are not likely to be needed in two nearly simultaneous contingencies, and large numbers of soldiers and marines will be needed on any given day for TEAA and stability activities.

The land components have taken steps to better prepare themselves for their expanded roles in unconventional operations. The Marines, for example, established the Fourth Marine Expeditionary Brigade (Anti-Terrorism)

> to provide Unified Combatant Commanders with a rapidly deployable and sustainable specialized Anti-Terrorism Force to deter, detect, defend, and conduct initial incident response to combat the threat of worldwide terrorism.[20]

The Army, meanwhile, has cut back on some "big war" capabilities, such as air defense artillery, to provide resources for civil affairs and other assets more useful in stability operations.[21] But both services need to take additional, bolder, steps to orient themselves properly to what the nation will require of them in coming years.

The Army should evaluate whether its envisioned future force structure adequately supports the demands it will face for TEAA and stability operations. In keeping with its projected status as a "one MRC" force, an option would be to reconfigure a substantial part of the Army's combat forces to a more focused concentration—in equipment, training, and organization—on nonconventional missions. Made more robust in civil affairs, law enforcement, psychological and information operations, multinational liaison, and foreign language and area knowledge, these units would be far more effective in both direct and indirect stability operations; they would remain "war-fighting units," merely reoriented to a different context. The MRC-aligned component, meanwhile, would be aggressively modernized to maintain or increase its dominance in traditional combat roles over any plausible adversary.[22] By explicitly dedicating troops to these two very different missions, the Army could improve its performance in both roles, build and train units sized and organized consistently with their primary jobs, and ensure that there was an institutional constituency within the service and among its senior leadership committed to maintaining and enhancing capabilities for both conventional warfare and TEAA and stability activities.

The equipping aspect of this transition should not be overlooked. Stability operations make heavy demands on individual soldiers, who must often operate on foot, in small units, and in very dangerous, dynamic, and uncertain tactical circumstances. In early 2007, the Army essentially killed its Land Warrior Program, which had been intended to field the next generation of soldiers' personal equipment, incorporating "the weapon system, helmet, computer, digital and voice communications, positional and navigation system, protective clothing and individual equipment."[23] Land Warrior was terminated after more than ten years of development but with a sum of only about $500 million invested; by comparison, the funding for the Future Combat System (FCS) in FY 08—even after a $3 billion cut—remains $3 billion, about six times the total spent on Land Warrior. FCS is the core of the modernization effort intended to sustain the Army's "overmatch" in conventional warfare, and is thus an important program. For many of the jobs that soldiers will be asked to do day in, day out in the post–post–Cold War world, however, the kinds of improved protective, communication, and weapons systems envisioned by Land Warrior are equally vital, and the Army should be careful not to underprioritize them versus platform-oriented development and acquisitions.[24]

For its part, the Marine Corps should consider expanding and deepening its already-strong commitment to special operations forces (SOF) and SOF-like missions.[25] Marine expeditionary units (MEUs)—typically a reinforced infantry battalion, a composite aviation component of fixed- and rotary-wing aircraft, and the appropriate command and support elements—provide steady-state presence afloat in the Mediterranean, western Pacific, and Arabian Gulf. These mobile, capable, and versatile combined-arms forces are a good match for supporting, via reinforcement, firepower, or both, SOF operations ashore. The amphibious shipping on which MEUs are based can provide secure basing for SOF personnel, boats, and aircraft, and a nearby, defended sanctuary if a SOF mission should go wrong. To take full advantage of this potentially powerful synergy, DoD should consider how to increase the coordination between SOF operations and MEU deployments, to include more tightly coupling the latter to the former, and routinely incorporating MEU and SOF assets into each other's exercises and training activities.

Given what will be a growing demand for intelligence, surveillance, and reconnaissance (ISR) around the world and around the clock, Marine amphibious assault ships—especially the larger LHA and LHD, but also the smaller LPD and LSD, vessels—should be configured to operate a variety of unmanned aircraft systems (UAS) for these purposes. It is probably impractical to employ the largest unmanned aircraft, such as Global Hawk, Reaper, or

Predator, off of even the biggest of these ships, and the Navy and Marine Corps already operate, or have tested, a variety of small shipboard UAS, such as Pioneer. Those deployments should become standard practice throughout the amphibious fleet to provide an additional level of flexible ISR capability to support both combatant commanders and local operators, including and especially SOF. It may also be worthwhile for the Navy and Marines to experiment with medium-sized UAS, such as the Israeli Aircraft Industries' Heron 1, which could offer substantial upgrades in payload and endurance compared to smaller platforms without requiring expensive and time-consuming modifications to amphibious shipping.[26]

Our work did not include any assessments of how big an Army or Marine Corps would be called for in the future, and rigorous analysis of these future demands might indicate the need for either larger land forces or smaller ones. What does seem clear, however, is that some skepticism may be appropriate toward plans for permanently increasing the size of U.S. land forces based on the operational and personnel tempo stresses arising from the protracted struggle in Iraq (and, to a lesser extent, in Afghanistan). While these problems are both real and serious, the likelihood of the U.S. engaging in any comparable undertaking in the near to midterm appears small. Given the price tag for the 62,000 troops slated to be added to the Army—estimated in January 2007 as $70 billion over five years—these plans risk becoming a case study of fighting the last war with a vengeance.[27] The opportunity costs to DoD and the nation, in forgone modernization across all the services, or displaced needs elsewhere in the federal budget, could be considerable, possibly for very little payoff in needed capability.

Concluding Remarks

The United States confronts an array of security challenges that go well beyond the "war on terror." The "five long wars" are diverse, and managing them will make substantial and sustained demands across all dimensions of America's national power and international posture. It appears that a new internal bargain with the Department of Defense—a new "division of labor"—is needed if the military is to bear its share of the burden effectively and efficiently.

The ability to fight and win "big wars" will remain important, but those wars will be very different from, and much more difficult than, recent experiences in Iraq, the Balkans, and Afghanistan. Success in these future scenarios will demand new and specialized capabilities from the force (e.g., effective defenses against large salvo attacks of accurate ballistic and cruise missiles), especially from the air and naval components. The burden of the day-to-day grind of TEAA and stability operations—the cruxes of the post-Iraq "war on terror"—will largely be borne by U.S. land forces, which will likewise require a higher degree of specialization to dramatically improve their performance in these roles.

The changes required across the joint force are daunting and institutionally difficult; they are also necessary if the military is to continue to serve as the ultimate protector of American interests and security in the face of the dangerous challenges looming in the post–post–Cold War world.

References

Army-Technology.com. n.d. "Land Warrior—integrated modular fighting system, USA." As of 9 November 2007: http://www.army-technology.com/projects/land_warrior/.

Cliff, Roger, Mark Burles, Michael S. Chase, Derek Eaton, and Kevin L. Pollpeter. 2006. *Entering the dragon's lair: Chinese antiaccess strategies and their implications for the United States.* Santa Monica, CA: RAND Corporation, MG-524-AF. As of 8 November 2007: http://www.rand.org/pubs/monographs/MG524/.

Cox, Matthew. 2007. "Army drops Land Warrior Program." *Army Times*, 8 February. As of 10 November 2007: http://www.armytimes.com/news/2007/02/ATLWcut070206/.

Dobbins, James, John G. McGinn, Keith Crane, Seth G. Jones, Rollie Lal, Andrew Rathmell, Rachel M. Swanger, and Anga R. Timilsina. 2003. *America's role in nation-building: From Germany to Iraq.* Santa Monica, CA: RAND Corporation, MR-1753-AF. As of 8 November 2007: http://www.rand.org/pubs/monograph_reports/MR1753/.

Economist. 2007. "Getting technical." 8 November. As of 8 November 2007: http://www.economist.com/world/asia/displaystory.cfm?story_id=10111682.

Embassy of the United States, Seoul, Korea. 2004. "U.S., Republic of Korea reach agreement on troop redeployment." 6 October. As of 8 November 2007: http://seoul.usembassy.gov/oct_6_2004.html.

——. 2007. "U.S., South Korea to transfer wartime force command in 2012: Defense ministers say operational control transition to begin in July 2007." 23 February. As of 8 November 2007: http://seoul.usembassy.gov/410_022307.html.

Hoehn, Andrew R., Adam Grissom, David A. Ochmanek, David A. Shlapak, and Alan J. Vick. 2007. *A new division of labor: Meeting America's security challenges beyond Iraq.* Santa Monica, CA: RAND Corporation, MG-499-AF. As of 7 November 2007: http://www.rand.org/pubs/monographs/MG499/.

Israeli Aircraft Industries. n.d. "IAI Malat Heron." As of 10 November 2007: http://www.iai.co.il/Default.aspx?FolderID=18900&lang=en.

Kahn, Joseph. 2007. "China shows assertiveness in weapons test." *New York Times*, 20 January. As of 8 November 2007: http://www.nytimes.com/2007/01/20/world/asia/20china.html.

Lague, David. 2007. "China announces gains in air defense." *New York Times*, 11 October. As of 8 November 2007: http://www.nytimes.com/2007/10/11/world/asia/11china.html.

Mueller, John. 2006. *Overblown: How politicians and the terrorism industry inflate national security threats, and why we believe them.* New York: Free Press.

Ochmanek, David. 2003. *Military operations against terrorist groups abroad: Implications for the United States Air Force.* Santa Monica, CA: RAND Corporation, MR-1738-AF. As of 8 November 2007: http://www.rand.org/pubs/monograph_reports/MR1738/.

Office of the Secretary of Defense. 2007. *Annual report to Congress: Military power of the People's Republic of China 2007.* Washington, DC, May. As of 8 November 2007: http://www.defenselink.mil/pubs/pdfs/070523-China-Military-Power-final.pdf.

O'Rourke, Ronald. 2007. *China naval modernization: Implications for U.S. Navy capabilities—background and issues for Congress.* Washington, DC: Congressional Research Service, October. As of 8 November 2007: http://www.fas.org/sgp/crs/row/RL33153.pdf.

Page, Susan. 2007. "Poll: Most want Iraq pullout deadline." *USA Today*, 9 September. As of 8 November 2007: http://www.usatoday.com/news/washington/2007-09-09-poll_N.htm

Reuters. 2007. "U.S. general sees $70 billion bill to expand Army." 23 January. As of 8 November 2007: http://www.reuters.com/article/politicsNews/idUSN2327124720070123.

Scobel, Andrew, and John M. Sanford. 2007. *North Korea's military threat: Pyongyang's conventional forces, weapons of mass destruction, and ballistic missiles.* Carlisle, PA: Strategic Studies Institute, April. As of 8 November 2007: http://www.strategicstudiesinstitute.army.mil/pdffiles/pub771.pdf.

Shlapak, David A. 2006. *Shaping the future Air Force.* Santa Monica, CA: RAND Corporation, TR-322-AF. As of 8 November 2007: http://www.rand.org/pubs/technical_reports/TR322/.

U.S. Army. 2004. "Building Army capabilities." Draft Army briefing for POTUS, 28 January. As of 8 November 2007: http://www.comw.org/qdr/fulltext/0401armstructbrief.ppt.

U.S. Department of Defense. 2006. *Quadrennial Defense Review report.* 6 February. As of 7 November 2007: http://www.defenselink.mil/pubs/pdfs/QDR20060203.pdf.

U.S. Department of State. 2007. "Background note: South Korea." September. As of 8 November 2007: http://www.state.gov/r/pa/ei/bgn/2800.htm.

U.S. Marine Corps. n.d. "4th Marine Expeditionary Brigade (Anti-Terrorism)." Briefing slides. As of 8 November 2008: http://www.dtic.mil/ndia/2001ewc/4thmeb.pdf.

Vick, Alan, Adam Grissom, William Rosenau, Beth Grill, and Karl P. Mueller. 2006. *Air power in the new counterinsurgency era: The strategic importance of USAF advisory and assistance missions.* Santa Monica, CA: RAND Corporation, MG-509-AF. As of 8 November 2007: http://www.rand.org/pubs/monographs/MG509/.

Notes

1. The author wishes to acknowledge the enormous contributions made by his colleagues Andrew R. Hoehn, Adam Grissom, David A. Ochmanek, and Alan J. Vick to the work on which this paper is based. The opinions expressed in this paper, however, are his alone and do not necessarily reflect those of RAND or the policies of its research sponsors. He must also insist on retaining sole credit for all errors of fact and judgment contained herein.

2. More thorough discussions of many of the points raised in this paper can be found in Hoehn et al. (2007), Shlapak (2006), Vick et al. (2006), and Ochmanek (2003). All RAND documents referenced in the paper can be downloaded from RAND's Web site, http://www.rand.org/.

3. U.S. Department of Defense (2006), p. 9.

4. Cogent arguments have been made both that the threat from terrorism has been overstated and that the "war on terror" is a suboptimal way of addressing such danger as does exist (see, for example, Mueller [2006]). There seems, however, little doubt that the nation has decided, or perceived itself as compelled, to mount a substantial and prolonged campaign against violent Islamic extremism.

5. It is important to note that we do not claim to have "discovered" any of these challenges; there is a rich and diverse array of books—both popular and learned—think tank reports, journal and magazine articles, and official discussions of each of the five challenges. Nor should we be understood as asserting that these are the only five security problems confronting the nation, or that all other problems are "lesser included cases" of this set. We believe, however, that the five we have identified define the core problems of the new security context.

6. One can argue that the war in Iraq actually had little or nothing to do with combating terrorism at its outset, but it has by now become a front in that conflict, even if largely by the United States' own doing.

7. Polls in the 2006–2007 period show that a small but consistent majority of those surveyed in the United States consider the invasion of Iraq to have been a mistake. See, for example, Page (2007).

   An occupation of Iran, with its population of more than 65 million, would require at least 325,000 troops even if the ratio of soldiers per thousand population were kept at five to one, roughly the level of "presurge" Iraq. Were the ratio set to twenty to one, which is consistent with that initially employed by NATO in Bosnia and Kosovo, 1.3 *million* troops would be needed. Even the smaller number is almost certainly beyond the capacity of the U.S. military to sustain for any prolonged period, with or without the planned increases in Army and Marine end strengths. North Korea has a much smaller population than Iran, but the main role in any occupation and stabilization operations there, whether resulting from the collapse of the regime in Pyongyang or a war on the peninsula, would almost certainly be played by South Korean forces. Data on force levels in "nation building" from Dobbins et al. (2003), pp. 149–151.

8. Ochmanek (2003), p. 10.

9. Hoehn et al. (2007), pp. 70–73.

10. The 2006 QDR calls for boosting the size of U.S. Army Special Forces by one-third. While this represents a significant boost in TEAA capacity, it still leaves the United States able to fill only a fraction of the projected demand. Thanks to colleague Adam Grissom for this insight.

11. The number of plausible MCO adversaries can expand with one's time horizon. Should Russia's relations with the West continue to deteriorate, for example, Moscow could rise in the rankings. A post-Musharraf Pakistan that supported radical Islamic groups might be another possibility, as might a future Syria with enhanced capabilities and larger strategic appetites. All of these scenarios would have more in common with the three cases described here than with the traditional Iraqi and prenuclear North Korean ones.

12. See, for example, Office of the Secretary of Defense (2007) and Cliff et al. (2006).

13. On China's growing capabilities to threaten U.S. air, sea, and space dominance see, for example, Lague (2007), Kahn (2007), and O'Rourke (2007).

14. RAND has conducted numerous games and analyses of the potential effects of North Korean nuclear weapons in a conflict scenario. See, for example, Shlapak (2006), pp. 5–6, and Hoehn et al. (2007), pp. 16–19. North Korea is thought to have separated sufficient plutonium for up to thirteen weapons; see *Economist* (2007), and Scobell and Sanford (2007), pp. 76–77.

15. A recent assessment of North Korea's military capabilities is Scobell and Sanford (2007).

16. "Air and maritime forces" include the U.S. Air Force and the surface, subsurface, and aviation components of the U.S. Navy. The U.S. Marine Corps and U.S. Army—including their organic fixed- and rotary-wing aviation components—we consider to be "land forces."

17. We emphasize that we are referring here to maneuver forces. Specialized Army capabilities—including, for example, missile defense or special forces—would be very valuable in these contingencies.

18. On the redeployment of U.S. troops from South Korea, see U.S. Embassy (2004); the repositioning is described in U.S. Department of State (2007); on the change in command structure, see U.S. Embassy (2007).

19. Hoehn et al. (2007), p. 45.

20. U.S. Marine Corps (n.d.), p. 3.

21. U.S. Army (2004), especially slide 7.

22. These ideas are discussed in much greater depth and detail in Hoehn et al. (2007), pp. 65–70.

23. Army-Technology.com (2007).

24. On the demise of Land Warrior, see Cox (2007).

25. Even before 9/11, for example, the Corps deployed a number of Marine expeditionary units (MEUs) prepared to undertake a subset of special operation missions, and dubbed "MEU-SOC," for "special operations capable."

26. We mention the Heron as an example, not to recommend a specific system for evaluation or procurement. For details on the Heron, see Israeli Aircraft Industries (n.d.).

27. On the cost of the proposed expansion of Army end strength, see, for example, Reuters (2007).

Panel III: Land Forces

Summary of Discussion

Dr. Mackubin Thomas Owens
Associate Dean of Academics for Electives and
Directed Research
Professor, National Security Decision
Making Department
U.S. Naval War College

The papers presented here concern force planning, the art of making decisions today about the size, composition, and mix of a future force structure, in light of plausible alternative security environments and resource constraints. These papers, along with the subsequent discussion, raised important issues regarding the makeup of the future U.S. force structure.

Colonel McMaster made the case for a large, flexible land force possessing the capabilities necessary to deal with, among other contingencies, a protracted series of irregular conflicts. He argued that effective force planning must entail an "explicit rejection of fantastical ideas concerning the nature of future conflict, ideas that gained wide acceptance in the 1990s and that recent and ongoing experiences have thoroughly discredited," e.g., that rapid advances in communications, information, and precision munitions technologies would provide U.S. forces with "dominant battlespace knowledge," permitting them to achieve "full-spectrum dominance" over potential adversaries well into the future.

Colonel McMaster contended that such flawed doctrinal thinking has resulted in unbalanced and vulnerable forces dependent on centralized resources and unable to overmatch the enemy in close combat. He argued that future forces ought to be designed explicitly to fight under conditions of uncertainty and despite capabilities degraded by enemy countermeasures and that they must also be designed for effectiveness rather than efficiency. Organizing units to operate in uncertain environments, however, will entail tolerating a higher degree of redundancy; autonomous organizations must be capable of not only employing but also controlling the full range of capabilities. If lower-level commanders have to rely on higher-level commands for assets and capabilities, those assets might not be available and capabilities might not be responsive under all conditions.

Mr. Shlapak argued that irregular war, as made manifest by the conflicts in Afghanistan and Iraq, is only one of five "long wars," the others being

- Dealing with nuclear-armed regional powers like North Korea . . .
- Managing a growing security competition in Asia, especially countering the growing power of a rising China
- Coping with a Russia that is increasingly both authoritarian and assertive

- Managing this complex set of challenges while the foundations of the network of U.S. alliances and partnerships are undergoing tectonic, historic shifts.

Regarding the size of future U.S. ground forces, Mr. Shlapak suggested that future major combat operations (MCOs) would not resemble those envisioned in the past, and that accordingly ground forces would play less of a role were such conflicts to occur. He also argued that even though ground forces are most appropriate for irregular war, "the experience in Iraq has almost certainly reduced American willingness to undertake similar ventures in the future, and it is difficult to identify serious candidate targets for the next 'regime change' that would or could be undertaken by the United States acting largely alone." In other words, Iraq and Afghanistan do not provide the proper template for sizing future ground forces. "Some skepticism may be appropriate toward plans for permanently increasing the size of U.S. land forces based on the operational and personnel tempo stresses arising from the protracted struggle in Iraq (and, to a lesser extent, in Afghanistan)." It might be the case that the most effective use of U.S. ground forces in the future would be training the forces of other countries rather than conducting MCOs.

The first question had to do with the Army's brigade combat team (BCT) organization and officer professional development. The respondent pointed out that the problem with the new BCT organization is that it seems to be based on the assumption that U.S. forces would possess a high level of knowledge about an adversary, enabling us to target him with a high degree of certainty employing long-range precision munitions. The new BCT lacks some elements, e.g., engineers, dismounted reconnaissance, and logistical capabilities, that experiences in Iraq and Afghanistan have demonstrated are necessary because we lack such perfect knowledge about our adversaries.

Regarding professional education for officers, the respondent indicated being an advocate of graduate education for officers, especially in such areas as international relations and military history, which would improve the ability of officers to think clearly about complex issues and to integrate with other government elements charged with nation building.

The next question raised the issue of the effectiveness of U.S. efforts to train the forces of friendly governments. The respondent observed that we have had successes in training such elements and that in the long run, it is better to improve the security forces of other countries rather than trying to take care of other countries' security on our own. As another participant put it, it is probably a better idea to train Pakistani forces than to invade Waziristan in an effort to get at the Taliban and al Qaeda.

A subsequent question concerned the relative advantages of capabilities-based and threat-based force planning. The respondent argued that the problem with the former is the impossibility of predicting the future since conflict involves the continuous interaction of U.S. force development and that of other countries. A questioner then asked if the problem was an overreliance on technology. The respondent observed that the real problem was not overreliance on technology per se but viewing war as an end in itself rather than the means to achieve particular political objectives.

Another participant pointed out that the way General Aideed had defeated the United States in Somalia was by exploiting the image of dead Americans in order to discourage the U.S. public. He invoked the observations of General Rupert Smith, British Army, that war had moved from being primarily "kinetic" to being primarily psychological. The respondent agreed, observing however that the use of force must always be consistent with one's political objectives. In the case of an insurgency, the principal battleground is in the areas of intelligence and perception. To deal with a broad array of contingencies, it is necessary to have a force that can operate at the high end of the spectrum of conflict but then transition rapidly to the low end. The respondent also defended the employment of heavy ground forces in a counterinsurgency setting. The key is flexibility and adaptability.

Another questioner raised the issue of the "five wars," wondering if these were the appropriate planning cases. The respondent replied that these were plausible cases in an admittedly uncertain security environment. The last comment involved the question of Iran and nuclear weapons. The commenter's point was that Iran's possession of nuclear weapons complicated U.S. strategy and force planning.

Panel IV

Maritime Forces

Dr. Geoffrey Till
Professor of Maritime Studies, Defence Studies Department, King's College London

Robert O. Work
Vice President for Strategic Studies at the Center for Strategic and Budgetary Assessments

Ronald O'Rourke
Naval Analyst, Congressional Research Service of the Library of Congress

Moderator:
Dr. Thomas R. Fedyszyn
Security, Strategy, and Forces Course Director, National Security Decision Making Department, U.S. Naval War College

'A Cooperative Strategy for 21st Century Seapower': What's New? What's Next? A View from Outside

Dr. Geoffrey Till
Professor of Maritime Studies
Defence Studies Department
King's College London

Navies everywhere are grappling with the security issues they confront in the post-9/11 world. This is a difficult task because they face issues that seem so much more complicated than we remember them to have been during the cold war. Partly because of its collapse but mainly because of the impact of globalisation, the concept of security has expanded from notions that are mainly military to encompass the dimensions of political security, economic security, societal security, and environmental security. All of these may apply at the levels of the individual citizen, groups in a national population, the nation, the region, and the world. Moreover these dimensions and levels are intimately connected with one another, vertically and horizontally, so that responses to a discerned threat at one of these intersections is likely to have a range of effects, both good and bad, everywhere else.[1]

Moreover there is a temporal dimension to all this; what a country does now, in response to a clear and immediate danger, may have untold implications for its ability to respond to other challenges further up the line. Such issues require a 'comprehensive approach' in which military action is carefully integrated with political and economic approaches in order to produce a range of desired effects. To make their full contribution, military forces will need to think about their traditional tasks in new ways and accept new ones. The searing experiences of Iraq and Afghanistan add urgency to the call. Or so at least the argument goes.

Other analysts, however, wonder how real, how new, or how permanent this development actually is. They argue that the cold war really didn't seem so simple at the time, and that while the major focus may have been on the potentially deadly confrontation between East and West over the established battle lines of Europe many other quite important things were going on elsewhere that called for Western forces to respond in a variety of ways far removed from the brutal simplicities of the central front. Moreover Colin Gray is not alone in writing of 'another bloody century'[2] in which many of these new threats may seem much less dominant when compared to the possible recurrence of traditional state-on-state wars. And these possible wars continue to call for a set of approaches, military disciplines, and capabilities that seem really quite traditional. What we have therefore, goes the alternative view, is at most a difference of degree, and it is far too early to conclude that the elements of change, to the extent that they exist, constitute a permanent trend for which military forces need to adapt, rather than a temporary blip that they need to absorb.

These two approaches have been labelled, respectively, the postmodern, or nontraditional, way of thinking about the role and character of military forces and the modern, or traditional. When it comes to sizing and shaping the fleet there are obvious tensions between these two approaches. Many navies around the world are thinking through their own answers to this set of conundrums, and there has been a great deal of interest in how the U.S. Navy would seek to square this particular circle. How will its strategic thinking develop? How will it structure the fleet? How will it operate? And how should everyone else respond? Accordingly, the rest of the world has awaited *A Cooperative Strategy for the 21st Century Seapower*, if not with bated breath, then at least with real interest in both the process and the outcome of the debate.

So What's New?

This approach to strategy making was certainly intended to be novel. The former chief of naval operations, Admiral Mike Mullen, launched the campaign for a new strategy in June 2006. 'When I initiated the discussion of what it should be,' he said, 'my view was that we needed one. We hadn't had one in 20-plus years and you need a strategy which is going to underpin how we operate, what our concepts were, and literally how we invest.' The scope and scale of new threats, the complexity of globalisation, and the staggering rate of change seemed to make a major rethink necessary. The task was handed over to Vice Admiral John Morgan, Deputy Chief of Naval Operations for Information, Plans and Strategy.

Rather like the British had done a decade earlier with their Strategic Defence Review of 1997, the U.S. Navy decided to make the process as inclusive of all major stakeholders as possible. 'One of the things I [Mullen] said when I came in as CNO [was that] I am not going to move ahead on major decisions without doing this with my other four stars.' So the US Marine Corps and Coast Guard were in the process from the start. The Navy also decided to hold a series of 'conversations with America.'[3] In some ways, the process was as important as the product since, if successful, it would yield not only a strategy but also a constituency of opinion that might be expected to help with its implementation later on. Finally, foreign engagement was sought in aspects of the strategy through the International Seapower Symposium of 2005 and that of 2007, a variety of naval staff talks, and academic engagements abroad. The new CNO, Admiral Gary Roughead, argued that 'This was an approach that was very different than in the past when we engaged more than just a very small cell of Navy thinkers. We heard from other leaders in our country about the use of maritime power.'[4]

The problem with this, paradoxically, was that the degree of prior involvement in the process and the extent to which developing concepts such as the Thousand-Ship Navy/Global Maritime Partnership were telegraphed in advance combined to make the new strategy appear less than wholly new when it finally appeared. Moreover at least some of the ideas it contained had appeared before in earlier formulations. Recognising the tectonic shifts in strategy caused by the end of the cold war, another doctrinal formulation, '. . . From the Sea,' had in 1992 already shifted the emphasis away from power *at* sea and towards power *from* the sea. This closer coordination of the Navy and the Marine Corps was symbolised by the equal positioning of their service logos on the front cover of the document. The shock of 9/11 caused another such shift, leading to a new emphasis on counterterrorism and asymmetric operations. Such thoughts had also been illuminated and advanced in the four broad naval mission areas identified by the Quadrennial Defense Review (QDR) 2005 process:

- Conducting an active and layered defense against aggression from forward locations not dependent on the land bases of other nations.

- Ensuring the access of joint forces to contested areas where adversaries seek to exclude US presence.

- Enabling the success of joint forces ashore through the provision of firepower, mobility, intelligence and logistics support.

- Defending the seaward approaches to the American homeland against an array of conventional and unconventional threats.[5]

Even the equal treatment given winning and preventing war can be seen as less than novel given the great stress on deterrence in the cold war era, which was, after all, about *preventing* war. However what *does* seem to be different is the much wider conception of what deterrence actually means and actually takes these days. The coercive approach of demonstrating denial capabilities against, or promising punishment for, prospective wrongdoers has been absorbed into a much wider concept of working against the social, environmental, and economic conditions that make wrongdoing more likely. These postmodern conceptions of seapower had, however, been signalled in parts of the *Naval Operations Concept* and the *Navy Strategic Plan* of 2006.

These conceptions are, nevertheless, key to the novelty, and indeed the attractiveness, of the strategy. It is much more comprehensive in its approach and seems much more aware of the implications and consequences of the broader concepts of security discussed earlier. The same might be said when it comes to the document's implementation. The extent of the stress on cooperation and mutual dependence amongst the three maritime services is new: it solidifies the emerging partnership between the Marine Corps and the Navy on the one hand and between the Navy and the Coast Guard on the other. It underlines the thinking behind the 'National Fleet' concept of, and, to some extent at least, operationalises the objectives contained in, the White House's *National Strategy for Maritime Security*. The admittedly brief discussion of distributed and disaggregated command decision-making may suggest something of a shift in naval thinking away from task force–centric operations characteristic of the Navy to the tactical platform-centric approach of the Coast Guard. The extent to which the Navy may be signalling a willingness to engage in what would elsewhere be regarded as constabulary operations is significant too. But, note, there are a lot of 'may be's' here.

The specific importance attached to humanitarian aid and disaster relief is however also quite novel. Instead of being an activity that is something of bonus when the need arises and assets are available because there is no decent war to fight elsewhere, the task is accepted as part of one of the six strategic imperatives and the ability to do it has apparently been elevated to equal standing with more traditional core capabilities, such as forward presence and sea control.

But perhaps the most striking departure of all is the consolidation of the Global Maritime Partnership initiative, which becomes one of the six strategic imperatives and which is clearly crucial to two of the six core capabilities, namely, those of Maritime Security and of Humanitarian Assistance and Disaster Response. Since this concept has grown out of Admiral Mullen's earlier concept of a 'Thousand-Ship Navy,'[6] this is not entirely new, of course. But the retitling of the concept is more than merely cosmetic. It suggests a significant move away from the traditional 'modern' thinking that probably explains the label originally given to the concept. Zappy as it was, the title 'Thousand-Ship Navy' was profoundly misleading since it seemed to exclude coastguard forces, had clear hierarchical connotations that inevitably sparked the unwelcome question of 'Who's in charge?' and raised equally unfortunate suspicions that the Navy's hidden aspirations were to re-create a grander vision of the '600-ship navy' of the Reagan years. Hence, in Admiral Morgan's words, 'we are beginning to distance ourselves from that moniker.'[7] Many people will therefore welcome the complete disappearance of the term from the document as the passing of a distraction from what is otherwise a persuasive concept. It is noticeable, also, that the Global Maritime Partnership would benefit significantly from all three of the document's implementation priorities.

It seems fair to conclude therefore that there are indeed new, postmodern elements to the new strategy that go alongside the old and that, in Loren Thompson's words, "It is hard to argue with such a reasonable approach to global security."[8]

Criticisms[9]

Nonetheless, there have been criticisms—in fact quite a lot. To a large extent this is inevitable as the document seeks to cover a vast subject in comparatively few words, no doubt on the assumption that no one would actually read anything longer. In less than four thousand words it reviews extraordinarily complicated changes in the world scene and seeks to lay down a strategy that defines, in doctrinal, operational, and procurement terms, the objectives, methods, and supporting implementation plans for the world's biggest Navy, Marine Corps, and Coast Guard. Moreover it was produced through a process of consultation with the widest range of maritime stakeholders imaginable. The new statement of strategy is essentially a compromise in length, in overall posture, and in detailed substance. Given the level of compression and the complexity of the subject, a measure of superficiality and possibly constructive ambiguity is perhaps inevitable.

Each of the major stakeholders consulted in the process could, however, argue with some justification that its particular interests have not been given due weight. The kinetic community preoccupied by the possible recurrence of interstate war with a strategic competitor in twenty or thirty years' time, or the possibility of a conflict with a country like Iran or North Korea in the nearer term, might well feel that the pendulum has swung much too far from hard to soft maritime power. The absence of reference to strike operations and amphibious assault in the discussion of power projection has already been noted. According to some observers earlier drafts of the document had even less reference to the sources of kinetic effect. References to theatre ballistic missile defence are hidden away rather uncomfortably in the discussion on deterrence, for example. This partly explains the emphasis given by Secretary of the Navy Donald Winter to the need to stick with 'the Mahanian insistence on U.S. Navy maritime dominance.'

'Let there be no mistake,' he said. 'We are not walking away from, diminishing, or retreating in any way from those elements of hard power that win wars—or deter them from ever breaking out in the first place. . . . The strength of a nation's navy remains an essential measure of a great power's status and role in the world.'[10]

Attitudes to where the balance between hard and soft power in doctrine and force structure is to be struck in the document may well partly depend on where the observer 'sits,' both in terms of geography and maritime discipline. Aviators may well tend towards a more kinetic approach, especially if they operate in areas where local conflicts against middle powers seem a quite possible contingency. The attention of submariners and those in the antisubmarine warfare (ASW) community will be fixated on the need to respond to the growing reach and sophistication of possible competitors like China, or middle powers with access to new and improved diesel-propelled submarines (SSKs) or even nuclear-propelled submarines (SSNs), and consequently may feel that still more could have been said about the future importance of their craft. Operators in regions such as Africa, Europe, or South America, simply by virtue of their operational priorities, will tend to be more interested in softer capacities like riverine or patrol operations or civil-military affairs; they too may feel, though, that their concerns could have been given greater emphasis.

Against this, the Coast Guard community might think that its side of the strategy has been played down in the document. It might well feel that the document uses 'seapower' as a synonym for naval power rather than as an alternative to 'maritime power' and that the default understanding of the term will tend to pay too little regard to the contribution made by the U.S. Coast Guard. The constabulary role and law enforcement are crucial aspects of maritime security in its newer and wider sense, but seem rather glossed over, at least in the sense that there are no specific references to the fact that, in the United States, such activities are the domain of the Coast Guard rather than the Navy. Given the evident importance attributed by the document to wider engagement with other countries, whose primary concerns in maritime security in fact tend to be about things like the protection of their fisheries and the interception of drugs, arms, and people smugglers, this apparent neglect would seem particularly unfortunate. For people of this persuasion, it would be no very great step from this to suspect that the Navy is using this wider concept of maritime security to help justify a building programme of ships that are, in fact, by no means appropriate to its enforcement.

The strategy could also be said to have paid insufficient regard to the perspectives of the shipbuilding and operating industries, for they are part of the maritime team and have objections and dissent to table, and strategic needs to be met. The U.S. Navy's construction programme has been relatively stable for the last two years not least in response to industry's requirements for some reliable planning baselines. Electoral as well as national considerations mean that members of Congress have a huge and, some suspect, determining political stake in such outcomes. For all these reasons, their concerns might have been more directly addressed.

There is a second set of criticisms that proceed not from particular constituencies and stakeholders who feel that their particular angles on the issue should have been given more weight but that focus instead on the document as a statement of strategy. Current events in Iraq and Afghanistan suggest that the United States and its allies have encountered real difficulty in coming up with a connected set of statements that provide seamless guidance to how broad policy objectives at the grand strategic end of the scale should be implemented at the other operational and tactical end, now and in the plannable future. The contention is that they have a set of visionary statements, and of detailed force structure plans, but that the two often do not match up.

As a result, the allies went to war in Iraq and Afghanistan with a broad sense of what needed to be done, but without the resources, or sometimes the institutional framework, needed to do it. In consequence, there is a great focus on satisfying the tyrannous demands of the immediate commitment. In consequence the future is being mortgaged to the urgent demands of the present. This is not a criticism of the new maritime strategy so much as a comment that it is by no means clear where it fits into the family of policy statements that the United States, or any other country for that matter, needs in order to translate policy into successful action.[11]

Relatedly, more specific questions can be raised about the connections between this document and force structure, particularly but not exclusively in the U.S. Navy. One angle, as already noted, is to argue that this document is actually an attempt to justify a set of building plans already established in the *Navy Strategic Plan*, which was introduced by Admiral Mullen in order to provide a measure of much-needed stability for the Navy's shipbuilding programme. Some are quite clear about this being

> [T]he Navy's latest attempt to articulate the role of maritime forces, and to provide a sensible justification for its plan to increase the current 278-ship fleet to 313 during the next three decades. Navy officials worry that fleet expansion efforts could be wrecked if the Defense Department cuts naval budgets to pay for the addition of thousands of troops to the Army and Marine Corps over the next four years.[12]

Indeed, Secretary Winter made the point that 'Our 30-year shipbuilding program remains unchanged; our aircraft purchasing schedule remains on track; and our end strength targets will not change as a result of this new strategy.'[13]

If this was indeed the intention, it was, arguably, the wrong way to go about things; the building plan should be derived from an open examination of need. The latter should not be crafted to suit the former.

Another angle of attack on the relationship between the document and the building plan, however, is to argue the exact opposite. Some make the point that this is not a 'strategy' at all in the sense that it does not relate ways and means in a manner that would offer much guidance to force planners in any of the three maritime services. The document is more of an overall 'vision' that seeks to establish general things that need to be done, but avoids discussion about what is needed to get those things done. A 'Former Senior Officer' quoted in one account reportedly complained: 'There's nothing in there about force planning. Do I build capital ships for major wars that don't occur often, or do I build for general purpose, lower-end ships for the kinds of events we encounter far more regularly?'[14] Nor does it give much clue about relative priorities between modern and postmodern maritime approaches that in an age of budgetary constraint must compete to some extent. According to some, 'By not including or even alluding to a recapitalization plan in the strategy, The Navy missed a golden opportunity to link its strategy and equipment needs in a single clear case for lawmakers.'[15]

But perhaps, some wonder,[16] there is a new accompanying, classified annex that does articulate and justify Navy building plans and that supports the aspiration to advance to a 313-ship navy, if not more. Vice Admiral Morgan offers a more subtle explanation. He has spoken of his hope that 'the new strategy will "lead strategic thinking" in the formation of future budgets. The intention is for the strategy to be "refreshed" every two years, right before long-term budget plans are finalized.'[17] In other words, the strategy is intended to provide a continuing means of on-course guidance for the existing programmes that they therefore accompany rather than precede or follow.

Moreover, the timing of the debate is interesting, seeming to imply a readiness on the part of the maritime services to get people thinking about American defence needs *after* Iraq and Afghanistan, by which time the political complexion of White House and Congress may be rather different.

For all that, it's clear that there's no pleasing everybody since the very nature of the document required major compromise by all the participants. The Navy could hardly make more specific claim to more ambitious force structure, in general or in particular naval discipline terms, in an abbreviated document it was producing jointly with the other two maritime services. Nor, of course, could the Marines or Coast Guard. The maritime services, in any collective bid to draw national attention to the importance of the physical environment in and across which they all operate, needed to be mindful of the fact that this was not a statement of *national* policy. The subject area this document sought to address is vast, geographically, substantively, and temporally; it required massive compression. Accordingly the statement could hardly have the crisp exactitude and the articulated performance indicators of *The Maritime Strategy* of the 1980s, for example. For all these reasons a final verdict on the importance and impact of this document will need to wait upon events. The proof of the pudding will be in the eating.

So What's Next?

For the new strategy to convince observers that it really is the significant departure from the norm that it was claimed to be, its progenitors will need to convince sceptics by what they do after its introduction. A serious and sustained campaign of strategic communication amongst the stakeholders themselves, between them and the rest of the country, and amongst the United States and other countries seems called for as a first step. The (mis)apprehensions noted above will need to be addressed.

In particular, this is an ideal time for the United States to progress a campaign of (re)engagement with the rest of the world, given the strains induced by the Iraq war. Here the problem is exemplified by global worries that the United States is not only too powerful but also inclined to often-self-defeating unilateralism. It is against this background that the debate about the ratification of the UN Convention on the Law of the Sea (UNCLOS) by the United States, significantly represented by its American adversaries as LOST (the Law of the Sea Treaty), is being followed by the outside world. Critics of the proposal to ratify clearly argue from a rigorous set of traditional, modern conceptions of U.S. sovereignty and national interest.[18]

White House and Navy proponents however believe UNCLOS provides an indispensable legal framework for most activities in support of maritime security. Some would go on to admit that the United Nations generally also lends authority for more ambitious acts in defence of the maritime system. The perception, whether it is true or not, that the United States and its allies are 'acting outside the law' undermines their prospects of success. Accordingly ratification of the Law of the Sea would indeed seem to imply acceptance by the United States of the notion that its maritime security is best provided in concert with everyone else's.

With this we approach the most postmodern aspect of American maritime thinking in this document: the continual references to its 'collaborative' nature. Although most countries find the notion of a global maritime partnership attractive,[19] there are residual suspicions about whether the United States really means it. This is manifested by Africa's hesitations about Africom: Africa, the locals say, is not about to be commanded by the United States. A real partnership will need to acknowledge this, that in many cases local alliances will provide the first response to local troubles and that local priorities in the maintenance of Good Order at Sea are not necessarily the same as those of the United States. Americans tend to put 'international terrorism' at the top of the list of threats; other countries are much more concerned about illegal fishing or people smuggling. Even Europeans often do not necessarily put counter-terrorism at the head of their priority list.[20]

Certainly in the strategy document, with its emphasis on building the trust that cannot be surged, and indeed in the public statements of regional commanders around the world, there is at least declaratory acceptance of the need to accommodate such differences of view. As Admiral Mullen said,

> [T]he changed strategic landscape offers new opportunities for maritime forces to work together—sometimes with the U.S. Navy, but oftentimes without. In fact, a greater number of today's emerging missions won't involve the U.S. Navy. And that's fine with me.[21]

Putting the concept of partnership into effect, however, will require practical steps. These may include a concerted effort to make 'maritime domain awareness' work, by moving from an information culture based on 'the need to know' to one based on 'the need to share' and by the open-handed provision of skills and equipment in a sophisticated capability-building campaign for those countries that need it. Sophisticated, in this case, means two things. First is a practical appreciation of the need fully to integrate naval efforts with coastguards, both foreign and domestic, in a manner that gives the latter full credit for their particular strengths in this area. Second, it will require particular awareness of the political and cultural sensitivities of the region in question. The current emphasis on language training and cultural awareness together with the creation of a 'civil affairs command' of foreign area officers is an encouraging step in this direction. And so were the demonstrations of intent evident in the recent cruises of the hospital ships *Mercy* and *Comfort*, when put alongside the effective reactions of the U.S. Navy towards natural disasters like the 2004 tsunami. Actions, after all, speak louder than words and this is the kind of thing likely to make a reality of the concept of 'Global Fleet Stations'[22] and persuade others that the maritime services really mean what they say in this document. All of this seems to presage a move away from the techno-centric thinking that seems to have characterised U.S. defence policy over the past few years.

But the rest of the world isn't the only constituency of concern that needs to be addressed in a continuing campaign of justification, as already remarked. Different sets of justification may need to be given to domestic stakeholders, and some of these may well compete with the messages that need to be transmitted to foreigners. For instance, the 'kinetic community' will need to be assured that their 'modern' but perfectly legitimate concerns about the need to continue to prepare for the prospect of normal interstate war are addressed.[23] Getting the right balance between 'hard' and 'soft' maritime power is particularly problematic when naval budgets are tight, partly because of the inevitable political concentration on the Iraq and Afghanistan wars and a building programme mired in continuing controversy. It exacerbates the concerns of people like Robert Kaplan who argue that the U.S. Navy is moving too far away from catering for the traditional naval threats from first- and second-class adversaries now and in the more distant future.[24] Instead it should focus its efforts on such 'modern' preoccupations as the acquisition of more sophisticated ASW, supercarriers and sea-based ballistic and cruise missile defence, the Zumwalt class, and the CG(X).

These of course are expensive and encourage the trend towards smaller fleets, particularly as fewer builds makes safe, incremental modernisation of the fleet more difficult. It forces the Navy into specifying 'transformational' leaps in platform specification as evidenced in the LCS, *Zumwalt*, and CG(X) programmes, which are inherently riskier and costlier to fix when things go wrong. Although the new maritime strategy does not go into this question, because it does not address relative priorities as remarked earlier, questions will have to be asked and answered about the balance that should be struck in the hi/lo mix.

The LCS programme is particularly important from this point of view and its current difficulties therefore especially unfortunate. But even within the programme, there are those who argue that something cheaper, less capable, and in greater numbers would provide a better solution. Lower-intensity postmodern operations would seem to many to call for still greater expansion of riverine capabilities, significant reentry into the small patrol craft area, and something of a de-emphasis on the mainly Mahanian aspects of the current shipbuilding programme. William Lind complains that 'the U.S. Navy is building a fleet perfectly designed to fight the navy of Imperial Japan. If someone wants to contest control of the Pacific Ocean in a war between aircraft carrier task forces, we are ready.' In support of his call for a major shift in resources he recalls Robert Kaplan citing a former deputy assistant secretary of defense, Jim Thomas, as saying, 'The Navy is not primarily about low-level raiding, piracy patrols, and riverine warfare. If we delude ourselves into thinking that it is, we're finished as a great power.' On the contrary, Lind argues that in today's postmodern fourth-generation world that *is* what naval power is all about—or ought to be.[25]

Getting these budgetary and force structure balances right, and giving real effect to the ideas sketched out in *A Cooperative Strategy for 21st Century Seapower* calls for the open debate it is already getting but also for a clear sense of *national* strategy in which the place of maritime forces in the overall response to the demands of a complex present and future world is seriously addressed. A major part of this would be the creation of an overall joined-up strategy that does two things. First, it should seriously address the task of deterring or winning today's conflicts while being able to secure the 'peace' that follows. Second, it should define and balance the needs of today's conflicts with those of tomorrow's. Easier said than done perhaps, but essential all the same. These issues are unlikely to be resolved quickly or easily, and this points to the need for the continued dialogue that preconditions ultimate agreement.

Likely Foreign Reactions

It is not easy to gauge likely foreign reactions. Inevitably some of these will be a response to the strategy-making process that produced and is succeeding production of the document, rather than to what the document actually says. In the course of this, some outsiders are bound to hear things that confirm existing suspicions about U.S. intentions. Statements intended to assuage the concerns of 'hard power' advocates in Congress, for example, will unnecessarily alarm those for whom American maritime dominance can be seen as a prospective threat and dismay those who instead wish to see the establishment of a real global maritime partnership against common threats and challenges. Hence the need for a strategic information campaign that explains what is actually, rather than apparently, going on. Moreover foreign navies are conducting their own strategic reviews; their views about the new U.S. strategy will tend to reflect their own preoccupations and emerging conclusions. This will tend to determine what parts of the process and the product they focus on.

A campaign of strategic communication would probably fall on receptive ears, at least amongst the United States' closer allies since many of them are facing identical problems. The United Kingdom, for example, has yet to develop a national strategy in which the resources available to defence match the political objectives set for it and in which future needs are secured against the immediate demands of an urgent present. Because of the focus 'on the here and now', the Royal Navy is facing acute difficulties in achieving a modern/postmodern balance it is happy with.[26] Here too the aim is to get people thinking about the world *after* Iraq. Inevitably, hi/lo mix issues dominate fleet structure questions. Having secured its future carriers, how many other top-class surface combatants does the Royal Navy need and can it afford? And when considering the Future Surface Combatant programme, what should be the ratio between the (relatively) cheap and cheerful C3 variants and the more ambitious C1s? This is in large measure a matter of resources, but getting the resources needed seems very much to be a question of getting the message across to a public, a media, and a political establishment largely focussed on present land/air, rather than future air/naval, needs.[27]

In a more general way, opinions differ over the extent to which it is safe and appropriate for the Royal Navy to get involved in the lower reaches of the spectrum of maritime security. Many of these issues apply to the other European navies as well. They all face growing gaps between the resources apparently available and the range of possible commitments they may be expected to fulfil. Their fleets are shrinking numerically but comprised of individual units that are ever more powerful.

To a degree, this reflects widespread acceptance in European navies of the expeditionary impulse that seems to flow naturally from the global security concerns that preoccupy their conceptions of necessary defence. Accordingly, they will tend to be broadly sympathetic to the aims and methods outlined in the strategy. Other European countries take a more geographically local view of their security priorities and, while not unsympathetic, will not see in this much that is directly relevant for them. Caveatted support of this kind will be much more common in the developing world where residual suspicions of U.S. foreign policy remain strong, although many such countries are as aware of the objective need for enhanced maritime security, broadly defined. A few other countries, such as Iran or North Korea, can be expected to take a dim view of a strategy much of which they will think, rightly or wrongly, is essentially aimed at them. It will be especially interesting to see the emerging reaction of China, and perhaps Mr Putin's Russia too.

Evidently, in the problems it is having in its quest to adapt to the difficult conditions of the twenty-first century, the U.S. Navy is not alone. Current uncertainties and differences of opinion are understandable, even inevitable. But the fact that even the U.S. Navy seems unable to square the circle on its own, perhaps, suggests that a *cooperative* strategy is indeed the way to go.

Notes

1. The views expressed in this article are my own and should not be taken necessarily to reflect official opinion in the United Kingdom or the United States.
2. Colin Gray, *Another Bloody Century* (London: Phoenix, 2005).
3. Geoff Fein, 'Maritime Strategy Still a Priority for Outgoing CNO,' *Defense Daily*, 26 September 2007.
4. 'Strategy Lacks Specifics, Covers Familiar Ground,' *Navy Times*, 29 October 2007.
5. Loren Thompson, *QDR 2005 Issues Facing the Navy* (Washington: Lexington Institute, 2005), p. 7.
6. ADM Mike Mullen formally launched this concept at the 17th International Seapower Symposium in September 2005. See John Hattendorf, ed., *Seventeenth International Seapower Symposium: Report of the Proceedings, 19–23 September 2005* (Newport, RI: U.S. Naval War College, 2006), pp. 3–8.

7. VADM John G. Morgan, quoted in 'Maritime Strategy to Be Unveiled Next Month,' *Navy Times,* 26 September 2007.

8. Loren B. Thompson, 'New Maritime Strategy: Three Cheers, and Three Complaints,' Issue Brief 3 (Washington: Lexington Institute, 23 October 2007).

9. The ideas that follow grew out of discussions with a range of colleagues in Washington and the United Kingdom. It is impossible to list them all, but they will know who they are and will, I hope, take this as evidence of my gratitude for their help.

10. Donald Winter, speech (18th International Seapower Symposium, Naval War College, Newport, RI).

11. Hew Strachan, 'Making Strategy: Civil-Military Relations after Iraq,' *Survival,* Autumn 2006, pp. 59–82.

12. 'Facing Uncertainty, Navy Contemplates Alternative Futures,' *National Defense Magazine,* 10 October 2007.

13. Winter, speech.

14. Christopher Cavas, 'New US Maritime Strategy Is Incomplete,' *Defense News,* 22 October 2007.

15. Ibid.

16. 'Analysts Question Navy Assertions about NMS,' *Inside the Navy,* 22 October 2007.

17. Cavas, 'New US Maritime Strategy Is Incomplete.'

18. William P. Clark and Edwin Meese, 'Another UN Power Grab,' *Wall Street Journal,* 8 October 2007.

19. See 'The Commanders Respond' in *Proceedings of the US Naval Institute,* 2007, pp. 14–31; and 'Charting the Course: World Navy Chiefs Look to the Future' in *Jane's Defence Weekly,* 2 May 2007, pp. 23–50.

20. Esther Brimmer, *Seeing Blue: American Visions of the European Union,* Chaillot Paper 105 (Paris: Institute of Security Studies, September 2007), p. 15.

21. ADM Mullen, speech at the 17th International Seapower Symposium, in *Seventeenth International Seapower Symposium: Report of the Proceedings, 19–23 September 2005,* ed. John Hattendorf (Newport, RI: U.S. Naval War College, 2006), p. 6.

22. 'Global Fleet Stations' may be another term that needs further examination. To some observers it implies something more akin to a floating naval base for possibly offensive action than a means of alleviating local distress.

23. This clearly lay behind Secretary Winter's assurances at the 18th International Seapower Symposium.

24. Robert D. Kaplan, 'America's Elegant Decline,' *Atlantic Monthly,* 3 October 2007.

25. William S. Lind, 'A "Little Ship" Navy,' United Press International, 29 October 2007.

26. VADM Sir Jeremy Blackham and Gwyn Prins, 'Storm Warning for the Royal Navy,' *Proceedings of the US Naval Institute,* October 2007.

27. ADM Sir Jonathan Band, 'The Strategic Vision for Navies,' *Journal of the RUSI,* February 2007.

The Global Era of National Policy and the Pan-Oceanic National Fleet

Robert O. Work
Vice President for Strategic Studies at the
Center for Strategic and Budgetary Assessments

Introduction

In May 1954, Samuel P. Huntington penned a remarkable article titled, "National Policy and the Transoceanic Navy." Huntington wrote the article during a time when the Department of the Navy was losing defense budget share to the newly created Department of the Air Force. His thesis was that a fundamental element of a military force was its strategic concept—a clearly rationalized and articulated explanation of how the service contributes to the nation's contemporary national (security) policy. With each new "phase" of national security policy, it was incumbent upon a service's leadership to adapt its strategic concept to the new contours of the security environment or risk losing relevance. Huntington then advanced two implicit arguments: that the Navy had not adequately adjusted its strategic concept to account for the observable changes in the post–World War II security environment, and that, until it did so, it would risk further marginalization in U.S. national defense policy debates and cuts in its resource allocation.[1]

Huntington's 1954 article continues to influence U.S. naval strategists. Indeed, it served as the intellectual North Star during the most recent search for a new U.S. maritime strategy. This short paper thus borrows and expands on the article's analytical framework to help discuss the general requirements for future U.S. maritime forces. However, it adopts a broader concept for maritime power than that espoused by Huntington. The major theme of this paper is that future maritime requirements must be considered within the context of an integrated *National Fleet* that includes the U.S. Navy, U.S. Coast Guard, and U.S. Marine Corps (along with their reserve components), as well as the Military Sealift Command (MSC) and the Maritime Administration's Ready Reserve Force (RRF).[2] The National Fleet derives additional maritime power and can be augmented with capabilities from many other sources—among them Army Transportation Command (which operates a variety of vessels and craft); American inland river and waterway operators and port authorities, merchant ships flying under the U.S. flag; allied and friendly navies; and, under certain conditions, even foreign-owned ship operators. However, this paper does not address these supporting capabilities, except tangentially. Its primary aim is to articulate the reason why an integrated maritime force consisting of the Navy, Coast Guard, Marines, and MSC/RRF is so relevant and important in the current phase of national security policy.

Before proceeding, it will help to quickly review the fortunes of the National Fleet in previous national security policy phases, which are referred to hereafter as eras. Accordingly, the following sections review the history of the fleet since the birth of the Republic. This history is written as though the National Fleet has been an enduring operational rather than conceptual construct. By so doing, it is easier to understand why a reformed and reinvigorated twenty-first-century National Fleet will be such a vital contributor to U.S. national security policy in the first decades of the twenty-first century—and why the leaders of all four U.S. maritime services and organizations should strive to make the fleet a reality rather than a slogan.

The Continental Era

From 1783 through 1889, the primary task of the U.S. armed forces was to establish American military supremacy on the North American continent. In diplomatic support of this task, the United States avoided entangling alliances with foreign states, announced the Monroe Doctrine to stake out U.S. hemispheric hegemony, and resisted any inclination to involve itself in great-power wars overseas. While implementing their task, the military was called upon to screen the national expansion to the limit of our current continental borders, and to secure them, once reached; to wage a century-long counterinsurgency and pacification campaign against North American Indians; to fight one war against an intervening foreign power (Great Britain) and another against the country's southern neighbor (Mexico); and to fight a bloody civil war to preserve the Union. These activities generally occurred north of Mexico City and south of the border with Canada. During both peace and war, the dominant service was the nation's land force—the U.S. Army.[3]

The Birth of the National Fleet

Throughout this era, the nation's maritime forces were assigned narrowly defined supporting roles. With the Continental Navy and Marine Corps having been disbanded in 1785, between 1790 and 1798 the Revenue Marine of the Department of the Treasury—the forefather of today's Coast Guard—was the only armed U.S. maritime service. The Revenue Marine operated in U.S. littoral waters, fighting pirates and suppressing smugglers. In 1797, its cutters were given a broader coastal defense mission against invading foreign states.[4] However, after the Department of the Navy was established in 1798, the newly reconstituted U.S. Navy and Marine Corps assumed primary responsibility for the coastal defense mission. In addition to defending the U.S. East Coast from naval attacks, the two reformed sea services supported Army operations on the North American continent (e.g., through blockading and amphibious and riverine operations) and conducted distant commerce raiding against the merchant fleets of U.S. adversaries. Throughout the era, just as they had in the Revolutionary War, Marines died alongside sailors during actions at sea and sailors died alongside Marines in landing parties ashore; their strategic concepts were as one.[5] Moreover, after 1798, ships of the Revenue Marine were to cooperate with the Navy under the direction of the secretary of the Navy during times of war. As a result, as early as the Quasi-War with France, revenue cutters fought alongside U.S. Navy combatants. Indeed, the U.S. revenue cutter *Pickering* captured ten of the twenty French ships ultimately seized by U.S. maritime forces during the war.[6] The powerful idea of a unified National Fleet, which combined the combat power and core competencies of each of America's three seagoing services, was thus an early one, forged in battle.

A Naval Expeditionary Posture

Although having a clearly subordinate role in U.S. national security policy on and near the North American continent, the U.S. Navy and Marine Corps took the lead in establishing America's first global defense posture—defined herein as the deliberate apportionment and global positioning and sustainment of forward-based and forward-deployed forces in order to facilitate the rapid concentration of forces in time and space across transoceanic distances, support and sustain U.S. military presence and operations in distant theaters, and establish a favorable global strategic balance.[7] Forward-deployed naval forces, operating from six to ten distant "fleet stations" established in regions of U.S. commercial and national interest, fought pirates, protected U.S. merchantmen and citizens, and upheld American honor.[8] While operating from these fleet stations, far beyond the range of effective communications, the Navy and Marine Corps team developed both its preference for forward operations and a unique expeditionary culture that defines it to this day. The two services fought numerous small actions and conducted several minor campaigns. Remarkably, the two services were able to sustain this *naval expeditionary posture* and these distant operations without the benefit of any formal forward bases. The Navy Department instead established fee-for-service "cooperative security locations" in friendly foreign ports.[9] This proved to be a cheap and effective way to establish U.S. forward presence around the globe.

Given the strategic focus on the North American continent, there was no great demand for a standing U.S. strategic sealift fleet. Throughout most of the era, the sail-powered Navy and Revenue Marine vessels that forward-deployed were largely self-sufficient, and ships' complements of sailors, augmented by their Marine detachments, were generally sufficient for most tasks ashore. When necessary, the Navy would simply charter U.S. merchant ships to augment fleet operations. When the Army needed to get anywhere, as it did in the War with Mexico, it too chartered its own ships. After the war, when the Army suggested that the Navy take on the sealift role in time of war, the Navy adamantly rejected the idea. Thus, aside from the U.S. merchant marine, the Continental-Era National Fleet lacked an integral strategic sealift component.[10]

In terms of aggregate combat capability, the National Fleet never threatened the top naval powers of the day. Although the Navy occasionally operated "ships of the line," these large vessels were generally too much ship and too expensive for the service's assigned missions. The primary National Fleet combatants were therefore frigates (later cruisers), sloops, brigs, and cutters. In terms of numbers of ships, the highest standing the Navy ever achieved among world naval powers was fourth. However, after the Civil War, the Navy languished in both numbers and technological prowess. By 1886, it was twelfth among the world navies.[11] The newly renamed Revenue Cutter Service (RCS) and U.S. Marines suffered similar declines in fortune. Although dispiriting to U.S. sea warriors, as argued by

Huntington, these circumstances were wholly consistent with the nation's national security policy needs in the Continental Era.

The Oceanic Era

In 1890, two things happened to help change the National Fleet's fortunes. For all intents and purposes, the Battle of Wounded Knee ended the Indian wars. With friendly or weaker neighbors to the north and south, the United States was "practically sovereign" on the North American continent, if not the entire Western Hemisphere. The primary national security objective of the Continental Era was achieved.[12] Just at this time, Alfred Thayer Mahan published *The Influence of Seapower on History*, which explained the importance of maritime power to both global commerce and war. These two events, among many others, helped spur a more active U.S. role in world politics and led to a radical expansion of U.S. national security interests. The new primary role of the U.S. armed forces would be to secure the Republic from threats originating from outside the Western Hemisphere and to project U.S. power and influence globally.

This new set of national security tasks was a boon for the National Fleet, and particularly the Navy. Since the only plausible exterior threats to the United States originated from across the seas, America's defended national security perimeter was expanded to include the maritime avenues of approaches in both the Atlantic and Pacific oceans. However, because the maritime approaches to the continent were too many to defend from the coasts, the only option was to build a powerful battle fleet capable of deterring or defeating possible attacks. In the blink of an eye, the Navy became the country's first line of defense. Under these circumstances, a strategic concept focused on coastal defense and *guerre de course* was no longer relevant. In its place, the Navy adopted a new strategic concept that emphasized sea control operations and a capability to project maritime power and to defeat advancing enemy battle lines in either the Atlantic (presumably in the Caribbean) or the Pacific.[13]

With a strategic concept perfectly attuned to the new national security environment, American political leaders vowed to build "incomparably, the greatest navy in the world," organized around powerful, all-big-gun, armored battleships capable of taking on any potential naval adversary.[14] By 1908, propelled by a sustained, two-decade-long national shipbuilding program, the "New Navy" leapfrogged over most naval powers and was competing with the Imperial German Navy for the number-two spot among world naval competitors, behind the British Royal Navy.[15] Fifteen years later, after Germany's defeat in the First World War, the Washington Naval Treaty recognized the U.S. Navy as being equal with the British Royal Navy—at least in terms of aggregate tonnage.[16]

A Service Expeditionary Posture

Consistent with requirements of the new national security policy phase, all Oceanic-Era wars were fought "over there," away from the North American continent. Moreover, the United States assumed its first true global posture during the era, with permanent exterior bases concentrated in the Caribbean Basin and the Pacific Ocean. It also built the Panama Canal, which linked its Atlantic and Pacific fleets, thus facilitating their concentration, if necessary. In World

War I, to deny the Germans the use of a forward submarine base and to help secure the Atlantic approaches, the United States added the Danish Virgin Islands to its exterior possessions. It also maintained sizable forces (for the time) in China. These bases were all located on U.S.-controlled territory or on territory governed under the principle of extraterritoriality—meaning territory under direct U.S. sovereign control with no operational strings attached.[17]

The Army's role changed as substantially as the Navy's. The Army shifted from being a peacetime frontier constabulary to a modern expeditionary force that fought in numbers beyond the confines of the North American continent for the first time. Army forces fought Cuban forces during the Spanish-American War, waged a three-year-long counterinsurgency campaign and then occupied the Philippines, and fought alongside the allies in World War I. Consistent with the precedent established in the Continental Era, the Army was forced to charter and operate its own sealift ships during wartime, except during the final stages of the First World War. Permanent Army garrisons were also established outside the confines of the continental United States, primarily in the Canal Zone, Hawaii and the Philippines, and later Alaska. In peacetime, forward Army garrisons were also supported by ships owned and chartered by the Army, not the Navy.[18]

During peacetime, while the U.S. battle fleet normally remained concentrated in U.S. home waters, U.S. Navy and Marine expeditionary forces continued to operate around the world, as they had since 1798.[19] However, during wartime, the National Fleet generally operated forward. During the Spanish-American War, Marines landed and occupied forward naval bases in Cuba and cut Spanish undersea telegraph cables that landed and originated there. Across the Pacific they served on the gun crews of Dewey's ships at Manila Bay. Ships of the RCS fought as part of naval task forces off Cuba and in the Battle of Manila Bay. Later, the 1915 Act to create the Coast Guard stated that the service would "constitute a part of the military forces of the United States and . . . operate as a part of the Navy, subject to the orders of the Secretary of the Navy, in time of war or when the President shall so direct."[20] During World War I, with Marines fighting alongside the Army in Europe, the Coast Guard protected convoys and helped train sailors under the operational control of the Navy. After the war, the Marines began to advance a new strategic concept—seizing advanced naval bases through amphibious assault—which blended seamlessly into the Navy's strategic concept of sea control. Moreover, the Coast Guard's famous Treasury-class cutters, designed in the 1930s, were based on the Navy's Erie-class gunboats and built in Navy-owned shipyards.[21] In other words, during the Oceanic Era the Navy, Marines, and Coast Guard gradually became a truly integrated fighting team, with complementary strategic concepts and visions. This circumstance was helped bureaucratically by the ranks of the top leaders of the three sea services. After 1915 the chief of naval operations was a four-star admiral, while the commandant of the Coast Guard was either a captain or rear admiral, and the commandant of the Marine Corps was a major general. This made the Navy the "senior maritime service" and helped to quell any major dissent when it came to charting the future pathway for the National Fleet.

As indicated above, the Oceanic Era's *service expeditionary posture* continued to see a National Fleet with two sealift fleets, not one. Even though the Navy resisted taking on the strategic sealift mission during most of the era, World War I demonstrated the need for a robust *national* sealift capability. By war's end, the Navy operated over four hundred ships capable of carrying over two million tons of cargo and equipment. However, this impressive force was not nearly big enough to transport a modern, mechanized army from the United States to Europe. In the end, due to a shortfall in U.S. strategic lift, over 50 percent of American troops were ultimately transported to Europe on British, French, and Italian troop transports. Although the U.S. Shipping Board Emergency Fleet eventually authorized the building of over two thousand cargo ships and tankers during the war, most of them were not completed before war's end. With the major cuts in U.S. defense spending after 1921, the majority of these cargo ships were scrapped, sold off to commercial operators, or placed into reserve, leaving the Army and Navy to operate their own small fleets of troop and cargo transports throughout the remainder of the interwar period.[22]

The National Fleet in World War II

World War II was the high-water mark for the National Fleet. Early in the war, enabled by two decades of operational experimentation, the aircraft carrier quickly replaced the battleship as the capital ship in the Navy's battle fleet, and fleet operations were radically changed. Every ship class designed before World War II, with the exception of minesweepers, performed a different role than it was originally designed for.[23] At the same time, the Navy–Marine Corps team, together with the Army, perfected the art of amphibious warfare and fought their way across the Pacific through a combination of naval strike and naval maneuver—the latter defined as the swift movement of forces [by sea] to successive positions the loss of which will hurt the enemy badly.[24] Once again, the Coast Guard fell under the operational control of the Navy, and it fought forward in both oceans. By 1945, the Navy operated nearly 6,800 warships of all types, 99 of them aircraft carriers.[25] The Marine Corps numbered six full divisions. The Coast Guard punched well above its weight, operating approximately 800 vessels of all types and manning 351 more Navy ships. It also developed the idea of using a newly developed aircraft called the helicopter as an ASW platform.[26]

The warships in the fighting fleet operated by the Navy and Coast Guard were supplemented by an enormous national sealift fleet. In addition to the huge numbers of personnel, jeeps, trucks, tanks, artillery pieces, and engineer equipment needed to support global allied attacks, every forward-deployed soldier consumed between 7 and 15 tons of supplies, ammunition, and support gear each year, depending on the theater of operations. With millions of men continuously deployed, the amount of equipment and cargo that needed to be transported across transoceanic ranges was staggering, and sealift provided the most reliable and efficient means for moving it.[27] The U.S. Merchant Marine alone operated more than 5,700 ships during the war, including 2,751 Liberty ships and 531 larger Victory ships—and these numbers do not include the attack cargo and personnel ships operated by both the Navy and the Army. This fleet, augmented by the equally large British merchant fleet, carried the majority of supplies, equipment, food, cargo, and ammunition necessary to sustain forward combat operations in multiple foreign theaters.[28]

As these numbers suggest, then, by 1945 the National Fleet was, incomparably, the greatest maritime force in the world—and likely the most powerful maritime force in history.

The Transoceanic Era (aka the Cold War)

The shift in the National Fleet's fortunes in the next era of national security policy was as dramatic as had been the shift from the Continental and Oceanic phases—but in the opposite way. Indeed, during the era's early years, the power and prestige of the National Fleet greatly diminished and its very relevance was often questioned—even by its own constituent organizations. The root cause of this development was, as predicted by Huntington's model, a radical change in the national security environment.

Soon after the end of the Second World War, it became increasingly clear that the primary future threat to the United States and its interests would be the Soviet Union—a continental land power that sat across the oceans, astride the Eurasian continent, with an authoritarian communist ideology and expansionist foreign policy. In 1947, President Truman committed the United States to protecting free nations on the Eurasian continent from being forcibly incorporated into the Soviet empire either through subversion or invasion. Also that year, the famous Mr. X article was published in *Foreign Affairs*, which explained to the American people the insidious nature of the Soviet threat.[29] These two events served the same purpose as the Battle of Wounded Knee and *The Influence of Sea Power on History*: they helped to spur a further widening of the American national security perimeter to include threats to allies and free countries on the opposite sides of the Atlantic and Pacific oceans. They therefore help mark the beginnings of the Transoceanic Era of national security policy, now most commonly referred to as the cold war.[30]

The primary tasks assigned to the U.S. armed forces during the Transoceanic Era were thus to deter any direct Soviet attack on the United States, to contain Soviet expansionism, and, if need be, to defeat both overt and proxy Soviet attacks. Given the Soviet Union's geographic position, this inevitably meant that much of the joint force—particularly units of the Army and Air Force—would need to be positioned overseas, essentially on a "wartime" footing, ready to repel a "bolt from the blue" Soviet attack into Europe.

The National Fleet in Nuclear Warfighting Phase

Containment of a land power with (at the time) a weak navy undermined the sea control concept that had so defined the Navy for the better part of five decades. With no fleet left to fight, a large navy no longer seemed relevant to national security policy makers. Moreover, the advent of atomic weapons appeared to make the idea of amphibious operations obsolete, which similarly demolished the Marines' primary *raison d'être*. Indeed, the appearance of atomic weapons seemed to upend the very way future warfare would be conducted. The first 15 years of the Transoceanic Era, which might best be termed its *nuclear warfighting phase*, saw all of the services struggle to adjust their strategic concepts to account for a new grand strategy of transoceanic containment in a world with atomic weapons.[31]

The service that most easily conformed to the nuclear warfighting phase was the upstart U.S. Air Force, with a ready-made strategic concept of strategic air bombardment and a growing fleet of long-range atomic bombers to implement it. As previously implied, each national security policy era was characterized by a dominant service—the service most attuned to the nation's national security needs. In the Continental Era, the dominant service was the Army; in the Oceanic Era, it was the Navy. Now, the Air Force would assume pride of place among the four services—a fact that contributed to dramatic cuts to the size of the National Fleet.[32] By June 1950, the active Navy fleet had shrunk to just 634 ships, the Marines had been reduced to two skeletal divisions, and the Defense Department's cancellation of the Navy's new supercarrier, the USS *United States*, had sparked a "revolt of the admirals."[33]

The major reductions in the size of the Navy's battle force caused a significant change to the Coast Guard's expected role in the National Fleet. In 1947, in the midst of the National Fleet's dramatic post-war decline, and perhaps to preempt any argument that Coast Guard ships available in wartime might justify further reductions in the number of active Navy ships, the chief of naval operations decreed that in future conflicts the Coast Guard should limit its future contribution to those *peacetime tasks* in which it specialized.[34] These duties included port security, maritime inspection and safety, search and rescue, and patrolling ocean stations. In other words, the Coast Guard would no longer be expected to fight the "away game" alongside the Navy. Consistent with this line of thinking, the Coast Guard provided only minimal support during the Korean War, where not a single "Coastie" was wounded or killed in battle.[35]

On the other hand, the Navy and Marines welcomed the Korean War, which rather dramatically demonstrated the continued relevance of the Navy–Marine Corps team in "limited wars" in an age of atomic weapons. Indeed, the war triggered a temporary resurgence for both services. In 1952, Congress set the minimum Marine Corps force structure at three division-wing teams, and by June 1953, the Navy's battle force had climbed quickly back up to 1,122 ships, primarily through the recommissioning of ships placed in reserve after World War II.[36] Moreover, the war helped to spur the building of an entirely new 20-knot amphibious landing fleet.[37] However, not even the demonstrated brilliant wartime performance of the Navy–Marine Corps team could fully resist the tides caused by the major changes in the national security environment. For example, the lack of any compelling naval competitor continued to work against any major expansion of the Navy. Moreover, although the Navy embraced the nuclear strike mission for its aircraft carriers, the relative lack of carrier aircraft range and the subsequent shift of the nuclear strike mission to the submarine fleet dampened Navy arguments to expand the carrier and surface fleets for the "big one."[38] As for the Marines, despite the success of the Inchon landing in the first months of the Korean War, with America's new willingness to enter into entangling alliances the U.S. global defense posture underwent a profound change. The post-war exterior-basing structure saw a dramatic expansion in land bases in Europe,

Africa, Latin America, and the Pacific.[39] For the first time, the United States stationed large combat garrisons on foreign soil in sovereign states. In such a *garrison posture*, forward access in expected combat theaters was relatively secure, and seizing advanced bases was no longer a pressing requirement.

In sum, then, containment of a continental power with a weak navy, the initial post–World War focus on nuclear warfighting, and the shift to the Transoceanic Era's new garrison posture all compelled the Navy and Marines to start seeking new strategic concepts to justify their continued defense budget share. In the process, the two services began to drift apart. The Navy began to focus on maintaining "combat credible" carrier battle groups (CVBGs) forward in peacetime. For wartime operations, it planned to protect the ocean bridge between the United States and Europe through aggressive antisubmarine operations and conduct independent carrier strike and attack submarine operations.[40] At the same time, the Marines began to tout their role as an "expeditionary force-in-readiness" for use in peripheral theaters. They were far less concerned about the mode of transport used to get them to a fight, as long as it got them there fast. True, amphibious ready groups (ARGs) with embarked Marine air-ground task forces (MAGTFs) routinely deployed as much as carrier battle groups—reflecting the strong Navy and Marine preference for forward expeditionary operations evident since the Revolutionary War. In the process, CVBGs and ARGs became two of the most important national tools for responding to rapidly developing third-world crises.[41] However, naval strike and maneuver forces seldom trained as integrated fighting teams, and officers assigned to the "Gator Navy" seldom made flag rank. As a result, the strong operational bonds that had linked the two services together since the Revolutionary War gradually began to fray.

Ironically, the bonds that held the National Fleet together were also somewhat weakened by the post-war elevation of the commandants of the Marine Corps and Coast Guard to four-star rank. This move, made to recognize the contributions of both services during World War II, made "consultations" and "negotiations" between and among the U.S. sea services more difficult. The Navy still boasted the largest budget, and its voice therefore often carried the most weight in maritime matters. Unquestionably, however, the elevation in rank of the two commandants made the Coast Guard and Marines more independently minded, and their strategic concepts less prone to Navy influence.

Indeed, one of the only clearly positive steps for the National Fleet during the Transoceanic Era's nuclear warfighting phase was the formation of a single, standing national sealift fleet. The Merchant Ship Sales Act of 1946 created the National Defense Reserve Fleet (NDRF), consisting of mothballed World War II ships that could be activated to meet shipping requirements during national emergencies. At its peak, the NDRF consisted of 2,277 ships laid up at twelve ports or anchorages throughout the United States.[42] Moreover, post-war new-construction U.S. merchantmen were specifically designed to be converted to fast amphibious transports in time of war.[43] Finally, in 1949, the forerunner of the Military Sealift Command—the Military Sea Transportation Service (MSTS)—was formed in "order to provide, under one authority, control, operation, and administration of ocean transportation . . . for all agencies or departments of the National Military Establishment."[44] The fourth leg of a true National Fleet was finally permanently constituted.

Continued Drift in the Flexible Response Phase

The nuclear warfighting phase of the Transoceanic Era ended abruptly in 1961. President Kennedy rejected the emphasis on nuclear warfighting in favor of a more balanced strategy of flexible response.[45] At the same time, he directed a major change in long-practiced U.S. defense allocation methods. Both the Truman and Eisenhower administrations had followed the remainder method for allocating defense resources: they started with tax revenues, subtracted domestic spending, and apportioned the remainder to defense. They then apportioned the greatest percentage of defense resources to a single service—which in practice turned out to be the U.S. Air Force. In contrast, with his new strategy of flexible response, President Kennedy approved across-the-board defense spending increases to support equally strong Army, Air Force, Navy, Marine Corps, and special operations forces.[46] The Transoceanic Era's *flexible response phase* thus saw the end of the dominant-service model and "locked in" a notional 1/3-1/3-1/3 budget split among the three departments (Army, Air Force, and Navy). From the mid-1960s on, with every service assured a relatively high peacetime allocation, the services no longer competed to be dominant in peacetime spending. Instead, they argued over only relatively minor shifts in budget shares.

The influx of new Department of the Navy money caused a temporary resurgence in Navy interest in naval maneuver, which may have arrested the further decay of the operational linkages that had so long connected the Navy and Marines. In 1964, the Navy–Marine Corps team landed a full Marine division of men and equipment across beaches in Spain, and the two services seemed poised to reforge the strong bonds developed during World War II and Korea.[47] However, that same year marked the start of the long Vietnam War, which saw only a few minor amphibious landings along the coast of South Vietnam.[48] While the Navy did provide Marines (and the Army) with close air and naval gunfire support as well as logistics support, the two services essentially fought independent wars, one from the sea and one on land. Tellingly, the huge riverine fleet developed during the war supported Army troops, not Marines. The worldviews of the two biggest partners in the National Fleet thus began to drift farther and farther apart.

This drift apart was slowed for a time after Vietnam, when a resurgent Soviet navy revived the dormant Mahanian spirit within the Navy. This new spirit led to a new Maritime Strategy that reinvigorated the service's rank and file and provided the rationale for an impressive 1980s naval buildup. The strategy called for a multidimensional sea control campaign that included offensive ASW operations in the Norwegian Sea and Arctic Ocean, Marine landings in Norway and Thrace, and aggressive carrier strike operations along the periphery of Soviet territory. Marines began to "heavy up" to fight Soviet motorized rifle divisions, and the amphibious lift requirement called for a fleet capable of carrying the assault echelons of a Marine amphibious force and a Marine amphibious brigade. For a time, it thus appeared the Navy and Marines were moving closer to the integrated fleet model that had worked so well in World War II.

However, in 1987, General Alfred Gray became the commandant of the Marine Corps. Eight years earlier, the commandant became a permanent member of the Joint Chiefs of Staff, which gave the commandant even more independence to express his thoughts and to set the direction of the Marine Corps. In General Gray's case, he rejected the notion that the United States would ever fight the Soviets, and decided to focus the Marines on the expeditionary force-in-readiness role. Although a staunch supporter of amphibious forces, he replaced the descriptor "amphibious" in MAGTF designators with the term "expeditionary" (e.g., Marine amphibious brigades were renamed Marine expeditionary brigades). The symbolic importance of this move should not be underestimated; it provides clear evidence that by the end of the 1980s the Marines' worldview was increasingly divergent from that of the Navy.[49]

The relationship between the Navy and Coast Guard also had its ups and downs in the Transoceanic Era's flexible response phase. One positive development was that during the Vietnam War, the Coast Guard once again made an impact as part of the battle fleet in forward wartime operations. Coast Guard Squadron One, consisting of twenty-six 82-foot patrol boats, worked under Navy operational control and alongside Navy patrol craft during Operation Market Time, the protracted maritime interdiction operation along South Vietnam's coast and inland waterways. Later, Coast Guard Squadron Three, numbering between two and five High-Endurance Cutters, performed coastal surveillance and naval gunfire support missions. A total of fifty-six different Coast Guard vessels saw action during the war.[50]

After the Vietnam War, as it turned its attention to fighting a world war against the Soviet Union and its allies, the Navy and Coast Guard continued to plan for integrated wartime operations. U.S. Coast Guard high-endurance cutters were given antisubmarine and antisurface warfare upgrades and included in Navy war plans. Moreover, in 1985, Coast Guard–patrolled Maritime Defense Zones (MDZs) were created along the Atlantic and Pacific coasts, rectifying a long-standing deficiency in harbor and inshore water defenses in time of war. Ironically, however, the creation of the MDZs may have helped to reinforce the idea that the proper place for Coast Guard vessels was in U.S. home waters, not forward alongside Navy combatants, which may help explain why the Navy rebuffed the Coast Guard's offer to send 110-foot patrol craft to the Persian Gulf during the so-called tanker wars between Iraq and Iran in the late 1980s.[51]

The fortunes of the MSTS/MSC were similarly mixed during the flexible response phase. Despite the aforementioned creation of the NDSF, for the first three decades after the end of World War II most new money devoted to strategic lift was given to the growing U.S. Air Force strategic airlift fleet. Moreover, during the 1960s, because U.S. forward garrisons were located in the theaters in which they were expected to fight, they could be reinforced far more quickly and safely by prepositioning equipment sets for reinforcing forces on land and flying their associated personnel across the oceans to man them. By the 1980s, the Army and Marines had no fewer than fourteen brigade sets of equipment— nearly five division equivalents—housed on the ground in Europe. While this garrison reinforcement scheme was eminently sensible (and quite expensive), it greatly dampened demand for sealift and for major investments in the NDSF, which by the mid-1970s was in very sorry shape.[52]

Starting in the late 1970s, however, U.S. planners began to worry about countering a potential Soviet thrust into the Persian Gulf, a theater with few forward garrisons. The Military Sealift Command thus helped to oversee a substantial investment in U.S. strategic sealift, the creation of a Ready Reserve Force of sealift ships, under the supervision of the Maritime Administration, capable of immediate activation, and the pursuit of Marine *maritime* prepositioned sets—brigade sets of equipment maintained on specially configured ships that could be sailed to a theater and off-loaded. Unfortunately, however, as maritime prepositioning force (MPF) operations were considered logistical in nature, they did little to strengthen the operational ties between the Navy and the Marines.[53] Indeed, because many Navy officers saw MPF ships as a cheaper substitute for amphibious landing ships, their appearance undoubtedly contributed to a further diminution of Navy interest in naval maneuver.

Thus, by 1989, the very idea of a globally deployable and integrated National Fleet had undergone substantive change since its heyday in World War II. The long cold war against a continental military superpower, along with its associated land-centric garrison posture, had gradually worked to diminish the importance of maritime power in its broadest sense in U.S. strategic thought, and had caused great stresses among the members of the National Fleet. Said another way, the Transoceanic Era helped to undercut the rationale for an integrated National Fleet and spurred each of its four component organizations to pursue semi-independent strategic concepts to preserve their own relevance and budget share.

The Global Era

As late as April 1989, the Central Intelligence Agency believed the Union of Soviet Socialist Republics (USSR) would remain America's principal future adversary through the 1990s and into the next century.[54] The agency, along with most Soviet experts, proved to be embarrassingly wrong. Although the Soviet Union did not officially dissolve until December 1991, for all intents and purposes the cold war ended in 1989 when joyous Germans began dismantling the Berlin Wall. Less than a year later, the Army's VII Corps was pulled out from the Fulda Gap and sent to Saudi Arabia to participate in Operation Desert Storm, the liberation of Kuwait—something unimaginable only a year prior. This event, perhaps more than any other, signaled the end of the one national security policy era and the beginning of another.

The abrupt and unexpected end to the Transoceanic Era triggered a period of great geopolitical uncertainty.[55] However, the collapse of the bipolar cold war competition left the United States alone atop the global pecking order, and well positioned to weather any unexpected strategic turbulence. The United States faced no state competitor remotely capable of matching its cultural, economic, and military power. Its large and growing population was vibrant and tech-savvy. Its gross domestic product was two to three times that of the closest economic competitor. American intelligence and research and development budgets dwarfed those of other countries. The U.S. armed services commanded the "global commons" of sea, air, and space—and, as demonstrated during Desert Storm, were without peer in conventional joint combined-arms warfare as well.[56]

If that were not enough, U.S. military power was poised to make a major jump in potency. Just as had happened during the transition between the Oceanic and Transoceanic eras, the transition to the new post–cold war era occurred simultaneously with the culmination of a revolution in war, marked by the maturation of conventional guided weapons and the battle networks that employed them. Operation Desert Storm thus served both as the benchmark for a new level of American joint operational excellence and the "defining battle" of the guided weapon/battle network regime, which rendered obsolete the massed, armored warfare characteristic of unguided weapons warfare. Moreover, since the only state then capable of remotely matching the scale of U.S. investments in guided weapons and battle networks was the Soviet Union, its unexpected collapse resulted in the rapid rise of an American monopoly in the new warfare regime. Indeed, such was the extent of the additive combat power supplied by the guided weapons/battle network revolution that even as each of the services struggled to contend with the inevitable post–cold war demobilization, the resulting smaller U.S. armed forces actually increased their relative superiority over both allies and potential adversaries—at least in conventional warfare.[57]

Finally, just as America was left standing as the sole global superpower and its military power was seeing exponential increase in conventional fighting power, the world was powering into a new phase of globalization, defined by MIT scholar Barry Posen as "the spread of capitalism across the globe along with the intensification of international trade and the diffusion of manufacturing, investment and finance that is . . . enabled by the crumbling of old political barriers and by the continuing improvements in information and all modes of transportation for goods and people."[58] Globalization was largely seen as a boon to the general U.S. pursuit of free and open global markets. Indeed, in the new Global Era of national security policy, globalization seemed to provide the best evidence that the "end of history," and the final victory for the twin U.S. visions of liberal democracy and free trade, was at hand.[59]

The Global Era's Unilateral Phase

As one strategist pointed out—echoing the same thoughts expressed by Huntington in the mid-1950s—"if the Cold War was a big deal (and it was), then the end of the Cold War had to be a big deal, too, requiring us to synchronize our policies and assumptions underlying them with a new reality."[60] At first glance, this is exactly what happened. The first decade and a half of the Global Era saw a succession of "strategic" reviews: the 1992 Base Force; the 1993 Bottom-up Review; the 1994 Commission on Roles and Missions; the 1997 Quadrennial Defense Review (QDR) and National Defense Panel; and the 2001 QDR. However, upon closer inspection, it is obvious that these reviews were all focused narrowly on policies and programs for the Department of Defense. They were not accompanied by the broader *national security* reviews suggested by Huntington's model. Moreover, in hindsight, and as will be discussed further shortly, these defense reviews were built on several key erroneous assumptions.

As a result, what passed for U.S. strategic thought in the immediate aftermath of the cold war was really nothing more than an exercise in congratulatory triumphalism: "With globalization advancing the secular trinity of American values, interests, and power, policy became a management function, not the expression of a strategy."[61] The best that might be said is that in order to preserve the "unipolar moment," successive U.S. administrations pursued policies that aimed to "lock in" America's global primacy. These policies sought to advance globalization through the aggressive expansion of free-market capitalism, to advance the cause of freedom and enlarge the community of democratic nations, and to directly confront both rogue nations and emerging transnational security threats, such as nuclear proliferation. Said another way, being no longer constrained by the intense two-way competition of the Transoceanic Era, the United States globalized the Monroe Doctrine, and U.S. national security interests became even broader, more global, and more expansive in scope.[62]

The first decade and a half of the new Global Era of national security policy was thus characterized by aggressive U.S. international activism and marked by an unprecedented operational use of "peacetime" armed forces for a variety of purposes. The joint force conducted major deployments to Somalia, Haiti, Rwanda, Bosnia, and Kosovo, and too many minor deployments to enumerate. Although Democratic administrations may have emphasized multilateral solutions to a greater degree than Republicans, Bill Clinton's idea of the United States being the "indispensable nation"[63] was only a shade less different from the neocons' notion of the United States' being a benevolent "global hegemon."[64] The horrific attacks of September 11, 2001, the first major attack on the U.S. homeland since the War of 1812, simply worked to widen the already-expansive U.S. national security aperture and to reinforce unilateralist and interventionist tendencies that had been steadily building since the fall of the Soviet Union.[65] During the *unilateral phase* of the new Global Era of national security policy, then, the United States became accustomed to going and getting its way, either without allied support or with "coalitions of the willing" that acquiesced to or supported U.S.-led efforts.[66]

During the first 15 years of the foregoing Transoceanic Era, it was the atomic revolution that loomed so large in national security debates and so distorted the development of the U.S. defense strategy and programs. In the first decade and a half of the Global Era, it was the guided weapon/battle network revolution that indelibly shaped defense policy and program debates. For example, in support of the U.S. aim for primacy, the joint force was sized to prevail in two simultaneous or overlapping regional wars. Importantly, however, future wars were seen primarily as variations of Operation Desert Storm—a conventional cross-border invasion of a U.S. ally or strategically important state. Just as importantly, since these wars would generally involve the rapid reinforcement of an ally, military planners continued to assume they would have ready operational access under most circumstances. Indeed, the only new wrinkle in early post–cold war defense planning was that dense guided-weapon salvos would allow the joint force to "rapidly halt" any future invasion without the need to base large numbers of troops forward. This thinking dampened the demand signal for ground forces and amplified the demand signal for aerospace and naval forces. Unsurprisingly, the Navy and the Air Force benefited and began to vie for the rapid halt mission.[67]

Soon, however, overwhelming U.S. conventional dominance caused the idea of rapidly halting cross-border invasions to be expanded into something even more fundamental: winning wars quickly and on the cheap. "Rapid halt" quickly morphed into the idea of "rapid decisive operations," which was just as quickly replaced by "shock and awe." By 2001, U.S. defense "strategy" assumed that joint multidimensional battle networks could win one war in 30 days, shift to another theater in 30 days, and win a second war 30 days after that.[68] As the 1990s progressed, the growing U.S. obsession with strategic speed and winning wars quickly gradually resulted in the "tacticization" of U.S. military strategic thinking. Servicing targets quickly became the epitome of operational art. The utter collapse of U.S. strategic and operational thinking in the 1990s helps to explain why U.S. strategists and military planners completely missed the inevitable adjustments that adversaries were making to account for, and offset, U.S. conventional dominance. It also helps to explain the disastrous "short-war mentality" and the disdain for so-called Phase IV, or postwar, planning, so evident before the invasion of Iraq in March 2003.

Stormy Seas for the National Fleet

During the Global Era's initial unilateral phase, the National Fleet sailed through stormy seas. A promising new convergence of Navy and Marine Corps strategic concepts espoused in . . . From the Sea and Forward . . . From the Sea (published in 1992 and 1994, respectively) was soon undone by the continued hold of cold war thinking.[69] The first war of the Global Era (i.e., Operation Desert Storm), just like the first war of the Transoceanic Era, saw the Navy–Marine Corps team assemble a large amphibious landing fleet. Although this fleet ultimately did not land any troops, its mere presence affected the Iraqis' plans and dispositions of forces. However, after the war, rather than conducting a serious debate over whether the ability to conduct naval maneuver might be more important in the *future* national security policy phase, OSD and the Department of the Navy instead clung to Transoceanic-Era assumptions like assured forward access. As a result, National Fleet naval maneuver capabilities continued to decline throughout the 1990s. This decline was accelerated by the Navy's keen interest in at least sharing the "rapid halt" mission with the Air Force.[70] As a result, the Navy began to conflate the narrower idea of missile and air strikes with the broader idea of power projection even more than it had at the end of the cold war. Indeed, by 1997, its shipbuilding plans emphasized aircraft carriers and surface ships with high-capacity guided-missile batteries; the *smallest* surface combatant in the planned future battle fleet was to be an 8,500-ton guided missile destroyer.[71]

The continued divergence of Navy and Marine worldviews was not the sole fault of the Navy. For its part, even though it developed new ideas for naval maneuver, during the 1990s the Marine Corps—guided by post–Desert Storm calls for more "jointness"—talked far more about building separate Marine components for the geographic combatant commanders than it did about rebuilding Fleet Marine Forces. Moreover, it purchased systems more suited for sustained operations on land than for operations from the sea. When the Marines abruptly removed the last Marine detachments from U.S. naval ships in 1998, relations between the two services were likely at a post–World War II, if not historic, low. Reflecting this circumstance, Navy and Marine Corps fights over "blue in support of green" budget allocations—such as for Marine aviation or Navy amphibious landing ships—turned poisonous.

At the same time, the Coast Guard began to recede in importance in National Fleet wartime planning. The only Coast Guard assets deployed forward during Desert Storm were Coast Guard port security units. In 1992, budget cuts compelled the Coast Guard to remove the antisubmarine and antisurface warfare systems that gave their cutters the ability to actively defend U.S. maritime defense zones and operate forward with battle force units.[72] While these moves were perfectly justifiable because of the lack of any apparent threat, they further accentuated the differences in Navy and Coast Guard warfighting capabilities and further distanced the two services.

Just as it had been during the earlier turbulent transition from the Oceanic and Transoceanic eras, one of the few bright spots for the National Fleet during the 1990s was the growing relevance and importance of the Military Sealift Command. Desert Storm was fought in a forward theater with no major U.S. land-based garrisons—a circumstance U.S. strategists believed would be the "new normal" in the Global Era. Under these conditions, the joint force would be much more reliant on sealift than it had been during the cold war. However, even after the substantial improvements made to the U.S. sealift fleet during the 1980s, Desert Storm revealed much more work needed to be done. Because of problems with ships in the RRF, Desert Storm logisticians were initially forced to rely more heavily on airlift than expected, and later had to charter over three hundred foreign-flagged ships to support the massive transport of equipment and supplies in support of combat operations to eject the Iraqis from Kuwait. To correct these problems and to account for sealift's growing importance, DoD made major investments in sealift forces after the war, primarily to procure nineteen large, medium-speed, roll-on, roll-offs (LMSRs) and to improve RRF ship readiness.[73] Mirroring these moves, sealift saw an increased emphasis in Department of the Navy strategy documents.

Perhaps more important for the National Fleet, however, was the thorough integration of Military Sealift Command ships into the active U.S. Navy. Civilian-crewed MSC ships were far cheaper to man and enjoyed much higher operational availability rates than active Navy ships. As a result, the Navy began to shift its entire combat logistics force and much of its mobile logistics force into the Military Sealift Command, making active fleet operations more dependent on the MSC than ever before.[74]

The Storm Begins to Break

The growing relevance of strategic sealift in U.S. national security strategies and the improved integration of the Navy and the MSC marked the first breaks in the storm that had buffeted the National Fleet for nearly five decades, and which had intensified since the end of the cold war. By the late 1990s and early 2000s, the turbulent post–cold war seas began to subside as the vague contours of the new national security policy era began to take more concrete shape. As these contours began to more fully form, the rationale for a reformed, revitalized National Fleet became much clearer. This rationale was derived from three "new" complementary conditions in the Global Era of national security policy:

First, and most fundamentally, the United States was shifting back to a global expeditionary posture. A posture that emphasizes forward bases can be characterized as a garrison posture, whereas one that emphasizes sovereign territorial bases and forward-deployed troops can be characterized as an expeditionary posture. Basing foreign troops inside their borders is an unnatural act for most sovereign countries. It generally occurs only if a nation faces an existential threat far beyond its own ability to counter, and it is almost always accompanied by a formal bilateral or multilateral security treaty between the host nation and the basing power. As the Soviet threat on the Eurasian continent receded, so did much of the overseas political support for large U.S. garrisons. By 1998, consistent with an early post–cold war decision to maintain 100,000 troops in both Europe and Asia for the immediate future, the number of U.S. forces based abroad had been cut by almost 300,000 personnel, dropping the total number of troops stationed abroad to 235,000, including 109,000 in Europe, 93,000 in Asia, and 23,000 in the Persian Gulf.[75] Most of these cuts were Army and Air Force personnel leaving bases in Germany, although the 1991 decision of the Philippines government to revoke U.S. access to the superb facilities at Subic Bay Naval Base and Clark Air Force Base resulted in a reduction in the overall number of troops based in the Pacific.[76]

The redeployment of troops from overseas bases back to U.S. territory accelerated after the 2001 QDR, when Secretary of Defense Rumsfeld announced a major review and "reorientation" of the U.S. global defense posture.[77] At the end of this reorientation, the vast majority of U.S. joint forces would be based inside the continental United States or on U.S. exterior sovereign bases located in Alaska, Hawaii, and Guam—just as they had been in both the Continental and Oceanic eras. The resulting U.S. exterior-basing network would be composed of far fewer U.S. main operating bases on foreign territory, far more numerous and lighter-footprint forward operating sites and cooperative security locations, and many "gas-and-go" agreements for transiting aircraft. Europe would serve as a "strategic trampoline," a logistics and transshipment hub that speeded the eastward and southern movement of forces from the United States (a role played by Brazil in World War II). An improved and expanded sovereign basing structure in the Pacific would serve a similar purpose, facilitating the western movement of forces.[78]

In other words, the Global Era would see the United States return to its more "normal" expeditionary posture. However, this expeditionary posture would be quite different in character from earlier ones. In essence, the Global Era's *joint expeditionary posture* would form a new "global coaling station network," backed by large strategic airlift and sealift forces, geared to support the rapid transoceanic, intertheater, and intratheater movement and sustainment of U.S. expeditionary forces around the globe.

Second, as the United States transitioned to this expeditionary posture, the all-volunteer joint force naturally began to emphasize expeditionary organizations and operations and to build sustainable rotational deployment bases. The decline in overseas bases was not accompanied by a concomitant decline in U.S. operations overseas. Indeed, as mentioned earlier, the pace of U.S. operational deployments picked up dramatically in the early years of the Global Era. As the U.S. Commission on National Security in the 21st Century concluded, this meant that future U.S. armed forces stationed in the United States needed to be able to "deploy rapidly, be employed immediately, and prevail decisively in expeditionary roles, prolonged stability operations, and major theater wars."[79]

Under these conditions, and with the joint force having shifted to all-volunteer recruitments and reenlistments in 1973, it became increasingly important for the services to organize their forces into sustainable rotational deployment pools. Failing to do so would put an enormous strain on the smaller joint force, which was increasingly made up of married members. The worry was that this strain might then translate into lower force recruitment and training and, in turn, lower force training and readiness.

The Navy and Marine Corps had the easiest time adjusting to the demands associated with this new expeditionary posture and forward-deployed mindset, as they had been deploying forward since the birth of the Republic and had organized to support routine rotational deployments since the late 1940s.[80] For the Air Force's part, after disparaging the Navy's rotational deployment model for its aircraft carrier fleet as being inefficient and costly throughout the Transoceanic Era, the new conditions of the Global Era spurred the Air Force to simply copy the model. It formed ten air and space expeditionary forces (AEFs) and gradually worked out a rotational assignment pattern that kept two AEFs ready for immediate tasking. The Army was the only service that resisted a move to a more effective rotational deployment pool, deciding instead to manage deployments from a smaller version of its cold war divisional force structure. It was not until the Army was bogged down in the prolonged two-front war in Afghanistan and Iraq that it began belatedly to move to reorganize the Army into a deployable pool of seventy-six active duty and National Guard brigade combat teams (BCTs), with a goal of maintaining twenty BCTs forward at any given time. Despite its delay in establishing an expeditionary rotation base, however, the Army trumpeted its move to a more expeditionary mind-set throughout the 1990s—a circumstance that irritated the Marine Corps, which believed it had cornered the ground force expeditionary market in the Transoceanic Era.

Third, an increasing number of defense experts began to question the continued assumption of assured forward access in the Global Era. In 1996, a Defense Science Task Force for Strategic Mobility pointedly noted that 96 percent of all cargo delivered by sea during Operation Desert Storm went through just two seaports, and 78 percent of all cargo delivered by air went through just five airfields. Although Iraq failed to attack these facilities, allowing a smooth uninterrupted delivery of the U.S. and allied invasion force, the task force doubted that future adversaries would be as accommodating.[81]

The notion that forward access would likely be contested or denied more often in the future was picked up by the 1997 National Defense Panel, which wrote in its final report that:

> For nearly a half a century, the U.S. military has relied upon access to forward basing and forward bases as a key element in its ability to project power. . .

However, U.S. forces' long-term access to forward bases, to include air bases, ports, and logistics facilities cannot be assumed. Access may be granted or denied for any number of political or military reasons. Moreover, U.S. forces may find themselves called upon to project power in areas where no substantial basing structure exists.[82]

The NDP's heightened concern over ready future access was soon driven home by actual events. During Operation Allied Force, the NATO operation against Serbia, Macedonia refused access to U.S. troops due to the influx of refugees from neighboring Serbia and Kosovo. Operation Enduring Freedom, the invasion of Afghanistan, was complicated by the lack of ready access in Central Asia. Perhaps most sobering, however, was the refusal by Turkey, a long-standing U.S. and NATO ally, to allow the United States operational access during Operation Iraqi Freedom. This decision greatly complicated U.S. operational plans for a two-front invasion of Iraq.[83] These events helped to underscore a key difference between the Transoceanic and Global eras: the far greater uncertainty over the availability of forward access. For example, even if the United States could ultimately negotiate forward access, the negotiations might not conclude easily or quickly. Therefore, to retain its global freedom of action, the United States would likely need a higher percentage of *access-insensitive forces*—forces that could operate, at least for some period of time, without support from forward bases—than it required in the Transoceanic Era.

A New Rationale for "Seabasing" and Naval Maneuver

In other words, in the Global Era of national security policy, U.S. planners would once again have to adjust to an expeditionary posture in an age of uncertain access. Because of simple geography, this meant that being able to operate over the oceans would become more important than it had been in the immediate past. The words of Winston Churchill, written in 1942, just as aptly described the basic Global Era problem as they did the U.S. expeditionary problem in an earlier age of uncertain and contested access:

> The whole power of the United States, to manifest itself, depends on the power to move ships and aircraft across the sea. Their mighty power is restricted; it is restricted by the very oceans which have protected them; the oceans which were their shield, have now become both threatening and a bar, a prison house through which they must struggle to bring armies, fleets, and air forces to bear upon the common problems we have to face.[84]

Under these conditions, as noted by the U.S. Commission on National Security in the twenty-first century, "the need to project US power globally with forces stationed in the United States, and those stationed abroad *and afloat in the forward presence role*" (emphasis added) would be a "fundamental" future requirement in the new national security policy era.[85] Indeed, this line of thinking helps explain why the Navy and Marines were able to persuade the Office of the Secretary of Defense during the 1993 Bottom-up Review that forward presence operations could be used to size the battle fleet.[86]

More importantly, however, under these conditions the National Fleet once again gained great relevancy in terms of national security policy. Once the shift to the new expeditionary posture was complete, by being able to claim command of the seas and to use the oceans themselves as a base for forward joint operations the National Fleet would provide the United States and the joint force with tremendous global freedom of action. Said another way, in the Global Era of national security policy, *seabasing*—in the broadest conceptual, not programmatic, sense—would once again become a key U.S. national security requirement and an essential component of the evolving joint expeditionary posture. As Huntington explained in 1954:

> . . . in a very real sense *the sea is now the base* from which the Navy operates in carrying out its offensive activities against the land. Carrier aviation is sea based (*sic*) aviation; the Fleet Marine Force is a sea based ground force; the guns and guided missiles of the fleet are sea based artillery . . . *The base of the United States Navy should be conceived of as including . . . the seas of the world right up to within a few miles of the enemy's shores.* This gives American power a flexibility and a breadth impossible of achievement by land-locked powers.[87]

The flexibility and breadth provided from seabasing derives from an ability to support naval strike and maneuver—combined arms attacks from the sea. With the shift to the guided weapons regime, the National Fleet had enormous, and increasing, strike capacity. In an era of uncertain forward access, one might expect an increased interest in naval maneuver to balance the fleet's strike capability. However, as has been discussed, the continued embrace of the cold war's condition of assured overseas access throughout the 1990s greatly dampened demand for naval maneuver forces. On the positive side, the assumption that wars would take place in theaters with few forward-based forces greatly amplified demand for strategic airlift and sealift forces, and spurred a gradual shift in emphasis from static land-based to mobile maritime prepositioned equipment and supplies. These capabilities were well matched for the rapid reinforcement of early arriving joint forces, in which reinforcing troops were generally delivered to a theater by air to marry up with equipment either already on the ground or, more likely, delivered by sea. However, once troops and equipment were together, it would take some period of time to assemble a ready combat force. The aforementioned DSB Task Force on Strategic Mobility believed that this primarily logistical operation would create a potential joint force vulnerability in the future, writing that ". . . the hand-off of personnel, equipment, and material from [U.S. Transportation Command] to the [Regional Combatant Commander] at points of debarkation appears to be the 'critical seam' where disruption of the deployment flow is most likely to occur."[88]

To help address this potential vulnerability, both the Army and the Marines began to search for new ways to deliver *intact combat units* capable of fighting as soon as they arrived in a forward theater. The Army referred to this as operational maneuver from strategic distances, while the Marines referred to it as operational maneuver from the sea. Both are distinct from the basic transoceanic movement of forces, which, as described above, can be efficiently accomplished by disaggregating and moving equipment, personnel, and supplies separately to a theater and then marrying them together. Despite claims from some zealots that transoceanic *aerial* maneuver of forces was the preferred solution, it seemed clear that for the foreseeable future both the maneuver of joint forces and the movement of joint equipment across transoceanic distances—not to mention their sustainment once ashore—would remain critically dependent on ships.[89] While jet transport aircraft held a great speed advantage over ships, buoyancy still gave vessels riding over the world's oceans a great advantage in delivered cubic feet of cargo and square feet of vehicles. This made ships far more effective platforms for the delivery of intact combat units.[90]

In summary, then, the move to a global expeditionary posture ineluctably made seabasing and naval maneuver more important than at any time since the end of World War II. Therefore, even though the late-1990s Navy still largely conflated the idea of air and missile strikes with power projection, the growing need for improved joint seabasing and naval maneuver and movement capabilities was becoming increasingly clear. As this happened, Navy planners found new Marine ideas about seabased maneuver capabilities much more difficult to ignore. Unfortunately, when the Navy did start to think about seabasing, it was more in terms of new programs than in terms of improving and expanding naval maneuver capabilities, and more about reducing the amount of resources dedicated to naval maneuver forces to help pay for additional strike capabilities. However, after a period of institutional infighting, by 2004–2005 the Navy and Marines were finally once again engaged in a meaningful debate about the extent and direction of naval and joint seabasing and naval maneuver capabilities.

The Coast Guard Rejoins the National Fleet

Things were also looking up for the Navy–Coast Guard relationship. By 1997, the Navy's active battle fleet was at 365 ships, down from the 1980s high of 594 ships.[91] Moreover, the number of ships in active commission was still falling, prompting Navy leaders to establish in the 1997 QDR a "red line" of 300 ships below which the fleet could not be allowed to fall. Under these trying circumstances, Navy leaders naturally began to think of the Coast Guard's 42 high- and medium-endurance cutters in a different way. With the Navy's decision to get out of the frigate business entirely and to concentrate on high-end, multi-purpose surface combatants, the Coast Guard's frigate- and cutter-sized ships could potentially provide forward-deployed naval task forces with smaller combatants suitable for a variety of presence and low-end tasks. As one joint Navy–Coast Guard document explained, "Especially at the low end of the spectrum of conflict . . . a combined and interoperable force will be needed to establish the numerical sufficiency required for effective global operations."[92]

At the same time, Coast Guard ships were proving to be quite useful in the peacetime "shaping," "engagement," and forward presence roles—roles that had risen in relative importance in the new Global-Era unilateral phase. As General Charles E. Wilhelm, USMC, then-commander of U.S. Southern Command, wrote in 1999:

> The United States Coast Guard brings tremendous capabilities and contributions across a wide spectrum of regional engagement activities. Its role in the Southern Theater is a significant one, and will only grow as we continue to pursue a National Security Strategy that directs us to engage and shape an extremely diverse, dynamic, and expansive environment.[93]

The decreasing size of the active battle fleet and the growing importance of peacetime shaping and engagement operations help to explain why, on 21 September 1998, the chief of naval operations and the commandant of the Coast Guard signed a joint Navy/Coast Guard policy statement on the "National Fleet" concept (more narrowly defined than in this paper). The statement committed the two services to the tailored operational integration of their multimission surface combatants and cutters, in order to reduce overlap and maximize our effectiveness across the range of naval and maritime missions. As the policy said, "All ships and aircraft of the National Fleet will be interoperable to provide force depth for peacetime missions, crisis response, and [major theater war] tasks."[94] Just as conditions in the Global Era suggested the needed reconvergence of Navy, Marine Corps, and MSC strategic concepts, they also suggested that the Transoceanic Era's notion of separate maritime "home" and "away" games for the Navy and Coast Guard was no longer valid.

As was the case for seabasing and naval maneuver, however, it would take additional time to overcome the inertia of Transoceanic Era thinking. As Colin S. Gray observed, despite the 1998 National Fleet policy statement, the Navy's April 2000 *Strategic Planning Guidance and Long Range Planning Objectives* was "all but oblivious to Coast Guard skills."[95] Unquestionably, however, the Navy and Coast Guard were well on their way toward a new integration of their respective capabilities—a move only accelerated by the 9/11 attacks. Soon thereafter, the Navy transferred five patrol coastal craft to the Coast Guard, marking the first time since the 1950s that the Navy and Coast Guard operated similar combatant vessels.[96] During Operation Iraqi Freedom, the Coast Guard deployed two high-endurance cutters, ten 110-foot patrol boats, and a 225-foot buoy tender in support of maritime interdiction operations in the northern Arabian Gulf. Six Coast Guard port security units provided security in the Kuwaiti and Iraqi ports, particularly the important southern Iraqi port of Umm Qasr. Finally, Coast Guard units relieved U.S. Marines and provided security to Iraqi offshore oil terminals.[97] As these developments suggested, although officially a part of the Department of Homeland Security, the Coast Guard was once again a vital part of the forward-fighting National Fleet.

The Global Era's Cooperative Phase

The further the United States moved into the Global Era, the stronger the case became for a revitalized National Fleet. This case became stronger still with the gradual change in U.S. strategic thinking that occurred in 2004–2005. At this time, the United States was bogged down in Afghanistan and Iraq, and both campaigns were increasingly unpopular at home. All of the governments that had supported the U.S. invasion of Iraq either had been thrown out of office or were in trouble at the polls. The opening of the Guantanamo Bay detention facility, reports of abuses at Abu Ghraib, revelations about secret overseas prisons, and persistent reports of U.S. interrogators torturing detainees all contributed to a sharp drop in U.S. approval ratings and moral standing around the world, particularly among Muslims.[98]

Moreover, by the end of 2004, the shallowness of 1990s thinking on future warfare had been convincingly revealed. Far from dissuading U.S. adversaries, the great U.S. lead in conventional guided weapons/battle network warfare merely spurred them to find ways to avoid or offset U.S. conventional dominance. One adversary approach, as seen in Afghanistan and Iraq, was to "atomize" and disappear in complex terrain or among local populations, and to practice various forms of irregular warfare—like insurgency, terror, or subversion—thereby denying U.S. battle networks any massed targets. Another approach, as practiced by North Korea and Iran, was to pursue nuclear weapons in order to deter the assembly of U.S. battle networks, or even the very idea of a U.S. intervention or attack. A third approach, as practiced by China, was to seek regional parity with the United States in the guided weapons/battle network regime, albeit asymmetrically, in order to deter or delay any U.S. regional intervention. Each of these observed approaches was problematic for a joint force born and bred to fight and win on conventional battlefields, with a marked advantage in guided weapons warfare and with ready forward operational access. Indeed, the idea of fighting and winning even one war within 90 days against an opponent adopting any of these three approaches was ludicrous.

In addition, despite the hyper U.S. international activity since the end of the cold war, the unipolar moment appeared to be passing with the rise of new great powers (e.g., China and India) and the resurgence of old ones (e.g., Russia). When combined with the general diffusion of military technology and weapons to lesser state and nonstate actors, it was increasingly clear that the potential cost of any direct future U.S. intervention was increasing—at the very time the U.S. diplomatic and economic position appeared to be weakening.[99] Under these circumstances, unilateralist, go-it-alone policies no longer seemed so wise (if they ever were). A change in strategic approach seemed warranted. In this regard, the idea of building global security partnerships and going to war with staunch allies and strong alliances was looking far more attractive.

Within this context, the 2005 National Defense Strategy (NDS) and the follow-on 2006 Quadrennial Defense Review mark the end of the Global Era's initial unilateral phase.[100] The 2005 NDS announced, "The United States follows a strategy that aims to preserve and extend peace, freedom, and prosperity throughout the world." In pursuit of this strategy, the United States would have four top national security objectives: securing the homeland from direct attack, especially attacks using weapons of mass destruction (WMD); securing strategic access and retaining global freedom of action; strengthening alliances and partnerships; and establishing favorable security conditions. The strategy explicitly recognized America's great dominance in conventional warfighting and, as indicated by the need to secure strategic access and retain global freedom of action, implicitly accepted the condition of more uncertain forward access. It also outlined a broad new range of national security challenges for which the joint force must prepare. These included irregular challenges (conflicts in which enemy combatants are not regular military forces of nation-states); catastrophic terrorism employing weapons of mass destruction (WMD); and disruptive threats to the ability of the United States to maintain its qualitative edge and to project power.[101] Note that these three challenges track closely with the three aforementioned reactions to U.S. dominance in the guided-weapons warfare regime.

The 2006 QDR then went on to identify the top four things DoD would need to do to "operationalize" the NDS: defend the homeland in depth; fight a Long War against radical extremists and defeat global terrorist networks; prepare for a wide range of weapons of mass destruction (WMD) elimination operations, including against nuclear-armed regional powers; and shape the choices of countries at strategic crossroads, such as a rising India or China or a resurgent Russia. As the QDR stated, "Strengthening capabilities in these areas [would] . . . improve the versatility of the force to perform a wider range of military operations than today."[102]

Notably, both documents signaled a shift from a defense capability portfolio focused on conventional warfighting to a more balanced portfolio capable of addressing the broader identified range of irregular, catastrophic, and disruptive challenges. Moreover, the QDR explicitly rejected the two-major-theater-war force planning construct associated with the Global Era's unilateral phase in favor of a more flexible construct that distinguishes between steady-state and surge expeditionary operations, and between irregular and conventional wars.[103]

Perhaps more important, however, was the tone taken in both documents toward allies and partners overseas. For example, the NDS states, "International partnerships continue to be a principal source of our strength. Shared principles, a common view of threats, and commitment to cooperation *provide far greater security than we could achieve on our own*" (emphasis added).[104] The QDR was even more explicit, saying, "Recent operations demonstrate the critical importance of being organized to work with and through others, *and of shifting emphasis from performing tasks ourselves to enabling others*" (emphasis added). The QDR explained this in terms of a new "indirect" strategic approach.[105] Consistent with this theme, both the NDS and the QDR emphasized the importance of existing and new alliances and allies, and seeking new authorities to help build partner capacities both in the U.S. government and around the world. Gone was any indication that the United States intended to continue the go-it-alone, direct strategic approach followed in the earlier unilateral phase.

In other words, the 2005 NDS and 2006 QDR mark the beginning of a new cooperative phase in the Global Era. Together, they play the same role as President Kennedy's strategy of flexible response, which brought an end to a similarly turbulent and distorted transition phase between the Oceanic and Transoceanic eras.[106]

The Growing Importance of the National Fleet in the Global Era's Cooperative Phase

The Global Era's new cooperative phase promises to be a new golden age for the National Fleet. For one thing, the importance of maritime power projection, which since the end of the Transoceanic Era has been steadily growing but largely unacknowledged, has finally once again been explicitly and implicitly recognized in the new U.S. national strategy. As the 2005 NDS said:

Our ability to operate in and from the global commons—space, international waters and airspace, and cyberspace—is important. It enables us to project power anywhere in the world from secure bases of operation. Our capacity to operate in and from the strategic commons is critical to the direct defense of the United States and its partners and provides a stabilizing influence in key regions.

> Such capacity provides our forces operational freedom of action. Ceding our historic maritime advantage would unacceptably limit our global reach.[107]

Moreover, once across the oceans, seabased forces are remarkably well suited for each of the major new defense challenges outlined in the QDR. After all, the QDR proposed *"measures to increase both strategic and operational freedom of action by combining a more indirect approach, stealth, persistence, flexible basing and strategic reach."*[108] With these goals, how could seabasing not be more relevant? Reestablishing fleet stations, from which naval and joint forces can prosecute the Long War and disrupt terrorist networks from over the horizon and through maritime partners, is the epitome of an indirect approach. Being able to operate from seabases against a nuclear-armed regional adversary preserves both U.S. strategic and operational freedom of action, even when regional countries are coerced into denying U.S. operational access. Demonstrating naval strike and maneuver capabilities that are totally independent of land bases can go a long way toward shaping the choices of countries at strategic crossroads, as they always have.

Aside from the warfighting advantages of being able to operate on and from the sea, the oceans remain one of the most pivotal, mission-critical links in the globalized supply chain, connecting manufacturing and crop-producing countries to global markets. Approximately 90 percent of all interregional trade, measured in tonnage, moves across the oceans. By 2005, the World Shipping Council estimated that ocean transportation moved about two-thirds the value of America's international commerce. Another report estimated that ocean carriers were carrying some $500 billion of annual trade.[109] Although the threat to the sea lanes is likely lower than at any time since 1890, when Mahan wrote his masterwork, ensuring that the sea lanes remain free and open will be an enduring U.S. and international security concern in the Global Era.

This is especially true since the entire ocean trading and transport system is on the verge of its greatest transformation since the advent of the Suez and Panama canals. Due to global warming, the Arctic Ocean's fabled Northwest Passage, which connects the Pacific and Atlantic oceans, opened up on 21 August 2007. A ship traveling from China to Europe through the Northwest Passage covers 5,000 fewer miles than if passing through either the Suez or Panama canals. Or, as calculated by London's *Financial Times*, "A ship traveling at 21 knots between Rotterdam and Yokohama takes 29 days if it goes via the Cape of Good Hope, 22 days via the Suez Canal and just 15 days if it goes across the Arctic Ocean."[110] The effects of the Northwest Passage on global trade might thus be immense. As one analyst wrote, "Much shorter shipping distances and quicker shipping times will lower the cost of doing business. It could lead to big increases in trade and, certainly, a major shift in sea lanes."[111] In the past, the only U.S. naval vessels that routinely ventured into the Arctic Ocean were nuclear submarines, which could navigate below the ice cap. In the Global Era's cooperative phase, cutters and warships from many navies will routinely ply the globe's northernmost waters, protecting this new oceanic trading route.

Precisely because the sea lanes are such a free and secure highway, knowing what is traveling or going on the world's oceans will be an increasingly important security imperative in the Global Era, from both a U.S. and international

149

perspective. As has been amply demonstrated in places like the Caribbean Basin, where drug smugglers carry their cargos on, over, and even under the seas, the oceans provide a ready thoroughfare for drug, contraband, illicit weapon, and human slave traffickers, and potentially for the transport of WMD. As Admiral William J. Fallon, then–Commander, U.S. Pacific Command, noted at the Fourth Annual Shangri La Dialogue in 2005:

> On today's globalized planet, the vast oceans and crowded littoral waters present a dichotomy of essential personal and economic sustenance on the one hand, and on the other, the very real security challenge of immense areas of ungoverned or weakly controlled space. For both dimensions of the challenge, maritime security is essential.[112]

This circumstance will likely demand a higher level of "maritime domain awareness" than in the past—from the brown and green waters of the world's littoral, to strategic maritime chokepoints like the Strait of Gibraltar, the Gulf of Aden, and the Strait of Malacca; to the relatively small number of super ports that serve as the global hubs for containerized trade, to the open ocean, to maritime approaches to the United States, and to U.S. ports and inland waterways. This is a daunting task—and not one remotely doable by any one navy.

The task will be made even more daunting because knowing what is going on under the sea and on the sea bottom is becoming as important as knowing what is happening on and over the seas. In 2002, undersea fiber-optic cables connected the global economy, transmitting 96 percent of all U.S. transoceanic long-range communications and "as high as 80 percent" of *all* international telecommunications.[113] By 2006, undersea cables carried greater than 90 percent of global telecommunications traffic.[114] Widespread disruption of the undersea cable network would literally stop globalization in its tracks. At the same time, the oceans—long the primary highways for the transport of the world's oil and gas supplies from one global market to another—cover an increasing percentage of the world's extractable energy supplies. In 1984, offshore oil and gas production provided 26 percent of world energy demand. By 2003, 30 percent of the world's oil and 50 percent of its natural gas came from offshore production.[115] The undersea fiber-optic communications grid and offshore energy platforms and wells thus comprise a new type of global strategic infrastructure that must be monitored and protected. The last time there was anything similar was a century ago, when the British Empire worried incessantly about attacks on or disruptions to the global undersea telegraph network.[116]

Because of the increasing importance of the security of the oceans to the continued growth of the globalized economy, the National Fleet will provide an important means to forge cooperative action in the current phase of the Global Era. As naval strategist Geoffrey Till wrote:

> One characteristic of the [emerging global sea-based trading system] is that it has hugely increased the level of economic interdependence and drastically decreased the importance of geographic distance—so that what happens "over there" matters far more to us "here" than it once did. *Hence, navies are being required to act together in common cause to project military power ashore, particularly in expeditionary operations at a distance from the home base.* Freed in

many cases from the . . . need to fight to make use of the open ocean, navies can now concentrate on exploiting that control. . . . But this requires them, to some extent at least, to shift priorities from the sea to the land, from power at sea to power from the sea (emphasis added).[117]

Following this line of thinking, it should come as no surprise whatsoever that fifteen of the next seventeen largest world navies, which together operate the preponderance of non-U.S. naval tonnage, are built and operated by democracies with as big a stake in globalization and the global seabased trading system as the United States. It should also come as no surprise that most of these navies are shifting from their cold war focus on antisubmarine warfare and local littoral operations to mounting and sustaining global expeditionary operations. In the process, they are discarding smaller surface combatants and submarines for larger, more capable oceangoing combatants and amphibious landing ships.[118] The Global Era will therefore likely see an increased level of cooperative patrolling and monitoring of the world's oceans by the world's democratic navies, the continued strengthening of existing democratic naval alliances, and the formation of new naval alliances and coalitions.

A strong National Fleet will also be an important national asset for dealing with the remaining large, nondemocratic naval powers—China and Russia. For China, a growing global actor increasingly dependent on open sea lines of communication for both its energy and trade, and Russia, which depends on open sea lines to get its ample energy supplies to global markets, a strong National Fleet serves at once as a strong lure for cooperative global action and as a deterrent against global mischief. And, as seen in the latter stages of the cold war, when the U.S. Navy planned aggressive forward naval operations along the flanks of the Soviet empire, strong and capable naval forces can have a powerful shaping effect on the choices of both Russia and China as they approach their own strategic crossroads.

Finally, establishing favorable security conditions is one of the four primary objectives of the 2005 National Defense Strategy. Keeping the sea lanes free and open, achieving a good degree of maritime domain awareness, working with global maritime partners to establish a high level of maritime security, and using maritime power to shape the choices of rising and emerging powers all support this objective. Another key National Fleet contribution is what Admiral Jim Stavridis, Commander, U.S. Southern Command, describes as Missions of Peace—using the National Fleet both proactively and reactively to relieve human suffering in the world's littorals, respond to humanitarian crises, and help build local capacities for good governance. Naval forces are particularly well adapted to these types of missions, due both to their mobility and flexibility and their light footprint ashore. Both attributes help prevent any perception of an American occupation or long-term stay, which in the postcolonial age often works against the overall objective of establishing favorable global security conditions.

In sum, then, the Global Era of national security policy calls for a powerful, well-balanced, *Pan-Oceanic* National Fleet, combining the complementary capabilities of the Navy, Coast Guard, Marines, and MSC/RRF, and capable of operating on, over, under, on the bottom of, and from the seas. With its already-large group of global maritime partners, the Pan-Oceanic National Fleet will work in peacetime to expand the community of peaceful maritime powers; develop a detailed understanding of what is happening on *every* ocean in the world; remove or dampen any major threat to maritime security; work to raise U.S. standing in the world and relieve human suffering in the world's littorals; deter regional fighting; and dissuade other global powers from becoming hostile global naval competitors. It will be one of the primary tools for a new indirect strategic approach in the ongoing struggle against radical extremists, serving as a base for low-footprint offshore operations and as a tool to increase partnership irregular warfare capacities on both the landward and seaward sides of the world's littorals. During wartime, the Pan-Oceanic National Fleet, along with the U.S. Air Force, will underwrite U.S. global freedom of action and mobility. It will create the conditions necessary to convert the world's oceans and littoral seas into a joint base for global expeditionary operations, help create access when needed through a powerful blend of naval strike and naval maneuver, support joint campaigns ashore, as it always has, and sustain the joint force.

The Tri-Modal Pan-Oceanic National Fleet

Despite its increasing strategic value, any thoughts or aspirations of trying to make the Pan-Oceanic National Fleet the Global Era's dominant service should be quickly stamped out. The great power of the joint force comes from its multidimensional character; it is indeed greater than the sum of its individual parts. As a result, resources will most likely (and rightly) continue to be distributed relatively equitably among all three of DoD's subordinate departments. Similarly, in the Department of Homeland Security, the Coast Guard will continue to compete for resources among a passel of disparate agencies. Moreover, any increases in *national security* resources may very well be devoted to non-DoD capabilities and capacities, such as the State Department and the U.S. Agency for International Development, both of which were cut precipitously in the Global Era's initial unilateral phase. Indeed, most prudent planners now presume that U.S. *defense* spending will, at best, simply level off over the next decade. As a result, the National Fleet leaders must make sensible and pragmatic investment choices designed to provide the maximum return on investment.

These leaders start from an enviable position. The Pan-Oceanic National Fleet numbers nearly 700 vessels of all types, including 280 warships in the U.S. Navy battle fleet; over 220 Coast Guard cutters, patrol boats, and tenders; and 172 active or reserve MSC ships—and these numbers do not include numerous smaller craft such as Navy patrol coastal ships and riverine craft, and smaller Coast Guard harbor and river craft.[119] The Marines are building to a force of 202,000, organized into three division-wing teams—an organization larger than the *entire* British active armed forces. As these numbers suggest, then, the National Fleet is in no danger of losing its position as the number-one world naval power, a position it has held continuously since 1945. In addition, the Navy, Marines, and Coast Guard together operate over 4,000 aircraft of all types. Indeed, the fleet's combined capabilities remain without equal in the world, and its margin of superiority over any potential naval competitor or group of competitors continues to be comfortably wide. However, given the broad range of potential challenges and duties it must cope with in the Global Era, the fleet is likely not well balanced for the future. The most pressing choices facing the leaders of the fleet therefore involve decisions over the proper mix of fleet capabilities and capacities, rather than any need to dramatically increase its size.

When thinking about the proper balance of capabilities and capacities, it is helpful to think of the Pan-Oceanic National Fleet as comprising three component fleets. These three component fleets, which define the fleet's overall operational and investment portfolio, include the Power Projection/Heavy Seabase Fleet; the Maritime Security/Light Seabase Fleet; and the Strategic Deterrence/ Dissuasion Fleet.[120]

- *The Power Projection/Heavy Seabase Fleet* will continue to define the heart of the National Fleet, as it has since 1890. In the Global Era, with its joint expeditionary posture, a battle fleet capable of projecting U.S. power across transoceanic distances will be like money in the bank. U.S. strategists may not be quite certain how they will spend it, but they are more confident knowing the money is there to be spent when needed.[121] This component is made up primarily of naval strike and maneuver capabilities, naval logistics forces, and joint sealift and seabasing capabilities. It therefore comprises mainly Navy, Marine, and MSC forces, although Coast Guard forces provide important deployable armed maritime interdiction and supporting security capabilities.

- *The Maritime Security/Light Seabase Fleet* is focused on the National Fleet's day-to-day shaping and maritime security activities. It does not require the high-end combat capabilities of the Power Projection/Heavy Seabase Fleet. Indeed, the capabilities in the Heavy Seabase Fleet are generally not cost-effective in the maritime security role and are ill suited for building maritime partnership capacity in the majority of world navies, which more resemble coast guards. In addition to shaping and maritime security missions, this component fleet is the primary National Fleet arm for Missions of Peace and for fighting the persistent global campaign against radical extremists. As a result, this fleet consists primarily of Coast Guard and Marine forces, augmented by Navy and MSC seabase, amphibious, and logistics ships and forces optimized for brown- and green-water operations along the world's littorals.

- *The Strategic Deterrence/Dissuasion Fleet* consists primarily of Navy forces designed to deter direct state-sponsored attacks on the U.S. homeland, sweep any opposing naval force from the surface or under the sea, and dissuade would-be adversaries from challenging U.S. naval supremacy. For deterrence, the fleet includes strategic ballistic missile submarines and ships assigned the national missile defense mission. For the sea control mission, the fleet relies mainly on its nuclear attack submarines, which remain the greatest naval predators in the world. The dissuasion mission adds a robust naval research and development (R&D) line and a vibrant fleet exercise and operational experimentation line. The focus of fleet R&D and fleet exercise and experimentations should be to demonstrate a capability to prevail against any naval opponent seeking guided weapons/battle network parity with the National Fleet. Although not an integral component of the National Fleet, the U.S. shipbuilding design and industrial base is a key national partner with the Strategic Deterrence/Dissuasion Fleet, since, barring a major national mobilization, it helps to define the overall limit of the size and capabilities of the future National Fleet.

Of course, this type of binning of capabilities is not absolute. Attack submarines can be used in support of the global campaign against radical extremists and to support a major maritime power projection operation. Similarly, the combat and mobile logistics force ships in the Heavy Seabase Fleet can be used to support both other National Fleet components. But by thinking of the National Fleet's operational and investment portfolio in terms of these three disparate types of needed capabilities, near-term decisions on the shape and character of the future fleet can be better framed, understood, and debated. For example, capabilities that are fungible across all three fleets are the most valuable and should attract the largest investments. Investments that work to further integrate the Pan-Oceanic National Fleet are also especially valuable, such as a single cutter/frigate that can be used by both the Navy and the Coast Guard, or increased numbers of amphibious ships that by their very nature strengthen the day-to-day collaborative operations of sailors, MSC personnel, and Marines. Any individual decision that weakens the shipbuilding design and industrial base will weaken the potential dissuasive effect of the National Fleet, since a withered design and industrial base might convince potential opponents that they will be able to take on and surpass the fleet as the number-one global naval power at some point in the future.

This operational/investment portfolio also aids in the development of time-based competition strategies. The primary choices for the Maritime Security/ Light Seabase Fleet are more immediate and near-term but likely require the fewest resources. The primary choices for the Power Projection/Heavy Sealift Fleet, which is already immensely powerful, is focused more on the midterm, when it may be asked to confront a regional adversary armed with nuclear weapons. This might, for example, require improved theater ballistic missile capabilities. A key part of the Strategic Deterrence/Dissuasion Fleet is focused on shaping the choices of countries approaching strategic crossroads, and preparing for the future. It therefore requires less immediate systems procurement than it does robust research, experimentation, and prototyping.

This operational/investment portfolio approach also suggests new ways of doing business. For example, as suggested by Frank Hoffman, a strategist and analyst working for the Center of Emerging Threats and Opportunities, the Navy Expeditionary Combat Command (NECC) might become more than a Navy type command: it might be renamed the National Fleet Engagement and Cooperation Command (NECC) and reformed as a joint Navy, Marine Corps, Coast Guard and interagency command focused on both day-to-day maritime security and partnership-building activities, and waging an indirect campaign against radical extremists. The NECC would operate from new fleet or partnership stations in regions around the world.[122]

Relevant and Ready

Regardless of how the component parts of the Pan-Oceanic National Fleet are conceptualized, however, one thing is certain: the rationale for the fleet is likely stronger than at any time since the end of World War II. As a consequence, the strategic concepts of the Navy, Coast Guard, Marines, and Military Sealift Command are once again converging, rather than diverging. The nation will benefit as a result. In the cooperative phase of the Global Era of national security policy, the Pan-Oceanic Fleet will be a national investment with a high rate of strategic return.

Notes

1. Samuel P. Huntington, "National Policy and the Transoceanic Navy," *U.S. Naval Institute Proceedings,* May 1954, pp. 483–493.

2. Today, the term "National Fleet" is associated only with the combined capabilities of the U.S. Navy (including the Military Sealift Command) and the Coast Guard. Hopefully, this paper will make plain why the definition of the National Fleet should be expanded to include the Marine Corps and explicitly recognize the MSC and MARAD's RRF as a separate National Fleet partner.

3. Derived from Huntington, "National Policy and the Transoceanic Navy," and Kenneth J. Hagan, *This People's Navy* (New York: Free Press, 1991). Hagan's book is one of two primary historical sources for this paper.

4. "United States Revenue Cutter Service," available at http://en.wikipedia.org/wiki/Revenue_Cutter_Service (accessed 26 October 2007).

5. The Constitution adopted in 1787 required the Congress to "provide and maintain a Navy." However, it was not until 1798 that the United States got around to forming a Department of the Navy. See Peter M. Swartz, *Sea Changes: Transforming U.S. Navy Deployment Strategy, 1775–2002* (Alexandria, VA: Center for Naval Analysis, 31 July 2002), p. 15. This is a wonderful piece of work, which explains in detail the changing deployment patterns of the U.S. Battle Force since 1775. It is packed with useful information, and is the second historical source used for this paper.

6. "United States Revenue Cutter Service."

7. For a thorough rationale behind this definition, as well as a detailed treatment of U.S. global defense postures, past and present, see Andrew F. Krepinevich and Robert O. Work, *A New Global Defense Posture for the Second Transoceanic Era* (Washington, DC: Center for Strategic and Budgetary Assessment, 2007). Since that work was published, the authors now refer to the current national security policy phase as the Global Era.

8. The most important of these stations were the East India Station (Western Pacific); Pacific Station (West Coast of South America); West India Station (Caribbean); Brazil Station (East Coast of South America/South Atlantic); Africa Station (West Coast of Africa); North Atlantic Squadron/Station (Western and Northern Europe); and the Mediterranean Station. Swartz, *Sea Changes: Transforming U.S. Navy Deployment Strategy, 1775–2002,* pp. 18–21 and pp. 65–67. For a wonderful description of these fleet stations, see Robert Albion, "Distant Stations," *Proceedings,* March 1954.

9. The term "cooperative security location" is a contemporary one, developed during the most recent Global Posture Review. Together with "main operating bases" and "forward operating sites," these terms describe the three main types of facilities the United States maintains overseas. Continental cooperative security locations included Port Mahon, in Spain's Balearic Islands; Valparaiso, Chile; Rio de Janeiro, Brazil; Callao, Peru; Luanda, Angola; Hong Kong and Macau, China; Magdalena Bay, Mexico (Baja California Sur); Colon and Panama City, Panama; Tenerife, Canary Islands; Cap Haitien, Haiti; St. Thomas in the Danish Virgin Islands; and Porto Prava in the Cape Verde Islands.

10. See "Merchant Marine in the Mexican-American War," available at http://www.usmm .org/mexicanwar.html (accessed 27 October 2007).

11. From Huntington, "National Policy and the Transoceanic Navy," and Swartz, *Sea Changes: Transforming U.S. Navy Deployment Strategy, 1775–2002.*

12. As Senator Henry Cabot Lodge declared in 1895, "We are a great people; we control this continent; we are dominant in this hemisphere: we have too great an inheritance to be trifled with. . . . It is ours to guard and defend."

13. Huntington, "National Policy and the Transoceanic Navy," and Norman Freidman, "The Real Purpose of Strategy," *Proceedings,* December 2007, p. 90.

14. The call for a Navy that was the "greatest in the world" came from none other than Woodrow Wilson, during his run for president. At the time, he was chided by many for being so bold as to challenge the primacy of the British Royal Navy. See Hagan, *This People's Navy,* p. 252.

15. Stephen Howarth, *To Shining Sea: A History of the United States Navy, 1775–1991* (New York, NY: Random House, 1991), pp. 295–296.

16. The Washington Naval Treaty stipulated a 5-5-3 ratio of aggregate naval tonnage for the British Royal Navy, the U.S. Navy, and the Imperial Japanese Navy, respectively. At least by treaty, then, the United States had achieved parity with the Royal Navy.

17. Krepinevich and Work, *A New Global Defense Posture for the Second Transoceanic Era,* pp. 48–50.

18. Ibid., pp. 52–54.

19. See Bernard D. Cole, "The Interwar Forward Intervention Forces: The Asiatic Fleet, the Banana Fleet, and the European Squadrons: The Battle Fleet Trains while the Gunboats Fight," a paper prepared for the U.S. Navy Forward Presence Bicentennial Symposium, 21 June 2001.

20. See "S.2337," available at http://www.uscg.mil/hq/g-cp/history/regulations/USCGBill .html (accessed 2 November 2007).

21. See "Ingham," U.S. Coast Guard, http://www.uscg.mil/history/webcutters/ Ingham_WPG_35.html (accessed 5 January 2008).

22. Paul Halpern, "The US Navy in the Great War," available at http://www.worldwar1.com/ tgws/usnwwone.htm; and Charles Dana Gibson, "The Ships and Men of the Army Transportation Service," available at http://www.usmm.org/atshistory.html. Both sites were accessed on 2 November 2007.

23. CAPT Wayne P. Hughes, USN (Ret), "LCS Isn't Right Yet. That's a Good Reason to Build It," a presentation to the 71st Military Operational Research Society, 10 June 2003.

24. CAPT Wayne P. Hughes, USN (Ret), "Naval Maneuver Warfare," *Naval War College Review,* Summer 1997, available at http://www.nwc.navy.mil/press/Review/1997/summer/ art2su97.htm.

25. "US Navy Active Ship Force Levels, 1945–1950," available at http://www.history.navy .mil/branches/org9-4.htm#1945.

26. Email from CAPT Bruce B. Stubbs, USCG (Ret), to Robert O. Work dated 29 October 2007.

27. "The US Merchant Marine in World War II," available at http://www.usmm.org/ ww2.html.

28. See "Ships for Victory," available at http://www.seawaves.com/bookreviews/ shipsforvictory.htm.

30. In his 1954 article, Huntington actually referred to this phase as the "Eurasian phase" of national policy, and the Navy as the Transoceanic Navy.

29. See Daniel Yergin, *Shattered Peace: The Origins of the Cold War* (Boston, MA: Houghton Mifflin Co., 1977), pp. 280–285.

31. For example, for a good description of the Navy's adjustment to atomic warfare, see Dr. Jeffrey G. Barlow, "The Navy and the Bomb: Naval Aviations' Influence on Strategic

Thinking, 1945–1950," available at http://www.history.navy.mil/colloquia/cch1e.htm (accessed 5 November 2007).

32. Derived from Huntington, "National Policy and the Oceanic Navy."

33. "US Navy Active Ship Force Levels, 1945–1950." Concerning the revolt of the admirals, see Hagan, *This People's Navy*, pp. 339–341, and Jeffrey G. Barlow, *Revolt of the Admirals: The Fight for Naval Aviation* (Washington, DC: Naval Historical Center, 1994).

34. His suggestion stated that the Coast Guard's "war time functions and duties assigned should be those which are an extension of normal peacetime tasks."Additionally, Coast Guard personnel, ships, aircraft and facilities should be utilized as organized Coast Guard units rather than by indiscriminately integrating them into the naval establishment." See Scott T. Price, "The Forgotten Service in the Forgotten War," available at http://www.uscg.mil/ History/Korean_War.html (accessed 4 November 2007).

35. See "FAQs from the Historian's Office," available at http://www.uscg.mil/history/faqs/ wars.html (accessed 4 November 2007).

36. "US Navy Active Ship Force Levels, 1951–1957," available at http://www.history.navy .mil/branches/org9-4.htm#1945.

37 For a complete account of the development of the 20-knot amphibious fleet, see chapter 11 in Norman Friedman, *U.S. Amphibious Ships and Craft* (Annapolis, MD: Naval Institute Press, 2002), pp. 311–346.

38. Indeed, after its rebound to 1,122 ships in 1953, the fleet steadily declined in size, reaching a post–World War II low of 521 ships in 1981 before rebounding during the mid- to late 1980s. Of course, each of these individual ships was far more powerful than the ships they replaced. See "US Navy Active Ship Force Levels," sections covering 1951–1989.

39. For a description of the Garrison Posture, see Krepinevich and Work, *A New Global Defense Posture for the Second Transoceanic Era*, pp. 100–105.

40. The significance of maintaining "combat credible" forces forward is well captured in Swartz, *Sea Changes: Transforming U.S. Navy Deployment Strategy, 1775–2002*, pp. 48–49.

41. In President Eisenhower's "New Look" Defense Strategy, the aircraft carrier and forward-deployed Amphibious Ready Groups played the same role for the United States in the Garrison Era as the frigate played for the British Empire during the age of sail. See Hagan, *This People's Navy*, p. 350.

42. "National Reserve Defense Fleet," available at http://www.marad.dot.gov/Programs/ NDRF.html (accessed 2 November 2007).

43 Friedman, *U.S. Amphibious Ships and Craft*, pp. 316–320.

44 Dr. Salvatore R. Mercogliano, "Sealift: The Evolution of American Military Sea Transportation" (30 September 2007), pp. 5–6, derived from Salvatore R. Mercogliano, "Sealift: The Evolution of American Military Sea Transportation" (PhD diss., University of Alabama, 2004).

45. See "Flexible Response," available at http://www.nuclearfiles.org/menu/key-issues/ nuclearweapons/history/cold-war/strategy/strategy-flexible-response.htm (accessed 6 November 2007). See also the discussion in Hagan, *This People's Navy*, p. 356.

46. Richard K. Betts, "A Disciplined Defense," *Foreign Affairs,* November/December 2007, pp. 69–70.

47. For a concise description of the 1964 landing in Spain, see Maj J. W. Hammond, Jr., "Steel Pike I," *Marine Corps Gazette,* January 1965, p. 51.

48. For a description of amphibious operations during Vietnam, see LtCol H. T. Hayden, USMC (Ret), "Amphibious Operations During the Second Indochina War: 1965–73," *Marine Corps Gazette,* August 2005, pp. 46–48.

49. For a more thorough discussion about the gradual weakening of Navy and Marine ties during the cold war, see Robert O. Work, *To Take and Keep the Lead: A Naval Fleet*

Platform Architecture for Enduring Maritime Supremacy (Washington, DC: Center for Strategic and Budgetary Assessments, December 2005), pp. 29–35.

50. Eugene N. Tulich, USCG, "The US Coast Guard in Southeast Asia during the Vietnam War," available at http://www.uscg.mil/history/h_tulichvietnam.html (accessed 3 November 2007).

51. Norman Polmar, *Ships and Aircraft of the US Fleet*, 16th edition (Annapolis, MD: Naval Institute Press, 1997), pp. 499–500.

52. Krepinevich and Work, *A New Global Defense Posture for the Second Transoceanic Era*, pp. 121–122.

53. Ibid., pp. 122–124.

54. Lorna S. Jaffe, *The Development of the Base Force 1989–1992* (Washington, DC: Joint History Office, Office of the Chairman of the Joint Chiefs of Staff, July 1993), p. 2.

55. The uncertainty that existed is well captured in John Lewis Gaddis, "Toward the Post–Cold War World," *Foreign Affairs*, Spring 1991, pp. 102–122.

56. For a good description of "the great concentration of capability in the United States relative to other consequential powers, see Barry R. Posen, "After Bush: The Case for Restraint," *The American Interest*, November/December 2007, pp. 8–9. Although I take issue with some of Posen's prescriptions, I think his diagnosis of the immediate post–cold war world is accurate.

57. Krepinevich and Work, *A New Global Defense Posture for the Second Transoceanic Era*, pp. 140–142. For a thorough discussion of the guided weapons/battle network revolution, see Barry Watts, *Six Decades of Guided Munitions and Battle Networks: Progress and Prospects* (Washington, DC: Center for Strategic and Budgetary Assessments, March 2007).

58. Posen, "After Bush: The Case for Restraint," pp. 10–11.

59. The term "end of history" comes from Francis Fukuyama, "The End of History," *National Interest*, Summer 1989. In Fukuyama's own words, he argued "that liberal democracy may constitute the 'end point of mankind's ideological evolution' and the 'final form of human government,' and as such constituted the 'end of history.' That is, while earlier forms of government were characterized by grave defects and irrationalities that led to their eventual collapse, liberal democracy was arguably free from such fundamental internal contradictions." His thesis is still roundly debated.

60. Attributed to Owen Harries in Adam Garfinkle, "Strategy on the Cheap," *The American Interest*, November/December 2007, p. 137.

61. Garfinkle, "Strategy on the Cheap," p. 138.

62. Many analysts and strategists have written on America's post–cold war drive for primacy. For just two examples, see Robert Kagan, "End of Dreams, Return of History," *Policy Review*, August/September 2007; and Tom Donnely's comments in "What's America's Grand Plan?" Armed Forces Journal, August 2007, pp. 17–18. The comment on globalizing the Monroe Doctrine is found in Garfinkle, "Strategy on the Cheap," p. 138.

63. William J. Clinton, Second Inaugural Address, 20 January 1997.

64. See Donnelly in "What's America's Grand Plan?" p. 17.

65. As described by Robert Kagan, the "Bush Doctrine" refers to three sets of principles: preemptive or preventive military action; the promotion of democracy, through regime change if necessary; and diplomacy tending toward "unilateralism." He argues that these principles are not that much different than those followed by previous administrations, Democratic and Republican. See Kagan, "End of Dreams, Return of History." For a critique that the Bush Doctrine differs materially from past administrations, see David C. Hendrickson and Robert W. Tucker, "The Freedom Crusade," *The National Interest*, Fall 2005, pp. 12–21.

66. As one analyst put it, "Ad hoc allies were to serve primarily as window dressing and hopefully pick up the bills." Graham E. Fuller, "Strategic Fatigue," *The National Interest*, Summer 2006, p. 38.

67. See Krepinevich and Work, *A New Global Defense Posture for the Second Transoceanic Era*, pp. 139–142.

68. See Greg Jaffe, "Battle Lines: Rumsfeld's Push For Speed Fuels Pentagon Dissent," *Wall Street Journal*, 16 May 2005.

69. The first of these two documents is conceptually the most important. *Forward . . . From the Sea*, published two years later, was merely an update of the basic document. See Sean O'Keefe, ADM Frank B. Kelso II, USN, Gen C. E. Mundy, . . . *From the Sea* (Washington, DC: Department of the Navy, September 1992), available at http://www.globalsecurity.org/military/library/policy/navy/fts.htm#INTRO.

70. As CNA's Peter Swartz reminded me, the Navy's intense focus on air and missile strikes during the 1990s was also spurred by the inability of its carrier force to share planning information with the Air Force during Desert Storm, the cancellation of the A-12 carrier-based stealth bomber, and the rapid increase in the number of vertical launch (missile) systems (VLS) cells in the surface combatant fleet.

71. In the 1997 QDR, the Navy's projected future surface combatant force was pegged at 116 combatants, including 27 Ticonderoga-class guided missile cruisers (over 9,000 tons full load displacment), 57 Arleigh Burke-class guided missile destroyers (over 8,000 tons FLD), and 32 DD-21 land attack destroyers (over 15,000 tons FLD). The force included no guided missile frigates of any kind.

72. Norman Polmar, *Ships and Aircraft of the U.S. Fleet*, 18th edition (Annapolis, MD: Naval Institute Press, 2005), pp. 571 and 577.

73. See "Logistics Fixes That Took Root"; and Eric Schmitt, "US Insists It Is Better Prepared to Ship Arms and Equipment to Gulf This Time," *New York Times*, 20 January 2003.

74. See Robert O. Work, *Seabasing: All Ahead, Slow* (Washington, DC: Center for Strategic and Budgetary Assessment, 2006), p. 96.

75. Col Stephen Schwalbe, "Overseas Military Base Closures," *Air & Space Power Chronicles Online*, 4 January 2005, available at http://zfacts.com/metaPage/lib/Overseas-Military-Base-Closures.pdf.

76. John Shimcus, "Changes in the Forward Deployment of the United States' Military and the Effects on the Transatlantic Alliance," available at http://www.nato-pa.int/default.asp?SHORTCUT=922.

77. Donald H. Rumsfeld, Secretary of Defense, Quadrennial Defense Review Report (Washington, DC: Office of the Secretary of Defense, 30 September 2001), pp. 25–28, available at http://www.defenselink.mil/pubs/pdfs/qdr2001.pdf (accessed 11 November 2007).

78. Krepinevich and Work, *A New Global Defense Posture for the Second Transoceanic Era*, pp. 185–195.

79. U.S. Commission on National Security/21st Century, *Seeking a National Strategy: A Concert for Preserving Security and Promoting Freedom: The Phase II Report on a U.S. National Security Strategy for the 21st Century* (Washington, DC, 15 April 2001), p. 15.

80. U.S. naval deployment patterns since World War II are covered in depth in Swartz, *Sea Changes: Transforming U.S. Navy Deployment Strategy, 1775–2002*.

81. As cited in Jon D. Klaus, *Strategic Mobility Innovation: Options and Oversight Issues* (Washington, DC: Congressional Research Service (order code RL32887), dated 29 April 2005), p. CRS-8. For those interested in reading the entire report, see The Defense Science Board, *Report of the Defense Science Task Force on Strategic Mobility* (Washington, DC: Undersecretary of Defense for Acquisition and Technology, August 1996).

82. National Defense Panel, *Transforming Defense: National Security in the 21st Century* (Washington DC: National Defense Panel, 1997). The Panel's final report can be found on the Defense Strategy Review Page, available at http://www.comw.org/qdr/97qdr.html.

83. Krepinevich and Work, *A New Global Defense Posture for the Second Transoceanic Era*, p. 165 and pp. 178–181.

84. Benjamin W. Labaree, et al., *America and the Sea: A Maritime History* (Mystic, CT: The Museum of America and the Sea, 1998), p. 9.

85. U.S. Commission on National Security/21st Century, *Seeking a National Strategy: A Concert for Preserving Security and Promoting Freedom: The Phase II Report on a U.S. National Security Strategy for the 21st Century,* p. 14.

86. See the section entitled "Overseas Presence" in Les Aspin, Secretary of Defense, *Report of the Bottom-Up Review* (Washington, DC: Office of the Secretary of Defense, October 1993), available at http://www.fas.org/man/docs/bur/part03.htm (accessed 2 November 2007).

87. Huntington, "National Policy and the Transoceanic Navy," p. 491.

88. Klaus, *Strategic Mobility Innovation: Options and Oversight Issues,* p. CRS-8.

89. For a critique of the idea of aerial maneuver, also now known as air mechanization, see LTC John Gordon IV, Ph.D., USA (Ret); COL David E. Johnson, Ph.D., USA (Ret); and Peter A. Wilson, "Air Mechanization: An Expensive and Fragile Concept," *Military Review*, January–February 2007, pp. 63–73.

90. As two of the leading thinkers of the Army After Next Project wrote: "Of all air and sea, current and future, lift capabilities, shallow draft high-speed ships (SDHSS)—because of their speed, throughput capability, and capacity—most significantly impacted force closure. Air deployment remains the only way to rapidly establish the initial crisis-response presence of air expeditionary forces and a division equivalent of ground forces needed to preclude enemy forces' early success. But after a few days, SDHSS had a distinct advantage. It was the only strategic platform that could deliver troops and equipment together in sufficient size to bring immediate combat power to bear. While in transit, commanders could conduct en route planning and receive intelligence updates. Moreover, the SDHSS did not require a fixed port because it could discharge its combat power wherever there was at least a 10-foot draft and an acceptable beach gradient or discharge site. Troops drove the future combat system (FCS) from the ship ready to fight onward to the tactical assembly area." See BG Huba Wass de Czege and LTC Zbigniew M. Majchrzak, USA (Ret), "Operational Maneuver from Strategic Distances," *Combined Arms Center Military Review,* May–June 2002.

91. "US Navy Active Ship Force Levels."

92. "National Fleet, a Joint Navy/Coast Guard Policy Statement, 21 September 1998," found in CAPT Bruce Stubbs, USCG, and Scott C. Truver, PhD, *America's Coast Guard: Safeguarding Maritime Safety and Security in 21st Century*, Appendix C, available at http://www.uscg.mil/news/AmericasCG/CG2000complete.pdf (accessed 15 November 2007).

93. Ibid., p. 5.

94. Stubbs and Truver, PhD, *America's Coast Guard: Safeguarding Maritime Safety and Security in 21st Century*, Annex C.

95. Colin S. Gray, "The Coast Guard and the Navy: It's Time for a 'National Fleet'," *Naval War College Review*, Summer 2001, available at http://findarticles.com/p/articles/mi_m0JIW/is_3_54/ai_80786337/pg_19 (accessed 28 November 2007).

96. Polmar, *Ships and Aircraft of the US Fleet*, 18th edition, pp. 585–586.

97. "Operation Iraqi Freedom," available at http://www.uscg.mil/hq/g-cp/comrel/factfile/Factcards/IraqiFreedom.htm (accessed 22 November 2007).

98. See for example "The US Seen through Muslim Eyes," *US News and World Report*, available at http://www.usnews.com/usnews/news/articles/070523/23muslims.htm (accessed 19 November 2007).

99. See for example Posen, "The Case for Restraint"; Christopher Layne, "Impotent Power? Reexamining the Nature of America's Hegemonic Power," *The National Interest,* September/October 2006, pp. 41–47; and Graham E. Fuller, "Strategic Fatigue," *The National Interest,* Summer 2006, pp. 37–42; Peter G. Peterson. "No Free Lunch," *The National Interest,* July/August 2007, pp. 19–22.

100. Interestingly, like the strategy of flexible response, these documents appeared approximately a decade and a half after the shift in national security policy eras, suggesting that it takes at least that long to take a measure of a new national security era.

101. Donald H. Rumsfeld, Secretary of Defense, *The National Defense Strategy of the United States* (Washington, DC: Office of the Secretary of Defense, March 2007), p. 1. The strategy can be found online at a number of different sites. One is http://www.globalsecurity.org/military/library/policy/dod/nds-usa_mar2005.htm, accessed for this paper on 30 November 2007. The embedded quote in this paragraph is found on page 1 of the strategy.

102. Donald H. Rumsfeld, Secretary of Defense, *Quadrennial Defense Review Report* (Washington, DC: Office of the Secretary of Defense, 6 February 2006), available at http://www.globalsecurity.org/military/library/policy/dod/qdr-2006-report.htm (accessed 30 November 2007), p. 19.

103. Ibid., pp. 35–40.

104. Rumsfeld, *The National Defense Strategy of the United States*, March 2005, p. 4.

105. Rumsfeld, *Quadrennial Defense Review Report*, 6 February 2006, p. 17.

106. In 2005, Richard N. Haass, the President of the Council on Foreign Relations, described the appropriate grand strategy for the cooperative phase of the Global Era (although he does not use these terms) as "integration." See Richard N. Haass, "The Case for 'Integration'," *The National Interest*, Fall 2005, pp. 22–29.

107. Rumsfeld, *The National Defense Strategy of the United States*, March 2005, p. 13.

108. Rumsfeld, *Quadrennial Defense Review Report*, 6 February 2006, p. 18.

109. April Terreri, "Ocean Freight Carriers Cope with Good Times, October 2005," available at http://www.worldtrademag.com/CDA/Articles/Ocean/abe9170abaaf7010VgnVCM100000f932a8c0 (accessed 28 November 2007).

110. Christopher Mayer, "NW Passage Opens Shipping Routes, with Global Economic Impact," available at http://www.bitsofnews.com/content/view/6264 (accessed 28 November 2007).

111. Ibid.

112. LtCol David A. Anderson, USMC (Ret), "Naval Forward Presence," *Marine Corps Gazette*, December 2007, p. 65.

113. Mel Mandell, "120,000 Leagues under the Sea," *IEEE Spectrum*, April 2000, pp. 50–54.

114. Email from Robert Bannon to Robert O. Work, in preparation for an Executive Seminar on undersea telecommunications, 11–12 February 2004.

115. John Temple Swing, "What Future for the Oceans?" *Foreign Affairs*, September/October 2003, p. 145.

116. For an outstanding review of British concerns over the global telegraphic cable net, see Paul M. Kennedy, "Imperial Cable Communications and Strategy, 1870–1914," *The English Historical Review*, October 1971.

117. Geoffrey Till, "Navies and the New World Order," *Proceedings*, March 2005, p. 61.

118. For an accounting of the capabilities of these next seventeen largest world's navies, see Chapter IV in Robert O. Work, *To Take and Keep the Lead: A Naval Fleet Platform Architecture for Enduring Maritime Supremacy* (Washington, DC: Center for Strategic and Budgetary Assessments, December 2005).

119. The active number of Navy ships was drawn from the Naval Vessel Register, available at http://www.nvr.navy.mil/nvrships/FLEET.HTM (accessed 30 November 2007). Coast Guard numbers were drawn from Polmar, *Ships and Aircraft of the US Fleet*, 18th edition, Chapter 32. Ships in the MSC inventory were found at the MSC website, http://www.msc.navy.mil (accessed 1 December 2007).

120. Wayne P. Hughes, a noted naval strategist, argues for a bi-modal fleet consisting of one fleet optimized for high-end warfighting and one fleet optimized for forward presence and supporting the Long War against radical extremists. The idea of a tri-modal fleet is a variation of his idea.

121. This is a metaphor often invoked by former Secretary of the Navy Richard Danzig. *See* his comments in "What's America's Grand Plan?" p. 18.
122. From discussions between Frank Hoffman and Robert O. Work.

A Key Challenge for the Navy—and Some Potential Options for Addressing It

Ronald O'Rourke
Naval Analyst, Congressional Research Service of the Library of Congress

Introduction[1]

A central challenge for the Navy in coming years will be to prepare for a range of potential future operations—including some operations that are not widely viewed as urgent near-term Defense-spending priorities but will nevertheless require substantial Navy investments beginning soon—and do this in a potentially less open-ended Defense budget environment where the services will be competing for resources and the Navy will not have the strongest obvious claim on the marginal Department of Defense (DoD) dollar. This paper discusses this challenge and then presents some potential options—some potential future directions, to borrow from the workshop's title—for addressing this challenge.

The Challenge

Range of Potential Future Operations. The Navy's range of potential future operations includes, among other things, the following:

- Day-to-day presence; engagement; and intelligence, surveillance, and reconnaissance (ISR) operations;

- Humanitarian assistance and disaster relief operations;

- Antipiracy and maritime intercept operations;

- Antiterrorism operations;

- Larger-scale, land-oriented combat operations;[2] and

- More purely maritime (as opposed to land-oriented) operations for countering improved Chinese naval and other military forces.

Navy capabilities required for conducting some of these operations overlap with, but are not identical to, Navy capabilities required for conducting others. In a situation of constrained resources, these overlapping but nonidentical sets of required capabilities can create a situation of potential Navy investment trade-offs. (For further discussion, see appendix A.)

Although China's military modernization and its implications for required U.S. Navy capabilities are a topic not frequently at the forefront of discussions over future U.S. defense spending, they are nevertheless a significant force-planning and budget issue for the Navy. Several of the Navy's most expensive potential investments are for capabilities associated partly or largely with countering improved Chinese military forces years from now. (For a discussion of the apparent goals of China's military modernization effort, and the implications of these goals for required U.S. Navy capabilities, see appendix B.)

Potentially less open-ended budget environment. The complexity of the current Defense-budgeting environment—which includes not only the "regular" or "base" budget for the coming fiscal year but also one or more supplementals for the fiscal year in progress, plus additional war-related funding for the coming fiscal year—has made it more difficult to track and understand total Defense-related spending. In addition, supplementals, being appropriation bills, can bypass the oversight provided by the defense authorization committees, and have been submitted with justification documents that have been light on line-item details and explanations. All these factors together may have served to create a more open-ended Defense budget environment in recent years.

The expected eventual reduction in the scale of the U.S. military efforts in Iraq and Afghanistan, and a corresponding reduction in the size of the supplemental appropriations bills financing those efforts, could work to reverse this situation, at least to some degree, producing a less open-ended Defense budget environment. Supporters of higher defense spending may argue in favor of converting current war-related spending into additional base-budget spending, but it is far from clear that the conversion factor will be 100 cents on the dollar or something close to that.

Navy position in competition for resources. In this potentially less open-ended budget environment, the military services will be competing for resources to execute their respective programs. While the services all face challenges in being able to finance their programs (the Navy's challenge, as illustrated through the lens of its shipbuilding plan, is discussed in appendix C), they are currently quite unequal in terms of their potential abilities to lay claim in coming years to marginal DoD dollars that do become available. The Navy appears to be the least well positioned of all the services in this regard, for at least four reasons:

- **The Army and Marine Corps come first.** Many observers expect that the Army and Marine Corps will have first claim on additional resources by virtue of being the services that have borne most heavily the burden of the fighting in Iraq and Afghanistan. Although the Navy contributes to the U.S. military efforts in Iraq and Afghanistan, and has worked to relieve the burden on the Army and Marine Corps where it can through the assignment of Navy personnel ashore and other measures, the Navy's direct role in these two military efforts is more modest and much less visible.

- **The Air Force has been publicly asking for more funding; the Navy hasn't.** Air Force officials in public statements have not been reticent about raising the issue of needing more money to fulfill their plans, and most recently have taken several public opportunities to stress their service's need for an additional $20 billion per year for five years. In contrast, the Navy under its two previous chiefs of naval operations (CNOs) has spent much of the past eight years generally refraining from publicly asking for more money and emphasizing instead how new business-efficiency measures and other cost-saving actions will permit the Navy to implement its program without an increase in its planned budget top line. The Navy has sometimes acknowledged that the executability of its shipbuilding program is "at risk," but has not followed such acknowledgments with any requests for additional funding. The Navy's approach of not asking for additional funding over the past several years may have been music to the ears of the Office of the Secretary of Defense (OSD) officials who regularly receive pleas for more funding, but it has not created much of a foundation for the Navy to start laying claim to additional DoD resources that might become available in coming years.

- **The 1,000-ship-navy concept can be viewed as partial solution.** The Navy's recent emphasis on international maritime cooperation in security issues (until recently referred to by the Navy as the 1,000-ship-navy concept) can encourage others to believe (or can be used by others as an excuse to argue) that shortfalls in Navy capacities for performing certain missions can be mitigated, at least in part, by relying more heavily on other navies to perform these missions.

- **Lots of talk about terrorism, not much about China.** Administration descriptions of U.S. security challenges are often dominated by references to the war on terrorism, while references to China as a potential security challenge are comparatively rare. In tracking testimony and other public statements from DoD and Navy officials, I have sometimes perceived a reluctance to talk directly and plainly about China's military modernization program, including sometimes an apparent reluctance to refer to China directly by name, as opposed to making vague references about potential regional peer competitors. This way of describing U.S. security challenges has prepared observers well for understanding arguments for additional spending related to counterterrorism operations, but has not prepared them as well for understanding arguments for additional spending prompted by Chinese military modernization.

Some Potential Options for Addressing This Challenge

Potential options for addressing this challenge include but are not limited to those listed below. These options aren't listed in any particular order, and some might not be consistent with others.

Talk more about China as a top defense-planning priority. One option would be for administration and Navy officials to begin talking more frequently in a plain and direct fashion about China's military modernization program, and thereby elevate China's military modernization in public discussions as a significant U.S. defense-planning issue, at least for the Navy. This includes mentioning China more frequently by name rather than referring to it indirectly as an unnamed potential peer competitor.[3]

Start asking for more money. A second option would be for Navy officials to emulate the Air Force and start talking more openly about needing more money. It is understandable for the Navy to want to be viewed as a responsible and helpful player in DoD budgeting. But if the Navy lags significantly behind the other services in terms of openly talking about how additional funding could help implement its program of record, it could distort U.S. defense planning by encouraging policy makers to misperceive the relative funding needs of the various services.

Shift responsibilities to other navies. A third option would be to transfer to other navies responsibilities for performing certain missions aimed at promoting general maritime security, so that the Navy can devote more of its resources to preparing for other kinds of operations. In other words, if some observers view the 1,000-ship-navy concept as a means for mitigating the Navy's missions-versus-resources situation, perhaps it would make sense to find out just how true that proposition is.

Shift responsibilities to the Coast Guard. In a similar vein, a fourth option would be to explore options for shifting a greater share of maritime-security responsibilities to the Coast Guard, so that the Navy could devote more of its resources to preparing for other missions. Although the Coast Guard is currently contending with its own missions-versus-resources challenge, the next administration might be willing to substantially increase spending on the Department of Homeland Security, including the Coast Guard. If so, then the planned size and capabilities of the Coast Guard could be increased, which might enable it to take on maritime-security operations that the Navy now plans to perform.

Pursue greater hull commonality in shipbuilding. As demonstrated this year by the Littoral Combat Ship (LCS) Program, the Navy could avoid some of the cost growth in its shipbuilding programs by simply not forgetting well-established lessons in Defense acquisition, such as avoiding concurrency in design and construction. But there are also some new ideas for reducing shipbuilding costs, and one of those is Vice Admiral Sullivan's concept for consolidating the Navy over time into a smaller number of common hull designs that are fitted out for various missions. As I stated in testimony this past July to the Seapower and Expeditionary Forces Subcommittee of the House Armed Services Committee, this concept could help recover economies of scale in shipbuilding that were lost when the rate of Navy shipbuilding declined after the end of the cold war. This idea has potential for being a powerful engine for reducing ship procurement costs, thereby permitting a larger Navy to be maintained for a given amount of money.[4]

In addition to pursuing a consolidation of hull designs within the Navy, another possibility would be to explore the potential for doing so across the Navy and the Coast Guard, where the two services are currently pursuing five different hull designs for smaller ships—two LCS designs for the Navy, and three cutter designs of different sizes under the Coast Guard's Deepwater acquisition program. Eric Labs, my counterpart at the Congressional Budget Office (CBO), is currently conducting a study on the potential merits of consolidating the two LCS designs and the two larger cutter designs into a reduced total number of designs.

Assign more ships to Pacific Fleet; forward-homeport more ships in western Pacific. Two additional options, both of which I discuss in my Congressional Research Service (CRS) report on China's naval modernization and its implications for required U.S. Navy capabilities,[5] would be to expand the Navy's plans for shifting ships from the Atlantic Fleet to the Pacific Fleet, and for forward-homeporting ships in the western Pacific. These options could improve the Navy's ability to respond to a contingency in the Taiwan Strait area with on-station or early-arriving forces, or to maintain desired levels of presence in the western Pacific for other purposes.

Consider adjusting some force-level goals. Another option would be to consider adjusting some of the force-level goals in the Navy's 313-ship plan. The Navy has emphasized stability in planned force levels as important for helping to reduce shipbuilding costs, but, as I have discussed in a CRS report, the Navy itself has indicated that it might make changes to certain parts of the plan,[6] and the concept of planning stability in any event does not automatically trump the notion of making needed changes in force-level goals.

One possibility for adjusting planned force levels would be to increase the planned number of amphibious ships (thirty-one) by a few or several ships so as to more robustly meet Marine Corps lift requirements—something that Marine Corps officials have made clear they would like to see. A second and somewhat related possibility concerns the Navy's plan to deploy a squadron of fourteen Maritime Prepositioning Force (Future), or MPF(F), ships to help implement the Navy–Marine Corps seabasing concept. Robert Work of the Center for Strategic and Budgetary Assessments (CSBA) has been arguing for the last two years that the seabasing concept is not well thought through, that the MPF(F) squadron is premature or ill advised, and that policy makers should consider the alternative of not pursuing the MPF(F) squadron and instead building a larger number of amphibious ships.[7]

Additional possibilities include increasing the attack submarine (SSN) force-level goal from forty-eight to a higher number, such as fifty-five (a previous planning goal), so as to better meet demands from theater commanders for forward-deployed SSNs; and increasing the cruiser-destroyer force-level goal from eighty-eight ships to some higher number, so as to reduce the risk of a future tension between demands for cruisers and destroyers to perform traditional surface combatant missions and demands for cruisers and destroyers to perform ballistic missile defense (BMD) operations in other locations.

Consider adjusting some programs. The above potential adjustments to planned ship force-levels could lead to corresponding adjustments in shipbuilding plans. In addition, even if the force-level goals for SSNs and cruisers/destroyers are not increased, one option would be to add up to eight SSNs and up to ten cruisers/destroyers to the Navy's 30-year shipbuilding plan so that the Navy could achieve and maintain (or come closer to achieving and maintaining) its current force-level goals for these two categories of ships. Another possibility would be to expand the application of nuclear power to a wider array of the Navy's surface ships, beginning with the CG(X) cruiser—an option supported by the House Armed Services Committee.[8]

An additional possible program adjustment that has been promoted by Thomas Ehrhard and Robert Work of CSBA would be to accelerate the development and expand the planned numbers and mission capabilities of the Navy's carrier-based Unmanned Combat Air System (UCAS).[9]

There are many other possibilities for making program-level adjustments. To pick just one warfare area as an example, potential options for making program adjustments relating to BMD include the following:

- Accelerate CG(X) procurement so as to introduce more quickly new Navy capabilities for countering tactical ballistic missiles (TBMs), including potential Chinese TBMs equipped with maneuvering reentry vehicles (MaRVs) that are capable of hitting moving ships at sea;[10]

- Create a more robust program than the current program of record for replacing the Navy Area Defense (NAD) System (the Navy's lower-tier BMD program), which was canceled in 2001;

- Increase the planned number of BMD-capable Aegis ships; and

- Increase the planned procurement quantity of SM-3 BMD interceptors.[11]

Notes

1. The views expressed in this paper are those of the author and do not necessarily reflect the views of the Congressional Research Service or the Library of Congress. Parts of this paper draw on some of the author's CRS reports for Congress.

2. The term "land-oriented combat operations" is used here to refer to naval operations that are oriented toward achieving or influencing outcomes on the continental landmass.

3. When I have suggested this option in the past, I have sometimes been asked whether talking more frequently in a plain and direct fashion about China's military modernization program and its implications might heighten Chinese concerns about its security, spur additional Chinese military modernization, and consequently be counterproductive. There is logic behind this concern, but there is also a converse risk that avoiding talking in a plain and direct fashion about China's military modernization program and its implications might spur additional Chinese military modernization by suggesting to Chinese leaders that its modernization activities are helping to intimidate U.S. policy-makers. The key is to talk about China's military modernization plainly and without self-censorship, but also respectfully and without exaggeration. You don't have to hype Chinese military capabilities to be concerned about them. China's military isn't 10 feet tall, and it isn't 6 feet tall either, but in relation to the goals that China appears to have in mind for its military modernization (see appendix B), its forces are on a path to becoming 6 feet tall.

   Speaking more plainly about China's military modernization will require an ability to understand China as a big, complex country, about which many things are true, some of them seemingly contradictory. China is a dynamic economy, a big trading partner, and an actual or potential partner on certain international issues. But it is also a potential major security challenge.

   China's perspectives and potential reactions on issues can and should be taken into account, but doing this does not necessarily require a general avoidance of openly identifying China in U.S. discussions as a potential regional peer competitor, or openly and fully discussing the defense-planning implications of China's military modernization effort. It is arguably not desirable in the long run for the United States, as a democracy that mediates its defense spending through public understanding of security challenges, to avoid a direct and open discussion among its own people about a country that may pose a potentially significant security challenge. Self-censorship on this matter could distort U.S. defense planning by reducing policy-making attention devoted to, and the justification for investments that might be needed to respond to, China's military modernization effort. Avoidance of this issue in public U.S. discussions on U.S. defense planning is arguably not desirable for China either. China is an emerging world power, and world powers have their actions commented on by others. The sooner China gets used to that, the sooner China will emerge as a fully mature, responsible world power. Paying excessive deference to Chinese expressions of sensitivity regarding comments that others make about Chinese actions could encourage continued and even strengthened expressions from China of such sensitivities, slowing China's maturation process as a responsible world power.

4. For a discussion of this idea, see Charles "Chuck" Goddard, Howard Fireman, and Christopher Deegan, "A Question of Cost," *Armed Forces Journal*, June 2007, pp. 24–27, 47. See also Emelie Rutherford, "Affordable Future Fleet Study Being Vetted by NAVSEA," *Inside the Navy*, 5 November 2007.

5. Ronald O'Rourke, *China Naval Modernization: Implications for U.S. Navy Capabilities—Background and Issues for Congress*, CRS Report RL33153. This report was first published in November 2005 and has been updated numerous times since. As of this writing, the most recent update was published on 18 October 2007. CRS reports are published for use by members of Congress and their staffs only.

6. Ronald O'Rourke, *Navy Force Structure and Shipbuilding Plans: Background and Issues for Congress*; CRS Report RL32665; see section entitled "Potential for Changing 313-Ship Proposal."

7. See, for example, Robert Work, *Thinking About Seabasing: All Ahead, Slow* (Washington: CSBA, 2006).

8. For a discussion of this issue, see Ronald O'Rourke, *Navy Nuclear-Powered Surface Ships: Background, Issues, and Options for Congress*, CRS Report RL33946.

9. Thomas P. Ehrhard and Robert O. Work, *The Unmanned Combat Air System Carrier Demonstration Program: A New Dawn for Naval Aviation?* CSBA Backgrounder (Washington: Center for Strategic and Budgetary Assessments, 10 May 2007).

10. This might be accomplished in part by procuring, in addition to the lead CG(X) in FY2011 and the second CG(X) in FY2013, three more CG(X)s in FY2011, FY2012, and FY2013, rather than the three DDG-1000s planned for FY2011, FY2012, and FY2013.

11. For discussions of these options, see Ronald O'Rourke, *Navy CG(X) Cruiser Program: Background, Oversight Issues, and Options for Congress*, CRS Report RL34179; and Ronald O'Rourke, *Sea-Based Ballistic Missile Defense—Background and Issues for Congress*, CRS Report RL33745.

Appendix A. Potential Future Navy Operations and Investment Trade-Offs

The Navy's range of potential future operations can be summarized in various ways; in my own work on the issue, I have found it helpful to organize it into three broad categories:

- Smaller-scale, widely dispersed counterterrorism operations and other operations to promote global maritime security or global security generally;

- Larger-scale, land-oriented combat operations;[1] and

- More purely maritime (as opposed to land-oriented) operations for countering improved Chinese naval and other military forces.

This three-part organizational scheme essentially consolidates into a single broad category the first four items of the list of potential future operations presented at the start of this paper. I first presented this three-part organizational scheme at a Naval War College symposium in December 2006.[2] While other schemes are certainly possible,[3] this one isn't too different from those that have been presented by some others.[4] Whatever the scheme, a key point that arises from a discussion of the Navy's range of potential future operations is that Navy capabilities required for conducting some of these operations overlap with, but are not identical to, Navy capabilities required for conducting others. In a situation of constrained resources, these overlapping but nonidentical sets of required capabilities can create a situation of potential Navy investment trade-offs.

Table 1 below is my own attempt to depict this situation of potential Navy investment trade-offs; it shows which of the three categories of kinds of operations above are more likely to be invoked as principal justifications for making certain potential naval investments. It is a slightly modified version of a table that I presented at the December 2006 symposium.[5] The table does not attempt to be comprehensive or systematic—the list of potential naval investment areas is far from complete, and it mixes together platforms, programs, and capabilities. Although every item scored in the third category is also scored in the second, the size of the investment required for some of these items might be greater for the third category than for the second. China-related operations, for example, might require investing in a larger inventory of antisubmarine warfare(ASW)–related systems than would be required for an operation in the second category. Some items not listed in the table—such as aircraft carriers, precision strike systems, special operations forces (SOF), and ISR—might be principally justified by all three types of operations.

Observers creating their own versions of the table might list other items, or score them differently against the justifying categories of operations. Some observers, for example, might argue that the first category of operations could be a principal justification for investing in SSNs because SSNs are used as intelligence-collection and SOF-insertion/recovery platforms, while other observers might argue that China-related operations could be a principal justification for investing in amphibious capabilities because certain potential operations relating to countering China as a peer competitor (such as, for example, presence and engagement operations designed to maintain U.S. presence and regional influence in the western Pacific) could involve the use of U.S. amphibious forces. While the details of the table are subject to debate and revision, I have found it useful for illustrating in graphic form the general issue of potential naval investment trade-offs in a situation of finite resources.

Table 1
Potential Naval Investment Areas and the Kinds of Operations That Are More Likely to Be Invoked as Principal Justifications for Making Them

Potential naval invest- ment areas and . . .	. . . Their more likely principal justifications		
	Smaller-scale counter- terrorism and general maritime/ global security	Larger-scale land-oriented operations	China-related operations
MDA and MIO	X		
Riverine force	X		
GFS	X		
Civil affairs/CBs/medical/ disaster relief	X		
AT/FP measures	X		
LCS	X	X	
Amphibious fleet	X	X	
MPF(F)	X	X	
NSFS		X	
BMD		X	X
Air-to-air combat		X	X
AAW		X	X
ASuW		X	X
SSNs		X	X
ASW and torpedo defense		X	X

Potential naval investment areas and . . .	. . . Their more likely principal justifications		
	Smaller-scale counter-terrorism and general maritime/ global security	Larger-scale land-oriented operations	China-related operations
MIW		X	X

Source: Prepared by the author. MDA is maritime domain awareness; MIO is maritime intercept operations; GFS is global fleet stations; CBs is construction battalions; AT/FP is antiterrorism/force-protection; LCS is Littoral Combat Ship; MPF(F) is Maritime Prepositioning Force (Future); NSFS is naval surface fire support; BMD is ballistic missile defense; AAW is antiair warfare; ASuW is antisurface warfare; SSNs is nuclear-powered submarines; ASW is antisubmarine warfare; MIW is mine warfare. Some items not listed in the table—such as aircraft carriers, precision strike systems, special operations forces (SOF), and ISR—might be principally justified by all three types of operations.

Notes

1. As mentioned earlier, the term "land-oriented combat operations" is used here to refer to naval operations that are oriented toward achieving or influencing outcomes on the continental landmass.
2. Ronald O'Rourke, "China's Naval Modernization: Potential Implications for Required U.S. Navy Capabilities," (presentation at a conference on maritime implications of China's energy future, U.S. Naval War College, Newport, RI, 7 December 2006).
3. To cite only two possible alternatives, some observers might place counterterrorist operations into a category of their own, while others might discount my second category as no longer important, or consolidate it with my third category.
4. See, for example, Wayne P. Hughes, Jr., "A Bimodal Force for the National Maritime Strategy," *Naval War College Review*, Spring 2007, pp. 29–47, which discusses future U.S. naval operations in terms of engaging China as the emerging peer competitor, conducting a large number of "'small' operations, expeditionary in nature, in which the Navy will continue to participate," and conducting "wars in between," though Hughes states that he "cannot imagine who the high-risk 'in between' enemy can be, so readers must specify their own foes. . . ." See also James Kurth, "The New Maritime Strategy: Confronting Peer Competitors, Rogue States, and Transnational Insurgents," *Orbis*, Fall 2000, pp. 585–600, which, as the title suggests, discusses future U.S. naval operations in terms of addressing China as a peer competitor, countering Iran and North Korea as rogue states, and countering radical Islamist transnational terrorist and insurgent networks.
5. A key difference in the new table shown here is the inclusion of the line item for SSNs. In the December 2006 version of the table, I treated SSNs as platforms that could be principally justified by all three categories of operations. Although SSNs are used in counterterrorism and other operations to promote global maritime security or global security generally, my current sense is that, as a practical matter, such operations are less likely than the other two categories of operations to be invoked as a principal justification for making major investments in SSNs.

Appendix B. Goals of China's Military Modernization Effort, and Implications for Required U.S. Navy Capabilities

The modernization of China's maritime-relevant military forces, and the implications of this modernization effort for required U.S. Navy capabilities, is a topic I cover at some length in a CRS report.[1] As discussed in that report, there is a consensus among observers that a near-term goal of China's military modernization is to develop military options for addressing the situation with Taiwan. Consistent with this goal, observers believe, China wants its modernized military to be capable of acting as a so-called antiaccess force—a force that can deter U.S. intervention in a military crisis or conflict in the Taiwan Strait area, or failing that, delay the arrival or reduce the effectiveness of U.S. intervention forces, particularly U.S. naval and air forces.[2] In light of this near-term goal, a crisis or conflict in the Taiwan Strait could place a premium on having a U.S. Navy with sufficient on-station or early-arriving naval forces and a capability to defeat Chinese antiaccess weapons and platforms, including modern, highly capable models.

As also discussed in the CRS report, DoD and other observers believe that, in addition to a near-term focus on developing military options for addressing the situation with Taiwan, broader or longer-term goals of China's military modernization effort, including its naval modernization effort, include the following:

- Asserting China's regional military leadership, displacing U.S. regional military influence, prevailing in regional rivalries, and encouraging eventual U.S. military withdrawal from the region;

- Defending China's claims in maritime territorial disputes, some of which have implications for oil, gas, or mineral exploration rights; and

- Protecting China's sea lines of communication, which China relies upon increasingly for oil and other imports.

These broader or longer-term goals are significant for two reasons. First, they imply that if the situation with Taiwan is somehow resolved, China will find continuing reasons to pursue its modernization effort.[3] Second, they suggest that even if China's military never fires a shot in anger at an opposing military, China's military forces, including in particular its naval forces, will still be used on a day-to-day basis to promote China's political position in the Pacific. This creates an essentially political (as opposed to combat-related) reason for the United States or other countries to maintain a competitive presence in the region with naval and other forces that are viewed by observers in the Pacific as capable of effectively countering China's forces.[4]

Notes

1. Ronald O'Rourke, *China Naval Modernization: Implications for U.S. Navy Capabilities— Background and Issues for Congress*, CRS Report RL33153. This appendix adapts a section from that report.
2. DoD, for example, states that "If a quick resolution [to a situation involving Taiwan] is not possible, Beijing would seek to deter U.S. intervention or, failing that, delay such

intervention, defeat it in an asymmetric, limited, quick war; or, fight it to a standstill and pursue a protracted conflict." U.S. Department of Defense, *Annual Report to Congress [on] Military Power of the People's Republic of China, 2007* (Washington: Office of the Secretary of Defense, released 25 May 2007), p. 32. See also pp. 15–18.

3. DoD states that "China's near-term focus on preparing for military contingencies in the Taiwan Strait, including the possibility of U.S. intervention, appears to be an important driver of its modernization plans. However, analysis of China's military acquisitions and strategic thinking suggests Beijing is also generating capabilities for other regional contingencies, such as conflict over resources or territory." Ibid., p. I (Executive Summary). Similar statements can be found on pages 8–9, 15, and 22–24. The director of National Intelligence has similarly stated: "Beijing continues its rapid rate of military modernization, initiated in 1999. We assess that China's aspirations for great power status, threat perceptions, and security strategy would drive this modernization effort even if the Taiwan problem were resolved." John D. Negroponte, Director of National Intelligence, "Annual Threat Assessment of the Director of National Intelligence," 110th Cong., 1st sess., 11 January 2007, p. 10.

4. It can also be noted that if these broader or longer-term goals eventually become more prominent in the mix of reasons for China's military modernization effort—either because the situation with Taiwan has been resolved, or because the buildup of Taiwan-related force elements has been completed—it could prompt a shift in the composition of the naval modernization effort toward a greater emphasis on force-structure elements that are more closely associated with these broader or longer-term goals, such as aircraft carriers, nuclear-powered attack submarines (SSNs) as opposed to non-nuclear-powered attack submarines (SSs), serial production of destroyers as opposed to the recent production of new destroyer designs in ones and twos, at-sea logistics, and overseas bases.

Appendix C. Affordability/Executability of Navy's Shipbuilding Plans[1]

Although the Navy is a lot more than just ships, ships are central to the Navy—you can't have much of a Navy without them—and a discussion of the current affordability and executability of the Navy's shipbuilding plans draws in other major categories of Navy spending, providing a reasonably good lens through which to view the Navy's overall program-versus-resources situation.

The Navy's 30-year shipbuilding plan, submitted to Congress in February 2007, does not contain enough ships to achieve and maintain all elements of the Navy's planned 313-ship fleet consistently over the long run. To do that, the total of 291 new ships included in the plan would need to be augmented by another 23 ships—1 LPD-17 amphibious ship, 4 cruise missile/SOF submarines (SSGNs), 8 attack submarines (SSNs), and 10 cruisers and destroyers. At today's prices, these 23 ships could easily cost an average of more than $2 billion each, meaning a total additional investment of more than $46 billion.

Navy officials have said that for its shipbuilding plans to be affordable and executable, five things need to happen:

- The Navy's overall budget needs to remain more or less flat (not decline) in real (inflation-adjusted) terms,

- Navy operation and maintenance (O&M) spending needs to remain flat (not grow) in real terms,

- Navy military personnel (MILPERS) spending needs to remain flat (not grow) in real terms,

- Navy research and development (R&D) spending needs to decrease from recent levels and remain at the decreased level over the long run, and

- Navy ships need to be built at the Navy's currently estimated prices.

The Navy says the first four things are needed for the Navy to be able to increase the shipbuilding budget from an average in FY2002–FY2007 of about $9.6 billion per year in constant FY2008 dollars to a long-term average of about $15.4 billion per year in constant FY2008 dollars—an increase of about 60 percent in real terms.[2]

Some observers have questioned whether all five of the above things will happen, arguing the following:

- The need in coming years to fund an increase in Army and Marine end strength could, within an overall DoD budget that remains more or less flat in real terms, require funding to be transferred from the Air Force and Navy budgets to the Army and Marine Corps budgets, which could, for a time at least, lead to a real decline in the Air Force and Navy budgets.

- DoD in the past has not been fully successful in meeting its goals for controlling O&M costs.

- The Navy does not have full control over its MILPERS costs—they can be affected, for example, by decisions that Congress makes on pay and benefits.

- While the Navy may be able to decrease R&D spending in coming years as a number of new systems shift from development to procurement, it may be difficult for the Navy to keep R&D spending at that reduced level over the long run, because the Navy at some point will likely want to start development of other new systems.

- Several Navy shipbuilding programs have experienced significant cost growth in recent years, and CBO estimates that Navy ships will cost substantially more to build than the Navy estimates.

A 1 October 2007 press article stated:

While the US Navy (USN) is set to receive at least USD13.2 billion for shipbuilding in the 2008 US defence budget, a confluence of budgetary and post-Iraq pressures leaves its 313-ship plan "at some risk," according to the head of US Naval Sea Systems Command (NAVSEA).

Congress is close to approving the Senate's shipbuilding budget, which is USD2 billion less than the sum proposed by the House of Representatives.

Either way, based on current cost estimates for the fleet, it may not be enough to realise the navy's plan without forcing cuts in other areas, Vice Admiral Paul Sullivan said.

The navy's "cost of future capability—new ships, new airplanes—is too high to meet and deliver all of the requirements we have for them," he told the 2007 Fleet Maintenance Symposium.

Vice Adm Sullivan warned that pressure to cut funding on programmes that run over-budget or behind schedule will intensify, with tough choices having to be made between maintaining older vessels or keeping a new programme on track.

For several years, the USN has avoided the need to choose between new-build or maintenance by receiving funds from wartime supplemental budgets. The remaining 2007–08 supplemental request, for example, is expected to total USD200 billion in addition to the regular defence request.

"We've been living the dream" of paying for ship maintenance through supplemental spending, Vice Adm Sullivan told the symposium. Soon, he said, the maintenance planners will have to make ends meet without recourse to supplemental funding.

"How do you decide which year [supplemental budgets will end]? We think it could be in the next couple of years. Looking out there it is about the same time that the army and marines will need to recapitalise. They are going to leave most of their equipment in the desert. They will need to reset, and they are going to feel like it is their time—they fought in Iraq and Afghanistan."

The admiral said of the USN's 313-ship plan: "I don't expect that to be tweaked, but it is at some risk." . . .

Vice Adm Sullivan said: "Particularly the HAC [House Appropriations Committee] has been beating on us to get our cost numbers right so they can add more ships to the budget. I am happy to have them add more ships to the budget, but if that means . . . we get three more ships but they kill readiness, or we get two more ships but we don't get the F-18 Es and Fs that we need, that's not going to work."

The USN has already reduced the number of uniformed personnel from 377,000 to 339,500 and transferred support services to the private sector in order to cut costs.

But Sullivan said the manpower cuts "haven't saved a nickel" due to rising personnel and healthcare costs. Likewise, of the seven new shipbuilding programmes underway to recapitalise the fleet, USN budget planners "don't have a really good handle on what they are really going to cost."[3]

If one or more of the Navy's five required things does not happen, it might become difficult or impossible to execute the Navy's shipbuilding plans. The risk of the plan becoming unexecutable may become particularly acute starting in FY2011–FY2013. In FY2011, the Navy wants to increase the destroyer-cruiser procurement rate from one ship per year to two. In FY2012, the Navy wants to increase the SSN procurement rate from one ship per year to two. In FY2013, the Navy wants to begin procuring both two destroyers-cruisers and two SSNs in a single year.

Regarding the fifth item on the Navy's list of required things, CBO estimates, as shown in table 2, that the Navy's shipbuilding plan could cost an average of about $20.8 billion per year in constant FY2008 dollars to execute—about 35 percent more than the Navy's estimate of $15.4 billion in constant FY2008 dollars. If aircraft carrier refueling overhauls are also included in the calculation, CBO's estimated cost of $21.9 billion per year in constant FY2008 dollars is about 33 percent higher than the Navy's estimate of $16.5 billion in constant FY2008 dollars. The table also shows that if the 30-year shipbuilding plan is augmented to include the extra ships needed to fully achieve and maintain all elements of the 313-ship plan over the long run, CBO estimates the average annual cost at $22.0 billion per year excluding carrier refueling overhauls, and $23.1 billion per year including carrier refueling overhauls, both figures in constant FY2008 dollars.

As shown in table 3, CBO in 2006 estimated that if the Navy in coming years does not receive or cannot devote more budgetary resources to ship construction, and if the Navy retains roughly the same proportionate mix of ship types as called for in the 313-ship proposal, the fleet could eventually be reduced to a total of 211 ships, or about 33 percent fewer than called for in the 313-ship proposal.

Table 2
Average Annual Shipbuilding Costs

(billions of constant FY2008 dollars per year)

	New-construction ships only	New-construction ships + carrier refueling overhauls
Navy shipbuilding budget in FY2002–FY2007	9.6	11.4
Navy estimate of cost of 30-year plan	15.4	16.5
CBO estimate of cost of 30-year plan	20.8	21.9
CBO estimate of cost of 30-year plan plus additional ships needed to fully support all elements of 313-ship fleet consistently over the long run	22.0	23.1

Source: "Statement of J. Michael Gilmore, Assistant Director for National Security, and Eric J. Labs, Senior Analyst, [on] The Navy's 2008 Shipbuilding Plan and Key Ship Programs, before the Subcommittee on Seapower and Expeditionary Forces, Committee on Armed Services, U.S. House of Representatives, July 24, 2007," 110th Cong., 1st sess., 2007, Table 2 on p. 8.

Table 3
CBO Estimate of Potential Fleet Size

Ship type	Proposed 313-ship fleet	CBO estimate
Ballistic missile submarines (SSBNs)	14	10
Cruise missile submarines (SSGNs)	4	0
Attack submarines (SSNs)	48	35
Aircraft carriers	11	7
Cruisers, destroyers, frigates	88	54
Littoral Combat Ships (LCSs)	55	40
Amphibious ships	31	15
MPF(F) ships	12	12
Combat logistics and support ships	50	38
Total battle force ships	313	211

Source: Congressional Budget Office, *Options for the Navy's Future Fleet* (May 2006), pp. xviii–xx.

Notes

1. This appendix adapts a section from Ronald O'Rourke, *Navy Force Structure and Shipbuilding Plans: Background and Issues for Congress*, CRS Report RL32665.

2. Source for dollars figures: CBO telephone conversation with CRS, 31 May 2006. *See also* "Statement of J. Michael Gilmore, Assistant Director, and Eric J. Labs, Principal Analyst, [on] Potential Costs of the Navy's 2006 Shipbuilding Plan, [Testimony] before the Subcommittee on Projection Forces, Committee on Armed Services, U.S. House of Representatives, March 30, 2006," 109th Cong., 2nd sess., 2006.

3. Tara Copp, "USN Faces Tough Choices on Fleet Plan, Warns NAVSEA Chief," *Jane's Navy International*, 1 October 2007. (Online version posted 24 September 2007.)

Panel IV: Maritime Forces

Summary of Discussion

Dr. Thomas R. Fedyszyn
Security, Strategy, and Forces Course Director
National Security Decision Making Department
U.S. Naval War College

The discussion of the future of maritime forces was significantly affected by the existence of the new U.S. maritime strategy, "A Cooperative Strategy for 21st Century Seapower." The papers discussed during this panel address discrete aspects of the Navy strategy, including an objective international appraisal, a historical perspective in terms of organizational relationships and required capabilities, and, finally, some considerations of its force planning implications.

Geoffrey Till's paper, "'A Cooperative Strategy for 21st Century Seapower': What's New? What's Next?" offers "a view from outside" on the new U.S. maritime strategy. Till addresses the impact of globalization and the changed concept of security driving America's sea services to put forth this new strategy. The author proposes that the security environment of the current century requires that naval leadership develop a "postmodern" conception of sea power. This might entail a wider notion of the concept of deterrence and a greater stress on mutual interdependence, as well as a willingness to conduct constabulary and humanitarian operations as primary missions of the Navy.

He is positive about the Global Maritime Partnership, sometimes known as the "Thousand-Ship Navy," since it is the most feasible naval response to the security challenges of the postmodern world. However, he voices one central concern related to nomenclature: the term "Thousand-Ship Navy" seems to exclude the world's coast guards and harbor police fleets, which will be responsible for many of the activities required by the strategy. The paper envisages that constabulary operations, law enforcement operations, and humanitarian operations will increasingly become a principal requirement for postmodern navies and happily embraces the notion of the National Fleet. Till is not unaware of the necessity to link strategic thinking to reality and is concerned that Navy shipbuilding has not yet responded to this imperative. He concludes that "[f]or the new strategy to convince observers that it really is the significant departure from the norm . . . its progenitors will need to convince sceptics by what they do after its introduction."

Robert Work's paper, "The Global Era of National Policy and the Pan-Oceanic National Fleet," provides a synopsis of the development of American maritime strategies over two hundred years and considers the new strategy a welcome and reasonable response to the security environment posed by the post-9/11 world. Trends in the new security environment, specifically the problematic nature of assured forward access, made the case for an improved Navy–Marine Corps expeditionary capability. Additionally, the confluence of the need for expanded law enforcement and homeland defense capability argued for the development of a national fleet, comprised of all three sea services. The strategy's idea of building global maritime partnerships was welcomed, creating a more balanced portfolio to address the broader range of irregular, catastrophic, and disruptive challenges through improved maritime domain awareness.

The paper criticizes the new strategy for not taking full advantage of the increased importance of *Seapower 21*'s seabasing concept. In fact, the paper argues that seabasing should be a cornerstone strategic concept in any American military strategy emphasizing expeditionary, as opposed to forward-based, warfare. The paper argues for three fleet components: Power Projection/Heavy Seabase Fleet; the Maritime Security/Light Seabase Fleet; and the Strategic Deterrence/Dissuasion Fleet.

Ronald O'Rourke's paper entitled "A Key Challenge for the Navy—and Some Potential Options for Addressing It" sets a pessimistic tone for the future of Navy shipbuilding, despite an expanding set of strategic requirements faced by the Navy. This restricted budgetary environment was adversely affected by a number of forces:

- Reduction in the size of budgetary supplementals

- Primacy of the Army and Marine Corps because of Iraq and Afghanistan

- Air Force's articulating of its need more effectively

- "1,000-ship-navy concept's" offsetting of the need to build U.S. Navy ships

- All the talk about terrorism; little about China.

A series of logical proposals for amelioration follows, which includes a stronger lobbying effort on the part of the Navy as well as the development of a more efficient shipbuilding plan that would include greater hull commonality with the Coast Guard.

Much of the follow-on discussion related to regional applications of the Navy's projected future force. In Africa, the Navy has already made huge strides in establishing a presence in the Gulf of Guinea and off the Somali coast. In both cases, naval missions are mostly nontraditional, including antipiracy and fishery and oil field protection along with navy training and nation building. Participants concurred that the U.S. Navy's activities need to be coordinated with local officials and be responsive to their desires. Activities deemed self-serving would do more harm than good in the region. There was also agreement that naval forces are preferable to any American military headquarters on the ground and its neocolonial association. The lighter the footprint the better. Further, this activity is best done with elements of all three sea services: the Navy alone does not have the capability to deliver the full spectrum of resources.

China represented the subject of greatest interest in that it represented the polar opposite to most of the previous discussion. Only China, it was felt, could pose the massive naval threat to the United States that would require the building of a "traditional" sophisticated power projection force. Most discussants agreed that China is indeed formidable, but that its naval power only could "puncture our dominance selectively." That is, we should not treat it as a "peer competitor" in a global sense across the spectrum of naval capability. The

Chinese view the term "deterrence" in terms of actual demonstrated capabilities. They respect American carrier battle groups and our ability to conduct long-range strike and most likely are not looking for a pretense to challenge us at sea. In a potential Taiwan scenario, all discussants agreed that it is difficult to imagine that the United States could match Chinese localized firepower.

Several discussants considered the possibility of developing a "cost-imposing strategy" on China, much like Reagan's strategy to defeat the Soviet Union in the cold war. Simply put, engaging in a building program that would threaten China to the point where it would be tempted to overinvest in defensive systems would be dramatically better than buying $3 billion destroyers "to operate within range of the China coast." This "cost-imposing strategy" might include developing space systems along with long-range unmanned combat aerial vehicles (UCAVs) launched from ships beyond the Chinese ability to project meaningful power. Panelists agreed that we were on the wrong side of this strategy today. Additionally, since Taiwan is the principal player in this situation, it must be coaxed to adopt a complementary strategy and to "spend on its own defense."

There was consensus that, irrespective of Chinese intent, its naval capability would continue to grow dramatically in the near future. This naval power could be used for aggressive purposes, but it certainly would be part of the international political calculus "even if China's military never fires a shot." This fact alone would argue for a strong American naval presence in the region, if for no other reason than to get used to operating in proximity to the People's Liberation Army Navy (PLA[N]).

As to future Navy funding, participants acknowledged that even the "Thousand-Ship Navy" would have huge budgetary implications. The Navy is not standing on firm financial ground especially when adding the imbalance created by the War on Terror (biased toward the Army and Marine Corps) and the age of the Air Force fleet. All agreed that there is "no free lunch in building the Thousand-Ship Navy." The domestic political difficulty is that congressional appropriators would have less compunction about shortchanging the "Thousand-Ship Navy" than the U.S. plan for 313 ships. The math is simple: deleting 50 ships from an inventory of 300 ships seems worse than a similar subtraction from a "Thousand-Ship Navy."

Tensions between the U.S. Navy and Coast Guard must be eliminated. The opportunities for a very constructive partnership are manifold, particularly in areas like tsunami relief operations, and would redound to the benefit of the United States. No single service can provide the resources; "you need numbers because you need constant . . . engagement."

The Navy's biggest credibility problem is that this radically new strategy continues to rest upon the force structure presented in the 1997 Quadrennial Defense Review. This suggests to Congress that the Navy isn't serious about the strategy driving force structure. If it were, the proposed shipbuilding plan would have taken a major revision. That is, we are chasing dhows off the coast of Somalia with billion-dollar destroyers and seem perfectly content to build more of them—only now for $3 billion. The principal message that Washington should get from this drill is that we need to match the future force to the strategy.

Panel V

Air and Space Forces

Lieutenant General David A. Deptula
U.S. Air Force, Deputy Chief of Staff for Intelligence, Surveillance, and Reconnaissance, Headquarters, U.S. Air Force

Barry D. Watts
Senior Analyst at Center for Strategic and Budgetary Assessments

Dean Cheng
Research Fellow, Center for Naval Analyses Corporation

Moderator:
Professor Roger H. Ducey
Associate Professor, National Security Decision Making Department, U.S. Naval War College

Air and Space Power Going Forward: Lead Turning the Future

Lieutenant General David A. Deptula, U.S. Air Force
Deputy Chief of Staff for Intelligence, Surveillance, and Reconnaissance
Headquarters, U.S. Air Force

Airpower was brought forth from its infancy by forward thinkers who envisioned roles for it that previously had not existed. Today, conversely, prospective roles for air and space power seem if anything to be *limited* by our ability to conceive of them, so vast are the capabilities yet to be harnessed.

Lt Col Suzanne Buono

As we explore optimizing security investment for the future, the Department of Defense (DoD) may need to revisit its persistence in providing each service with relatively equal slices of the military budget. Such an approach does little to reward judicious spending, and even less to encourage the services to jointly forge a coherent plan for confronting our collective future. Instead, the divvied-up monies are all too often used to procure more or improved versions of what was needed in the last war. What is needed, particularly in these times of rising costs and shrinking budgets, is a plan for going forward that is centered on a shared vision of the spectrum of threat conditions we are likely to face, and a mature appraisal of what will be required to deal with them.

This is not to suggest we devote ourselves to anticipating the detailed specifics of every future threat in order to develop the best means to specifically counter each type individually. *Rather, we need to dedicate ourselves to crafting an overall defense strategy that will allow us to shape the environment and act flexibly across the entire spectrum of operations, and that will also provide a framework upon which to base our jointly focused resource and investment decisions.*[1]

Basing Future Direction on the Direction of the Future

Garnering unanimity from our four services on what our future security environment will look like presents no small challenge. Still, a reasonably common view of what the future is likely to hold is required in order to chart a proactive national security course. One approach is to begin by drawing out some of the more incontrovertible trends and realities in evidence today as a means to identify broad areas of agreement upon which a rational defense strategy can then be based. For example, there can be no denying that the geostrategic landscape of today is significantly different from the cold war bipolarity it supplanted. Accordingly, our future defense strategy must take into account the increasing prevalence of nonstate and transnational actors; insurgencies; emerging peer competitors; declining states; regional powers with nuclear weapons—and the potential for proliferation; and a dynamic web of terrorism.

Likewise, the pace and tenor of our lives today have been irrevocably altered by the acceleration of change. Global trade, travel, and telecommunications have produced dramatic shifts in the way we live; speed and complexity have merged and now permeate the conduct of warfare. The profound effects of globalization and the information revolution are mirrored, if not magnified, in the realm of conflict—where they have recast the character of our adversaries, redefined the fabric and scope of the battle space, and reinvented the tools and techniques used to conduct warfare. The future will hold more of the same. Notwithstanding the inherent contradiction, rapid and deep-seated change has been, and will continue to be, a reliable constant. Consequently, one implication for our future force structure is that it must be able to respond rapidly anywhere on the globe.

Additional realities we will have to contend with are increasing military costs and decreasing military budgets. Perhaps most of all, these realities necessitate our immediate consideration of a revised defense strategy and associated force structure. We simply do not have the resources to move down multiple, divergent paths in an attempt to meet our nation's future security requirements. The DoD can afford only the most judicious of spending plans; therefore, our expenditures must be geared toward underwriting the appropriate force structure that is required to realize the National Security Strategy. Recognizing fiscal constraints, and acknowledging the increasing complexity and adaptability our adversaries already exhibit, it is clear that force structure planning must give significant consideration to the flexibility various options offer. We must prepare to counter enemies that have yet to emerge in a battle space that has yet to materialize; accordingly, the provision of flexibility of response across a wide spectrum of circumstances should be foremost among the decision criteria we apply to force structure.

Another trend is that large numbers of U.S. forces on foreign soil may be counterproductive to securing our goals and objectives. Consider the array of domestic negatives resulting from ongoing operations in Iraq and Afghanistan.[2] Invariably, anti-American backlash plays out on the world stage any time U.S. military forces are involved in the affairs of a sovereign state, no matter how justifiably.[3] Moreover, large deployments of U.S. force may create destabilizing effects within the very state or region they are intended to secure.[4,5] Such second- and third-order effects, visible even among our allies, increasingly result any time the United States exercises power unilaterally. Such trends are not likely to subside in the future and, given the transparency and growing access to communication in the information age, they most likely will continue to be considerations in large force deployments. We must move toward force structure options that project power without projecting mass with all its related challenges and vulnerability. At the same time, for the purposes of countering terrorism, and achieving stability in a region—actions taken so that governments can effectively control their own territories—significant numbers of deployed forces may be required.

In addition to the stated problems associated with deploying large numbers of forces into foreign theaters, there is the likelihood that our forces will increasingly confront antiaccess challenges and strategies. Few states can contest U.S.

military power in force-on-force combat. Rather, the means by which our adversaries will attempt to counter our strengths are likely to take the form of efforts designed to counter our presence.

Prescriptions for the Future

Our future defense strategy, and by extension the force structure it necessitates, must be driven by the requirements set forth in our National Security Strategy. The broad trends identified above provide a starting point for considering the types of circumstances that our future strategy must be designed to contend with. To summarize, these are

- More complex and erratic geostrategic realities (compared to those of the cold war)
- The acceleration of change and its effects in the realm of conflict
- Fiscal constraints and rising prices
- Increasing adversary access to chemical, biological, radiological/nuclear, and explosive materials
- Negative ramifications of large deployments of U.S. forces
- Growth in antiaccess and asymmetric challenges.

Include All the Pillars of National Security

One of our first—albeit indirect—efforts toward drafting a viable defense strategy should be to strengthen the other, *nonmilitary* elements of our security architecture to shape the security environment. Bolstering and better integrating our diplomatic, economic, military, and informational elements of power are an absolute must as we move into the future. Our defense strategy must be embedded in a multifaceted approach to international engagement and alliance building, the goal of which should be to achieve international stability—a condition directly related to securing our national defense. In this way we can make sure that when the requirement to use our military is levied, it will be as a last resort, and it will not be accomplished in a vacuum.

This perspective was reinforced recently by Admiral Mullen, the chairman of the Joint Chiefs of Staff (CJCS), when he stated that "The needs are pretty striking to me, including the preventative, deterrent, dissuasion kinds of things that a global presence and engagement permits or tries to achieve."[6]

Embrace Interdependence—the Next Level of Jointness

Crafting our nation's future defense strategy requires first codifying and solidifying the nature of the joint force framework in which our services operate. The extent to which we leverage or move away from jointness—and by extension the synergies it creates—will have cascading effects on how we arm our services, and on which roles and missions each will be expected to execute. For the same reasons we cannot afford to prepare dedicated counters to every scenario we may face, we must also come to fully embrace the tenets of joint force operations. In particular, we must make *interdependence* the centerpiece of our nation's defense strategy and the DoD's force planning construct in order to maximize the capabilities we can bring to bear within the constraints under which we must operate.

Full appreciation for the importance of embracing an interdependent approach requires an understanding of the joint force construct America uses to fight, and the resultant synergies promised by its diligent application. In short, we do not fight wars as individual services. Under our joint force construct, each of our four services offers a unique array of capabilities to a joint force commander who is responsible for assembling a plan that draws from this "menu" of capabilities to apply the right force, at the right place, at the right time for a particular contingency. Joint operations entail—and *require*—much more than simply deploying separate service components to a fight and aligning them under a single commander.

From a force structure–planning perspective, the greatest value to be gained from joint employment results less from bringing separate service components together during an operation than it does from having deconflicted their strengths and specialties well in advance. This gets at the heart of why joint force operations create synergies—because embracing an interdependent approach allows each service to focus on its own core competencies while relying on the other services to do the same.

The requirements of interdependence are that our services must define and adhere to specified lanes in the road, and that each must then rely upon the others for the capabilities outside its lane; the opportunity costs of *not* embracing this approach include mission overlap and confused responsibility areas, redundant capabilities, lost opportunities for specialization, and the associated costs that invariably result. These latter reasons underscore why we cannot afford anything but the most dogged perseverance of interdependence as our frontline defense against resource limitations and growing threats.

Advocacy for interdependence among our services would seem non-controversial—particularly in light of the obvious advantages. However, it has been next to impossible to get services to relinquish mission-area real estate, or discipline themselves from encroachment, even when those areas are a function of another service. What creates this situation is the drive by some services to attain self-sufficiency—the antithesis of jointness, but the desire of many unit commanders. Accordingly, one of our biggest priorities going forward must be to wrestle the intricacies of jointness to the ground, and to mandate service adherence to clearly defined and delineated capability sets.

The days of sustained real defense budget growth facilitating equitable service budget shares are long gone. DoD and national leadership—including Congress—must understand the exigencies of fully committing to the tenets of joint force operations—and their leadership in enforcing those tenets will be necessary. To be sure, we have made solid strides toward jointness since the days of the failed Iranian hostage rescue attempt—owing in large measure to the 1986 Goldwater-Nichols Act—yet some of the most critical ground remains to be covered. What we have not done is to internalize the requirement to elevate the interests of *jointness*. The services must become willing to cede market share where required. We can alleviate costly overlaps and excessive redundancies once the services are given, and adhere to, clear and distinct lanes in the road, and once the leadership takes an active role in enforcing the traffic rules. That is the price of admission if we are serious about optimizing our force structure for the future.

Invest for Mission Flexibility

Flexibility of forces offers another means of preparing for a wide range of missions despite budgetary constraints that preclude large force buildups. Mission flexibility is a function of how we size our services, balance our forces, and select our equipment. It also derives from creatively teaming multidomain forces and capabilities together to achieve powerful effects while minimizing the number of forces employed. An example of such a strategy-to-forces arrangement was used with success in Operation Enduring Freedom. Relatively small, tailored special operations forces; conventional ground-based forces; and airborne strike and intelligence, surveillance, and reconnaissance (ISR) forces defeated disproportionately large numbers of adversary forces.

Likewise, employing our forces to train and assist indigenous forces in defending their own countries would be another prudent and highly effective use of our resources. This approach makes optimal use of local language and culture familiarity that will always be a challenge to U.S. forces. Devising such combinations of highly capable forces, specifically tailored to dominate the circumstances they will be operating in, should be a mainstay of our strategy and employment repertoire. The more versatility we can build into our force structure, the greater will be the range of operations in which our military can be effectively employed.

Selecting and arraying our forces for flexibility of response is our best means of girding against the twin evils of complex adversaries and reduced resources to counter them. Add to that what will undoubtedly continue to be a sizable role for our military in the provision of disaster relief and humanitarian aid around the world, and the rationale for ensuring our forces will be capable of carrying out full-spectrum operations is clear. Lacking the virtually infinite resource base required to arm up for *every* possible contingency, posturing for flexibility will provide our best means, and best odds, for successfully meeting the demands of "big world, not so big budget."

Assure Access

In order to counter the increasingly advanced antiaccess strategies our adversaries are likely to employ we should be actively pursuing and investing in options that negate these strategies. It is perhaps in this regard that air, space, and cyber forces yield some of their greatest benefits and strengths. They allow us to deliver a wide variety of kinetic and nonkinetic effects in forward areas around the world, doing so largely from locations that are well outside adversary reach.

Forces of the future must be able to operate on short notice from austere locations over long distances. Additionally, once our forces are within engagement range, the tactical, antiaccess threats posed by the proliferation of modern technology will have to be dealt with to create a permissive environment for friendly force operations. Continued investment in stealth, speed, standoff, and other technologies for aerospace vehicles—manned and/or unmanned—and increased numbers and coverage of space-based systems are required if we are to remain out in front of the antiaccess systems our adversaries are seeking to field.

Balance Sensors and Shooters

Similar in fashion to denying U.S. forces access are adversary efforts to deny us the opportunity to use our forces. Adversaries have worked to thwart our asymmetric advantages with asymmetries of their own. They target civilians, hide in population centers, don't wear uniforms, etc. They have assiduously worked to deny us the ability to "find" and "fix" them, fully aware that there can be no "finish" piece of that equation until the first two have been satisfied. To counter these efforts we must acknowledge that our ISR capabilities will be required as a heavy lifter in our future strategy and must be integrated into all elements of our forces. Today, and in the future, the time and resource expenditure required to *find* our enemies eclipses anything required to *deal* with them.

ISR capabilities have labored under the mantle of "low density, high demand" for far too long now—and our reliance on ISR will only continue to grow. One of the main challenges in planning our future force structure is to consider the balance in investment between sensors and shooters. Our problem is no longer how to engage a set of targets to achieve a particular set of effects but rather to determine where the appropriate targets are, and what kind of actions are required to achieve the desired effects. That may mean an increase in the investment share allotted to ISR systems and architectures is required. The percentages of investment that we allocate between *"Find-Fix"* and *"Finish"* must be brought closer to the proportions in which these mission types require resources. We clearly need to increase our emphasis on the ISR capabilities that are increasingly relied upon by all of our joint forces.

A complementary approach is to examine the sensor-to-shooter balance, not in terms of dollars, but in terms of concepts of operation. Today's technology may allow us to accomplish this rebalance in a fashion that does not reduce our force application capacity or necessarily require dramatic budget shifts. If we are smart about the design of future systems we can increase our ISR capability while retaining a robust shooter force. The potential exists to do that by ensuring every platform is designed as an integral element of a distributed sensor architecture. Consider the F-22 as an example. It is not only a *fighter*—it possesses the capability to act as an F-, A-, B-, EA-, RC-, and E-22. Both it and the F-35 are flying sensors that will allow us to conduct sensor operations inside adversary battle space any time we want, in addition to using their vast array of attack capabilities; *and* the fact that they are *not* opposed by like aircraft means we can make use of those robust sensor capabilities all the more.

The inherent challenge then is to effect a change in acquisition and operations perspectives that have historically viewed "fighters" and "bombers" as force application assets, to ones that view—and design and build—aircraft as sensors that feed an architecture designed to enhance our knowledge of the battle space. We are in the nascent stages of moving in this direction. Almost *every* force application aircraft flying in Southwest Asia today has a targeting pod on it that is used more for acquiring information (ISR) than for specific weapon employment. Such capabilities have become known as *"non-traditional* ISR." By taking advantage of capabilities such as these that are inherent on platforms we already have, we can increase our sensor capacity before a single investment dollar changes between program elements. Now we need to build the concepts of operation that will take us from viewing such capacity as *non-traditional* ISR to conceiving of, and employing it, as *routine* ISR.

Structuring the Air Force for the Future

Two *enduring* elements of our National Security Strategy—regardless of administration—are that America will engage forward in peacetime, and fight forward in wartime. Accordingly, to execute our National Security Strategy the Air Force requires sufficient force structure to maintain a rotational base that is sustainable to accomplish these elements. The mechanism for doing that is the Air and Space Expeditionary Force—or AEF—construct. AEFs provide joint force commanders with ready and complete air and space forces to execute their plans.

Ten AEFs provide the *framework* to achieve sufficient expeditionary aerospace forces to sustain rotational base requirements to meet our defense strategy requirements at a sustainable personnel tempo. The *key* to Air Force expeditionary force structure is to ensure those ten AEFs are each structured, equipped, and equal in capability and capacity for each of the Air Force's mission areas: Aerospace Superiority, Global Attack, Rapid Global Mobility, Precision Engagement, Cyber Superiority, and Agile Combat Support. Aerospace capability does not stop with expeditionary assets. Space, ISR, cyber, national missile defense architecture, intertheater airlift, and others are the foundation upon which the AEF structure stands. What the Air Force will require in the future is sufficient force structure to maintain both an adequate rotational base of expeditionary capabilities, and its foundation.

Enemies and potential adversaries have not stood idly by as the Air Force has been growing older. The Air Force has become a geriatric force with bombers older than the pilots that fly them, fighters that are thirty years old, and tankers over forty-five years of age—and with the current program plans, the average age of AF aircraft (twenty-four years—much older than the average ages of Navy ships and Army vehicles) will continue to grow. The impact of this aging is becoming dramatic. "It was a looming crisis, and now, because of Iraq and Afghanistan, it's a looming disaster," notes Richard Aboulafia, an analyst with the Teal Group.[7] That was written before the entire Air Force F-15 fleet was grounded in early November 2007 due to an F-15 falling apart in midair from structural failure. Today, nearly eight hundred aircraft—14 percent of the Air Force fleet—are grounded or operating under restricted flying conditions.[8] As defense analyst Loren Thompson notes, "after 20 years of neglect by both political parties, a period of consequences has arrived for American air power. We either spend more [on recapitalization of the Air Force], or in the very near future we lose our most important war-fighting advantage. The Air Force that prevented any American soldier from being killed by enemy aircraft for half a century may not be up to the task in the years ahead due to lack of adequate investment."[9]

General Barry R. McCaffrey, U.S. Army, retired, calls the Air Force "badly under-funded[;]its manpower is being drastically cut and diverted to support of counter-insurgency operations, its modernization program of paradigm shifting technology is anemic—and its aging strike, lift, and tanker fleets are being ground down by non-stop global operations with an inadequate air fleet and maintenance capabilities."[10] His vision of the future includes creating "a US national security policy based principally on the deterrence capabilities of a dominant, global Air Force and Naval presence which can: near guarantee the defense of the continental United States; provide high levels of assurance for the security of our key allies from air, missile, space, cyber, or sea attack; and which can guarantee a devastating punitive air, sea, and cyber strike using conventional weapons capable of devastating the offensive power of a foreign state—and which can hold at risk their vital national leadership and economic targets."[11] It is imperative that the Air Force modernize and replace its aging air- and spacecraft to ensure America's freedom to maneuver, operate, and command and control expeditionary forces in the face of emerging, highly sophisticated threats.

A future defense strategy based on the trends identified earlier points to the following *capability* demands on the Air Force:

- Rapidly dominate (within days) adversary air defenses to allow freedom to maneuver, freedom to attack, and freedom from attack

- Render an adversary's cruise and ballistic missiles ineffective

- Rapidly reconstitute any loss to friendly space capability, and negate adversary space capability

- Create desired effects within hours of tasking, anywhere on the globe

- Provide deterrence against WMD attack and coercion by maintaining a credible nuclear, and flexible conventional, strike capability

- Create precise effects rapidly, with the ability to retarget quickly, against large, mobile, hidden, or underground target sets anywhere, anytime, in a persistent manner

- Assess, plan, and direct aerospace operations anywhere in near real time, tailored across the spectrum of operations and levels of command

- Provide continuous, tailored information within minutes of tasking with sufficient accuracy to engage any target in any battle space worldwide

- Ensure our use of the cyber domain unhindered by all attempts to deny, disrupt, destroy, or corrupt it; and ensure our ability to manipulate an adversary's information in pursuit of friendly objectives

- Provide the airlift, aerial refueling, and en route infrastructure capability to respond within hours of tasking

- Build an aerospace force that enables robust, distributed military operations with time-definite sustainment

- Build a professional cadre to lead and command expeditionary aerospace and joint forces

- Implement innovative concepts to ensure we recruit and retain the right people to operate our air, space, and cyber forces of the future

- Achieve an unrivaled degree of innovation founded on integration and testing of new concepts, innovations, technologies, and experimentation.

Finally, we will also need to address some difficult questions as we move into the future: How do we deal with the fragility of our space architecture? Do we need to seek legislation to unshackle the constraints that force us to operate outside an adversary observe-orient-detect-act (OODA) loop, and constrain our ability to lead in the invisible but ongoing cyber war? How do we move from a national security architecture designed in the aftermath of WWII to one more relevant for the twenty-first-century security environment? What needs to be done regarding our ability to counter "unrestricted warfare?"[12] Do we need to readdress the expectations of collateral damage? How should we deal effectively with an adversary when women and children are combatants? How can we deter suicide bombers? How do we ensure that air and space perspectives get heard in a DoD that does not have a single Air Force officer among the top ten-plus military positions on the U.S. military joint staff (CJCS, vice CJCS, director of staff, and J-1 through J-8)?

Conclusion

Just as combat tomorrow will look different than it did yesterday, so, too, should the military that we prosecute it with. We should take maximum advantage of the asymmetric capabilities we possess with our air, space, and cyber forces. A concerted focus on further developing and expanding these forces would serve us well, as they are uniquely positioned to underpin the kind of defense strategy and force structure appropriate to our future.

Capabilities employed through air, space, and cyberspace allow us to project precision effects over great distances, with an advantage in speed over any other domain, and without projecting the degree of vulnerability inherent with surface forces—they allow us to project power without projecting vulnerability—decreasing the requirement to put surface forces at risk. Adversaries have a limited opportunity to contest our presence when we are delivering effects from outside their reach, and often operating outside their awareness. That allows aerospace power to impose a degree of psychological advantage not available by any other force.

Additionally, the nature of our air, space, and cyber platforms is such that they can be directed, redirected, prepositioned, repositioned, and even recalled. They offer virtually limitless targeting possibilities, both in terms of the effects levied and the recipients they can be levied upon. Air, space, and cyber systems deliver the kind of flexibility in which we should be making substantial investment—both in terms of planning and in terms of system acquisition—as they provide options that will be key to our security future.

The capabilities resident in all four services must be retained, but that does not mean that all four services require an equal or simultaneous increase in their resources. We can, however, all simultaneously gain if our collective efforts result in the creation of an appropriate defense strategy for our nation that can then guide the appropriate corresponding resource investment.

Notes

1. In a recent publication entitled "A New Division of Labor: Meeting America's Security Challenges beyond Iraq," Andy Hoehn et al. suggest a number of changes in our DoD architecture based on the emerging security environment of the future. These recommendations "are aimed at generating greater breadth in needed capabilities while maintaining needed depth to contend with particular challenges." Their recommendations focus on "reallocating risk to produce needed capabilities," and deserve serious attention by Defense and national leadership as they establish an appropriate defense strategy blueprint for the kind of security future we are likely to encounter. Andrew R. Hoehn, Adam Grissom, David A. Ochmanek, David A. Shlapak, and Alan J. Vick, "A New Division of Labor: Meeting America's Security Challenges beyond Iraq" (Santa Monica, CA: RAND Corp, 2007).

2. For examples see ABC News/Washington Post, poll, 29 October–1 November 2007, http://www.pollingreport.com/iraq.htm (accessed 7 November 2007); Pew Research Center, poll, 9 May 2007, http://www.pewtrusts.org/news_room_ektid21014.aspx (accessed 7 November 2007); World Public Opinion, poll, 29 September 2005, http://www.worldpublicopinion.org/pipa/articles/brunitedstatescanadara/77.php?nid=&id=&pnt=77 (accessed 7 November 2007).

3. Even during the well-documented atrocities the Serbian military perpetrated against Albanians in the province of Kosovo in 1998, China and Russia opposed United States–led action being taken under the auspices of the UN; military action to halt the destruction had to be conducted under the NATO flag instead.

4. One need only consider current events in Iraq, and, to a lesser extent, Afghanistan.

5. Of note, U.S. deployments are not the only catalyst for such destabilizing effects; negative effects have been evident for years when "great powers" have sent forces into smaller, sovereign states.

6. ADM Michael Mullen, from remarks on 25 October 2007 as quoted in AFP report "US Military Chief Sees Expanding Missions, Big Military Budgets," Google.

7. Dave Montgomery, "An Aging Fleet Has Air Force Worried," *Seattle Times*, 4 March 2007.

8. A4MY data from USAF Inventory Groundings & Restrictions (GARR), current as of 13 November 2007. POC Mr. Guy Fowl, (703) 697-9232.

9. Loren Thompson, "The Slow Death of American Airpower," Lexington Institute Issue Brief, 16 January 2007.

10. Barry R. McCaffrey, General USA (Ret), memorandum for U.S. Military Academy, 15 October 2007.

11. Ibid.

12. *Unrestricted Warfare* is a book on military strategy written in 1999 by two Air Force colonels in China's People's Liberation Army. Its primary concern is how a nation such as China can defeat a technologically superior opponent (like the United States) through means other than direct military confrontation. These other means include using international law and a variety of economic and unconventional measures to place one's opponent in a bad position and circumvent the need for direct military action.

Implications of the Changing Use of Orbital Space for Future Air and Space Forces

Barry D. Watts
Senior Analyst at Center for Strategic and Budgetary Assessments

This paper explores what ongoing changes in the use of space since the 1980s may imply for America's air and space forces over the next couple decades. The central argument is that the military and civilian exploitation of satellites has undergone enormous transformation since 1985 with far-reaching implications for future American air and space forces. On the one hand, the U.S. military's dependence on near-earth space for ongoing combat operations has grown by leaps and bounds since the mid-1980s. This dependence includes satellite-based intelligence, surveillance, and reconnaissance (ISR); global communications and networking for a range of command-and-control functions; and precision navigation and timing for everything from targeting and weapons guidance to Blue-force tracking. On the other hand, precious little has been done to preclude this dependence from becoming a major strategic vulnerability that adversaries will exploit in future conflicts.

Because the bulk of the changes in the use of space have occurred gradually and outside of the immediate awareness of most people in the United States—even within the military—their extent and gravity have not yet been sufficiently appreciated in terms of the enforceable implementation of U.S. national strategy: declaring freedom of action in space to be as important to the United States as air and sea power is not tantamount to being able to achieve the desired freedom of action in the face of hostile efforts to deny it.[1] Among other reasons, this potential vulnerability has not escaped the attention of prospective adversaries. Ashley Tellis has articulated the problem as well as anyone. As he wrote in May 2007 *after* the People's Republic of China (PRC) had demonstrated a direct-ascent antisatellite (ASAT) capability in January:

> Chinese analyses of U.S. military operations in the Persian Gulf, Kosovo, and Afghanistan have yielded one crucial insight. The advanced military might of the United States depends inordinately on a complex, exposed network of command, control, communications, and computer-based systems that provide intelligence, surveillance, and reconnaissance; and these systems operate synergistically in and through the medium of space. These space-based capabilities enable American forces to detect and identify different kinds of targets, exchange vast and diverse militarily relevant information and data streams, and contribute to the success of combat operations by providing everything from meteorological assessment to navigation and guidance to different platforms and weapon systems to early warning and situational awareness. Yet the very key to America's unrivaled military strength is also its greatest vulnerability. Accordingly, Chinese strategists quickly concluded that any effort to defeat the formidable military power fielded by the United States should aim not at its capacity to deliver overwhelming conventional

firepower from long distances but at its Achilles heel: its space-based capabilities and their related ground installations.[2]

If Tellis is right, then considerably more than declaratory policy will be needed in the long run to ensure that the U.S. military will continue to enjoy the unfettered use of space that has become so vital to the American way of war.

The Use of Space: 1985 versus Today

For purposes of documenting just how much the military and commercial use of near-earth space has changed since the cold war's final decade, 1985 has been chosen, albeit somewhat arbitrarily, as a useful year for comparison with 2006.[3] Various metrics have been selected as comparative benchmarks. They include such things as space launches, government spending on and commercial revenues from space, the use of navigation satellites, and the accessibility of high-resolution imagery.

From the successful orbiting of the first artificial satellite (Sputnik or Спутник) by the Soviet Union in 1957 through at least the early 1980s, access to space was a major barrier to entry for the majority of nation-states and, hence, offers a crude measure of whether a given country is a first-tier competitor in the use of space. Launching a satellite using essentially German rocket technology from the 1940s was—and remains—a risky, expensive proposition. In 1985, access to space was still dominated by the two cold war superpowers. Of the 122 space launches that year, 98 were Soviet and 17 American; of the other 7, the European Space Agency (ESA)[4] accounted for 4 launches, Japan 2, and the PRC 1.[5] The year 1985 also witnessed nine orbital missions by U.S. space shuttles, a peak that has not quite been equaled in any subsequent year.[6] By comparison, during 2006 there were only 66 launches worldwide: 25 Russian, 23 American, 6 Japanese, 6 Chinese, 5 European, and 1 Indian.[7] Moreover, of the 25 Russian launches, 11 were missions on which the Russian Federation provided commercial launch services to orbit the satellites of other nations, and 5 other Russian launches went to the International Space Station. Thus, whereas the Soviet Union and the United States accounted for the preponderance of worldwide satellite launches in 1985 (80 and 14 percent, respectively), their former duopoly on access to orbital space has long since been eroded by the entry of other major competitors.

This observation is especially striking with respect to the launching of military satellites. In 1985 the Soviet Union conducted sixty-four military launches as compared with only seven in 2006. Granted, the severe contraction of the Soviet space program in the early 1990s was largely the result of a steep decline in funding due to the collapse of the Soviet economy. Still, by 1999 questions were being raised in the United States as to whether the Russian Federation still had operational satellites capable of providing warning of ballistic-missile launches from the continental United States or the Pacific and Atlantic oceans.[8] In terms of launches, therefore, the Soviet/Russian military presence in orbital space has undergone a substantial contraction since 1985 relative to other nations.

The change with regard to the aggregate of spending on space by governments plus commercial revenues from satellites and related services is even more striking. In 1985, the Futron Corporation has estimated that governments invested some $32 billion (in current dollars) in space worldwide, while commercial revenues were a mere $3 billion (less than 9 percent of the total).[9] For 2006, the Space Foundation put worldwide government spending on space at over $74 billion and worldwide commercial revenues at $145 billion (66 percent of total government and commercial space activity).[10] Granted, U.S. government spending on space in 2006 made up more than 80 percent of government space budgets worldwide.[11] However, government investment in orbital space no longer dominates what is in orbit and what satellites do, and that is a startling change from 1985. Consider, as one case in point, the University of Surrey's space center: located in the United Kingdom rather than either the United States or Russia, it has emerged as the undisputed world leader in "microsatellites" and "nanosatellites" since its founding in 1981.[12]

An equally dramatic change in the use of space since the mid-1980s has been the shift from geosynchronous (GEO) communications satellites (comsats) for long-haul communications to greater reliance on terrestrial fiber-optic cables. In the early 1980s, INTELSAT's GEO satellites alone carried upwards of 70 percent of worldwide overseas telephone traffic.[13] By 2000, satellite transponders were carrying only about 25 percent of voice traffic between countries along with essentially all of the television traffic.[14] This sharp change in the use of comsats for long-haul communications was precipitated by the rapid laying of high-capacity fiber-optic cables between continents. The first transatlantic fiber-optic cable was laid between the United States and Europe in 1988. By 2001–2002, the capacity in gigabits per second of existing fiber-optic cable exceeded that of comsats by at least a factor of fifty.[15] True, even today only a small fraction of the upgradable capacity of installed fiber-optic cables is being used (or "lit"). Nevertheless, it is clear that the era of GEO comsats' exclusive domination of long-haul communications is over.

A further consequence of this development is that it is no longer sensible to separate comsats from fiber-optic cables in terms of market share. INTELSAT, for example, has integrated its some fifty deployed comsats with terrestrial fiber-optic cables, telco-grade bandwidth switches, and Juniper routers. The resulting GXS Telecom network can rapidly reroute traffic whenever an individual satellite fails. Moreover, by 2006 roughly 90 percent of the international bandwidth in use was devoted to Internet traffic rather than voice communications or other networks.[16] Thus, long-haul communications have undergone remarkable transformation in capacity, use, and robustness over just the last decade. In the mid-1980s the operators of comsats sold transponders; today, with the rise of fiber-optic cables, they sell bandwidth—complete communications and data systems.[17]

Another area that has changed radically since 1985 is access to high-resolution satellite imagery. After twelve failures, in August 1960 the first American photo-reconnaissance satellite returned a film capsule containing images of facilities in the Soviet Union taken from space. Resolution from the first successful KH-1 Corona mission was 35–40 feet.[18] The Soviets returned pictures from orbit on the third Zenit-2 mission in 1962, almost two years after Corona's initial success.[19] Resolution of the early Zenit-2 images is believed to be similar to that of the KH-1's: around 32–50 feet. These events ushered in an era, which lasted almost to the end of the twentieth century, in which the U.S. and Soviet governments enjoyed exclusive use of the highest-resolution images available from orbit.

This era underwent at least one significant technological transition. Starting in December 1976, the United States orbited the first KH-11 spy satellite. This satellite has been widely reported as being able to achieve, under ideal conditions, a theoretical ground resolution of 6 inches; it also replaced prior film-return satellites with electro-optical, digital technology operating in both the visible and infrared bands, thereby permitting high-resolution imagery to be transmitted back to the United States through a satellite-relay network in near real time.[20] Due to difficulties with digital electronics, the Soviets probably did not achieve a comparable capability until the first Yantar-4KS1 (Cosmos 1426) went into orbit in December 1982. However, even by 1985 the only commercial earth-imaging satellites whose images were widely available were those of the LANDSAT-1, with a resolution of some 80 meters (262 feet), and the Soviet Resurs-0, a Russian version of LANDSAT. Not until early 1986 did the first French SPOT satellite begin transmitting images back to earth. SPOT-1 and SPOT-2 offered 10-meter (33-foot) resolution in the panchromatic mode and 20-meter resolution in their multispectral mode. However, even 10-meter-resolution imagery is of limited value in identifying aircraft, armored vehicles, mobile missile launchers, or even many surface ships.[21] Only when the U.S. government decided, in the 1990s, to encourage the development of commercial imaging satellites capable of 1-meter resolution or less did the American and Russian duopoly on high-resolution imagery begin to unravel.

This unraveling can be dated from the successful orbiting of Space Imaging's Ikonos-2 satellite in September 1999. (Reiterating the risks of launch using 1940s German rocket technology, Ikonos-1 ended up in the southern Pacific when the satellite's shroud failed to separate.) By late 1999, Space Imaging was offering 1-meter-resolution black-and-white imagery as a commercial commodity. Two more U.S. companies, DigitalGlobe and ORBIMAGE, soon followed. Today, the French SPOT-5 offers 2.5-meter resolution, Taiwan's FormoSat-2 2-meter resolution, DigitalGlobe's Quickbird 0.62-meter (2-foot) resolution, and Korea's KompSat-2 will provide another source of global 1-meter imagery.[22] Further, commercial resolutions are likely to continue improving. ORBIMAGE has recently petitioned the National Oceanic and Atmospheric Administration "to let the satellite companies sell the currently restricted 0.25-meter data to the civil market to provide a more level playing field with airborne sensors."[23] Thus, high-resolution electro-optical and infrared imagery is rapidly becoming a public commodity.

How soon high-resolution radar imagery may follow suit remains to be seen. Currently the United States' National Reconnaissance Office (NRO) is reported to have four Lacrosse satellites capable of providing all-weather synthetic-aperture-radar (SAR) imagery with resolutions of 2–3 feet (in addition to four optical-imaging KH-11 variants).[24] The European Union countries are considering a 1-meter-resolution radar-imaging satellite for their defense needs. In addition, the TerraSAR-X satellite, launched by the Russians but operated by the German DRL company, has been returning 1-meter-resolution SAR images since July 2007.[25]

Another far-reaching change in the use of space since 1985 has been the emergence of the U.S. Global Positioning System (GPS) as a global source of accurate geo-spatial information for both military and civilian users. The space and ground segments of GPS, which are operated by the U.S. Air Force (USAF), were originally developed to provide position location, navigation, and timing information to military users—initially for en route navigation, but later increasingly for weapons guidance.[26] In 1985, GPS was still in development. Eleven Block I Navstar satellites had been launched, but the first Block II was not orbited until 1989, and the Air Force did not declare initial operational capability (IOC) until 1993. Nevertheless, by the time Operation Desert Storm began on 17 January 1991, eleven Block II and five Block I satellites were available, their orbits optimized to maximize the hours per day U.S. forces in the Persian Gulf would have four satellites in view (the minimum number for three-dimensional positioning).[27] While the use of GPS for weapons guidance during this conflict was limited to the thirty-five AGM-86C Conventional Air-Launched Cruise Missiles (CALCMs) launched by B-52s on the opening night of the war, almost 4,500 commercial GPS receivers were sent to the Persian Gulf to supplement the roughly 840 military handheld sets.[28] These receivers enabled American ground units to grid maps with accurate latitude and longitude markings, navigate across trackless desert terrain without getting lost, pinpoint key Iraqi positions, and reduce fratricide by keeping clear of each other's fields of fire. Besides its use in guiding the thirty-five CALCMs to their targets, Air Force strike aircraft used GPS to navigate to their targets through adverse weather, while the Navy exploited it to clear mines in the Persian Gulf and provide more precise launch coordinates for their Tomahawk Land Attack Missiles (TLAMs). Suffice it to say that the 1991 Persian Gulf War was a watershed for the U.S. military insofar as widespread recognition of the immense value of the Global Positioning System was concerned. In fact, Desert Storm was billed as the first "space war."

Since 1991, the dependence of the American military services on GPS has grown exponentially. Perhaps the most striking area of change has been in the increasing exploitation of GPS for precision munitions, which have become increasingly central to the American way of war in the early twenty-first century. Excluding air-to-air missiles and 30 mm rounds fired by A-10s, U.S. forces expended nearly 231,000 guided and unguided munitions in air-to-surface and surface-to-surface strikes during Desert Storm; only about 7.5 percent of these 231,000 munitions were precision guided.[29] Of the more than 17,160 guided munitions expended during the campaign, the 9,283 laser-guided bombs (LGBs)—some 97 percent of which were dropped by forty-two F-117s, sixty-four F-111Fs, and the dozen or so F-15Es equipped with LANTIRN (Low-Altitude Navigation and Targeting Infrared for Night) systems—proved, by far, to be the most effective overall.[30]

Despite the spectacular success achieved with LGBs in Desert Storm, most in the U.S. Air Force did not immediately foresee that later air campaigns would be increasingly dominated by guided munitions. Yet that is precisely what happened over time, primarily because the mounting use of relatively inexpensive guided munitions such as LGBs and, later, Joint Direct Attack Munitions

(JDAMs) obviated the need to expend a couple hundred thousand unguided or "dumb" munitions that mostly missed their targets, as had happened in 1991. In 1999, during the North Atlantic Treaty Organization's (NATO's) campaign against Serbia (Operation Allied Force), guided munitions constituted 29 percent of air-campaign expenditures; during Operation Enduring Freedom against the Taliban and al Qaeda in Afghanistan, the guided share grew to almost 52 percent; and, during Operation Iraqi Freedom in March–April 2003, guided munitions were over 64 percent of expenditures (17,887 of 27,834).[31]

The significance of GPS in this trend toward mostly guided strike operations is that munitions such as JDAMs overcame the clear-air limitation of LGBs. As a result, during Operation Enduring Freedom in 2001–2002, JDAM expenditures exceeded the number of LGBs employed (figure 1). Starting in the Vietnam War, during which the U.S. Air Force expended over 28,000 LGBs with consistently good results, laser-guided bombs have been highly effective munitions. But they cannot be employed through clouds, smoke, fog, sandstorms, or other atmospheric obscurations. Because JDAM uses inertial guidance to home in on coordinates in GPS space, it obviated the clear-air restrictions of LGBs. In the words of the Third Infantry Division's after-action report following the major-operations phase of Operation Iraqi Freedom:

> Precision-guided munitions proved to be a lethal combat multiplier. Joint direct attack munitions . . . repeatedly proved . . . [their] value as an all weather weapon. JDAM was the weapon of choice for troops in contact and to destroy structures in an urban environment.[32]

Figure 1
U.S. Guided-Munitions Trends, 1991–2003

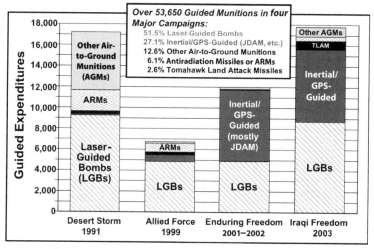

Information from orbital systems has become increasingly central to the American way of conventional warfare. Both for finding and fixing targets, as well as for striking them accurately, reconnaissance satellites and the GPS constellation are fundamental to the conventional predominance of the American military in the post–cold war era. This dramatic change in the exploitation of space by the U.S. military has occurred, however, during a period in which the global use of orbital systems has undergone a revolutionary transformation, as the comparison of 1985 with 2006 documents. The former U.S.-Soviet duopoly on national technical means (NTM) has unquestionably fallen by the wayside as high-resolution imagery evolves toward becoming a public utility, and GPS is, arguably, already part of what might be termed the "global commons." The development of differential GPS by companies like Garmin has enabled nonmilitary users to achieve location accuracies of 3–5 meters, well below the nominal 15 meters intended for civil users.[33] Thus, neither the military nor civilian use of orbital space today bears much resemblance to its use in 1985.

Growing Dependence, Growing Vulnerability

From the U.S. military's standpoint, however, the most important aspect of this transformation has not yet been mentioned: the changed role of satellite systems during ongoing American military operations. Throughout the cold war, national technical means were primarily viewed as a peacetime intelligence asset. The downing in 1960 of Francis Gary Powers' U-2 by SA-2 surface-to-air missiles (SAMs) showed that photoreconnaissance overflights of the Soviet Union with manned aircraft would have to be abandoned. The NRO's spy satellites, therefore, became the primary means of tracking the evolution of Soviet intercontinental nuclear forces over time.[34] They proved well suited to this task given the sizes of Soviet long-range bombers and their bases, launch pads and silos for intercontinental ballistic missiles (ICBMs), and ballistic-missile submarines (see figure 2). But from the outset in 1960 to the cold war's end, U.S. war planners generally assumed that use of the NRO's low-earth-orbit reconnaissance satellites would not survive the opening moments of any major nuclear exchange between the United States and the Soviet Union.[35] Despite efforts of the U.S. Army and Congress in the 1970s to make NTM imagery available to theater commanders during conventional operations, the cold war assumption was that reconnaissance satellites in particular were primarily a peacetime intelligence-collection activity.

This cold war assumption about the NRO's imaging reconnaissance satellites has long since been overtaken by the war-fighting needs of theater commanders.[36] Today, reconnaissance satellites and unmanned aerial vehicles (UAVs) such as Global Hawk have become integral, key components of virtually all ongoing U.S. conventional military operations. The main uses of these sensor assets are, first, to find and fix targets of all sorts and, second, to conduct battle-damage assessment after the targets have been struck by shooters.

To be stressed is that, currently at least, an air-breathing ISR platform such as Global Hawk cannot function effectively in the complete absence of certain orbital systems. To begin with, both command and control of the platform and real-time transmission of its sensor data to command echelons orchestrating strike operations require comsats capable of handling fairly high data rates. In addition, GPS is required for the sensor data to be usable: only if the UAV knows precisely where it is in GPS space can any targets it detects also be readily located precisely. So while a UAV like Global Hawk can provide staring surveillance over an area that any single reconnaissance satellite cannot, it is as dependent on the use of space as the NRO's "overhead" systems. Also worth noting is that while the Pentagon operates some protected military comsats, around 80 percent of the long-haul bandwidth utilized by American forces during Operation Iraqi Freedom was provided by commercial satellites.[37]

Figure 2
KH-4A Imagery of Dolan Airbase, 20 August 1966[38]

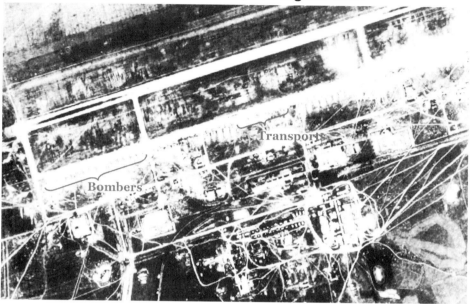

For 24-7 precision attack of individual aimpoints regardless of weather or other atmospheric obscurations, the shooters, too, are increasingly dependent on the GPS constellation for navigation to the target and munitions guidance. As more and more GPS-aided munitions enter the U.S. inventory, this dependency cannot help but grow. Starting in August 2005, the U.S. Army began employing the XM30 Guided Multiple Launch Rocket System (GMLRS) in Iraq. GMLRS is a guided rocket that provides an all-weather precision-attack capability to ranges of more than 70 kilometers with a circular error probable (CEP) of less than 10 meters.[39] The GPS-aided Excalibur artillery shell, first used in Iraq in 2007, provides a similar accuracy to shorter ranges for 155-millimeter artillery.[40] By comparison, the design CEP of the JDAM during development was 13 meters (43 feet) or less. However, during the initial testing of some 450 munitions, JDAM achieved a 9.6-meter CEP.[41] Subsequently, it proved even more accurate when first employed from the B-2 against Serbian targets in 1999. By exploiting the bomber's onboard SAR radar to eliminate most of the target location error, the B-2's GPS-Aided Targeting System (GATS) achieved CEPs "closer to four meters on average" with JDAM.[42] Since declaring IOC in 2006, the Air Force has had similar success with its 250-pound-class, coordinate-seeking Small Diameter Bomb (SDB), whose small size reduces collateral damage and allows a single platform to carry more munitions on a given sortie. So far the SDB has demonstrated CEPs around 1.2 meters, which makes the munition attractive even in urban environments provided airspace-control requirements can be met.[43]

Inertially guided/GPS-aided munitions such as JDAM, GMLRS, Excalibur, and SDB require two things in order to achieve their best accuracies. First mensurated GPS coordinates of the target or aimpoint must be developed and fed to the munition. Second, once fired or released, the munition needs to acquire signals from the GPS satellite constellation. Smart adversaries have already demonstrated awareness of both requirements.

The simplest way to counter inertially guided/GPS-aided munitions is to deny U.S. forces target coordinates. In 1991, Iraq's mobile Scud launchers spent most of their time hidden. By and large, the launchers only emerged from their "hides" at night, traveled quickly to presurveyed launch locations, fired their extended-range ballistic missiles (extended-range versions of the Soviet Scud), and then began moving away from the launch location within minutes. Even when U.S. aircrews were able to observe visually nearby launches, the sensor limitations of the best available strike aircraft at the time, the F-15E, precluded crews from acquiring the fleeing launcher with onboard systems. The upshot was that, contrary to wartime aircrew claims of having destroyed as many as 100 Iraqi mobile-missile launchers, Gulf War Air Power researchers were unable to find solid evidence that even one had definitely been destroyed by a fixed-wing aircraft.[44]

The Serbs used similar tactics with considerable success during Operation Allied Force in 1999. In the case of their mobile SAMs, for example, they discovered that periodically displacing the launchers just a few hundred yards sufficed to render them relatively survivable due to the long sensor-to-shooter timelines—hours to a day or more—that NATO required due to a combination of technical limitations and the delays caused by coordination among the participating nations. These tactics did not always work as the campaign progressed. Beyond flex targeting intended to shorten sensor-to-shooter timelines by passing targets to B-2s as they neared Serbia, B-2 crews also began utilizing the bomber's radar in the immediate target area to detect any displacement of targets such as Serbian SA-3 SAMs and early-warning radars.[45] When the crews did so, they effectively reduced the sensor-to-shooter time to a few minutes—far too brief an interval for the Serbs to be able to relocate.

These two examples underscore an important point. While all-weather accuracy is a problem the U.S. military has solved for *fixed targets*, mobile or moving targets that can limit their exposures to targeting sensors or change their locations inside the attacker's sensor-to-shooter cycle time remain a challenge. Moreover, the burden of dealing with emergent, mobile, moving, time-sensitive, or fleeting targets tends to fall on the ISR portion of the U.S. military's precision-engagement capabilities. This is why a time-sensitive-targeting cell emerged in the U.S. Combined Operations Center in Saudi Arabia during Operation Enduring Freedom, and why such cells have grown increasingly important ever since. They strive to address the simplest and most obvious adversary countermeasures to the U.S. military's formidable precision-strike capabilities.

Yet, precisely because the task of dealing with emergent/time-sensitive targets falls disproportionately on ISR capabilities, this class of adversary responses further increases U.S. dependence on space. Today U.S. forces can put ordnance on just about any target they can find and fix. True, LGBs and

JDAMs were not the first guided munitions to provide a capability to hit fixed targets day or night, regardless of weather, with precision or near-precision accuracy.[46] But in contrast to comparatively expensive missiles such as CALCM, TLAM, and the Army Tactical Missile System (ATACMS), LGBs and JDAMs proved to be cheap enough to procure and expend in tens of thousands (as opposed to hundreds). Still, the very success of relatively affordable guided munitions such as LGBs and JDAMs—and, more recently, GMLRS—gives opponents powerful incentives to do everything they can to undermine the ability of U.S. sensor networks to find and fix them.

A more recent and technological approach to reducing the accuracy of inertially guided/GPS-aided munitions has been to deploy jammers in the immediate vicinity of the target to try to interfere with the ability of either the strike platform or the munition itself to receive the GPS signals needed for maximum accuracy. Prior to Operation Iraqi Freedom, the Russians provided the Iraqis with a small number of GPS jammers. Coalition forces quickly began destroying these jammers.[47] Additionally, U.S. aircrews also discovered that, even when the munition was denied GPS signals after release, the CEP only increased somewhat, which is to say that, unlike LGBs without laser illumination of the aimpoint, JDAMs "degrade gracefully." In large part, this graceful degradation stems from the increasing accuracy of microelectronic inertial-guidance systems.

Last but not least, another enemy option for negating the growing U.S. stable of inertially guided/GPS-aided munitions would be to attack the satellites themselves. GPS satellites, however, do not use low-earth orbits. Instead, they orbit some 20,200 kilometers (12,600 miles) above the earth's surface. Consequently, trying to take out even a portion of the GPS constellation with direct-ascent ASATs would be a considerable chore. Moreover, the simplest and cheapest way of augmenting the loss of a portion of the constellation would be to install pseudo-GPS satellites at a few locations on the ground around the theater, an idea that retired Air Force general Mike Carns has been advocating unsuccessfully since at least 2000.

Unquestionably, American dependence on orbital systems is both complex and growing. As the Chinese ASAT test in January 2007 demonstrated, space is no longer the sanctuary it once was. Indeed, the Chinese appear to be working diligently to develop a wide range of techniques to turn this growing American dependence into an exploitable vulnerability. And, even in the case of lesser adversaries, tactics of the sort employed by Iraq in 1991 or the Serbs in 1999 can provide a significant challenge to the preferred American way of war. The U.S. dependence on orbital space, therefore, no longer appears to be a tactical issue but a strategic one. How the United States copes with this potential vulnerability in coming decades may very well be critical to the country's ability to sustain the large margins of advantage in major, conventional combat operations that the American military enjoyed at the cold war's end.

The Challenges of the Future Security Environment

Before offering any thoughts regarding the possible implications that growing U.S. dependence on orbital space may have for America's air and space forces, certain aspects of the likely future security environment and foreseeable constraints warrant mention. To start with the early twenty-first-century security environment, there appear to be three major challenges that will occupy American strategists and the Department of Defense in coming decades:

1. The possibility of an increasingly disordered and violent world in which small groups of religiously inspired extremists succeed in mounting ever more destructive attacks against civilians and various soft infrastructure targets in the American homeland and other Western nations, as well as against U.S. forces and diplomats overseas;

2. The possibility of an increasingly proliferated world in which the number of states and transnational groups with access to nuclear, biological, and other advanced weaponry grows; and

3. The rise of an increasingly rich and militarily capable China, which, with growing demands for energy and other resources, may embolden PRC leaders to embrace more assertive behavior in East Asia and the western Pacific.

The first of these challenges is already upon us and our allies, first in Afghanistan and subsequently, as a matter of choice, in Iraq. Here the retired British general Rupert Smith has gone so far as to argue that the era of interstate industrial-age warfare—in which strategic goals can be secured (at least for the victors) by the outcome of a single massive contest of arms—is over.[48] Instead, adversaries have sought to confront Western nations with wars "amongst the people" in which the most military force can achieve is to establish "conditions in which an outcome may be decided."[49] As a result, we find ourselves fighting "amongst the people" rather than on the battlefield, our conflicts seem to go on interminably, preserving the force takes priority over risking all to achieve a decisive victory, the sides involve nonstate groups, and the strategic objective is to capture the will of the people and their leaders rather than to prevail in open battle.[50]

There is a point that is often overlooked in considering the kinds of conflicts the United States has been engaged in since al Qaeda's September 11, 2001, suicide attacks on the World Trade Center and the Pentagon. It is that Western military superiority has left our enemies and prospective opponents with few choices. They cannot hope to hold their own in open battle against Western forces and advanced weaponry—particularly those of the United States. Terrorism and insurgency, therefore, are one of the few avenues of attack open to nonstate groups or even to smaller nations against Western secularism and domination. Moreover, this line of attack has been greatly aided by technological progress (figure 3). As Martin Shubik emphasized in the late 1990s, the amount of death and destruction a small group can achieve in a single attack has increased exponentially since the 1950s.[51] Cell phones and the Internet facilitate the ability of disaffected groups to plan and coordinate terrorist attacks; they are far harder to find than the traditional military forces; and it is simply impossible, resources being finite, to render every soft civilian or infrastructure target nearly impervious to attack, especially in open societies.

The other line of attack open to small groups or even nations inclined to threaten Western societies is to acquire weapons of mass destruction. Iran, for example, has now witnessed at least three demonstrations—two in adjacent

Iraq and one in Afghanistan—of the formidable military capabilities of the United States. In 2003 these capabilities were used to overthrow Saddam Hussein's regime in some three weeks. However much as the leaders of the United States and Israel may desire to prevent Iran's rulers from acquiring nuclear weapons, the mullahs have strong incentives to do so. Of course, the revelation from the U.S. intelligence community in December 2007 that Iran shut down its nuclear weapons program in 2003 suggests that Iran may be more susceptible to outside influence than some in the West had thought. So, even if Iran does eventually acquire a few nuclear weapons, it may still be possible to deter the Iranians from any direct, attributable violation of the post-Nagasaki taboo against nuclear use insofar as the ruling mullahs view preservation of their Shiite theocracy as a religious duty.[52] On the other hand, John Bolton is probably right in arguing that the distinction between Iran's "military" and "civilian" nuclear programs is artificial and, in any case, it is the civilian program that still poses the main risk of a nuclear "breakout."[53]

Figure 3
Martin Shubik's Notional Depiction of the Growing Lethality of Small Groups

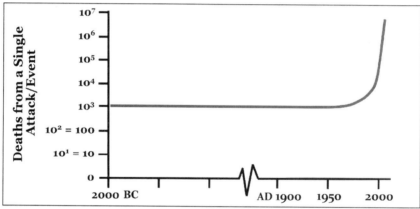

Moreover, these conjectures regarding Iranian intentions do not preclude terrorist organizations such as al Qaeda or Hezbollah acquiring a nuclear device or two from one source or another. Besides Iran, North Korea, Pakistan, and Russia are other possible sources of a "loose nuke" or two. Obviously the detonation of one or more nuclear weapons—even if they were only crude, low-yield fission devices—in major American cities would be a catastrophe of horrific proportions. Still, in the case of a country as large and powerful as the United States, one or two such detonations in major urban centers would not necessarily entail the end of the American republic. Put more cold-bloodedly, the long-term threat of terrorist organizations' gaining access to these particular weapons of mass destruction do not pose an inherently existential threat to the United States. Troublingly, a small state such as Israel may be another matter.

The detonation of crude nuclear devices in one or more American cities by suicidal terrorists is, of course, perhaps the most extreme form of the proliferation challenge. A less extreme—and, hence, more likely—form of proliferation is the possibility of organizations such as Hezbollah acquiring guided mortars, rockets, or missiles. Recall that from 12 July to 13 August 2006, Hezbollah fighters fired around four thousand unguided rockets into northern Israel from Lebanon.[54] It does not take a great deal of imagination to appreciate how much more devastating these attacks would have been with guided rockets having a CEP of, say, 10 meters. Since 1991, the U.S. military has enjoyed a virtual monopoly on air-to-surface and surface-to-surface guided munitions. American forces have had them in large quantities while U.S. opponents have not. It is highly unlikely, however, that this happy situation will persist indefinitely given the willingness of many countries to sell these weapons to anyone with enough cash. Moreover, one can envision a time in the not-too-distant future when access to a variety of navigation satellites—GPS, the Russian GLONASS constellation, Europe's planned Galileo system, and perhaps some version of China's Beidou—will render the positioning information for accurate weapons guidance more or less a public commodity. Already, manufacturers are building receivers able to access GPS, GLONASS, and Galileo signals. And once these systems are integrated into modernized air-traffic-control and precision-landing systems, it will be nearly impossible to shut them down completely even in time of war. Thus, there are other proliferation challenges than a dirty atomic weapon in the hands of terrorists.

What about the rise of China? The challenge posed by ongoing PRC military modernization aimed at fighting "hi-tech local war with information technology at its core" is probably best characterized as a mid- to long-term threat.[55] This particular "wolf" is probably not yet "at the door." As Dennis Blasko emphasized in 2006, a close reading of Chinese military writings suggests that the senior leaders of the People's Liberation Army (PLA) probably desire another 10–15 years of modernization before they would have much confidence in their capabilities to take on an opponent such as the United States in a high-tech local conflict.[56] Moreover, Blasko is also on firm ground in arguing that straight-line projections of current PRC modernization trends are not a solid basis for estimating where the Chinese rulers and their military will be by 2020 or 2025.[57] There are simply too many uncertainties between then and now.

Nonetheless, the possibility of a more militarily capable and aggressive China is one against which the United States must hedge, and PRC military writings are relatively unambiguous about the challenges the Chinese hope to be able to pose. First, Chinese writings consistently emphasize the critical role played by networks and information in Western military prowess, especially in the case of the United States. An early, fundamental, high-priority task for the PLA in any high-tech local war, therefore, would be to attack enemy "nodal points and break up the network" to paralyze the adversary's information systems.[58] Disrupting or negating American use of orbital space for everything from ISR to munitions guidance will, logically, figure prominently in Chinese war planning. Presently the PLA is exploring, among other avenues of attack, satellite jamming, collisions between space bodies, kinetic-energy weapons, high-power laser and microwave weapons, electromagnetic pulse, and particle-beam weapons.[59] Further, in light of Russia's successful cyberattack on Estonia in early 2007, attacks on information networks and computer systems should probably be added to the list of potential countermeasures. While these observations simply repeat in more detail Tellis' assessment, they do serve to underscore the strategic imperative for the United States of being able to preserve its use of space even in the face of concerted attack by a near-peer competitor.

The other salient feature of PLA modernization is China's sustained drive to build area-denial/antiaccess capabilities that can "interdict, at long ranges, aircraft carrier and expeditionary strike groups that might deploy to the western Pacific."[60] The Chinese are seeking a capacity to hold surface ships, air bases such as Kadena on Okinawa, and other facilities at risk as far out into the western Pacific as the so-called second island chain running south from Japan, through Guam, toward Australia. The obvious implication of this effort for U.S. air and space forces is a growing need to be able to fight over distances of at least 1,500 nautical miles (nm), if not over even greater distances. For both the U.S. Air Force and U.S. Navy, this prospect argues for some shift in force modernization away from short-range platforms and toward longer-range systems.

Resource and Institutional Constraints

Two long-term goals for American air and space forces emerge from this brief look at the future security environment. The first is to be able to preserve the use of orbital space by American forces despite the best efforts of future adversaries to convert U.S. dependence on satellite systems into a major vulnerability. The second is the need to shift platform modernization plans more in favor of long-range systems, meaning recoverable strike platforms with unrefueled combat radii of at least 2,500 nm.[61]

Over the next 10–20 years, however, there are likely to be major resource constraints affecting the ability of the American military to meet these challenges. First of all, there are the cumulative costs of military operations in Afghanistan and Iraq together with spending for enhanced-security measures. According to the Congressional Research Service, the spending on post-9/11 operations through the Fiscal Year 2008 request totals almost $760 billion.[62] Next, however the surge of ground forces in 2007 turns out, and regardless of the decisions taken on troop levels in Iraq by the new administration after the 2008 presidential election, the eventual bill to the U.S. government will surely reach $1 trillion before all is said and done. Moreover, this figure is only the direct monetary cost of 9/11. As Anthony Cordesman and Ionut Popescu observed in 2007:

> The economic cost of the war is less important than the human costs. The Iraq War alone has so far cost the lives of roughly 100,000 Iraqi civilians and wounded many times more. It has driven over two million out of the country, displaced more than two million within Iraq, and reduced eight million Iraqis to dire poverty. It has killed over 3,700 Coalition forces, including over 3,600 American military personnel, and wounded well over 27,000.[63]

Over and above these relatively direct costs is a discernible shift in the Pentagon's priorities away from air and space forces and toward "boots on the ground." In January 2007, Defense Secretary Robert Gates decided to add, over a five-year period, some 65,000 soldiers and 27,000 Marines, whereas the Air Force has cut some 30,000 airmen in the past two years and plans to cut more by 2009 in order to free up funds for modernization.[64] Most observers have estimated that adding 92,000 more "boots on the ground" would cost $100–110 billion over five years with an annual sustainment cost thereafter of $15–20 billion. Given the stress that troop levels in Iraq have put on American ground forces since 2003, the decision to increase the Army and Marine Corps is understandable, even if most of those troops are not available until after U.S. troop levels in Iraq will have been substantially reduced. Still, they suggest that American airmen will have difficulties over the next decade or two finding funding for major new initiatives in space or long-range strike.

A further complication is the strong preference of the U.S. Air Force, Navy, and Marine Corps for short-range tactical fighters. The Navy and Marines, of course, do not operate long-range strike aircraft at all. Only the Air Force retains some 180 heavy bombers (B-52Hs, B-1Bs, and B-2As). But just over half of the Air Force's bombers are venerable B-52s, the last of which was delivered in 1962. Only the sixteen combat-coded B-2s possess the all-aspect low observability needed to persist in defended airspace long enough to locate mobile, time-sensitive, fleeting, and emergent targets, or to attack fixed targets beyond the reach of short-range strike platforms. Officially the Air Force is committed to fielding a follow-on to the B-2 by 2018. However, a survey of the ninety-three major Defense acquisition programs (MDAPs) on the Pentagon's books as of 30 September 2007 does not reveal a major bomber program. Instead, what figure 4 points out is that the most expensive single Defense program over the next couple decades in terms of cost-to-go is the F-35 Joint Strike Fighter (JSF), which anticipates procuring over 2,440 short-range fighters for the Air Force, Navy, and Marine Corps. The second-most-expensive program on the books is the Army's Future Combat Systems (FCS), but even FCS is a distant second to the JSF. Thus, the Department of Defense's "Number 1" priority in terms of major acquisition programs is buying short-range tactical fighters. To quote Rebecca Grant: "Not since World War I has the USAF's force-structure balance been tipped so dramatically toward short-range force structure."[65]

Figure 4
Top Twenty-five MDAPs Ranked by Total Program Cost[66]

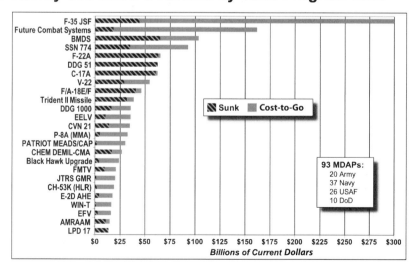

Constraints and Strategic Choice

This paper began by emphasizing how much the military and commercial use of near-earth space has changed since 1985. Insofar as the U.S. military is concerned, the current American way of war is *critically* dependent on orbital assets for the sorts of information-rich, networked operations to which the U.S. commanders and operators have become accustomed. Indeed, the manifest advantages conferred by this style of warfare go far to explain why American adversaries have been increasingly relegated to terrorism, insurgency, and the acquisition of nuclear weapons as the principal avenues for directly contesting U.S. military power. During March–April 2003, for example, so pronounced were the advantages of the U.S.-led coalition in ISR and precision munitions that Saddam Hussein's divisions were able to do little more than present targets for coalition forces to service from a distance or destroy in close combat. It is also difficult to imagine that Operation Iraqi Freedom would have been more successful if it had been prosecuted since 2003 *without* guided munitions. Extrapolating from the guided-unguided ratio in Desert Storm, a wholly unguided approach to counterinsurgency and stability operations in post-Hussein Iraq would have entailed dropping at least an order of magnitude greater number of munitions, and the likely result would have been to "rubblize" most of Iraq's cities and infrastructure. Given the amount of collateral damage and civilian casualties that has occurred to date with a heavy use of guided munitions, it is difficult to imagine that such an approach would even remotely have offered a more strategically efficacious alternative.

Today, however, space is neither the exclusive domain of the American and former Soviet (now Russian) militaries nor a sanctuary. One problem arising from these facts is that as capabilities such as precision-navigation systems and high-resolution imagery become more and more like global utilities, U.S. adversaries will eventually be able to acquire some of the ISR and precision-strike capabilities that the United States has been increasingly relying on since 1991. Space-based ISR and precision attack will not remain an exclusive advantage of the United States and its allies indefinitely. A Hezbollah armed with guided rockets, artillery, and mortars is but the most obvious manifestation of a foreseeable proliferation threat that American forces are far more likely to face in the near to midterm than, say, a nuclear-armed Iran openly employing such weapons. True, against a terrorist organization with guided munitions, American forces would still have considerable dominance in precision attack. Certainly terrorist organizations are not going to be able to match the United States' capacity for the prompt, precision attack of large numbers of targets anywhere on the globe. Nevertheless, the era of America's near monopoly on being able to employ tens of thousands of guided munitions by exploiting information and connectivity from satellites appears to be coming to an end.

The other problem arising from the transformation in the use of space is that the enormous day-to-day war-fighting advantages the U.S. military now derives from orbital systems represents a growing dependency that adversaries such as the People's Republic of China seem determined to convert into a vulnerability. Given China's emerging antiaccess/area-denial capabilities and the growing importance of Asia in the post–cold war security environment, the base-to-target distances that U.S. military forces are going to face in coming decades are four or five times greater than those that would have been demanded of NATO tactical air power if war with the Warsaw Pact had erupted in Central Europe. This problem could prove especially acute in the western Pacific should U.S. forces be forced to operate from bases as far from the Asian mainland as Guam against targets deep in defended airspace. For example, China's original spaceport at Jiuquan is located on the southern edge of the Gobi Desert some 1,600 nm from Kadena and over 2,800 nm from Guam.

These problems have major implications for U.S. air and space forces in coming decades. The first, of course, is the imperative to retain relatively unfettered use of information and connectivity based on orbital systems. The other is the need to give greater priority to long-range strike systems in Air Force and DoD modernization plans. Regarding American dependency on space, obvious first steps toward ensuring unfettered use would be to seek greater redundancy and develop a rapid-reconstitution capability in the event that critical orbital systems are neutralized or destroyed. One possibility would be to duplicate some orbital capabilities inside the atmosphere. Doing so could include fielding very-high-altitude surveillance systems with capabilities comparable to NRO imaging satellites and developing the hardware to augment a degraded GPS constellation with ground-based pseudosatellites positioned around the theater of operations. Another possibility would be to move away from large, capable, long-lived satellites like the KH-11 and Lacrosse to larger numbers of smaller, less-capable satellites. A longer-term possibility would be to distribute the functionality of a single large satellite across a number of micro- or smaller satellites, thereby enabling the system to degrade gracefully should one or two elements be lost. Next, it would seem prudent to invest in rapid-reconstitution capabilities, meaning having some backup satellites that could be orbited in hours should the functionality of critical U.S. space systems be lost. And, finally, bolstering U.S. capabilities for space situation awareness so that American decision-makers have better knowledge of what is happening in orbital space would appear to be a prudent step regardless of what else is or is not done to secure the use of orbital space.

These steps toward reducing the vulnerability of American military dependence on space stop short of deploying weapons there, even if the intent is merely to defend American satellites against kinetic or other kinds of attacks. One reason for stopping short of "weaponizing" space is that a LEO reconnaissance satellite as large and nonstealthy as the Hubble Space Telescope—which is a fair stand-in for the advanced KH-11 or Lacrosse satellites—probably cannot be defended at a reasonable cost at the end of the day. The other reason is the political furor that would undoubtedly erupt in response to any explicit American decision to put weapons in space, both domestically and internationally. The sentiment remains strong in some quarters that orbital space, like Antarctica and Yellowstone National Park, should not be polluted even with defensive weapons.

As for the matter of rebalancing the U.S. force structure more in favor of long-range systems, the obvious solution is to do what the Air Force has been directed to do by the 2001 and 2005–2006 quadrennial defense reviews: namely, to field a follow-on long-range-strike system to the B-2 by 2018. Figure

4, however, argues that, from a programmatic standpoint, this rebalancing may not yet have acquired the necessary priority. On the one hand, taking steps to guarantee unfettered use of orbital space by the American military and rebalancing platform modernization more in favor of long range appear to be compelling strategic needs. On the other hand, according these particular needs sufficient priority is a matter of making choices among competing priorities. As Charles Hitch and Roland McKean wrote in 1960:

> Resources are always limited in comparison with our wants, always constraining our action. (If they did not, we could do everything, and there would be no problem of choosing preferred courses of action.)[67]

What Hitch and McKean's insight highlights is that there is more to effective strategy than merely identifying desirable goals. In any competitive situation, strategy is ultimately about finding ways to achieve one's goals in the face of existing constraints as well as the best efforts of thinking adversaries to attain their goals instead. So while ensuring relatively unfettered access to space by the U.S. military and giving greater priority to long-range strike are unquestionably laudable goals, they do not constitute anything approaching a strategy despite what has been said regarding plausible steps toward achieving them. In fact, reflection on existing resource constraints and the institutional preference of the Air Force for short-range fighters suggests that the probability of space and long-range strike's getting sufficient programmatic priority in the near future is relatively low—perhaps no more than 20 or 30 percent.

Given the critical importance of unfettered use of orbital systems and long range to the prevailing American way of war, one wonders how this could possibly be. The answer is that in recent decades, the U.S. government's competence at long-term strategy seems to have atrophied, if not been all but lost. The growing consensus on this depressing conclusion has been captured by Aaron Friedberg:

> The U.S. government has lost the capacity to conduct serious, sustained national strategic planning. Although offices and bureaus scattered throughout the executive branch perform parts of this task for their respective agencies, no one place brings all the pieces together and integrates them into anything resembling a coherent, comprehensive whole. Worse still, to judge by the lack of any real effort in recent years to correct this shortcoming, there appears to be very little concern about what it may mean for the nation's security.

> These institutional and intellectual deficiencies have existed for some time and cannot be blamed entirely on the current administration or its immediate predecessors. Nevertheless, the consequences of an eroding capacity for strategic planning and an apparently dwindling recognition at the highest levels of government of its importance have become painfully evident in recent years. At a minimum, the absence of an institutionalized planning process seems certain to lead to a loss of efficiency: misallocated resources, suboptimal policies, duplication of effort, lost opportunities, and costly improvisations. At worst, it raises the risk of catastrophic failure.[68]

Perhaps the most fundamental error behind the decline in American strategic competence is confusion among political and military leaders alike about what strategy is. As already indicated, identifying strategic goals—however desirable or laudable—is not strategy. Yet when one reviews the 2002 and 2006 versions of *The National Security Strategy of the United States of America*, all one finds are lists of goals. These documents offer not a hint as to how these various goals might actually be achieved in light of available resources, institutional constraints, and the countervailing efforts of U.S. adversaries. True, the documents in question are public ones, not internal national-security-decision memoranda such as the Truman administration's National Security Council Paper NSC-68, "United States Objectives and Programs for National Security," or the Reagan administration's National Security Decision Directive 32, "U.S. National Security Strategy." But judging from the strategic mistakes the United States has made in Iraq, starting with the Pentagon's failure to do any serious planning beyond the major-combat phase of regime change, it seems unlikely that the U.S. government's classified strategy documents were appreciably better than the public ones.[69]

The strategic imperatives to take steps to secure more or less unfettered use of information and connectivity based on satellites for the American military, and to give greater priority to long-range strike, seem clear. Whether they will receive sufficient priority is another matter entirely. At this point in time, however, it is difficult to be optimistic despite all the revolution-in-military-affairs and transformation rhetoric of the last fifteen years.

Notes

1. In 2006, the United States declared its "space capabilities—including the ground and space segments and supporting links—vital to its national interests" (National Security Presidential Directive 49, "U.S. National Space Policy," 31 August 2006, p. 1). This document directed the secretary of defense to "Maintain the capabilities to execute the space support, force enhancement, space control, and force application missions" (ibid., p. 4).

2. Ashley J. Tellis, "Punching the U.S. Military's 'Soft Ribs': China's Antisatellite Weapon Test in Strategic Perspective," Policy Brief 51 (Carnegie Endowment for International Peace, May 2007), p. 3.

3. Andrew D. May, currently with the Office of Net Assessment, Office of the Secretary of Defense, deserves credit for suggesting this comparison.

4. ESA was founded in 1975. It is an intergovernmental organization dedicated to the peaceful exploration of space. It currently has seventeen member states.

5. Tamar A. Mehuron, "Space Almanac 2000," *AIR FORCE Magazine*, August 2000, pp. 44, 53. Note that based on comparing *AIR FORCE Magazine*'s historical launch data for 1998 with that kept by the National Aeronautics and Space Administration since 1998, it appears that *AIR FORCE Magazine*'s annual space almanacs exclude manned orbital missions and launch failures.

6. The shuttle *Challenger* was destroyed during launch in January 1986. Eight shuttle missions were flown in 1992 and 1997, and seven in 1994, 1995, and 1996. However, since the loss of *Columbia* on reentry in February 2003, only seven more successful shuttle missions had been flown through early November 2007.

7. National Aeronautics and Space Administration (NASA), "2006 Worldwide Space Launches," http://www.hq.nasa.gov/osf/2006/launch06.html.

8. See, for example, Pavel Podvig, "The Fire May Be Serious, but There Is No Reason for Concern," http://www.armscontrol.ru/start/comments/pp051001.htm. This Web site has extensive coverage of the controversy over Russian missile-warning capabilities triggered by David Hoffman's reporting in *The Washington Post*, which began on 10 February 1999. See Hoffman, "Russia 'Blind' to Attack by U.S. Missiles," *Washington Post*, 1 June 2000, p. A1.

9. In 1999 Futron's Greg Lucas provided Barry Watts with data on government spending on space and commercial revenues from space for 1970–1998.

10. Space Foundation, *The Space Report: The Guide to Global Space Activity (2007 Update)*, pp. 4–6, available at http://www.spacefoundation.org/TheSpaceReport07.pdf.

11. The Space Foundation's estimate of U.S. government spending on space in 2006 includes the Department of Defense ($22.5 billion), the National Reconnaissance Office ($9.9 billion), the National Geospatial Intelligence Agency ($2.67 billion), the Missile Defense Agency ($9.3 billion), NASA ($16.6 billion), the National Oceanic and Atmospheric Administration ($0.96 billion), the Department of Energy ($0.04 billion), and the Federal Aviation Administration ($0.01 billion).

12. The Surrey Space Centre's first satellite, UoSAT-1 weighed 50 kilograms (110 pounds) and cost less than 500 million pounds. The Surrey Nanosatellite Application Platform (SNAP), launched in June 2000, weighed 8.5 kilograms (19 pounds). At that time it was the world's smallest fully functional nanosatellite. SNAP included a miniaturized attitude control system for three-axis stablization using a miniature momentum wheel, a miniaturized Global Positioning System (GPS) receiver for autonomous orbit control, a propulsion system for formation flying maneuvers, a complementary metal-oxide semiconductor (CMOS) machine-vision system for automated inspection, and an intersatellite communication system for receiving GPS data from other satellites in a formation (see http://www.ee.surrey.ac.uk/SSC/achievements).

13. John V. Evans, "RE: Question on Sat Comms vs. Terrestrial Comms," e-mail to Erwin Godoy, 11 June 1999. At the time, Evans was vice president and chief technical officer of the Communications Satellite Corporation (COMSAT). The International Telecommunications Satellite Organization was founded in 1964 by a consortium of eleven nations. INTELSAT became a private company in 2001 and is the world's largest provider of satellite communications services.

14. John V. Evans, "Satellites for Personal Communications" (lecture abstract), available at http://www.cv.nrao.edu/~jhibbard/Colloq/abs/jevans.html.

15. Source: TeleGeography, *International Bandwidth 2000* (Washington, DC: TeleGeography, 1999), pp. 43, 46.

16. Alan Mauldin, "Backbone Supply and Demand: The End of the Glut?" (presentation, annual conference of the Pacific Telecommunications Council, Honolulu, HI, 15 January 2006), slide 7.

17. My colleague Chris Sullivan pointed out this change in the business model of comsat firms.

18. Dwayne A. Day, John M. Logsdon, and Brian Latell, eds., *Eye in the Sky: The Story of the Corona Spy Satellites* (Washington and London: Smithsonian Institution Press, 1998), pp. 10, 38.

19. Ibid., p. 164.

20. Source: Wikipedia, "KH-11," at http://en.wikipedia.org/wiki/KH-11.

21. See Yeaya A. Dehqanzada and Ann M. Florini, *Secrets for Sale: How Commercial Imagery Will Change the World* (Washington, DC: Carnegie Endowment for International Peace, 2000), pp. 5, 26; this study can be downloaded as a pdf file at http://www.carnegieendowment.org/publications/index.cfm?fa=view&id=160. The figure on page 26 shows a Yannan-class Chinese ship at 5-meter, 1-meter, and 20-centimeter resolutions. At 5-meter resolution, the ship is a blur, nearly impossible to identify based strictly on the image. From a military standpoint, the situation is altogether different at resolutions of 1–2 meters.

22. Clark Nelson, "The Global Balancing Act," *Earth Imaging Journal*, available at http://www.eijournal.com/Nelson.asp (accessed November 2007). This article contains 2-meter-resolution images from FormoSat-2.

23. William E. Stoney, "Markets and Opportunities?" *Earth Imaging Journal*, available at http://www.eijournal.com/Markets_Opportunities.asp (accessed November 2007). In 2005, ORBIMAGE acquired Space Imaging. The acquisition led to the formation of GeoEye in

2006, which is the largest commercial remote-sensing company in the world. DigitalGlobe orbited WorldView-1, the follow-on to Quickbird, in September 2007, and WorldView-2 is under construction.

24. Craig Covault, "Final Cape Titan Propels NRO's Secret Operations," 8 May 2005, available at http://www.aviationweek.com/aw/generic/story_generic.jsp?channel=awst&id =news/05095p04.xml (accessed November 2007); and Craig Covault, "Space Recon Dwindles as Iran, China Advance," 15 May 2006, available at http://www.aviationweek .com/aw/generic/story_channel.jsp?channel=space&id=news/aw051506p02.xml (accessed November 2007).

25. TerraSAR-X appears to be primarily intended for earth observation. For samples of TerraSAR-X images, see http://www.scanex.com/en/news/News_Preview.asp?id= n196242142.

26. Scott Pace, Gerald P. Frost, Irving Lachow, David R. Frelinger, Donna Fossum, Donald K. Wassem, and Monica M. Pinto, *The Global Positioning System: Assessing National Policies* (Santa Monica, CA: RAND, 1995), pp. 20, 238–247.

27. U.S. Space Command, *United States Space Command Operations Desert Shield and Desert Storm Assessment* (January 1992), p. 28; redacted version at http://www.gwu.edu/ ~nsarchiv/NSAEBB/NSAEBB39/#doc (accessed November 2007). During Desert Storm, U.S. forces in the theater of operations had four GPS satellites in view about 18 hours a day.

28. Ibid., pp. 26–27, 29.

29. *Gulf War Air Power Survey* [GWAPS], vol. 5, *A Statistical Compendium and Chronology*, pt. 1, *A Statistical Compendium* (Washington, DC: U.S. Government Printing Office, 1993), pp. 553–554. Note that the figures cited also exclude 3,063 ATGM-114 Hellfire missiles and 293 BGM-71 TOW missiles expended by U.S. ground forces.

30. Ibid., p. 27. The judgment that the LGB was the guided munition that proved the most effective in Desert Storm is based on having headed the GWAPS task force on operations and effects.

31. LtGen T. Michael Moseley, *Operation Iraqi Freedom—By the Numbers* (CENTAF-PSAB, Kingdom of Saudi Arabia: U.S. Central Command Air Forces, 30 April 2003), p. 11. The guided totals cited for Iraqi Freedom exclude 566 TOWs and Hellfires expended by ground forces. Of the data sets for 1999, 2001–2002, and 2003, the best is for Iraqi Freedom. Note that while the number of guided munitions expended in 1991 is only slightly smaller than in 2003, the total munitions expended (guided plus unguided) is eight times larger (227,600 total munitions in 1991 versus only 27,800 in 2003). The dramatic reduction in the expenditures of unguided munitions from 1991 to 2003 not only reduced collateral damage but the number of strike sorties as well.

32. Third Infantry Division (Mechanized), *After Action Report: Operation IRAQI Freedom*, (July 2003), p. 30.

33. See Garmin, "What Is GPS?" http://www8.garmin.com/aboutGPS/.

34. The first successful Corona mission returned more coverage of the USSR than had all prior U-2 overflights combined—Day, Logsdon, and Latell, *Eye in the Sky*, p. 24.

35. The Defense Support Program satellites, which orbit at geosynchronous altitudes and provide warning of missile launches and nuclear detonations, were thought to be more survivable—at least for a time.

36. The first Lacrosse radar-imaging satellite is believed to have been deployed from the space shuttle *Atlantis* in December 1988, making it available for Operation Desert Storm. It was deorbited in 1997.

37. Patrick Chisholm, "Buying Time: Disconnects in Satcom Procurement," *Military Information Technology*, 29 November 2003.

38. Image available online at http://www.nro.gov/corona/corona8.jpg. The annotations compare transports located on the airfield with Tupelov Tu-16 "Bear" bombers of Soviet Long Range Aviation. Dolan had two Tu-16 regiments at the time. The base is now

located in the Republic of Kazakhstan. The camera system of the KH-4A had a resolution of 9–25 feet.

39. See Scott R. Gourley, "Guided MLRS Unitary," *Army*, December 2006, available at http://www.ausa.org/webpub/DeptArmyMagazine.nsf/byid/KHYL-6VJRL3 (accessed November 2007).

40. The U.S. Army is also developing a GPS-aided fuze, the Precision Guidance Kit (PGK), for 155-millimeter artillery rounds. PGK is less ambitious but also simpler to use than Excalibur. Instead of homing in on target coordinates in GPS space like Excalibur, PGK uses GPS to make the CEP of each round 50 meters or less regardless of range (MAJ John S. Moorhead, "Precision Guidance Kits [PGKs]: Improving the Accuracy of Conventional Cannon Rounds," *Field Artillery*, January–February 2007, pp. 31–33).

41. U.S. Air Force, "Joint Direct Attack Munition GBU-31/32/38" (fact sheet), available at http://www.af.mil/factsheets/factsheet_print.asp?fsID=108&page=1 (accessed November 2007). B-2s expended 652 2,000-pound JDAMs (GBU-31s) in 1999 plus 4 5,000-pound GBU-37s, which used the same inertial/GPS guidance (509th Bomb Wing, "Operation Allied Force," August 1999, slide 22).

42. William M. Arkin, "Belgrade Hit Earlier Than Previously Reported," *Defense Daily*, 27 October 1999.

43. U.S. Air Force, "Small Diameter Bomb I Delivered Ahead of Schedule," 6 September 2006, http://www.af.mil/news/story.asp?storyID=123026454.

44. *GWAPS*, vol. 2, *Operations and Effects and Effectiveness*, pt. 2, *Effects and Effectiveness* (Washington, DC: U.S. Government Printing Office, 1993), p. 340.

45. Rebecca Grant, *The B-2 Goes to War* (Arlington, VA: IRIS Press, 2001), pp. 78–82.

46. The U.S. Air Force defines precision munitions as those with CEPs of less than 9.9 feet. By this definition, LGBs are precision munitions. JDAM, with official CEP of 13 meters (42.7 feet), which is greater than 9.9 feet but less than 66 feet, is a near-precision munition (John A. Tirpak, "Precision: The Next Generation," *Air Force Magazine*, November 2003, p. 46).

47. Jeremy Singer, "U.S.-Led Forces Destroy GPS Jamming Systems in Iraq," *Space News*, 25 March 2003, http://www.space.com/news/gps_iraq_030325.html.

48. Rupert Smith, *The Utility of Force: The Art of War in the Modern World* (New York: Alfred A. Knopf, 2007), pp. 20, 107, 148, 177, 269.

49. Ibid., p. 271.

50. Ibid, pp. 271, 279.

51. Martin Shubik, "Terrorism, Technology, and the Socioeconomics of Death," Cowles Foundation Paper 952, (New Haven: Cowles Foundation for Research in Economics at Yale University, 1998), pp. 406–408.

52. In this regard, the portion of the recent national intelligence estimate on Iran's nuclear efforts released to the public stated: "Tehran's decision to halt its nuclear weapons program suggests it is less determined to develop nuclear weapons than we have been judging since 2005. Our assessment that the program probably was halted primarily in response to international pressure suggests Iran may be more vulnerable to influence on the issue than we judged previously." National Intelligence Council, "Iran: Nuclear Intentions and Capabilities," news release, November 2007, p. 6, available at http://www.dni.gov/press_releases/20071203_release.pdf (accessed November 2007).

53. John R. Bolton, "The Flaws in the Iran Report," *Washington Post*, 6 December 2007, p. A29.

54. Uzi Rubin, *The Rocket Campaign against Israel during the 2006 Lebanon War*, Mideast Security and Policy Studies 71 (Begin-Sadat Center for Strategic Studies, Bar-Ilan University, June 2007), pp. 10–14, 38.

55. Peng Guangqian and Yao Youzhi, eds., *Science of Strategy* (Beijing: Military Science Press, 2001), p. 363.

56. Dennis J. Blasko, "Observations on Military Modernization and International Influence—an Alternative View" (paper prepared for the National Defense University Conference on China's Global Activism, 20 June 2006), p. 6.

57. Ibid., p. 10.

58. Guangqian and Youzhi, *Science of Strategy*, p. 416; *see also* Peng Guangqian and Yao Youzhi, eds., *Science of Military Strategy* (Beijing: Military Science Press, 2005), pp. 463–466.

59. Larry M. Wortzel, *The Chinese People's Liberation Army and Space Warfare* (American Enterprise Institute, 2007), p. 7.

60. Office of the Secretary of Defense, *Military Power of the People's Republic of China 2007*, annual report to Congress, p. 16.

61. The Center for Strategic and Budgetary Assessments (CSBA) has taken to defining short-range aircraft as those with unrefueled combat radii of 500–1,499 nm, medium-range aircraft as those with unrefueled combat radii of 1,500–2,499 nm, and long-range aircraft as those with unrefueled combat radii of 2,500 nm or more. See Barry D. Watts, *Long-Range Strike: Imperatives, Urgency and Options* (Washington, DC: CSBA, April 2005), p. 4.

62. Amy Belasco, *The Cost of Iraq, Afghanistan, and Other Global War on Terror Operations since 9/11* (Congressional Research Service [CRS], 16 July 2007), p. CRS-3.

63. Anthony H. Cordesman, *The Uncertain Cost of the Global War on Terror*, with Ionut C. Popescu (Center for Strategic and International Studies, August 2007), p. 2.

64. Jim Garamone, "Gates Call for 92,000 More Soldiers, Marines," American Forces Press Service, 11 January 2007, available at http://www.defenselink.mil/news/NewsArticle.aspx?ID=2651; Greg Grant, "Desperate for Money," *Government Executive*, 15 November 2007.

65. Rebecca Grant, "When Bombers Will Be Decisive," *AIR FORCE Magazine*, November 2007, p. 43.

66. Office of the Under Secretary of Defense (Acquisition, Technology and Logistics), Acquisition Resources and Analysis/Acquisition Management, *Selected Acquisition Report (SAR) Summary Tables: As of Date: September 30, 2007* (Department of Defense, 14 November 2007), pp. 10–11. The Evolved Expendable Launch Vehicle (EELV) is the only space program currently among the top twenty-five MDAPs.

67. Charles J. Hitch and Roland N. McKean, *The Economics of Defense in the Nuclear Age* (New York: Atheneum, 1986), p. 23.

68. Aaron L. Friedberg, "Strengthening U.S. Strategic Planning," *Washington Quarterly*, Winter 2007–2008, p. 47.

69. For a stunning example of strategic shortsightedness during the run–up to Operation Iraqi Freedom, see Bob Woodward, *State of Denial* (New York: Simon and Schuster, 2006), pp. 90–91. This passage describes the meeting in which General Tommy Franks cheerfully acquiesced to Donald Rumsfeld's decision to put Douglas Feith, the under secretary of defense for policy, in charge of everything after OIF Phase III, decisive combat operations.

Setting Future Directions in Space

Dean Cheng
Research Fellow
Center for Naval Analyses Corporation

Introduction

Recent conflicts suggest that the ability to access space is of increasing importance to the ability to fight and win modern wars. The concept of space power is arguably one that will be as important as that of sea power or airpower.

Despite a fifty-year history, space systems' impact on everyday lives has mushroomed only since the end of the cold war. The decision to allow broad public access to the Global Positioning System (GPS), and the proliferation of privately owned imaging satellites, coupled with the Internet and the broader telecommunications revolution, has made space-based assets as commonplace as computers. This is in marked contrast to the cold war, when space-based systems were largely seen as national assets providing strategic warning and surveillance, coupled with some commercial uses (primarily in terms of television transmissions and telephone/telex connectivity).

If the use of space is more commonplace today, however, the development of strategic concepts to govern its exploitation has not kept pace. In particular, the near monopoly on space access that the United States and its coalition partners have enjoyed has limited the need for such development. As that monopoly recedes, however, it is likely that this situation will change.

This paper will review the concept of space power and its importance, discuss evolving conditions, and conclude with some thoughts on the future of space power.

Defining Space Power

Although the space age has existed for fifty years, since the launch in October 1957 of Sputnik, there has not been a formal definition of "space power." Some working definitions have included:

- "The ability of a state or non-state actor to achieve its goals and objectives in the presence of other actors on the world stage through . . . exploitation of the space environment";[1]

- "The pursuit of national objectives through the medium of space and the use of space capabilities";[2]

- "The total strength of a nation's capabilities to conduct and influence activities to, in, through, and from space to achieve its objectives."[3]

In most discussions of space power, there are several elements deemed essential. These include the political will and high-level support to sustain the high costs of developing a space infrastructure; the actual financial, industrial, and human resources necessary to fund, build, and staff said infrastructure; and finally mission support capacity, comprising

- Launchers,
- Satellites, and
- Mission control facilities.

Within this framework, it is not clear precisely which attributes are necessary to make an entity a space power. Very few states possess the ability to manufacture satellites and launchers, as well as the capacity to launch and operate satellites. On the other hand, several states own satellites, which they purchased and arranged to launch from third-party vendors. Further complicating the issue, one of the largest satellite constellations in the world, the Iridium system with nearly seventy operational satellites, is owned by Motorola—a private corporation; another company, Inmarsat, is one of the largest providers of global mobile satellite communications.[4]

For the purposes of this paper, the primary focus will be on nation-states that possess the ability to manufacture both satellites and launchers, and can launch and operate satellites on their own. The major space-faring powers are the United States, Russia, the European Union (with a large French component), the People's Republic of China (PRC), Japan, and India.

Benefits of Space Power

The ability to access space confers several benefits to those who possess it. These include enhanced prestige, direct and indirect economic benefits, and military capabilities.

Prestige

Arguably one of the most important drivers for developing space power has been the political prestige that attends possession of a space capability. Given the expense involved, a space program has been available only to those states whose economy can generate a surplus, not only financially, but also in terms of human capital. Fielding a space program therefore symbolizes a nation's achieving a certain level of development where it can now afford to engage in more advanced forms of national endeavor.

This, in turn, has both domestic and foreign impact. At home, space achievements serve to improve a nation's self-confidence. They may also serve to enhance regime legitimacy, especially for newly industrializing and developing countries.

Abroad, space achievements serve to garner international respect, including enhancing deterrence. In general, few nations with the ability to launch their own space systems are seen as "backwards" or underdeveloped. Indeed, in some cases, it is a capability beyond those of more developed nations. In addition, a robust space launch capability implicitly means that a state also has a significant ballistic missile capability. It may also suggest that a nation can field more advanced surveillance systems. Both of these elements may contribute to a deterrent posture.

Finally, in a more globalized world economy, prestige carries not only a price tag but also an economic benefit. Not only does prestige enhance a nation's apparent standing, but it may lead to investments that actually improve the nation's economy. As NASA administrator Michael Griffin has noted,

> Success in an economic competition depends upon image as well as substance. Companies the world over have a choice as to where to do deals, and with whom to do them. The nation that appears to be at the top of the technical pyramid has taken a large step toward being there.[5]

Space power, in short, is emblematic of the concept of "soft power."

Economic Benefits

Beyond the benefits derived from prestige, there are also economic gains from fostering a domestic space industry. The manufacture of space systems, including satellites and launchers, represents a direct economic contribution to an economy. Manufacturing satellites and launchers, and the provision of satellite services, constitutes a $220 billion industry.[6]

In addition, satellite applications represent the fastest-growing portion of the space industry. Direct satellite television, provision of precision navigation and positioning services, and satellite communications all have become significant industries.

These, in turn, undergird much of the modern globalized economy. Just-in-time logistics, for example, involving global production and distribution requires a global communications system. This can only be achieved through the use of space-based assets. Precision agriculture, involving the spot application of pesticides and fertilizers at variable rates, and the tailoring of crops to soil and topographical features, requires GPS data.[7] Distance learning and telemedicine meanwhile facilitate the leveraging of scarce intellectual capital, and can reach every corner of the globe.

Space technology is also seen as providing the basis for many "spin-offs," technological advances that ultimately benefit the entire economy. The impetus to develop better microchips, advanced materials, and new metals was based in part on the space program. Nor is it just physical products that may be spun off. Given the requirements for operating in the harsh environment of space, production of space systems requires a level of precision manufacturing, quality control, and advanced design. These qualities, in turn, may benefit terrestrial industries and products.

Space as a Military Resource

The early days of the space age were focused not only on economics nor even primarily on prestige but on the military advantages to be gained from a space capability. This was a consideration even before the launch of Sputnik. "Developing space capabilities dates back to World War II and, in the United States, predates NASA."[8] The military interest in space is based on the advantages available to those who are able to use space-based platforms and systems.

- In the first place, they are able to gain the highest vantage point from which to observe an opponent.

- Moreover, this observation ability is sustainable for a prolonged period, especially for a satellite placed in a stable orbit.

- If one has a network of satellites, then it is also possible to support a global or regional observation ability, providing simultaneous observation of multiple points.[9]

Despite its strategic and military importance, however, for most of the cold war space was not generally seen as a battleground. While both the United States and the USSR developed satellites for early warning, imaging, communications, meteorology, and navigation, both sides generally refrained from deploying extensive antisatellite capabilities.

When the Soviet Union imploded, and its space systems eroded due to lack of funding, it appeared that the United States had secured a major advantage in space. There were few states that were in any position to challenge the United States, either in terms of accessing space, using space-based assets to gain information, or integrating information derived from space systems into their weapons.

At the same time, advances in computing power, telecommunications, and space systems conferred enormous new capabilities upon militaries that could access space. The unprecedented display of space power in the first Gulf War entailed U.S. forces coordinating military operations across a sprawling battlefield, engaging enemy forces with precision-guided munitions while navigating across the desert. To achieve these ends, the United States arrayed over a hundred satellites, including military communications satellites, navigational satellites, and meteorological satellites, supplemented by French SPOT satellites, European Space Agency METEOSATs, and American civilian systems.[10]

Similarly, the United States exploited space-based assets heavily in the air war against Serbia on behalf of Kosovo. This included navigation, meteorological, and communications satellites. In the *Kosovo/Operation Allied Force After-Action Report*, it is noted that "space support was instrumental to our success. . . . Reliance on space continues to grow in our military operations."[11]

For over a decade, it appeared that the U.S. advantage in space would be unassailable for some time to come. Neither Serbia nor Iraq, much less Afghanistan, could deploy its own satellites. And although Serbia and Iraq tried to deploy countermeasures, their records were mixed. In at least one instance, Iraqi active GPS jammers were pointedly neutralized by the use of a GPS-guided weapon.[12]

On the other hand, passive denial and deception techniques against Western surveillance systems, including space-based assets, were apparently effective. Despite a massive NATO surveillance effort, including various satellite systems, it would appear that the Serbian Third Army successfully deceived NATO forces as to its whereabouts. "Because future adversaries are likely to study Serbian denial and deception tactics and could present more advanced threats to future operations, the Department [of Defense] is working on a variety of techniques to further improve our capability to counter an adversary's use of camouflage, concealment, and deception."[13]

Prospects for the Future

Desert Storm first showed what space power could confer to the side that could better exploit it. Fifteen years later, the situation has further evolved. Where the United States was the unrivaled leader in terms of space capabilities, there are now a number of states with clear ambitions for space. Perhaps the space-faring nation that raises the greatest concern is the People's Republic of China. The PRC has exhibited an interest and ability to develop its space power across the areas of prestige enhancement, economic development, and military capability.

The Chinese Challenge in Space

In terms of prestige, the PRC has shown itself to be one of the most advanced space-faring nations in Asia, with a range of indigenously produced satellites and the only manned space program. Domestically, the Chinese Communist Party (CCP) has sought to use its space capabilities, especially its manned program, to garner additional legitimacy. The space program is touted as embodying the CCP's philosophy of "two bombs, one satellite," including Hu Jintao's variant of "autonomous innovation" (*zizhu chuangxin*; 自主创新). Diplomatically, China has used its space capability to help organize the Asia-Pacific Space Cooperation Organization (APSCO), which also helps underscore China's position as the preeminent Asian space power. The space program has also been the basis for securing some of China's first overseas bases in order to secure tracking, telemetry, and control (TT&C) sites, including at Swakopmund, Namibia; Kiribati (since closed); Malindi, Kenya; and Karachi, Pakistan.

Economically, the Chinese have also sought to leverage their space program both domestically and abroad. The main Chinese aerospace manufacturers, the China Aerospace Science and Technology Corporation (CASC) and the China Aerospace Science and Industry Corporation (CASIC), employ a workforce of nearly two hundred thousand for these two entities alone.[14] Meanwhile, the Chinese are not only part of the international launch services market but also now export satellites, including to Nigeria and Venezuela.

In terms of military space challenges, the PRC provided a clear signal of its capabilities when it tested a direct-ascent antisatellite weapon (ASAT) on 11 January 2007, destroying one of its own weather satellites. While this attracted enormous attention, it merely served as a capstone for a larger, more extensive effort on the part of the Chinese People's Liberation Army (PLA) to incorporate space into its planning.

PLA Views on Space

According to Chinese military writings, and based on their observation of American and NATO military operations in Kuwait, the Balkans, Afghanistan, and Iraq, there is a transformation in military affairs (*junshi biange*; 军事变革) under way. Whereas the PLA of the Mao era relied on mass, and the belief that the individual soldiers infused with the teachings of Mao's *Little Red Book* were paramount, today, the Chinese military is increasingly sophisticated. In response to perceived changes in modern warfare, the PLA has undertaken fundamental reforms, many codified in PLA regulations set forth in 1999. Most relevant to the space issue is the PLA's conclusion that future wars will be joint and will turn on information.

According to PLA assessments, future wars will be "Local Wars Under Modern, High-Tech Conditions." That is, they will be limited wars, fought with advanced technologies. In order to successfully fight such wars, the PLA has concluded that joint operations are essential, in order both to exploit various service specialties and technologies, and to ameliorate individual service weaknesses. This requires, however, the ability to coordinate the component elements of the joint force, which in turn requires a common situational awareness, while denying an opponent the same. Consequently, since 2004, according to PLA writings, the key to winning future wars is the ability to control information space (*xinxi jian*; 信息间). At the same time, Chinese descriptions of future wars now describe them as "Local Wars Under Informationalized Conditions"; the most important high technologies, according to Chinese assessments, are those related to information acquisition, information transmission, and information exploitation.

The ability to exploit information is of special import. Both the 2004 and 2006 Chinese defense white papers emphasize that informationalization, *which involves more than just information technologies*, is a key part of Chinese military modernization. The idea is that not only information technology but the easy accessibility of information itself represents a qualitative shift in how wars are conducted.

This combination of joint operations and high technology leads to an increased emphasis on space systems and space operations. The same information technologies and improved sensor systems that make modern weapons that much more destructive effectively make outer space a key battleground as well. Thus, Chinese writings emphasize that there are *five battlespaces* in which the PLA must operate: land, sea, air, the electromagnetic spectrum, and outer space. Similarly, when they talk about high technology, PLA authors are discussing information collection, transmission, and management and analysis systems, and space is a key arena for each of these functions.[15] Some Chinese authors even refer to the concept of "space information warfare," (*taikong xinxi zhan*; 太空信息战), because of the intimate relationship between space warfare and information warfare.[16]

Moreover, according to Chinese assessments, the importance of space for successfully fighting such wars is increasing. One Chinese article in 2005 noted that

- In the 1991 Gulf War, the United States used fifty-two military satellites,

- In Kosovo, the United States and NATO used eighty-six satellites, and

- In the 2003 Iraq War, U.S.-UK forces used over one hundred satellites.[17]

For the 2003 Iraq War, another Chinese article estimates that the United States relied on satellites for 95 percent of recon and surveillance information, 90 percent of military communications, 100 percent of navigation and positioning, and 10 percent of meteorological and weather forecasting.[18] Similarly, the Russian military is estimated, by PLA sources, to rely on satellites for 70 percent of its strategic intelligence and 80 percent of its military communications.[19]

For the PLA, there appear to be lessons for both space exploitation and space denial. In observing American military experience, the conclusion is striking.

> We can conceptualize that, without space systems support, the United States could conduct only a high-level mechanized war, and could not implement informationalized warfare. Therefore, we can reach the following conclusion: Without space technology breakthroughs and space technical preparations, the shape of warfare cannot move from mechanized combat towards informationalized combat.[20]

At the same time, key space systems and missions as identified by PLA authors include

- Communications satellites,

- Meteorological satellites,

- Reconnaissance satellites,

- Navigation satellites, and

- Earth observation satellites.[21]

Each of these systems is currently part of the Chinese inventory of space assets. The more limited, dual-use nature of China's space systems has not prevented them from developing the systems that they believe are necessary to sustain their own military operations.

Other Challenges to the U.S. Space Advantage

While ASATs provide a visible threat to U.S. space assets, other, less-obvious challenges to the U.S. space advantage have also emerged. One is soft-kill attacks against U.S. space systems; rather than attempting to destroy U.S. satellites, one could seek instead to disrupt the software that controls them, or even to interfere with the data flowing through the space-based systems.

Loss of information from satellites can prove as disruptive as losing the satellite itself. When the Galaxy-IV communications satellite suffered a thruster failure, there was significant disruption across portions of the United States. This included a loss of service to 40 million pagers, interruptions to financial networks, and disrupted TV network audio feeds and wireless Internet connectivity.[22]

Ironically, the PRC has already been the target of such attacks. The religious group Falun Gong has repeatedly overridden Chinese television signals, transmitting its own programming to Chinese audiences. In 2002, for example, its members jammed one of China's main television satellites for eight days, and even forced the cancellation of a speech by then-president Jiang Zemin.[23]

Beyond soft- and hard-kills, however, there is also the prospect of simple provision of information. In the past, so long as an opponent had no space capability of its own, the United States did not have to worry much about either countering its space systems or defending its own space assets. Supplemented by checkbook diplomacy, there was effective shutter control over most information derived from space. This will become much more problematic as the number of nations, and even nonnations, with the ability to gather information from space increases.

Even if the United States could afford to buy up access to all the information gained from commercial satellites, it is not clear that it can prevent information from national systems, be they Chinese or Indian, from passing to third-party hands. In the event of a U.S. conflict with Iran, for example, that occurs over the objections of Russia and China, there is some potential of Moscow or Beijing supplying Tehran with space-based intelligence about U.S. force deployments. Similarly, in the event of a Sino-U.S. confrontation, it is not clear that the United States would necessarily be able to outbid the PRC for shutter control over commercial satellite imaging systems.

The Other Challenge of Space: Modernization, Innovation, and Transformation

While the United States is likely to confront more potential challenges to its space advantage in terms of proliferating capabilities, it is the bureaucratic and doctrinal challenge posed by space that is arguably more worrisome.

While the U.S. military has been using space for nearly fifty years, it has not necessarily been transformed *by* space. In particular, in the wake of the cold war, the focus has been on *modernization*, with varying degrees of *innovation*, but much more limited *transformation*.

As it is not possible to review the extensive and rich literature on the issue of military innovation, and the distinctions between wartime and peacetime innovation, instead, we will confine ourselves to peacetime innovation, and focus on organizational (or social) innovation.[24] Within this context:

- *Modernization* will refer to the application of current or additional resources, to accommodate evolving requirements and incorporate additional capabilities. The focus of modernization is usually on the acquisition of new equipment, but generally does not entail changes to doctrine or organization.

- *Innovation*, on the other hand, is much more complex and harder to define. It can involve technical, tactical, or operational changes. Innovation refers to more than just incorporating new equipment and technology, tactics, or operational methods into an extant set of doctrine or practices. Rather, innovation involves changing concepts of missions and operations.[25]

- *Transformation*, for the purposes of this paper, should be seen as the institutionalization of innovations. It involves altering organizational structures, promotion patterns, and budgetary allocations in order not only to accommodate a given innovation but to support its continued application. In essence, transformation constitutes an "ideological" change within an organization, fundamentally redefining core values and attendant resourcing and staffing.[26] Of special import is the establishment of not only new doctrine and concepts of operations that would incorporate these new capabilities, but also the creation of "a new, stable career path for younger officers not committed to the old way of war."[27]

The United States and Space

Since the end of the cold war, the U.S. military use of space has been much more along the lines of modernization, leavened with some innovation, rather than transformation. Space assets have been used to provide better information, but the military continues to view space primarily as a force enabler and enhancer. While the Air Force has discussed "transforming outer space force into a *spacecontrol force*," the discussion is about how to provide "*persistent* intelligence, surveillance, and reconnaissance around the globe."[28] This is a function of using forces better, but not necessarily differently, from how they have been used in the past.

Indeed, if innovation requires a "new theory of victory, an explanation of what the next war will look like, and how officers must fight if it is to be won," then it is open to question whether such innovation has occurred in the context of U.S. space forces since the end of the cold war.[29] Instead, new systems and capabilities seem to be applied to traditional tasks, without accompanying changes to mind-sets—suggesting that modernization, rather than innovation or transformation, has been the watchword for U.S. military space endeavors.

In many ways, this is understandable. An essential common denominator among cases of successful innovation and transformation has been the existence of an actual, rather than purely hypothetical, opponent, complete with actual capabilities. The innovations and transformations occur in pursuit of real strategic and political objectives.[30] Few of these conditions exist in the context of current U.S. space planning.

To begin at the most fundamental, it is not clear who the United States should focus upon as the main enemy. Is the primary shaping factor for the foreseeable future terrorist actors? Or are nation-states, especially a rising China, the foremost and most likely challengers to U.S. security? The types of space systems, and military forces in general, required for countering terrorists are different than those necessary to deter and defeat the world's largest developing state.

Nor does recent history provide a good guide for how to develop American space forces. Recent wars have involved few real challenges to U.S. space supremacy, with countermeasures largely limited to terrestrial attempts at concealment and jamming. Space warfare, the struggle for dominance of the space ways, has not yet occurred in a meaningful sense. In the absence of an actual opponent exhibiting real capabilities, it is difficult to sustain the institutional commitment necessary to undertake transformation, or to establish the necessary constituency for "a major organizational embrace of a new mission."[31]

Moreover, with the rapid pace of technological change, determining precisely which technologies are best exploited, or what doctrines and organizations would best facilitate such exploitation, is difficult. This is further complicated by the extended time frame typical of government acquisition programs. In the midst of unceasing technological change, without historical precedent in the form of actual opponents or wars, it is a major challenge for U.S. space forces to avoid spending scarce resources on "technological sophistication irrelevant to the war actually being fought."[32]

The Challenge of Rising Space Powers

By contrast, for rising space powers such as the PRC, India, or Japan, the situation is much simpler. Their strategic threats are much more specific, and the kinds of space capabilities, whether for exploitation or denial, can therefore also be much more focused. The PLA, for example, has the advantage of being able to carefully monitor and assess American use of space in its wars, avoiding American missteps while extracting the most useful or applicable lessons.

The advantage of being a relative newcomer applies not only to technology but also to organization. As one of the earliest inventors of bureaucracy, it would be wrong to believe that any Chinese institution, least of all the military, is any less stove-piped than the U.S. military. Yet, in the space arena, precisely because they are relative newcomers to space and especially military space, they may well have fewer preconceived notions of what the right method is for conducting military space operations. Thus, the Chinese may be in a position to avoid the pitfall "where military organizations and high commands 'knew' the answers and drove the solutions."[33] Instead, they may well be more open to effective innovation, and focused more on achieving particular results than on following an established bureaucratic path.

Conclusions

Pierre Joxe, French minister of defense at the time of the 1991 Gulf War, concluded that that conflict had shown that "the stakes in space go beyond the strict definition of defense. They are national. Not to possess this capacity would affect the very status of the nation."[34] In essence, a state seeking to be a major power must be a space power.

To be a space power in the second decade of the twenty-first century will require not just the physical assets necessary to access and exploit space, but also the ability to think about space and the information that flows through it in new, transformative ways. America's rivals are already trying to do so. It remains to be seen whether, and how, the United States will as well.

Notes

1. James L. Hyatt III et al., *Space Power 2010*, Research Report, 95-05 (Maxwell AFB, AL: Air Command and Staff College, May 1995), p. 5.

2. Dana J. Johnson, Scott Pace, and C. Bryan Gabbard, *Space: Emerging Options for National Power* (Santa Monica: RAND, 1998), p. 8.

3. Joint Publication 3-14, *Joint Doctrine for Space Operations* (Washington, DC: Joint Staff, 9 August 2002), p. GL-6.

4. "Iridium Goes for Next Generation LEO Satellites," *SatNews Daily*, 15 February 2007, http://www.satnews.com/stories2007/3985.htm; and "Our Business: MSS Market Leader," INMARSAT, http://www.inmarsat.com/About/Our_business.aspx?language=EN&textonly=False.

5. Michael Griffin, "The Space Economy" (NASA 50th Anniversary Lecture Series, 17 September 2007).

6. Loring Wirbel, "2006 Space Expenditures of $220 Billion Show 18% Increase," *EETimes Online*, 10 October 2007, http://www.eetimes.com/news/latest/showArticle.jhtml?articleID=202400985.

7. Michael Rasher, "The Use of GPS and Mobile Mapping for Decision-Based Precision Agriculture," GIS Development, http://www.gisdevelopment.net/application/agriculture/overview/agrio0011.htm.

8. Joan Johnson-Freese, *Space as a Strategic Asset* (New York: Columbia University Press, 2007), p. 83.

9. LTC David E. Lupton, *On Space Warfare: A Space Power Doctrine* (Maxwell AFB, AL: Air University Press, 1988), p. 19.

10. U.S. Department of Defense, *Gulf War Air Power Survey*, vol. 5, *A Statistical Compendium and Chronology* (Washington, DC: GPO, 1993), pp. 126–132.

11. Secretary of Defense William Cohen, *Kosovo/Operation Allied Force After-Action Report* (Washington, DC: GPO, 2000), p. 155.

12. Secretary of Defense Donald Rumsfeld and GEN Richard Myers, DoD news briefing (25 March 2003), http://www.defenselink.mil/transcripts/transcript.aspx?transcriptid=2141.

13. Cohen, *Kosovo/Operation Allied Force After-Action Report*, p. 94.

14. Figures compiled from various articles drawn from *Zhongguo Hangtian* (China Aerospace) and CASC and CASIC Web sites.

15. Dong Zhenyu, "The Development of Space Power and Assessing Space Dominance," *Zhongguo Hangtian*, November 2004, p. 35.

16. Fan Xuejun, "Militarily Strong Nations Are Steadily Developing 'Space Information Warfare,'" *Jiefangjun Bao*, 13 April 2005.

17. Zhang Yuwu, Dong Zean, et al., "Informationalized Warfare Will Make Seizing the Aerospace Technology 'High Ground' a Vital Factor," *Jiefangjun Bao*, 30 March 2005.

18. Wang Yao and Shi Chunming, "Regarding 'Space Information Combat,'" Jiefangjun Bao, 19 December 2002.

19. Wang Yao and Shi Chunming, "Regarding 'Space Information Combat.'"

20. Zhu Wenhao, "An Exploration of the PLA's Military Equipment Construction Leapfrogging Development Concept," *Junshi Xueshu*, no. 2 (2004). Zhu was with the General Armaments Department at the time the article was published.

21. Wang Yao and Shi Chunming, "Regarding 'Space Information Combat.'"

22. Phil Scott, "Space Rescue," New Scientist.com, 16 September 2000, http://space.newscientist.com/article/mg16722564.700-space-rescue.html; "Galaxy 4 Satellite Not Expected to Be Restored," CNN, 20 May 1998, http://www.cnn.com/TECH/space/9805/20/satellite.update/.

23. Philip P. Pan, "Banned Falun Gong Movement Jammed Chinese Satellite Signal," *Washington Post*, 9 July 2002, p. A18.

24. For further discussion of military modernization, innovation, and transformation, see Stephen Peter Rosen, *Winning the Next War* (Ithaca, NY: Cornell University Press, 1991); Williamson Murray and Allan R. Millett, eds., *Military Innovation in the Interwar Period* (New York: Cambridge University Press, 1996); and Williamson Murray and MacGregor Knox, eds., *The Dynamics of Military Revolution, 1300–2050* (New York: Cambridge University Press, 2001).

25. Williamson Murray, "Innovation: Past and Future," in *Military Innovation in the Interwar Period*, ed. Williamson Murray and Allan R. Millett (New York: Cambridge University Press, 1996), p. 306.

26. Rosen, *Winning the Next War*, p. 20.

27. Stephen Peter Rosen, "New Ways of War," *International Security* 13, no. 1 (Summer 1988), p. 136.

28. MG David A. Deptula, "Air Force Transformation: Past, Present, and Future," *Aerospace Power Journal*, Fall 2001.

29. Rosen, *Winning the Next War*, p. 20

30. Williamson Murray and MacGregor Knox, "The Future behind Us," in *The Dynamics of Military Revolution, 1300–2050*, ed. Williamson Murray and MacGregor Knox (New York: Cambridge University Press, 2001), p. 192.

31. Allan R. Millett, "Assault from the Sea: The Development of Amphibious Warfare between the Wars—the American, British and Japanese Experiences," in *Military Innovation in the*

Interwar Period, ed. Williamson Murray and Allan R. Millett (New York: Cambridge University Press, 1996), p. 94.

32. Murray and Knox, "The Future behind Us," p. 185.

33. Murray, "Innovation: Past and Future," p. 326.

34. Bob Preston, *Plowshares and Power* (NDU Press: Washington, DC, 1994), p. 4.

Panel V: Air and Space Forces

Summary of Discussion

Professor Roger H. Ducey
Associate Professor
National Security Decision Making Department
U.S. Naval War College

The Ruger Workshop's Air and Space Panel began with presentations given by Lieutenant General David Deptula, Mr. Barry Watts, and Mr. Dean Cheng. Their presentations generated a lively discussion that concentrated on two main issues: the future of U.S. intelligence, surveillance, and reconnaissance (ISR) capabilities in light of the Chinese antisatellite test and how current operations in Iraq and Afghanistan, as well as the long war on violent radicalism, will affect future defense budgets, specifically regarding the need for more forward-deployed "boots on the ground" today balanced with future antiaccess scenarios that require standoff capabilities.

A leadoff question began the discussion of the vulnerability of our satellites in low earth orbit and possible U.S. responses to an attack on these satellites by a potential adversary such as China. The participant asking the question offered a couple of responses including punishing the attacking nation for the escalatory move or compensating for the loss of reconnaissance capability from space, which would allow the United States to continue to obtain necessary information needed to conduct operations. A participant agreed that it would be difficult to completely protect our space assets in low earth orbit and that we should be ready to respond in a couple of different ways. One way would be to "rapidly reinsert the same capability below earth orbit." At the same time we should be ready to quickly "take out" the adversary's antisatellite capabilities after the first attack before they are able to destroy any more of our satellites. Developing the capability to reestablish our ISR capability with an airborne asset versus a space asset from a budget standpoint, this participant asserted, will present a challenge to existing organizational budgetary processes. The Air Force, as well as the Department of Defense in general, tends to look at space differently. "We tend to be hindered by the bureaucracies that we've built in terms of looking at the balance of investment between the space piece and the air piece." "And we've got other stuff," such as the way we describe the information we use to plan and conduct operations. On the ground and in the air we refer to it as ISR; Air Force Space Command refers to it as "space situational awareness." "It's the same thing." "So we need to better figure out how we can rapidly adapt to those kinds of potential challenges and not just replace it in that particular domain." "The product is what is important, not necessarily how we do it." The other thing that concerned this participant was that we tend to be constrained by the way we classify information based on sources. "As Barry Watts indicated in his presentation, there are a number of nations that have access to information down to 1-meter accuracy obtained from commercial satellites." "We're still treating a lot of that" as highly classified information, which prevents "one office from talking to another office."

Another participant felt that by destroying one of our satellites another nation may be escalating the conflict to a level beyond one that is desired. It might be more advantageous to "conceal, jam, dazzle, or soft kill" our satellites before it would attempt to "hard kill" them. The participant also noted "going after" another country's antisatellite launch sites presents a "couple of problems," especially in a China scenario. The first would be that you would be "of course striking continental China," which we've avoided over "the past 50 years." The participant maintained that you would "really have to wonder whether it would be worth it," and the other issue would be that the Chinese have been testing mobile antisatellite weapons "so now you have the additional problem of how much of China are you willing to lay waste to."

Another question focused on information dominance and whether the Chinese were more dependent on it than the United States and whether they would be more disadvantaged by a lack of information dominance than the United States in a conflict. One participant argued that the Chinese had in their writings expressed the belief that they need to be able to assert information dominance in future wars. The participant went on to suggest that a more important question might be about the differences each side will make in trying to achieve information dominance in the future. The difference, he maintained, is that China is still currently a regional power and will be for the foreseeable future. Because of that, its focus will be a hundred miles off its shore, on the island of Taiwan. This removes the need to develop global command and control and global sensor capabilities and allows it to focus on regional capabilities. This will make its approach different from ours. The Chinese may not be able to completely "deny us access so much as they can make it very costly." The participant still felt that yes, if we were "fighting in their front yard," they would want to achieve information dominance to the extent possible.

The other issue that dominated the conversation was how to achieve greater efficiencies and savings through more and better interdependence. A question asked by one of the workshop participants was how to achieve these synergies and savings. One participant felt that the services are working outside of their core competencies. The Navy and the Air Force in trying to assist the Army and Marine Corps in Iraq and Afghanistan have developed redundant capabilities. The Navy has set up a "naval expeditionary command and [is] building another infantry element in addition to the Marines." "The Army is spending billions of dollars and investing thousands of people to create its own medium-altitude UAV [unmanned aerial vehicle] structure and is procuring a plane to conduct airlift." "At the same time the Air Force has already invested twenty thousand people to drive convoys and do prisoner interrogations and detention operations." The participant felt we need to establish "some discipline in terms of where our competencies are because as we move into a world of constrained resources, it just makes sense." Even though many have described this as an Air Force–versus–Army argument, "it's really an argument between smaller units controlling aircraft versus a joint force commander."

"There are no Air Force targets in Iraq." "There are only joint force targets." "The joint force commander should operate the aircraft to provide the effect the joint force wants to accomplish." This participant maintained that it was important for each service to provide the capabilities that were inherently core to its charter and to eliminate the redundancies that had sprung up in the past few years.

The panel ended with a discussion regarding the tension that is forming between the need to fund the programs that provide the capabilities that are needed to conduct present operations in Iraq and Afghanistan and the need to look into the future and fund the capabilities that may be needed to address antiaccess scenarios and major force-on-force engagements. There was a spirited discussion of what portion of the defense budget should be allotted to each, as one would imagine.

The presentations made by General Deptula, Mr. Watts, and Mr. Cheng, along with the subsequent discussion, were of great benefit to all those who attended. The panelists were commended for their presentations and for bringing such important national security issues to the forefront of debate.

Panel VI

Joint Special Operations Forces

Dr. Richard Shultz
Professor of International Politics, and Director, International Security
Studies Program, The Fletcher School, Tufts University

Dr. David C. Tucker
Associate Professor, Department of Defense Analysis, Naval Postgraduate
School

Moderator:
Commander Thomas C. Sass
U.S. Navy, Professor of Joint Military Operations, U.S. Naval War College

The Evolving International Security Environment of the 21st Century: Armed Groups and Irregular Warfare

Dr. Richard Shultz
Professor of International Politics
Director, International Security Studies Program
The Fletcher School
Tufts University

Introduction

Over the last two decades non-state armed groups—terrorists, insurgents, militias, and criminal organizations—have proliferated in number and importance. Today, armed groups can pose major security challenges to the United States, even without acquiring weapons of mass destruction (WMD). And these challenges are not confined to distant lands. Some armed groups have developed power projection capabilities; they can strike across the globe, to include against the U.S. homeland.

Moreover, the security challenges posed by armed groups are not temporary. To the contrary, they will continue to present serious and dangerous security problems for states, including the United States. Armed groups will be a significant part of the twenty-first-century global security landscape, having broadened the nature and scope of their activities.

Through the 1990s the expanding threats posed by armed groups were a low priority for the U.S. government and its national security institutions. When considered at all, armed groups were treated as minor problems, not as complex and interrelated security phenomena. Indeed, it is fair to say that as armed groups expanded their power and capabilities during and in the aftermath of the cold war, U.S. agencies concerned with national security dealt with them in an *episodic, transitory*, and *ad hoc* manner. Armed groups were a low-priority and negligible security issue.

In response to 9/11 this stance has undergone change. There now is a major focus on al Qaeda and its associated movements (AQAM), which constitute the global Salafi Jihad. The same is true of armed groups in Iraq and Afghanistan. However, there is only limited recognition that other armed groups present serious security threats and opportunities to the United States in key regions of the world where America has vital interests. And only segments of the American national security system have begun to consider the capabilities needed to effectively manage these nontraditional security challenges. There is no consensus on the priority of the problem or on how to deal with it.

This paper examines the complex and diverse nature of armed groups within the context of the twenty-first-century security environment, assesses the challenges they pose to U.S. security, and explores the extent to which the

Department of Defense is developing the foundations for meeting these threats and opportunities. The paper has the following objectives:

- To provide an overview of the global security environment in the early twenty-first century and to highlight the types of conflict taking place within that environment

- To present a brief tutorial on armed groups as a category of non-state actors that consists at minimum of four sub-types—insurgents, terrorists, militias, and organized crime

- To draw attention to the major and even strategic challenges that armed groups can pose to the United States

- To examine how the Department of Defense is responding to the armed group threats it has faced since 9/11 and to assess whether the concept of irregular warfare (IW) is an appropriate foundation to guide the development and integration of military strategy and capabilities for responding to these threats.

Twenty-First-Century International Security Environment

Before the cold war ended, non-state actors—armed groups—were of growing importance in an evolving international security environment. By the end of the 1990s, a handful of public policy centers and academic specialists were, to varying degrees, pointing out their impact on stability and conflict. A common theme running through these studies was that non-state actors were proliferating in number and significance.[1]

For example, James Rosenau explained that the broad scope of global politics, the arena within which political activities occur, and the relationships among actors were all changing, and would continue to do so in the twenty-first century. Rosenau outlined the parameters of a new international security environment.[2] Three key developments were said to have accelerated the growth of non-state armed groups: *integration/fragmentation*, *state failure*, and *lawless/ungoverned territory*.

At the center of this new global milieu were the contradictory processes of *integration* and *fragmentation* and the bifurcation of world politics. While the 1990s were marked by the globalization of capital and markets, expansion of transnational organizations, and spread of shared norms—all key aspects of the international integration of states—other sources of power challenged those developments.[3] They included, most importantly, the growing influence of non-state actors at both the sub-state and transnational levels.

With the end of the cold war this process of fragmentation escalated as sub-state actors increasingly contested the authority, legitimacy, and capacity of states to rule. According to Robert Rotberg: "The decade plus since the end of the cold war has witnessed a cascading plethora of *state failures*, mostly in Africa but also in Asia. In addition, more and more states are at risk, exhibiting acute signs of weakness and/or the likelihood of outright failure."[4]

This has been documented in various data sets, including "The Failed State Index," which is compiled annually by the Fund for Peace. Using twelve social, economic, political, and military indicators, this index ranks 148 states in order of their vulnerability to violent internal conflict and societal dysfunction.[5] To be sure, in a given year individual states can make progress—2005 was a good year for many fragile and developing states[6]—but the study's authors caution that the decline of individual conflicts has to be seen within a larger global context. Many millions of people live in countries that run a significant risk of collapse. "They are alienated by corrupt and ineffective governments and see little hope for economic improvement. These insecure and unstable states are breeding grounds for terrorism, organized crime, weapons proliferation, humanitarian emergencies, environmental degradation, and political extremism."[7]

Chester Crocker summarizes the situation found within these states as follows: "Self-interested rulers . . . progressively corrupt the central organs of government." And they "ally themselves with criminal networks to divide the spoils." The authority of the state is "undermined . . . paving the way for illegal operations." In conjunction with these developments, "state security services lose their monopoly on the instruments of violence, leading to a downward spiral of lawlessness." Finally, "when state failure sets in, the balance of power shifts . . . in favor of armed entities [groups]" who are "outside the law." They "find space in the vacuums left by declining or transitional states."[8]

This latter development—the expansion of lawless and ungoverned areas beyond the authority of government—creates safe havens in which armed groups can establish secure bases. Within and/or across the borders of several (not all) weak and failing states are areas in which the government in question has no presence or authority. Increasingly, this ungoverned territory provides secure bases in which various armed groups train, plan, and launch operations locally, regionally, and globally.[9]

This is the "new sanctuary" for armed groups. It covers significant territory—both urban and rural—and is attractive to a range of armed groups.[10] Central and South America is illustrative. This area has significant ungoverned territory and armed groups are making widespread use of it.[11] In his 2006 posture statement General John Abizaid likewise highlighted how in the Central Command region armed groups were taking advantage of ungoverned space in the Horn of Africa.[12]

Due to the developments described above, internal conflicts, many with transnational dimensions, burgeoned in the 1980s and 1990s. And especially since the cold war ended, the interrelated factors of globalization, information-based technologies, and network-based approaches to organization have provided armed groups with capabilities and opportunities that were not available to their earlier counterparts.

The frequency of these conflicts has been documented by several research organizations, most notably the International Institute for Strategic Studies (IISS). Its *Armed Conflict Database* provides information on conflicts worldwide. Of the seventy conflicts that IISS has followed since the early 1990s nearly all involve insurgent, militia, terrorist, and criminal armed groups fighting against states. IISS also traces the growth of "Selected Non-State Armed

Groups," providing detailed data and links for more than 270 insurgent, militia, and terrorist organizations.[13]

The International Peace Research Institute in Oslo (PRIO), in association with the University of Uppsala Conflict Data Program in Sweden, records global armed conflicts annually, dividing them into four categories: interstate, intrastate, extrastate, and internationalized internal conflicts. Their database also illustrates the rise in the number of conflicts fought between states and armed groups. According to PRIO, in the 1950s they represented only between a third and half of all conflicts, whereas by the 1990s they accounted for nearly all armed conflict.[14]

In the 1990s, Martin van Creveld and a small number of conflict specialists proposed that a transformation was under way and conflict was changing (or at a minimum diversifying). In *The Transformation of War* Van Creveld asserts that unprecedented changes in international affairs were altering the causes

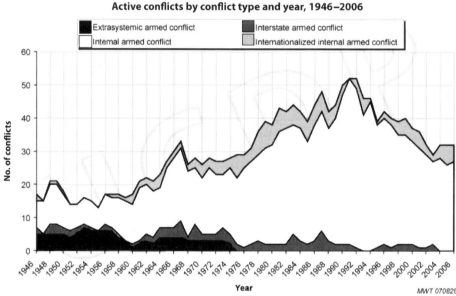

Active conflicts by conflict type and year, 1946–2006

and conduct of war across the global landscape, and new actors were emerging—tribal, ethnic, and religious factions—to challenge the dominance of state power. Nation-states would increasingly be confronted by non-state actors that refused to recognize the states' monopoly over armed violence.[15]

Throughout the 1990s this proposition generated a spirited debate within the U.S. defense community. Most military professionals and civilian security studies specialists rejected his thesis. Despite tectonic shifts in the global landscape during the 1990s, the institutions that constitute the U.S. national security system continued to treat armed groups as ancillary matters.

To illustrate this point, consider the following. Even as terrorist attacks against the United States escalated in the final decade of the twentieth century to the point that in one operation they nearly sank a Navy guided-missile destroyer, units within the Pentagon's Special Operations Command, which had been established for offensive—preemptive—counterterrorism operations against terrorists to prevent such attacks, were never employed. Within the military there was great reluctance to do so. Attacks such as that on the USS *Cole* were law enforcement problems, not ones necessitating military force.[16]

Damage to the USS Cole.[17]

Even in the aftermath of 9/11, raising the salience of armed groups to a tier-one security challenge and adapting U.S. national security institutions to meet these challenges have come slowly. Thus, with great difficulty and mounting frustration the United States has found itself mired down in major protracted conflicts in Afghanistan and Iraq, as well as confronting lesser armed-group challenges in several other regional contexts in Asia, the Americas, and Africa.

For the U.S. military, Afghanistan and Iraq have been extremely vexing. But it is not alone. The other agencies that constitute the American national security system have likewise found themselves ill equipped to deal with armed groups, let alone to address the larger issues of legitimacy and nation-state viability that characterize the environment in which armed groups are now major actors and sources of instability.

This situation calls for systemic change within U.S. national security institutions to meet these new challenges. The United States now faces major security challenges from non-state armed groups (and states supporting them) who employ a full range of irregular warfare methods. But America's national security system—how it thinks about war and organizes, trains, and educates for it—is not calibrated to prevail against these threats.

The starting point—the keystone—for bringing this transformation about is the development of new security operating concepts that (1) *explain* major contemporary challenges posed by non-state armed groups and (2) *identify* the principles, strategies, and capabilities needed to meet these challenges. To date, coming to a clear understanding of these developments and how to address them has proved extremely difficult for U.S. national security institutions. As we will see later in this paper, only in 2006 did the Department of Defense begin to move in this direction. And other national security agencies continue to lag behind the Pentagon.

Armed Groups—a Brief Tutorial

To both understand the contemporary threats posed by armed groups and develop effective strategies and capabilities to meet them, it is first necessary to develop analytic tools for defining and differentiating these violent non-state actors.

Increasingly, the term "armed groups" is being adopted to describe non-state actors that employ unconventional violence and asymmetric tactics to attack states. The media's coverage of both Afghanistan and Iraq is illustrative. Likewise, a number of nongovernmental organizations (NGOs) concerned with both the human costs of internal war and conflict-management measures to resolve them have adopted the term "armed groups." Finally, as noted above, research organizations like IISS and PRIO are also establishing databases on these non-state actors.

Here we will briefly (1) suggest a definition of armed groups that is based on a set of characteristics that all such organizations have in common; (2) propose a classification or taxonomy of armed groups that divides them into four sub-types: insurgents, terrorists, militias, and criminal organizations; and (3) illustrate how armed groups in each of the four categories are not static but dynamic organizations that can transform and morph from one sub-type into another or play multiple roles simultaneously.

Developing this understanding is critical from an operational perspective. Before one can identify the principles, strategies, and capabilities needed to meet the challenges posed by armed groups, an analytic understanding of the dimensions of the armed group phenomenon is the necessary starting point. Here we will only provide an overview—a brief tutorial.

Common Characteristics of Armed Groups

What constitutes an armed group? Is there a common set of characteristics that all armed groups share? We have identified eight specific features, based on research conducted with Roy Godson at the National Strategy Information Center. All armed groups, to varying degrees:

1. Challenge the authority, power, and legitimacy of states, seeking to either undermine or co-opt them.

2. Do not adhere to but seek to manipulate the rule of law and democratic principles.

3. Have at least a minimum degree of independence from state control.

4. Believe in the maintenance and use of force and violence to achieve political, religious, economic, and personal aims. Challenge the state's monopoly on legitimate coercive power.

5. Use violence in unconventional, asymmetric, and—in certain cases—increasingly indiscriminate ways.

6. Operate within and across state boundaries, across geographical regions, and, sometimes, globally. May exercise some degree of territorial control.

7. Maintain a secret or clandestine infrastructure as their key organizational method, although they may maintain overt political fronts as well. Clandestine infrastructure includes "intelligence-counterintelligence" capabilities, as well as financial, logistical, and communications networks. These clandestine organizations have varying levels of cohesion.

8. Have factional and external rivalries that affect cooperation, interaction, and effectiveness.

Categorizing Armed Groups: A Taxonomy

These common characteristics withstanding, there are important differences among various types of armed groups. How should specific types of armed groups be defined, differentiated one from another, and categorized? In previously noted research completed under the auspices of the National Strategy Information Center a taxonomy of armed groups was conceptualized. It consists of four categories of actors—insurgents, terrorists, militias, and criminal organizations.[18]

These four sub-types—while sharing the common features identified above—have important differences among them. This is true in terms of the following six elements: (1) leadership, (2) rank and file membership, (3) organizational structure and functions, (4) ideology/political code of beliefs, (5) strategy and tactics, and (6) linkages with other non-state and state actors. How armed groups approach each will vary. Understanding these differences is critical to meeting the challenges they may present.

Different specialists have described and assessed insurgents, terrorists, militias, and organized crime in various ways. It is beyond the scope of this paper to review these different efforts. What follows are basic working definitions for each that sets out key differences among them. It is presented here as a starting point for the kind of analytic understanding that is necessary for the development of effective countermeasures.

Insurgents

Insurgents can threaten the state with complex political and security challenges based on the ways in which they organize and the strategies they employ. *There is no generic type of insurgent.* They can differ based on their organizational forms, which can range from ones with complex political, intelligence, and military dimensions to ones that are more narrowly structured along conspiratorial lines. Insurgents can also be distinguished by the aspirations they seek to accomplish.[19]

In the aftermath of 9/11 several specialists proposed that the nature of insurgency was evolving from its primarily national-level focus in the twentieth century to a global one today.[20] Other specialists, focusing on Iraq, have argued that the insurgency there has the characteristics of "netwar" as described in an earlier work by Arquilla and Ronfeldt, and cannot be described in terms of the structural command relations of past insurgencies. This presents a serious challenge for those formulating a counterinsurgency response.[21]

Insurgency is defined as protracted political and military activities with the objective of gaining partial or complete control over the territory of a country through the use of irregular military tactics and illegal political activities. Insurgents engage in actions ranging from guerrilla operations, terrorism, and sabotage to political mobilization, political action, intelligence and counterintelligence activities, propaganda, and psychological warfare. These instruments are employed as part of strategies designed to weaken and/or destroy the power and legitimacy of a ruling government while at the same time increasing the power and legitimacy of the armed insurgent group.

Terrorists

Terrorism and those armed groups who employ this form of violence have been defined in a myriad of ways. Definitional disagreements persist over a range of issues, including (1) the line of division between terrorism and other forms of political violence, (2) whether the concept of terrorism should distinguish between the nature of the act or the nature of the perpetrator, (3) whether terrorism should be defined as a criminal or a political act, (4) how terrorist organizations differ from other organizations that sometimes employ terrorism.[22]

The definition that follows concentrates on the nature and target of the act. In doing so, we can contrast terrorists with insurgents to see how they differ. Terrorism is the deliberate creation and exploitation of fear by an armed group through the threat and/or use of the most proscribed kind of violence for political or criminal purposes, whether for or in opposition to an established government. The act is designed to have a far-reaching psychological effect beyond the immediate target of the attack and to instill fear in a wider audience. The targets of terrorist groups increasingly are noncombatants, and large numbers of them, who under international norms have the status of protected individuals and groups.

Scrutiny reveals important differences between insurgent movements and terrorist organizations. Understanding these dissimilarities is not simply an academic exercise. Such an appreciation is essential for those governments faced with having to combat each type of armed groups.

Important distinctions exist between terrorist groups and insurgents with respect to tactics and targeting. It is the case that insurgent use of violence can include terrorism. But they also rely on guerrilla warfare tactics, defined here as irregular small-unit attacks against the state's military and security forces to harass, exhaust, and force them to overextend their resources.

In conjunction with violence, insurgents employ a number of political tactics to reallocate power within the country. They may do so for revolutionary objectives—to overthrow and replace the existing social order. Or they may have less-grandiose aspirations, such as removing from power an established government without a follow-on social revolutionary agenda, establishing an autonomous national territory, forcing the withdrawal of an occupying power, or extracting political concessions that are unattainable through less-violent means.

These differences are captured graphically in the diagram below. Here we can see that there is some overlap between terrorism and insurgency, but there are also large areas where they do not intersect.

In terms of motivations, terrorist groups have evolved from the cold war to the post–cold war to the post-9/11 environment. Terrorist groups in the 1990s were increasingly motivated by ethnicity and religion.[23] This trend has continued

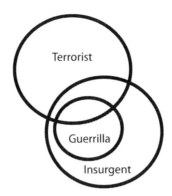

in the first decade of the twenty-first century, as reflected in the use of terrorist tactics by Salafi Jihad groups.[24]

Militias

With the growing number of weak and failing states, a third category of armed groups—militias—has become increasingly numerous and prominent. They appear to thrive in states with ineffectual central governments and to benefit from a global black market in various commodities that facilitates their growth.

Militias and those who lead them represent in some cases, such as Hezbollah, an alternative political authority to that of the state.[25] In other situations they are the product of a failed state that is not easily reconstructed, and the militias that emerge take the form of local gangs.[26] While individual militias have received attention, particularly those in sub-Saharan Africa and central Asia, there have been very few attempts to define this type of armed group in an analytically precise way or to develop a typology that identifies and categorizes different militia sub-types.[27]

Based on post–cold war examples, armed militia groups can be defined as recognizable irregular armed forces operating within the territory of a weak and/or failing state. The members of militias often come from the disadvantaged or underclasses and tend to be young males who are drawn into this milieu because it gives them access to money, resources, power, identity, and security. Not infrequently they are forced to join. In other instances becoming a member is seen as an opportunity. Finally, membership may be viewed as a duty based on identity.

Militias can represent specific ethnic, religious, tribal, clan, or other communal groups. They may operate under the auspices of a powerful factional leader, clan, or ethnic group, or on their own after the breakup of the states' forces. They may also be in the service of the state, either directly or indirectly. Generally, members of militias receive no formal military training. Nevertheless, in some cases they are highly skilled unconventional fighters. In other instances they are nothing more than a gang of extremely violent thugs that prey on the civilian population.

Within the parameters of this description, militias vary widely, revealing the diversity and complexity that exists within this category of armed groups. They can be differentiated in terms of the following four characteristics: (1) how they are led, (2) the bases on which they are organized, (3) the objectives they seek to achieve, and (4) the ways they operate and conduct themselves.

Consider the first factor, the relationship between militia leaders and individual members, more specifically between warlords and the militias from which they derive their power.[28] This relationship spans a complicated continuum that stretches from ethnic- and clan-based militias whose allegiances for commanders are based on personal prestige and ability to provide security and benefits for their followers to smaller militarized gangs mobilized behind their local strongmen who provide their members with access to money and security.

Likewise, how militias organize themselves can take a number of forms. What the case study literature reveals is that this can range from relatively small, informal, and part-time self-defense forces to formal, hierarchical, almost state-like entities with full-time members, specialization, and a chain of command. And these organizations can be based on pure patronage or some other unit of identity, to include clan and tribe.[29]

Understanding such distinctions with respect to militias in today's security environment can be very challenging. But it can also be critical to do so, and failing to do so can have serious consequences for those engaging militia groups. Consider the difficulty the United States has had since 2003 in coming to grips with Iraq's various militias and their Kurdish, Sunni Arab, and Shia Arab subcultures.[30]

Criminal Organizations

Perhaps the most pervasive category of armed groups in the taxonomy is that of organized crime. These groups have burgeoned over the last twenty-five years and several have established international linkages and networks. Organized criminal groups are characterized by (1) an identifiable structure operating outside the law; (2) engagement, in a region or globally, in more than one criminal enterprise; (3) internal cohesion and loyalty derived from ethnicity and family ties; (4) employment of violence to promote and protect interests; and (5) profit maximization.

The following definition captures these dimensions: An armed criminal group possesses a clandestine or secret hierarchical structure and leadership that operates outside the law in a particular criminal enterprise. Such groups frequently engage in more than one type of criminal activity and can operate over large areas of a region and globally. Often, these groups have family or ethnic bases that enhance the cohesion and security of their members. These armed groups typically maintain their positions through the threat or use of violence, corruption of public officials, graft, or extortion. The widespread political, economic, social, and technological changes occurring within the world allow organized crime groups to pursue their ultimate objective—to make as much money as possible from illegal activities.

A significant development since the end of the cold war has been the increased involvement of insurgents, terrorists, and militias with international criminal organizations (ICOs) in order to diversify their resource bases. For ICOs these linkages are equally valuable and widen the scope and profitability of their enterprises.[31]

Yet an additional linkage is that between international criminal organizations and political actors, to include officeholders and the staff of the legal governmental establishment of a state. Godson has described this linkage as a political-criminal nexus (PCN).[32] This involves collaboration between a local political establishment and armed criminal groups to undermine the rule of law and democratic development. A case in point can be found in the region encompassing Colombia, Mexico, Central America, and the Caribbean.[33]

The Dynamic Nature of Armed Groups

Armed groups are not static organizations. Here we have divided them into four categories to analytically differentiate one from another. In the real world these distinctions are not always static or long lasting but often the opposite.

For example, at one point in time an armed group may be classified as a terrorist organization based on its operational and organizational profile, while at another point it morphs into a militia or criminal enterprise. In other instances, an armed group can simultaneously be described as fitting into more than one of our four sub-types. In other words, at the same time it corresponds to the definitions of both a terrorist organization and a criminal enterprise or some other combination. Consider the following examples.

In Iraq these complexities and transformations can be seen in the different armed groups that are currently active. There are several armed groups that are playing multiple roles in various combinations. Other armed groups are morphing.

The different armed groups confronting Israel within the West Bank and Gaza, as well as regionally, likewise illustrate these complexities and transformations. Because of their operational and organizational activities, they can be classified in more than one of our four categories simultaneously.

Armed Groups: Threats and Opportunities

Thus far this paper has highlighted how, through the 1990s and now in the twenty-first century, conflicts pitting armed groups against states have been on the rise. Moreover, those clashes have had a significant impact on the once-dominant role of states, to include the United States (and its allies). Here we will suggest a way of classifying those threats and also include a brief comment on the proposition that armed groups might also be considered as opportunities for advancing policy objectives.

There are some armed groups that can strike at high-value targets locally, regionally, and across the globe. They have a global presence and global power projection capabilities. Consequently, such groups constitute a *direct strategic threat*. Consider the following examples:

- *Al Qaeda.* One of the first to establish a global reach, it attacked U.S. targets across the world in the 1990s. And on 9/11 it leveled direct strategic blows against the American homeland.

- *Hezbollah.* In the 1990s, it developed a global network of active and sleeper cells. Through this network it was involved in the Khobar Towers bombing and a failed attack on U.S. ships in the Singapore Strait. Its attacks against Israeli targets in Buenos Aires in 1992 and 1994 were the largest in the Western Hemisphere prior to 9/11.

- *Global Salafi Jihad Movement.* This expanding clandestine network of local/regional Islamist groups is spreading across the globe. Inspired by al Qaeda, they organize and carry out attacks on their own. Examples include the Madrid (March 2004) and London (July 2005) bombings.

Al Qaeda's 9/11 attack had both a strategic impact and strategic consequences, triggering a radical change in American policy toward terrorism.[34] Hezbollah has demonstrated a similar strategic capacity against Israel, a major ally of the United States in the Middle East. Hezbollah has expanded its arsenal and security arrangements with other regional actors to become a player with clear strategic goals in the Lebanese arena and the Israeli-Palestinian conflict.[35]

Armed groups can also present *direct regional threats* to the United States and other major powers that likewise can have strategic effects. To do so, they employ standard clandestine terrorist, insurgent, and criminal practices. This was true during the cold war and remains true in its aftermath. Armed groups can attack American facilities and personnel deployed abroad (in conjunction with those of local U.S. allies) with the goal of undermining major U.S. policies and strategic commitments. Current examples include:

- *Iraq.* Armed groups seek to inflict a strategic defeat on the United States by undermining political reform, reconstruction, and the establishment of democracy and the rule of law.[36]

- *Afghanistan.* Warlords and their militias, narco-traffickers, and resurging Taliban and al Qaeda forces challenge long-term stability, development, and regional progress.[37]

Finally, armed groups can pose *indirect threats* as well by destabilizing states and/or regions that are important to the United States. They do so through activities short of the kind of combat that is taking place in Iraq. Their tactics include political action, subversion, corruption, criminal enterprise, and low-level violence. These indirect threats can affect important U.S. interests in various ways. One way in which this can occur is through collaboration between local political leaders and institutions and armed groups. The following are examples of this kind of indirect threat:

- *Colombia, Mexico, Central America, and the Caribbean.* Collaboration ranges from the chronic to the acute, and often dominates political, economic, and social life even on the U.S. border. It creates zones of opportunity for armed groups inside and outside the region.[38]

- *Former Soviet Union.* Political-criminal collaboration can facilitate the acquisition of WMD by armed groups hostile to the United States.[39]

- *West/Southern Africa.* Local government officials, insurgents, and criminal syndicates collaborate to exploit the illegal diamond trade and undermine development. And both Hezbollah and al Qaeda have cooperated in this enterprise.[40]

Armed groups are not always threats. Sometimes they may provide opportunities to further a state's policy objectives through (1) exploitation of the military forces of armed groups against rival armed groups and states, (2) temporary control and security of local territory by an armed group so other armed groups or states cannot use it, and (3) intelligence on state and non-state adversaries.

The United States cooperated with armed groups in these ways during the Vietnam War, and again in the 1980s through assistance to armed groups in Afghanistan and Nicaragua. More recently, in 2001, U.S. cooperation with the Northern Alliance helped to topple the Taliban and destroy al Qaeda's base in Afghanistan.[41]

Viewing armed groups as opportunities is highly controversial. But the option should not be eschewed on those grounds. On a case-by-case basis it should be given careful scrutiny.

Irregular Warfare

In the mid-1990s the commandant of the Marine Corps, General Charles Krulak, in what has turned out to be a prophetic presentation titled "Not Like Yesterday," warned that war in the future would not mirror Desert Storm. He asserted that in the last decade of the twentieth century the conduct of war was evolving and the United States must adapt to the notion that wars would differ from those of yesterday. Within that changing context, the commandant singled out "the rise of non-state actors."[42]

This paper has proposed that over a decade later, what the commandant envisaged has evolved and burgeoned in ways that call for systemic change within U.S. national security institutions to meet these new challenges.[43] But even in the aftermath of 9/11 the United States has found it difficult to do so. Complex irregular warfare followed initial American successes in toppling the Taliban and Baathist regimes in Afghanistan and Iraq. And those protracted fights have demonstrated how the asymmetrical battlefield imposes demands on U.S. armed forces, in particular the Army and Marines, that have proved to be well beyond the kind of conventional war they had planned to fight.

Irregular conflicts in Afghanistan and Iraq revealed serious limitations in U.S. military planning and forced the Pentagon to seek to adapt. But adaptation has come haltingly. Only in 2006 did signs of change begin to appear. That year's *Quadrennial Defense Review* (QDR) stresses the need to prepare for unconventional and irregular warfare. The "long war," in which the United States is now engaged, is characterized in the QDR as "irregular in its nature." And enemies in that fight are "not traditional conventional military forces." Moreover, says the QDR, current and future U.S. military missions will feature counterterrorism, counterinsurgency, and stability operations. In each, the main adversary is an armed group, often more than one as Iraq has illustrated.[44]

However, as the Institute for International Strategic Studies has observed, the QDR contains major inconsistencies. "The QDR did little to make the DOD's long-term plans more realistic and affordable. Although it outlined 'transformational' areas where new investment will be required, there were no corresponding cuts in more traditional expenditure areas, suggesting that difficult budget decisions regarding expensive equipment programs have yet to be made."[45] U.S. emphasis has remained focused on programs and capabilities for conventional contingencies.

Other Pentagon initiatives, such as the 2006 *National Military Strategy for the War on Terror* have also acknowledged the need to expand U.S. forces capable of effectively engaging in irregular warfare activities. These include capabilities for long-duration unconventional warfare, counterterrorism, counterinsurgency, and military support for stabilization and reconstruction efforts.[46]

These nascent first steps have been followed by other initiatives, to include a new counterinsurgency manual and the *Irregular Warfare (IW) Joint Operating Concept (JOC)*, the latter of which was recently approved by Secretary of Defense Gates. The *IW JOC* is intended to "guide the development and integration of Department of Defense military concepts and capabilities for waging protracted IW on a global or regional scale against hostile states and armed groups."[47] Here we will briefly comment on the degree to which it is the right concept to provide the foundation for doing so.

Above we noted that in the 1990s irregular conflicts were considered by most military professionals and civilian specialists as ancillary security matters—sideshows—and not warfare. These were situations "other than war," lesser forms of conflict that did not reach the threshold of real combat.

The *IW JOC* rightly rejects this perspective, describing IW as "a form of warfare." Like its conventional counterpart, IW is characterized as "a violent clash of interests between or among organized groups characterized by the use of military force."[48] But irregular warfare differs in important ways, according to the *IW JOC*. It is not state-versus-state combat but rather "a violent struggle among state and non-state actors for legitimacy and influence over the relevant populations."

The center of gravity in IW is "the relevant populations to the nature of the conflict." Both parties to the conflict—armed groups and states—seek to enhance their legitimacy and credibility with the population and to exercise authority over it.[49] As General Rupert Smith has argued in his recent book—*The Utility of Force*—the key in irregular warfare is the population and not control of the enemy's armed forces or territory. Thus, as the *IW JOC* highlights, the focus of political, psychological, economic, and military operations must be centered on the population.

In terms of means, irregular warfare "favors indirect and asymmetric approaches, though it may employ the full range of military and other capabilities, in order to erode an adversary's power, influence, and will."[50] The following diagram, drawn from the *IW JOC*, captures these key characteristics—actors, methods, strategic purpose—of irregular warfare.

Next, the *IW JOC* highlights the kinds of indirect operations and activities that fall within the parameters of this form of warfare. In terms of core IW roles and missions for U.S. military forces, these include

- Counterinsurgency (COIN)
- Unconventional warfare (UW)
- Counterterrorism (CT)

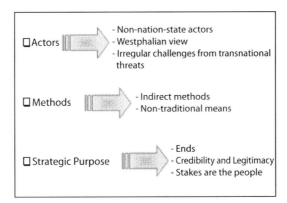

- Stabilization, security, transition, and reconstruction operations (SSTRO)

- Foreign internal defense (FID).

In light of the earlier discussion in this paper of the threats and opportunities posed by armed groups to the United States, these core missions make sense. And the UW mission ensures that the option exists for approaching armed groups as opportunities to further policy objectives. Finally, FID provides the means for assisting friends and allies to deal with armed group threats in their embryonic or incipient phases of development.

The remainder of the *IW JOC* concentrates on the "capabilities and capacities" American military commanders will require for prosecuting protracted irregular warfare effectively in the future. These include interagency and international requirements, both of which are considered essential. Reviewing these details is beyond the scope of this paper.

In sum, the *Irregular Warfare Joint Operating Concept* is a step forward. It is a useful guide that methodically describes the unconventional security threats posed by armed groups, defines the parameters of irregular warfare, and lays out the joint force requirements in terms of missions and capabilities needed for a twenty-first-century conflict environment where "irregular warfare will become the dominant form of warfare."[51] Whether it will reach fruition remains to be seen.

Notes

1. Some examples include Zalmay Khalilzad and Ian O. Lesser, eds., *Sources of Conflict in the 21st Century: Regional Futures and U.S. Strategy* (Washington, DC: RAND, April 1998); Ted Robert Gurr, *Peoples versus States: Minorities at Risk in the New Century* (Washington, DC: United States Institute of Peace, 2000); Donald L. Horowitz, *Ethnic Groups in Conflict* (Los Angeles, CA: University of California Press, 2000); Mary Kaldor, *New and Old Wars: Organized Violence in a Global Era* (CA: Stanford University Press, July 1999); Sudhir Kakar, *Colors of Violence: Cultural Identities, Religion and Conflict* (IL: University of Chicago Press, February 1996); Charles W. Kegley, Jr., and Eugene R. Wittkopf, *World Politics: Trends and Transformations*, 9th ed. (Belmont, CA: Wadsworth Press, 2004); John Bailey and Roy Godson, eds., *Organized Crime and Democratic Governability* (Pittsburg: University of Pittsburg Press: 2000); Roy Godson, ed., *Menace to Society: Political-Criminal Collaboration around the World* (New Brunswick, NJ: Transaction, 2003).

2. James Rosenau, *Along the Domestic-Foreign Frontier: Exploring Governance in a Turbulent World* (Cambridge, UK: Cambridge University Press, 2000).

3. Fragmentation is the result of a continuing allegiance to traditional or particularistic values and practices (e.g., ethnicity, ethno-nationalism, and religious fundamentalism) that challenge and weaken state authority.

4. Robert I. Rotberg, "Nation-State Failure: A Recurring Phenomenon?" This paper was prepared for the National Intelligence Council's project on the shape of the world in 2020, the NIC 2020 Project. Available at http://www.cia.gov/nic/NIC_home.html. Also see Rotberg, ed., *When States Fail: Causes and Consequences* (Princeton, NJ: Princeton University Press, 2004).

5. "The Failed State Index," *Foreign Policy* (May/June 2006). The data set can be accessed at http://fundforpeace.web.cedant.com/programs/fsi/fsindex.php. A failing state is defined as one where the government does not have control of its territory, is not seen as legitimate by a significant portion of its population, does not provide domestic security or basic public services, and lacks a monopoly on the use of force.

6. Ibid. "By most accounts, 2005 should have been a good year for many fragile and developing states around the world. A slew of countries—including many with limited democratic experience, such as Afghanistan, Egypt, Iraq, and Kazakhstan—held elections. The number of serious armed conflicts worldwide continued to fall. The world's richest countries agreed to forgive billions in developing-country debt. Robust world trade aided China's rise as an exporting powerhouse. And yet, trends that should have been boons for stability have often been busts." Why? Because "there are few quick fixes on the path to stability."

7. Ibid.

8. Chester Crocker, "Engaging Failing States," *Foreign Affairs* (September/October 2003), pp. 34–35.

9. For detailed maps of six ungoverned areas in six different regions of the world see Richard H. Shultz, Douglas Farah, and Itamara V. Lochard, *Armed Groups: A Tier-One Security Priority*, INSS Occasional Paper 57 (Colorado Springs, CO: U.S. Air Force Academy, Institute for National Security Studies, 2004), pp. 59–63.

10. Ungoverned territory is not confined to remote rural regions. It can also be found in cities that provide safe havens for armed groups, such as Mogadishu or Karachi. Members of al Qaeda redeployed to these urban sanctuaries after they were ousted from Afghanistan.

11. Philip Abbott, "Terrorist Threat in the Tri-border Area: Myth or Reality?" *Military Review* (September–October 2004). The author discusses the opportunities that lawless area provides to armed groups in the tri-border region.

12. General John Abizaid, *2006 Posture of the United States Central Command* (14 March 2006), pp. 3–12, 26–29. For a discussion of ungoverned territory in various parts of Africa see Council on Foreign Relations, *Backgrounder—Africa: Terror's Haven* (30 December 2003).

13. International Institute for Strategic Studies, *Armed Conflict Database*. For each conflict, IISS identifies the parties fighting, current status, the number of fatalities, costs, and the weapons used. It also provides an annual update of the year's trends and incidents. Criminal groups and gangs are excluded from this database, and hence, the full extent of armed conflicts is considerably greater than IISS reports.

14. Uppsala Conflict Data Program chart is available at http://www.prio.no/cwp/ArmedConflict/ and at http://www.pcr.uu.se. Mikael Eriksson, Peter Wallensteen, and Margareta Sollenberg, "Armed Conflict, 1989–2002," *Journal of Peace Research*, no. 5 (2003), pp. 593–607. This study documents that a total of 226 armed conflicts have been recorded for the years 1946–2002. Of these, 116 were active in the period 1989–2002, including 31 in 2002. The data for this study are drawn from the Uppsala Conflict Data Program Armed Conflict Web page at http://www.prio.no/cwp/ArmedConflict/ and at http://www.pcr.uu.se.

15. Martin van Creveld, *The Transformation of War* (New York: Free Press, 1991).

16. On this point see Richard H. Shultz, Jr., "Showstoppers," *Weekly Standard* 9, no. 19 (26 January 2004). Also see *The 9/11 Commission Report: Final Report of the National Commission on Terrorist Attacks upon the United States* (New York: W.W. Norton, 2004).

17. This and other photos of hull damage to the USS *Cole* are available at http://www.owlnet .rice.edu/~nava102/presentations/cole.ppt.

18. The National Strategy Information Center has developed an analytic framework that divides armed groups into four categories—insurgents, terrorists, militias, and organized crime—in order to spell out important differences among and within each of these four prototypes. It has also developed another framework for constructing systematic profiles of how an armed group organizes and functions. These analytic tools are described in Shultz, Farah, and Lochard, *Armed Groups*. These concepts were employed in Richard H. Shultz, Jr., and Andrea Dew, *Insurgents, Terrorists, and Militias: The Warriors of Contemporary Combat* (New York: Columbia University Press, 2006).

19. See Bard O'Neill, *Insurgency & Terrorism* (Washington, DC: Brassey's, 1990); Max G. Manwaring, "Toward an Understanding of Insurgency Wars: The Paradigm," in *Uncomfortable Wars: Toward a New Paradigm of Low-Intensity Conflict* (Boulder: Westview Press, 1991); and Ian F. W. Beckett, *Insurgency in Iraq: A Historical Perspective* (Carlisle, PA: Strategic Studies Institute of the U.S. Army War College, March 2005).

20. See John Mackinlay, *Globalization and Insurgency*, Adelphi Papers 352 (London: International Institute for Strategic Studies, November 2002); and Richard Shultz, *Global Insurgency Strategy and the Salafi Jihad Movement*, INSS Occasional Paper (Colorado Springs, CO: U.S. Air Force Academy, Institute for National Security Studies, forthcoming 2008).

21. See Bruce Hoffman, "Insurgency and Counterinsurgency in Iraq," *Studies in Conflict & Terrorism* (March/April 2006).

22. Bruce Hoffman, "Defining Terrorism," in *Terrorism and Counterterrorism: Understanding the New Security Environment*, ed. Russell Howard and Reid Sawyer, 2nd ed. (New York: McGraw-Hill/Dushkin, 2006), pp. 3–23; and Boaz Ganor, "Defining Terrorism: Is One Man's Terrorist Another Man's Freedom Fighter?" (International Institute for Counter-Terrorism, 2002).

23. Mark Juergensmeyer, "The Logic of Religious Violence," in *Terrorism and Counterterrorism: Understanding the New Security Environment*, ed. Russell Howard and Reid Sawyer, 2nd ed. (New York: McGraw-Hill/Dushkin, 2006), pp. 168–186.

24. Quintan Wiktorowicz, "Anatomy of the Salafi Movement," *Studies in Conflict & Terrorism* (April–May 2006), pp. 207–239; and Mark Sedgwick, "Al-Qaeda and the Nature of Religious Terrorism," *Terrorism & Political Violence* (October–December 2004), pp. 785–814.

25. Andrew Exum, *Hizballah at War: A Military Assessment* (Washington, DC: The Washington Institute for Near East Policy, December 2006).

26. International Crisis Group, "Côte D'Ivoire: The War Is Not Yet Over," Africa Report 72, (International Crisis Group, November 2003), available at http://www.crisisgroup.org/ home/index.cfm?1=1&id=2389.

27. Paul Jackson, "Warlords as Alternative Forms of Governance," *Small Wars & Insurgency* (Summer 2003), pp. 131–150; Paul Rich, ed., *Warlords in International Relations* (New York: St. Martin's Press, 1999).

28. John Mackinlay, "Defining Warlords," *International Peacekeeping* (Spring 2000), pp. 48–62; Kimberly Marten, "Warlordism in Comparative Perspective," *International Security* (Winter 2006–2007), pp. 41–73.

29. Alice Hills, "Warlords, Militias, and Conflict in Contemporary Africa," *Small Wars & Insurgency* (Spring 1997), pp. 35–41.

30. Thomas Mowle, "Iraq's Militia Problem," *Survival* (Autumn 2006), pp. 41–55.

31. See Thomas Sanderson, "Transnational Terror and Organized Crime: Blurring the Lines," *SAIS Review*, no. 1 (2004), pp. 49–61. The author examines how transnational terrorist

organizations are moving deeper into organized criminal activity and transforming into hybrid criminal/terror entities that partner with criminal syndicates. Robert Looney, "The Business of Insurgency: Expansion of Iraq's Shadow Economy," *National Interest*, Fall 2005, pp. 1–6. The author examines the convergence of segments of the Iraqi insurgency with organized crime and how this has important implications for the Iraqi economy. He concludes that the impact of these developments may have significant consequences beyond their direct impact. By creating an unstable security situation, their actions are retarding the development of the formal banking system. "Afghanistan: The Organized Narco-State," *Jane's Islamic Affairs Analyst*, 24 January 2007. This piece asserts that Afghanistan's lucrative opium trade is now controlled by a professionalized network of politicians and traffickers. This includes high-ranking provincial and central government officials.

32. Roy Godson, "The Political-Criminal Nexus and Global Security," in *Menace to Society: Political-Criminal Collaboration around the World*, ed. Roy Godson (New Brunswick, NJ: Transaction, 2003). The author describes how the active partnership between political actors—officeholders and the staff of the legal-governmental establishment of a state—and criminal actors functions in various parts of the world and the threats this collaboration poses for both local and regional states. These arrangements are termed the political-criminal nexus (PCN) by Godson. They consist of varying degrees of cooperation among political and criminal participants at the local, national, and transnational levels.

33. John Bailey and Jorge Chabat, eds., *Transnational Crime and Public Security: Challenges to Mexico and the United States* (San Diego, CA: Center for U.S.-Mexican Studies at the University of California, San Diego, 2002), ch. 1. This provides a case study of the political-criminal nexus and its impact on public security in the United States and Mexico.

34. Chairman of the Joint Chiefs of Staff, *National Military Strategic Plan for the War on Terrorism* (Washington DC: Department of Defense, February 2006), pp. 3–19. The first part of this document provides an excellent assessment of the post-9/11 global challenge posed by the al Qaeda Associated Movement (AQAM). It outlines the strategic environment, the dimensions of the war, how the AQAM has evolved, and the threats it poses to the United States and its allies. It describes the functions, processes, and resources that provide the AQAM with the capacity to do so. In sum, this document shows the direct strategic impact al Qaeda has had on the United States.

35. Ely Karmon, "Hizbollah as a Strategic Threat to Israel," *Heartland: Eurasian Review of Geopolitics* (July 2005).

36. Ahmed Hashim, *Insurgency and Counterinsurgency in Iraq* (Ithaca, NY: Cornell University Press, 2006), ch. 3; Shultz and Dew, *Insurgents, Terrorists, and Militias*, ch. 7.

37. Shultz and Dew, *Insurgents, Terrorists, and Militias*, ch. 6.

38. Stanley Pimental, "Mexico's Legacy of Corruption," in *Menace to Society: Political-Criminal Collaboration around the World*, ed. Roy Godson (New Brunswick, NJ: Transaction, 2003). This is a case study of the political-criminal nexus in Mexico.

39. Robert Orttung and Louise Shelley, "Linkages between Terrorist and Organized Crime Groups in Nuclear Smuggling: A Case Study of Chelyabinsk Oblast," PONARS Policy Memo 392 (NTI, December 2005), available at http://www.nti.org/e_research/cnwm/threat/russia.asp. This is an analysis of the "closed cities" in Russia's Chelyabinsk Oblast, where weapons of mass destruction are researched and produced, and of their increasing vulnerability to the threat that terrorist groups could use existing criminal networks and corruption to steal nuclear material.

40. Douglas Farah, *Blood from Stones: The Secret Financial Network of Terror* (New York: Broadway Books, 2004).

41. Henry Crumpton, "Intelligence and War: Afghanistan, 2001–2002," in *Transforming U.S. Intelligence*, ed. Jennifer E. Sims and Burton Gerber (Washington, DC: Georgetown University Press, 2005), ch. 10.

42. See the foreword by General Charles Krulak to Richard H. Shultz, Jr., and Robert L. Pfaltzgraff, eds., *The Role of Naval Forces in 21st Century Operations* (Washington, DC: Brassey's, 2000), pp. xi–xii.

43. A caveat about the changing paradigm of war debate is necessary. While the small wars of the 1990s, 9/11, and all that has followed since 9/11 make clear that war is evolving into new irregular forms, this does not mean that past conventional wars are passé. They are not. The United States will have to prepare for those fights as well. Thus, for example, the Marine Air-Ground Task Force (MAGTF) and combined-arms warfare will still be needed. But the Marines will also need the means to prevail in future irregular warfare against armed groups like those they have been fighting in Anbar. The same is true for the other services.

44. *Quadrennial Defense Review* (Washington, DC: Department of Defense, 6 February 2006).

45. International Institute for Strategic Studies, *The Military Balance, 2006* (London: Routledge, 2006), p. 20.

46. *National Military Strategic Plan for the War on Terrorism*. With respect to counterinsurgency, 2006 saw a joint Army–Marine Corps effort to establish a new manual designed to help operators face the challenges of armed groups employing asymmetric means: FM 3-24/MCRP 3-33.5, *Counterinsurgency* (Department of the Army, December 2006).

47. *Irregular Warfare (IW) Joint Operating Concept* (Department of Defense, July 2007).

48. The terms "organized" and "military force" refer to a group's ability to mobilize support for its own political interests and its ability to generate violence on a scale sufficient to have significant political consequences.

49. *IW Joint Operating Concept*, p. 4.

50. Ibid.

51. Ibid., p. 3.

The Present and Future Strategic Utility of Special Operations Forces[1]

Dr. David C. Tucker
Associate Professor, Department of Defense Analysis
Naval Postgraduate School

The war on terrorism has brought new prominence to special operations forces (SOF). Elements of SOF were critical to the destruction of the Taliban, played an important role in the invasion of Iraq, and have the lead in killing and capturing terrorists. These missions have shown the versatility of SOF. In Afghanistan and Iraq they achieved success by working with indigenous forces, while their targeting of terrorists depends on their perhaps-unequaled tactical skills. In part because of the strategy of the Bush administration, the most prominent or valued of SOF's missions in the war on terrorism so far has been the capturing or killing of terrorists and other individuals. If we look to the future, however, should this continue to be the case? What is SOF's greatest strategic utility likely to be?

We can begin to answer this question by considering SOF's roles and missions. SOF have two roles. They support conventional forces or they act independently. When SOF support conventional forces, their special missions are executed to facilitate achieving conventional force objectives. For example, in the Gulf War, some SOF elements helped clear the way for the advance of general purpose forces. In World War II, Navy underwater demolition teams conducted beach surveys and mining of underwater obstacles. These special missions were undertaken with the explicit purpose of assisting the assault on the beach by general purpose forces. In contrast, independent SOF operations may receive some support from conventional forces, but the entire effort is organized according to SOF principles and preferences. A well-known example would be the effort to capture Mohamed Farah Aideed in Somalia. Often, SOF perform their independent role without the support of conventional forces. SOF counterinsurgency efforts in El Salvador would be an example.

SOF conduct two kinds of missions. They engage the enemy either directly or indirectly. Two examples given above—the effort to capture Aideed and clearing beach obstructions—were SOF direct action missions because SOF were engaging an enemy or helping others to do so. An example of an indirect mission would be leading, or training others to lead, a counterinsurgency effort or the work of civil affairs and psychological operations forces in reestablishing effective civilian control of an area.

In making this distinction between direct and indirect missions, we must keep three things in mind. First, while these missions may occur separately, they may also be mutually supportive, producing a greater effect together than separately. For example, successful counterinsurgency will likely need to combine operations against the insurgents with efforts to protect a local population. Second, not all core SOF tasks fall neatly within one approach. Unconventional warfare, normally understood to be an indirect approach because it focuses on working with an indigenous population or military force, might include direct engagement of enemy forces by U.S. personnel. Psychological operations can achieve effects by working directly on the motivation of enemy forces or indirectly on the willingness of the population to support them. Third, as we are using it, the term "indirect" denotes not just a way of targeting the enemy (for example, by training other forces to do it) but a difference in strategy. The indirect approach aims primarily to defend or protect a population or help that population defend itself from an enemy, rather than to target the enemy, as does the direct approach.

The following table depicts SOF's roles and missions

	Independent Role	**Supporting Role**
Direct Missions	Attempted capture of Aideed in Somalia	Attack on Iraqi border radar to open first Gulf War
Indirect Missions	Training El Salvador's forces in counterinsurgency	Leading Kurdish tribesmen in Operation Iraqi Freedom

Given this breakdown of SOF roles and missions, how should we understand SOF's strategic utility? Generally speaking, SOF activities in a supporting role have less strategic utility than SOF activities in an independent role. When SOF perform in an independent role they are the strategic actor, if anyone is. In a supporting role, SOF make a strategic contribution only to the extent that the conventional force operations depend upon SOF for success. If the overall conventional force campaign plan is critically dependent upon SOF's contribution, then SOF's strategic value would be almost as high as when they perform independently, but this is almost never the case. Seldom would it make sense for a power like the United States, whose conventional military forces are currently unrivaled, to build a war strategy around SOF.

In addition to this almost-axiomatic sense in which SOF are less strategically useful in a supporting role, they are also less useful in this role because of the increasing capabilities of general purpose forces. The development of surveillance and targeting technology, for example, has reduced the importance of some SOF direct action missions, while improvement in the quality of general purpose forces has reduced the importance of SOF's indirect skills summarized under the tag "cultural awareness." Ongoing counterinsurgency operations by conventional forces in Iraq exemplify this development and also, perhaps, indicate its limits. In short, general purpose forces can now do things that in the past only special or elite forces could do or did so much better than general purpose forces that the missions had to go to special or elite forces if they were to have any chances of success.

The shrinking domain of missions exclusively in SOF's domain carries over from their supporting to their independent role. First, as our ability to identify and destroy individual targets continues to improve, the number of instances in which commanders will need SOF independent direct missions will decrease. The strategic utility of these missions will not reach zero. It will make sense to risk SOF when the situation requires human on-the-scene judgment to obtain the desired effect when this effect is something other than the mere destruction of the target without regard to collateral damage. An example of such a task might be the propagation or retrieval of critical information.

Second, it has become increasingly clear that the most prominent independent direct action mission (capturing or killing high-value targets) is at best of only limited strategic utility in countering terrorism. In some circumstances, it may even be counterproductive. In those cases where it is not counterproductive, it is likely to be effective only as a subordinate part of an essentially political strategy.[2]

How likely are these various trends to continue? It seems likely that the development of technology will continue, increasing our ability to target with precision. If the abilities of the volunteer force do not erode, then it is also likely that the effectiveness of general purpose forces in counterinsurgency and stability operations will also remain a fact of defense life. If, in addition, the Army's general purpose forces do not need to focus again on large-scale conventional operations, then it is likely that these forces will continue to be ready to take on the missions once thought to be SOF's. The key to success will be as it is now: understanding of counterinsurgency, for example, among officers and, through them, noncommissioned officers, combined with sufficient training to instill this understanding through the ranks.

If these trends continue, then it will become increasingly clear that SOF's greatest strategic utility is in their independent indirect missions, such as the counterinsurgency effort in El Salvador or the similar effort in the Philippines against the Abu Sayyaf Group on Basilan Island following 9/11. In these cases, the ability of SOF to operate in numbers limited for political reasons will give them an advantage over conventional forces. Concluding that SOF's independent indirect missions are likely to be most useful is paradoxical, since it is precisely these missions that historically have been most suspect in the eyes of military professionals and least respected and resourced in the special operations community. This suspicion and neglect is not without reason. These operations are not fully military, as military professionals, including many SOF, understand what is military; are often slow to produce results; and seldom produce decisive results. If the trends outlined above continue, this prejudice is likely to dissipate, at least somewhat.

To conclude that independent indirect missions provide and will provide SOF's greatest strategic utility does not mean that independent direct missions will not also be important. If the principal problem we confront is the combination of terrorism and weapons of mass destruction, and terrorism (the deliberate targeting of noncombatants for political ends) is a self-limiting strategy, then the principal focus of our National Security Strategy should be preventing the proliferation of weapons of mass destruction. In this case, SOF's direct action capabilities would or should gain renewed prominence. Generally speaking, the kind of targeting that SOF's premier tactical forces are capable of is more likely to be effective as part of a counterproliferation, rather than a counterterrorism, strategy.

SOF's independent direct action capability will also attain new importance if, as seems likely, the development of technology continues to put greater and greater power into the hands of smaller and smaller groups. This is part of the counterproliferation challenge we face. Small groups with great lethal power are likely to see the technological power they possess as a substitute for the political power that terrorists and insurgents sought in the past. This will make them terribly dangerous but also highly vulnerable. They will be terribly dangerous because they will possess terrible destructive power and, since unconcerned with a political constituency, will be uninhibited in its use. But as terribly dangerous and uninhibited, they will appear to many, if not most, people to be menaces. Destroying them will carry little political cost, therefore, and will make them perfect targets for SOF's discriminating tactical-strike capabilities.

SOF's direct action capabilities will achieve their fullest utility, however, only if the goals and restraints of policy inform operational planning and the possibilities and problems of operations inform policy making. For a number of reasons, this kind of mutual understanding is hard to achieve. Frequent, realistic simulations of the approval, conduct, and possible consequences of direct action missions would help, but only if those involved were the actual decision-makers and operators who will be involved when the real operations are under consideration and in progress. Such exercises would give the civilian decision-makers an opportunity to ask questions about the planning and thinking of SOF in settings that should reproduce the operational and political risk involved in potential missions. This interaction also would educate military leaders about the civilians for whom they work and the political realities that must govern military operations. Combined with a decision-making process better integrated across the various domains of the national security establishment, these exercises would help make SOF's direct action capabilities as effective as we will need them to be.[3]

However useful SOF's direct action capabilities become, they are likely to be less strategically useful than SOF's indirect action capabilities if these are allowed to develop in new directions. This may not happen because the military and even the Special Operations Command (SOCOM) have neglected them historically and this neglect might continue. There is nothing comparable in the world of indirect missions and capabilities to the training and effort that goes into making Navy SEALS proficient at their direct action missions. There are indications that SOCOM understands now, if it did not in the past, both the importance of SOF's indirect capabilities and the neglect they have suffered. There are some signs that SOCOM wants to remedy this neglect.

One way that this renewed focus on indirect capabilities or, to use a common term, unconventional warfare has manifested itself is an increased focus on information gathering. Deployed SOF have always gathered information on local conditions and circumstances. For example, an innovative use of SOF in the 1990s was to return them as assessment teams to areas in Haiti where they had worked after the invasion. Unlike this case in Haiti, much of SOF's information gathering has been done informally and has not moved beyond the units that work in a particular country or region. SOF are now taking a more formal approach to this information gathering and working with other U.S. government agencies that also collect and analyze information. This is an important effort, since we face serious difficulties gathering the kind of information we need. Our opponents operate in our world, the modern world of individualism, electronic media, centralized bureaucratic control, and cellular phones. They also operate in a traditional, nontechnical world of family and tribe and decentralized, socially based authority and communication. We have optimized our information collection capabilities for our world, the modern world of the nation-state. The terrorists operate in two worlds; we operate in only one. Thus, they have more strategic depth than we do.[4]

While SOF's new information collection efforts are welcome, they raise two concerns. First, the efforts appear to be keyed to the requirements of the strategy of killing and capturing high-value terrorist targets. To the extent that this strategy is not effective, SOF's information-gathering efforts will be wasted. Second, SOF's increased efforts in this domain appear to be copying techniques and approaches that have not worked for SOF or other agencies in the past. There is no reason to think they will work better now. Just as disturbing, perhaps, is that those approaches and techniques have, at least in the American context, led to a host of problems, such as shirking and fraud. While these problems are sometimes noted they are most often treated as cases of individual malfeasance, when they are in fact inherent in the kinds of activities that SOF are now increasingly engaging in.[5] Since much of SOF's work takes place in risky situations far from any kind of senior oversight, SOF depend on the trust of their military and civilian leaders for the room to maneuver that they require. SOF's efforts in information gathering could thus prove to be of no avail, because tied to a defective strategy, and corrosive of the trust that SOF require to achieve their true strategic utility.

The difference between what needs to be done with regard to improving SOF's information gathering and what SOF appear to be doing is, perhaps, a manifestation of the neglect that SOF's indirect capabilities have suffered from. Enhancing all of these capabilities, and not just those related to information gathering, is a major task for SOCOM and future administrations. Accomplishing it is not primarily, if at all, a question of more money but rather a matter of thinking anew about SOF's indirect capabilities, the capabilities that are most distinctive of SOF and most strategically useful.

Notes

1. This paper draws on David Tucker and Christopher J. Lamb, *United States Special Operations Forces* (New York: Columbia University Press, 2007); David Tucker and Christopher J. Lamb, "Restructuring Special Operations Forces for Emerging Threats," *Strategic Forum*, no. 219 (January 2006), http://www.ndu.edu/inss; and David Tucker, *Confronting the Unconventional: Innovation and Transformation in Military Affairs*, (Strategic Studies Institute, U.S. Army War College, October 2006). The opinions expressed in this article are the author's alone and do not represent the position of the Naval Postgraduate School, the Department of the Navy, or the Department of Defense.

2. I base this assessment in part on Daniel Byman, "Do Targeted Killings Work?" *Foreign Affairs* (March/April, 2006), pp. 95–111; Edward H. Kaplan, Alex Mintz, Shaul Mishal, and Claudio Samban, "What Happened to Suicide Bombings in Israel? Insights from a Terror Stock Model," *Studies in Conflict and Terrorism* 28 (2005), pp. 225–235; Steven R. David, "Israel's Policy of Targeted Killing," *Ethics and International Affairs* 17 (2003), pp. 111–126; and Peter C. Soderberg, "Conciliation as Counter-terrorism Strategy," *Journal of Peace Research* 32 (August 1995), pp. 295–312.

3. For further details on the exercises and integration of desicision making, including a discussion of common objections to such proposals, see Tucker and Lamb, "Restructuring Special Operations Forces for Emerging Threats."

4. For more detail on the points in this paragraph, see Tucker and Lamb, *United States Special Operations Forces*, pp. 207–209.

5. See David Tucker, *Why Human Intelligence Operations Fail and Some Suggestions for Improving Them* (Center on Terrorism and Irregular Warfare, Naval Postgraduate School, 2007).

Panel VI: Joint Special Operations Forces

Summary of Discussion

Commander Thomas C. Sass, U.S. Navy
Professor of Joint Military Operations
U.S. Naval War College

Panel VI addressed the role that the United States Special Operations Forces should play in the future U.S. defense establishment. Professor Shultz presented an overview of the global security environment, a summary of armed groups and the strategic challenges that they present to the United States, and an assessment of the Department of Defense's concept of irregular warfare. Then Professor Tucker presented his view of the strategic utility of United States Special Operations Forces by examining their conduct of direct and indirect methods of engaging the enemy and argued that their indirect capabilities are the most distinctive and strategically useful. The lively discussion that followed Professors Shultz's and Tucker's presentations revolved around the roles and missions of the United States Special Operations Forces in the context of irregular warfare and focused on four principal themes.

The initial series of comments focused on the conflicting efforts made by Special Operations Forces conducting direct action counterterrorist assaults in the joint operations area while conventional forces conduct counterinsurgency operations. Resources, mission priority, and command and control mechanisms were identified as the sources of the conflict. Operation Iraqi Freedom quickly became a discussion point and the regional fusion cells were identified as a means to diminish the conflicting efforts of the two forces across a broader area as well as a means to identify trends in the complex population. Additionally, redirecting intelligence-gathering functions away from emphasizing counterterrorist operations requirements toward supporting counterinsurgency operations was suggested as a potentially constructive means to increase the understanding of the population and the events on the ground. Specifically, increasing low-level human intelligence collection, broadening intelligence-gathering subjects, and improving reporting mechanisms were highlighted. The role that the Special Operations Forces would naturally gravitate toward is finding the targets, developing the intelligence, and training the indigenous force capability to address the insurgent threat while cultivating a broad level of support from the affected population. A broader intelligence picture would increase the ability to understand the impact of and assist in the prioritization of counterterrorist operations and counterinsurgency operations.

A brief conceptual discussion on irregular warfare itself and the soundness of the interagency joint operating concept designed to confront the threat followed. Specifically, the questions of whether irregular warfare is truly warfare and whether countering the threat is necessarily a military mission were debated. The idea is that since the relevant population is the center of gravity, vice an opposing military force, the lead effort should shift to an organization outside of the Department of Defense. Irregular warfare was argued to be misnamed because the means to alter the conditions where the threat persists require civilian, not military, efforts. Additionally, it was proposed that it should be called something other than warfare, particularly if the country specified holds full diplomatic relations with the United States. Developing a level of trust between the Department of State and the Department of Defense as the foundation of a working relationship was highlighted as in need of improvement and essential to the conduct of irregular warfare. Additionally, an overall increase in the U.S. government's capacities outside the Department of Defense is needed.

The related topic of the strategic threat posed by armed groups was also raised. They had been labeled as a tier-three security concern prior to September 11, 2001, and not important enough to employ Special Operations Forces against. That trend has since been reprioritized to tier one and operations have been ongoing since.

The remainder of the discussion revolved around the nature of the Special Operations Forces, their roles and missions, and the organization of their force structure. The premise for this discussion is that the role of the Special Operations Forces only makes sense when examined against the roles of the military as a whole and of the other elements of national power. If one considers the concept of a culminating point of efficiency, then the Special Operations Forces become inefficient if they kill too many people. To operate within their culminating point of efficiency in the future, Special Operations Forces would need to precisely kill only a limited number of unconditional terrorists, those terrorists with intractable issues that cannot be bridged.

It was argued that those Special Operations Forces should not dilute their status as the premier direct action force with indirect activities. The point was emphasized by an assertion that the Special Operations Forces culture values direct action over indirect action activities and that it is extremely difficult to train a Special Operations Forces operator to do both to the same level of competency. Furthermore, it was asserted that a new organization is needed to reverse the status pyramid and effectively conduct operations through the indirect method. That reasoning was questioned with a comparison against the conventional forces, who train their forces to conduct high intensity combat as well as counterinsurgency operations. In the end, consensus was not achieved in articulating the future roles and missions of the United States Special Operations Forces or their future organizational structure.

Panel VII

Joint Interagency

Michèle A. Flournoy
President and Cofounder, Center for a New American Security

Donna L. Hopkins
Plans and Policy Team Lead in the Office of Plans, Policy, and Analysis, Bureau of Political-Military Affairs, Department of State

Captain Kevin C. Hutcheson
U.S. Navy, Deputy Director for Interagency Integration, J9 Interagency Partnering Directorate, U.S. Southern Command

Moderator:
Deborah A. Bolton
State Department Advisor to President, U.S. Naval War College

Navigating Treacherous Shoals: Establishing a Robust Interagency Process for National Security Strategy, Planning, and Budgeting

Michèle A. Flournoy
President and Cofounder,
Center for a New American Security

In the post–cold war, post-9/11 security environment, the United States faces a broad and complex range of challenges, from the rise of violent Islamist extremism to the proliferation of nuclear weapons, from the emergence of new powers on the global stage to the prospect of catastrophic global climate change. This wide and diverse array of challenges has at least one thing in common: dealing effectively with them will require the United States to integrate the use of all of its instruments of national power in support of a sustained, long-term strategy.

Unfortunately, the U.S. government (USG) finds it exceedingly difficult to do so. While there is no shortage of so-called strategy documents—the National Security Strategy, the National Defense Strategy, the National Military Strategy, the Homeland Security Strategy, and the National Strategy for Combating Terrorism, among others—these tend to be either glossy, coffee-table documents that articulate an administration's aspirational goals and philosophy or single-agency documents that describe how one particular instrument of power should be employed. What is most needed is what we currently lack: an integrated and rigorous strategy, planning, and budgeting process for national security that would enable the United States to assess long-term threats and opportunities, set clear priorities, allocate and manage risk, develop long-term "whole of government" approaches, identify critical capability areas in which to invest, and make course corrections along the way. Without such a process in place, the world's greatest power is left navigating the treacherous shoals of the new international security environment without a map or even the most basic of navigational tools.

This state of affairs presents the next administration with both a challenge and an opportunity. The next president should come into office with a detailed plan to establish a truly interagency strategy, planning, and budgeting process for national security. This paper explores what such a process might look like and the changes it would require to be effective.

The Nature of the Problem

Today, U.S. national security policy is developed and executed in a highly stove-piped national security apparatus that was designed sixty years ago to meet the needs of a very different, post–World War II security environment. Most importantly, there is no rigorous interagency process that enables senior leaders to assess the national security challenges and opportunities the United States faces, develop a comprehensive U.S. strategy that sets priorities and makes clear judgments about where to place emphasis and where to accept or manage a degree of risk, and identify critical capabilities and capacities necessary to protect and advance U.S. interests, now and in the future. While some might argue that our system of divided government and distributed power makes such a process unworkable in the American political context, there is precedent for such a process. During the Eisenhower administration, the National Security Council (NSC) had a planning board that conducted long-range planning for the president. Eisenhower himself presided over key elements of the process, including the so-called Solarium exercise in which alternative strategies for dealing with the then Soviet Union were developed and debated. So there are some historical best practices on which to draw.

The lack of a comparable capacity and process in today's NSC undermines the U.S. government's unity of effort and effectiveness in several ways. Absent a long-term assessment of the country's strategic objectives and priorities, the urgent crowds out the important and the tyranny of the in-box goes unchecked. Absent clear guidance on the president's national security priorities, agencies fill the vacuum with their own agendas, with the right hand often working at cross-purposes with the left. Absent a process that enforces strategic priorities in the resource allocation process, rhetoric and reality quickly diverge, leaving the president saying one thing and his administration doing another. Finally, absent a process that engages senior leaders in looking over the horizon together to anticipate developments that may require some adaptation or change of course, the United States risks being blindsided by events or prone to driving off cliffs.

This challenge of taking a more strategic and integrated approach to national security is made even more difficult by decades of imbalanced investment that have effectively put one instrument of U.S. power—the armed forces—on steroids while leaving everything else—from diplomacy to development assistance—on life support. The Department of Defense's (DoD's) annual budget tops $430 billion[1] while the Department of State and the U.S. Agency for International Development (USAID) receive annual funding in the range of $20 billion.[2] To offer just one vivid example, the United States has fewer foreign service officers than it does military band members. While it makes sense for a global power with global interests like the United States to field the best military in the world, it makes no sense for the world's sole superpower to have anemic tools of diplomacy, public diplomacy, and foreign assistance. This imbalance leaves the United States without the capacity, particularly in the civilian agencies, to address the threats and opportunities at hand.

The U.S. government is in dire need of a more integrated approach to national security that includes the following elements:

- An NSC-led strategy and planning process for national security,

- An NSC–Office of Management and Budget–led (OMB) process to develop an integrated, multiyear national security budget, and

- Congressional oversight that can consider funding proposals for specific mission areas that cut across multiple agencies.

A More Robust Strategy and Planning Process for National Security

Not since the Eisenhower administration has the National Security Council been empowered and resourced to lead a robust, interagency strategy and planning process for national security. Given the number of complex and consequential security challenges the United States now faces, and the competing demands for limited resources, it is imperative that the United States reinstitute a more robust strategy development and planning process for national security at the highest levels. Such a process should include the following elements:[3]

Conduct Semiannual "Over the Horizon" Reviews for Agency Deputies to Anticipate Potential Future Crises and Challenges, and to Stimulate Proactive Policy Development

In an effort to establish an interagency process that enables senior leaders to regularly assess mid- to long-term threats, challenges, and opportunities in the international security environment, the deputies should convene twice a year for the express purpose of looking beyond today's challenges to anticipate tomorrow's. In these meetings, the director of national intelligence would be responsible for presenting the deputies—representing NSC, OMB, and all of the agencies involved in national security—with an "over-the-horizon look" at possible developments in the international security environment one year, five years, and ten years or more in the future. This material would be developed in concert with the broader intelligence community and would aim to highlight not only points of consensus within the intelligence community but also areas of uncertainty and debate that should inform national decision-making. This review would increase the visibility of longer-term trends, plausible developments, and potential discontinuities in order to stimulate more proactive consideration of ways the United States could shape the international environment and prevent crises from emerging. The results of the review should be briefed to the president and the National Security Council. This review process could also stimulate interagency contingency and capability planning efforts and provide scenarios for the exercise program described below. In the first year of each presidential term, this over-the-horizon review should kick off the Quadrennial National Security Review (QNSR) process.

Conduct a Quadrennial National Security Review to Set Priorities, Develop U.S. National Security Strategy, and Determine the Capabilities Required to Implement the Strategy

Every four years, at the outset of his or her term, the president should designate a senior national security official (most likely the national security adviser) to lead an interagency process to develop a U.S. national security strategy and identify the critical capabilities required—economic, diplomatic, military, informational, and so on—to implement the strategy. The review would engage all of the national security agencies in an effort to produce both the unclassified National Security Strategy already mandated by Congress and the National Security Planning Guidance described below.

The review would begin with an assessment of the future security environment and the development of national security objectives and priorities. The heart of the exercise would be engaging senior leaders in devising a national security strategy for achieving these priorities, identifying the most essential capabilities required to implement the strategy, and clearly delineating agency roles and responsibilities. The QNSR should logically precede and provide the conceptual basis for agency reviews like DoD's Quadrennial Defense Review.[4]

Several factors will determine the success or failure of the QNSR. First, such a review will have to be driven by the president, the national security adviser, and the leaders of the key departments involved in national security. The degree to which this process is owned by senior leaders will in large part determine both its utility and its impact. If the QNSR is an exercise that the cabinet uses to create a shared approach to national security, it will likely succeed; if, however, it devolves into a bureaucratic staff exercise divorced from the senior leadership, it will undoubtedly fail. Second, the review must frame, rather than gloss over, the hard choices that the next administration will confront in the national security domain. Rising and competing demands for resources coupled with downward pressures on the federal budget will force some exceedingly difficult trade-offs. If the review helps the leadership team work through these tough risk allocation decisions, it will succeed; if it enables the team to kick the proverbial can down the road, it will be judged a failure. Finally, the process must be designed to create buy-in from key stakeholders. As a rule, any agency with responsibility for implementing an element of the review should be provided an opportunity to participate in the process.

Create a Classified National Security Planning Guidance to Be Drafted by the NSC, Signed by the President in the First Year of a New Administration, and Updated on a Biannual Basis

The primary product of the QNSR would be the president's National Security Planning Guidance (NSPG), which would articulate his or her national security objectives and the strategy and capabilities required to achieve them. As a classified guidance document, the NSPG would direct the national security adviser and relevant cabinet secretaries to develop particular courses of action and undertake specific activities in support of the strategy. It would also provide guidance—developed in conjunction with OMB—identifying the capabilities that each agency should give priority to developing in its budget submission for that year. This document would provide the conceptual basis for the unclassified National Security Strategy, the development of interagency concepts of operation for priority mission areas, and the conduct of interagency mission area reviews as described below. It would also be the starting point for all of the departments involved in national security to develop their own implementing strategies, such as DoD's defense strategy. To be effective, the development of this National Security Planning Guidance would have to be a top-down, rather than bottom-up, effort that would engage the president and the national security principals.[5]

Establish an Annual Tabletop Exercise Program for Senior National Security Officials to Practice Managing Future National Security Challenges and Identify Capability Shortfalls That Need to Be Addressed on a Priority Basis

This exercise program would build on the over-the-horizon reviews and serve several functions. It would allow senior national security officials an opportunity to experience managing a crisis or complex operation without the costs and risks involved in a real-world situation. In addition, each exercise would enable these officials to identify courses of action that might prevent or deter a crisis as well as policy responses the United States should explore further. Furthermore, these simulations would enable the participants to identify critical gaps in U.S. capabilities and task development of action plans to address them. Progress in implementing these action plans could be reviewed in subsequent exercises or as part of the biannual National Security Planning Guidance process.

Institute a Scenario-Based Planning Process to Assess U.S. Capabilities for National Security and Inform Long-Term Resource Planning

For decades, the U.S. military has used scenarios to help assess the adequacy of its capabilities for the future and to inform resource allocation and investment decisions. More recently, the Department of Homeland Security has begun to use scenarios to assess its preparedness for various contingencies. The U.S. government as a whole would benefit greatly from an interagency scenario-based planning process that would bring agencies together to assess the strengths and weaknesses of their collective capabilities to deal with a future crisis. This process could be used to identify and prioritize capability and capacity shortfalls that should be addressed in the budget process, as well as unnecessary duplication that could enable a redirection of resources to higher-priority areas. Such a process could build on the recent, albeit low-profile, success of Project Horizon[6] and would best be coordinated by the NSC. It should also be supported and supplemented by more robust scenario-based planning efforts undertaken by individual agencies.

Toward an Integrated National Security Budget

Based on the priorities set in the course of a more robust strategy and planning process, the NSC and the OMB should partner to lead an effort to develop a more integrated, multiyear national security budget. At the heart of this process would be a number of mission area reviews that would endeavor to rationalize spending and enhance unity of effort across agencies in support of the president's highest national security priorities. This process should include the following elements:

Conduct NSC/OMB Mission Area Reviews for Top National Security Priorities That Require Interagency Implementation

Interagency reviews of priority mission areas (such as counterterrorism, counterproliferation, democracy promotion, etc.) would help to identify capability gaps; counterproductive areas of overlap; and misalignment among agency responsibilities, authorities, and resources. With NSC providing the policy focus and OMB the fiscal focus, the mission area reviews should be conducted for critical presidential priorities that require implementation across multiple USG agencies.

Specifically, these mission area reviews would include the following elements:

- First, the NSC staff, in coordination with key agencies, would help develop planning and capabilities guidance for the mission area as part of the president's National Security Planning Guidance described above. This guidance would, among other things, describe the priority capabilities needed to support this mission area and delineate agency responsibilities for providing those capabilities. It would be issued in the spring, prior to development of agency budgets.

- Second, once the president's National Security Planning Guidance is issued, OMB would track planned resource allocation against presidentially mandated priorities before agencies submit their budgets to OMB.

- Third, OMB and the NSC would cochair interagency mission area reviews before agency budgets are finalized. These reviews would build on the "hearing" process already in place, but would be held on a more regular basis and with broader participation. Such reviews might be conducted in two phases: in the early summer, before agency submissions to OMB; and in the fall, as part of the process of finalizing the president's budget submission to Congress. Extra reviews could be held as needed for crisis issues not foreseen in the budget.

- Finally, this process would enable significant unresolved budget issues to be raised to the president for decision as necessary.

This process argues for not only strengthening OMB's partnership with the NSC but also raising the level of "budgetary literacy" among senior national security policy officials through targeted training and hands-on experience.

Create and Submit to Congress an Integrated, Multiyear National Security Budget

An integrated national security budget would include, at a minimum, all U.S. spending for defense, international affairs, intelligence, and homeland security. In principle, it would enable the executive branch and Congress to look across the interrelated, if not interdependent, spending and programs of multiple agencies to determine whether the nation's investment in national security matches its policy priorities and manages risk appropriately. For high-priority mission areas, a "crosscut" of spending in that area across agencies would also be presented. Such a presentation would enhance the ability of the executive branch to defend its submissions in these areas based on a more integrated and presumably more robust rationale.[7]

Crosscutting Congressional Oversight

Even if the executive branch adopts a robust strategy and planning process and develops a more integrated national security budgeting process, these gains could be lost if Congress remained unable to consider resource allocation trade-offs that cross the jurisdictional boundaries of its current committee structure. Creating greater unity of effort and truly whole-of-government approaches in national security requires substantial changes to the way business is done at both ends of Pennsylvania Avenue.

Thus, the last and perhaps most difficult set of reforms would need to occur on Capitol Hill. In order to provide effective oversight of a more integrated national security budget, Congress would need to develop new processes or mechanisms for examining mission area funding streams that cut across multiple agencies. Some have suggested a complete overhaul of the existing committee structure. Others have proposed merging the authorization and appropriations processes. Since neither of these approaches seems feasible in the near term, a more pragmatic approach might be to form new House and Senate select committees on national security (similar to the select committees on intelligence or the committees on homeland security) that would enable Congress to evaluate and approve funding proposals for specific mission areas that cut across multiple agencies.

Implementing Change

The single most important requirement to implement these changes is the committed leadership of a president and key members of his or her National Security Council. Establishing an effective strategy and planning process and a more integrated approach to national security will require the next president to commit his or her most precious resources: time and attention.

The president must also be willing to assertively use his or her National Security Council staff to orchestrate the interagency process and to act as chief integrator of national security policies and programs. Doing so will also require creating capabilities and capacity on the NSC staff that have not existed since the Eisenhower era. Specifically, the next president should create a new NSC senior director with a small but empowered office dedicated to strategic planning. The proposed senior director for strategy and planning would be responsible for working with other NSC senior directors to draft the president's National Security Planning Guidance, working with the director of national intelligence to prepare the semiannual "over the horizon" reviews, and overseeing scenario-based planning and the annual national security exercise program.[8] The senior director for strategy and planning could fail either by being sucked into day-to-day crisis management, or by being so disconnected as to be irrelevant; striking the right balance will be a continuing challenge and will require top-cover from the national security adviser and the president.

In addition, the president should work with Congress to enhance the capacity of the various agencies involved in national security to engage in a sustained and robust strategy and planning process. In practice, this means providing additional personnel, training, and incentives to build up strategy and planning staffs in agencies other than the Department of Defense. This will require a modest expenditure of additional resources, but one that is likely to be well worth the investment.

Politically, moving down this road will likely require a national dialogue and debate on a way forward. Historically, major government reforms have followed some undeniable failure or period of paradigm-shifting events. Think the 1947 National Security Act, the 1986 Goldwater-Nichols Act, or the 1987 Nunn-Cohen Amendment. Today, we have experienced both the paradigm-shifting events of the end of the cold war and the 9/11 terrorist attacks, and a decade and a half of repeated interagency failures in the national security arena. In principle, this combination of events should create the space for candid dialogue on lessons learned and options for change. Unfortunately, the fact that we are now in the middle of a presidential campaign, where discussion of failures and lessons learned quickly becomes political footballs, means that this critical and urgent discussion will likely be delayed until after the 2008 election. Nevertheless, the moment of opportunity for interagency reform will come when a new administration, Democratic or Republican, takes office and realizes the urgent need for a new approach to navigating the shoals of a complex and dangerous security environment. Between now and then, we must identify and assess alternative approaches and determine the best way forward, so we know what to build when the time comes.

Notes

1. Office of the Under Secretary of Defense (Comptroller), *National Defense Budget Estimates for FY 2006* (U.S. Department of Defense, April 2005), available at http://www.defenselink .mil/comptroller/defbudget/fy2006/fy2006_greenbook.pdf.

   See also Office of Management and Budget, "Budget of the United States Government, FY 2007," http://www.whitehouse.gov/omb/budget/fy2007/defense.html.

2. The State Department's budget for FY 2007 was approximately $9.5 billion and the budget for USAID in FY 2007 was approximately $9.3 billion. See U.S. Department of State, "FY 2007 Budget in Brief," http://www.state.gov/s/d/rm/rls/bib/2007/pdf/; and USAID, "International Affairs FY 2007 Budget Briefing for ACFVA," http://www.usaid.gov/about_usaid/acvfa/022206_intaffairsbudget.pdf.

3. Many of these specific recommendations were first described by Michèle Flournoy in the CSIS report *Beyond Goldwater-Nichols, Volume II*.

4. In practice, the process often works the other way around, with the defense strategy being written first, in the course of the QDR, and then becoming the intellectual basis for the National Security Strategy.

5. Perhaps the best historical analogue for this process was President Eisenhower's Solarium Project as described in Tyler Nottberg, "Once and Future Policy Planning: Solarium for Today," The Eisenhower Institute, available at http://www.eisenhowerinstitute.org/programs/livinghistory/solarium.htm; and in Robert Bowie, "President Eisenhower Establishes His National Security Process," in *Triumphs and Tragedies of the Modern Presidency: Seventy-six Case Studies in Presidential Leadership*, ed. David Abshire (Westport: Praeger, 2001), pp. 152–154.

6. Project Horizon was an interagency scenario-based strategic planning exercise conducted in February and March of 2006, and included participants from the departments of Agriculture, Commerce, Defense, State, Energy, and Labor, as well as the NSC, the Environmental Protection Agency, Health and Human Services, Homeland Security, the Office of the Director of National Intelligence, the Millennium Challenge Corporation, National Defense University/ITEA, and USAID. For more information, see Sid Kaplan,

"Project Horizon: A New Approach to Interagency Planning," *Federal Times*, 13 February 2006, available at http://www.epa.gov/OSP/futures/ProjectHorizon.pdf.

7. There is some precedent for this approach. In the 1990s, OMB developed budget "crosscuts" for several priority mission areas, such as combating terrorism, counternarcotics, and counterproliferation. More recently, it has developed crosscuts for homeland security and combating terrorism. For another proposal to strengthen NSC and OMB planning and coordination to build capabilities to meet new threats, see John Deutch, Arnold Kantor, and Brent Scowcroft, "Strengthening the National Security Interagency Process," with Chris Hornbarger, in *Keeping the Edge: Managing Defense for the Future*, ed. Ashton B. Carter and John P. White (Cambridge, MA: MIT Press, 2001), pp. 265–284.

8. The recent reorganization of the NSC staff includes a new "Senior Adviser for Strategic Planning," but the responsibilities of this position do not appear to be as expansive as what is proposed here.

The Interagency Counterinsurgency Initiative: Meeting a Need

Donna L. Hopkins
Plans and Policy Team Lead in the Office of Plans, Policy, and Analysis, Bureau of Political-Military Affairs, Department of State

State, Defense, and the United States Agency for International Development (USAID) are collaborating in a significant new effort to fuse diplomacy, defense, and development to help address a problem that is both age-old and newly threatening—insurgency. Historically, insurgencies have threatened particular governments, and the governmental response to the threat—counterinsurgency, or COIN—has been focused on targeting identifiable individuals and groups that were relatively cohesive, both geographically and culturally. While conveniently homogeneous insurgencies still pose problems in many places around the world, globalization coupled with the rise of Islamist extremism and the spread of weapons of mass disruption and destruction has enabled a starkly new and lethal kind of insurgency that threatens governments both regionally and globally. One could make a good case, as some theoreticians have done, that the Global War on Terror is actually a global counterinsurgency campaign. Whether or not that paradigm is precisely accurate or politically palatable, counterinsurgency theory can in fact usefully inform national, alliance, and coalition efforts to work together both internally and among themselves to defeat insurgent-like activities of individuals, groups, and networks that seek to undermine or supplant the legitimate governance by nation-states of their populations and sovereign territories. We created the Interagency Counterinsurgency Initiative, or ICI, in order to export COIN theory to a wider, and specifically to a civilian, audience, and to update and adapt it to the contemporary sociopolitical environment.

For purposes of the ICI, insurgency is defined as a protracted political-military campaign by an organized movement seeking to subvert or displace a government and completely or partially control the resources and/or population of a country through the use of force and alternative political organizations. COIN is the combination of measures adopted to defeat an insurgency, and ideally will include integrated or synchronized political, security, economic, and informational components that reinforce governmental legitimacy and competence while reducing insurgent influence over the population.

Many Western nations have long and painful experience with COIN—the French in Algeria, the British in Malaysia, the Australians in Timor; the very word carries significant baggage for governments and populations that suffered on both sides of these conflicts. The United States' own experience in Southeast Asia so scarred our government that the lessons that we could and should have applied to Afghanistan and Iraq over the last several years are just now being pulled out of books found mainly on the shelves of military historians. When one examines COIN case studies, a single glaring fact becomes both obvious and compelling—COIN is an inherently *interagency* undertaking. It requires *interagency* planning and *interagency* collaboration and *interagency* capabilities. It requires military and civilian cooperation, interoperability, and mutual support. It requires patience, commitment, and resources. COIN requires deep understanding of the cultural context and the social and cultural fabric of the society or societies in which it is undertaken. Most important, it requires a profound comprehension that complex problems require multidimensional solutions that only *interagency* efforts can deliver.

There is widespread recognition that our national security structures are not sufficiently agile to address complex security challenges. While agencies struggle to implement a plethora of national strategies to address terrorism, failed and failing states, poverty, pandemic disease, weapons proliferation, and other existential threats, initiatives like the creation of the Office of the Coordinator for Reconstruction and Stabilization and the Project on National Security Reform attempt to create architectures, organizations, and legislation to deal with current and future problems. The ICI takes a different approach: it examines how, using COIN thought and theory, we might apply our rich and varied national and international capabilities to problems of inadequate governance that fuel or generate popular support for insurgencies.

The ICI, initiated in 2006 by then–assistant secretary of state for political-military affairs John Hillen and Deputy Assistant Secretary of Defense Jeffrey Nadaner, was initially intended to develop a national COIN framework analogous to the 1962 Overseas Internal Defense Policy and National Counterinsurgency Strategy. This ambitious goal was viewed by some as competing with the National Strategy for Countering Terrorism and by others as undermining the implementation of the *National Security Presidential Directive on Management of Interagency Efforts Concerning Stabilization and Reconstruction (NSPD-44)*. However, the direct relevance of COIN theory to current challenges and the intense interest across the interagency and among international partners has resulted in the ICI's maturing into something more than just a good idea—it is starting to produce results, not the least of which is healthy and growing interagency community of practice focusing on COIN.

The ICI consists of several primary components and a variety of related activities. These include outreach and education through conferences, workshops, consultations, and international collaborations; publication of a COIN guide for civilian policy makers; COIN training modules for inclusion in curricula at the Foreign Service Institute and other education and training venues; collaboration with the Department of Defense (DoD) on the nascent Consortium for Complex Operations; and the maintenance of the U.S. government (USG) COIN Web site (www.usgcoin.org). The ICI is implemented by networks of staffs within State, Defense, and USAID, and augmented and supported by the intelligence community and interested participants from other executive branch departments and agencies, including Justice, Homeland Security, Agriculture, Transportation, and Treasury.

Conferences and Outreach

In September 2006, State's Bureau of Political-Military Affairs (PM) and the Office of the Secretary of Defense (OSD), Stability Operations hosted in Washington, D.C., the inaugural U.S. Government Counterinsurgency Conference, at which expert speakers such as the Under Secretary of Defense for Policy Eric Edelman, General David Petraeus, Dr. David Kilcullen, Dr. Kalev Sepp, Ms. Sarah Sewall, and Assistant Secretary Hillen, among others, articulated the need for a national framework, capabilities, and capacity to deal with COIN challenges. In March 2007, DoD and State cohosted a similar conference in Munich, Germany, entitled "A Comprehensive Approach to Modern Conflict" This event, focusing on Afghanistan as a case study, has generated seminal efforts in NATO to produce NATO COIN doctrine and by individual member nations to develop national doctrine on the subject. State is planning another regional conference for mid-2008, possibly focusing on Southeast Asia or Latin America, to widen the dialogue among like-minded nations regarding COIN in particular and good governance more broadly. Complete reports of the 2006 and 2007 conferences are available on www.usgcoin.org under the Events tab.

As a mark of the importance placed on the ICI by the United Kingdom, the British embassy in Washington seconded to the PM Bureau's COIN team a Royal marine from the embassy's Defence staff, who operated as an adviser to State and liaison to Her Majesty's government in this initiative. The position proved so valuable to both governments that a full-time position was created for assignment to the Bureau of Political-Military Affairs at State and is now filled by a lieutenant colonel, Royal Marines, whose recent operational experience in Afghanistan and Iraq, among other conflict-affected regions, has been exceptionally helpful. The USG recently hired the renowned Australian counterinsurgency and counterterrorism expert, Dr. David Kilcullen, as a senior adviser on COIN to Dr. Eliot Cohen, counselor to the secretary of state. The possibilities for useful collaboration in this context with our closest allies are unlimited. The PM team has also received preliminary inquiries from Italian and French military officers on the initiative, and we view these overtures as very positive signs of renewed interest in counterinsurgency among our allies.

Interagency COIN Guide

State PM funded a nine-month interagency effort to produce a pamphlet, published in October 2007, entitled "Counterinsurgency for U.S. Government Policy Makers: A Work in Progress." A collaborative effort of policy and program officers and field operators from various bureaus and offices in State, Defense, and USAID, as well as the departments of Justice, Homeland Security, Treasury, Agriculture, and Transportation, and the intelligence community, this "Interim COIN Guide" will serve as the basis for more fully fleshed-out, detailed, and prescriptive documents for strategic, operational, and tactical planners from across the government. The first in a series of workshops to begin this onward development process is planned for 15–16 November in Washington, D.C., with delivery of output planned for the 2008 calendar year. The "Interim Guide," like all ICI products, can be found at the aforementioned Web site.

Consortium for Complex Operations

Arguably the most important component to issue from early ICI planning, the nascent Consortium for Complex Operations (CCO) holds exceptional promise for knitting together into effective communities of practice the disparate educational and training organizations that deal in complex operations, to include stabilization and reconstruction (S&R), counterinsurgency, and irregular warfare. The CCO represents a convergence of ideas issuing from the Quadrennial Defense Review, the ICI, efforts by State's Office of the Coordinator for Reconstruction and Stabilization to implement NSPD-44, and USAID's and the Foreign Service Institute's efforts to deliver training to people deploying to provincial reconstruction teams in Afghanistan and Iraq.

To be funded initially by DoD—because State and USAID do not have the legal authorities to create such an entity—the CCO will be an interagency association of organizations that educate and train professionals, and/or distribute lessons learned, for complex operations. There are literally hundreds of institutions that work on some facet of complex operations, but we lack a venue for the effective sharing of curricula, schedules, findings, studies, and related activities that could and should inform our national ability to plan for and conduct complex operations. The CCO will have a small support center staff led by an executive director in the Office of the Deputy Assistant Secretary of Defense for Stability Operations; the executive director and staff will report to an interagency executive steering committee and will provide such services to the larger consortium as a robust information clearinghouse on curricula, syllabi, and class schedules; a vehicle for real-time discussion and information searches; a "yellow pages" for functional experts; warehousing and distribution of Web-accessible knowledge and information; the facilitation of course sharing; the hosting or sponsoring of studies and academic competitions; and the holding of targeted events for the benefit of the consortium. The actual establishment of the CCO is anticipated in April 2008, and information on the CCO will be posted on the www.usgcoin.org Web site until the center develops its own Web presence, at which time it will likely subsume the www.usgcoin.org Web site.

Moving Interagency Thinking Forward

In the best sense, the ICI is an attempt to breach the walls between executive department agencies that, for structural and cultural reasons, do not easily interrelate. Collaboration on a topic of currency and urgency is already yielding new and productive working relationships. In support of this effort, USAID has drafted a blueprint paper that outlines its new thinking on COIN engagements, acknowledging the critical role broad-based economic development can play as part of the whole-of-government response to insurgency. This parallels USAID programming that addresses the root causes of instability, conflict, and terrorism in a number of hot spots around the globe. The intelligence community is now regularly providing briefings and analytical reports on incipient and ongoing insurgencies around the world to working-level staffs in interagency meetings. Staff from an increasing number of executive branch departments and agencies are reaching out to each other to collaborate on various aspects of this topic of particular current interest.

While other initiatives focus on more general planning, policy making, and capacity-building processes, the ICI has a narrow and singular focus: to connect the people, policies, and programs that support and enable governments to provide for and protect their people from armed and violent competitors for influence and resources. COIN, to be effective, truly must be joint diplomacy-defense-development efforts, and COIN theory and practice can certainly help us to analyze and understand the second- and third-order effects of activities of one or more of these efforts on the others. As a forcing function for habitual interagency consultation, COIN planning is hard to beat.

U.S. Southern Command in Transition

Captain Kevin C. Hutcheson, U.S. Navy
Deputy Director for Interagency Integration
J9 Interagency Partnering Directorate
U.S. Southern Command

U.S. Southern Command is currently working to expand interagency and nongovernmental-organization collaboration. Accordingly, it is developing a more integrated structure to achieve U.S. national security objectives in the emerging twenty-first-century security environment of transnational and unconventional threats.

Globally, small radical organizations currently pose the most significant threat to U.S. national interests. Of greatest concern is the possibility of a terrorist organization obtaining and using weapons of mass destruction. Radical actors will continue to attempt to coerce representative governments through terrorist tactics. Yet even with all this talk of asymmetric warfare, transnational, and unconventional threats, the United States must maintain the capability to fight and win conventional wars.

Preventing terrorism and defeating terrorists require a multifaceted approach that reduces terrorist resources and capabilities while simultaneously addressing the underlying conditions of poverty, inequality, and corruption that create the conditions that terrorists seek to exploit. This requires unprecedented levels of cooperation across the full spectrum of governance, not only within the U.S. government, but also within and among our partner nations in the region—a unified effort.

Admiral James Stavridis, Commander, U.S. Southern Command, has identified several fundamental conditions of the twenty-first-century security environment:[1]

- Attacks by radical organizations bent on religious or ideological domination

- Nation-states fighting in unconventional settings with unfamiliar tool sets

- The "war of ideas" at the root of conflicts, requiring sophisticated strategic communication

- A globalizing economy with perceived winners and losers

- Environmental concerns rising and coupled to globalization

- Diffusion of weapons of mass destruction—including biological and chemical

- 24-7 news coverage with satellite radio and television

- Satellite information and instant, global communication at everyone's fingertips

- Exploding Internet with bloggers, hackers, and chat rooms

- Cell phone cameras and recorders, making everyone a "reporter"
- Sophisticated media engagement by transnational terrorists and organizations

Each day, we are in a struggle of ideas where every activity attributable to the United States communicates to some audience. Effective strategic communication is critical to address this reality.

Latin America and the Caribbean

Southern Command's area of responsibility is notable by its current lack of conventional military threats; but the region's persistent conditions of poverty, inequality, and corruption provide fertile soil in which international criminals and transnational terrorists can flourish.

Throughout this area of responsibility—32 countries, 13 territories, 500 million people, 15 million square miles—security threats most often take forms that we more readily associate with crime than war. In the region's growing gang activity, criminals and the disenfranchised band together and combine traditional criminal activities in ways that threaten U.S. national security. Kidnapping, counterfeiting, human trafficking, and drug trafficking combined with extremist ideologies to create a dangerous blend. All of these conditions can undermine fragile democracies.

Latin America and the Caribbean are much different today than they were just over a generation ago. Back then, most Latin American countries were ruled by authoritarian regimes. Internal strife and instability pervaded the region and created a near-continuous flow of new governments. Over 250 constitutions were created in Latin American countries since independence. Many of these fledgling governments promised—yet failed—to deliver a better future.

But during the 1980s, significant changes started taking place across the region. Authoritarian rule failed to meet people's expectations in response to economic crisis.

There are extensive cultural and economic linkages to the United States throughout the region. Additionally, we share a social and political respect for democracy, freedom, justice, human dignity, human rights, and human values. We share the belief that these democratic principles must be at the core of what we accomplish in the region and that free governments should be accountable to their peoples and govern effectively. This common belief is most evident as expressed in the first article of the Inter-American Democratic Charter: "The peoples of the Americas have a right to democracy and their governments have an obligation to promote and defend it. Democracy is essential for the social, political, and economic development of the peoples of the Americas."[2]

This consensus document of the Americas goes on to further reinforce our shared values and our goal of strengthening representative democracy in the region. We have made great strides over the last two decades in helping democratic values spread, with all but one leader in the Americas having been democratically elected.

Democracy is now a force that binds us together in the Americas. It provides opportunity for regional peace and stability in the Americas. It creates a more open framework for dialogue, negotiation, and cooperative engagement—thereby reducing the sources of mutual distrust, suspicion, and ultimately international conflict. At the same time, democracy paves the way for free-market economies to flourish. In fact, 2006 marked the fourth consecutive period of economic growth in the region, and prospects for 2007 are also encouraging. Growth of 6.3 percent is projected for the Caribbean, and we expect to see 4.5 percent in Latin America.[3] Latin America and the Caribbean are inextricably linked to the economic, political, cultural, and security fabric of the United States.

This is very encouraging—but there are immense challenges as well.

Regional Challenges

There are significant challenges confronting the region—challenges such as crime, gangs, and illegal drug trafficking. These challenges loom large for many nations in the region; they are transnational, adaptive, and insidious threats to those seeking peace and stability. By their natures, these challenges cannot be countered by one nation alone. Therefore, they require cooperative solutions involving a unified, full-spectrum governmental and international approach in order to best address them.[4]

In many cases, the main source for these challenges stems from the underlying conditions of poverty and inequality that are prevalent in most of the area. According to 2005 United Nations statistics, about 40 percent of the region's inhabitants are living in poverty, defined as an income of less than two U.S. dollars per day. Of that number, about 16 percent are living in extreme poverty—less than one dollar per day. Couple these poverty figures with the most unequal distribution of wealth for any of the world's regions, and you have a catalyst for potential social and political insecurity and instability.[5]

Stemming from these underlying conditions, illegal drugs and crime are the most pressing security concerns for this part of the world—and based upon the region's proximity and linkages to the United States, a security concern in the United States as well. The Andean Ridge in South America is the world's leading source of coca cultivation, and despite international efforts and record interdictions and seizures, the region still produces enough cocaine to meet demand here in the United States and a growing demand abroad. Cocaine trafficking leads to over ten thousand deaths each year in the United States.

A close corollary to the illegal drug trade is the alarming growth of criminal activity in the region—some of which is a by-product of the drug trade, but which also stems from the region's extensive poverty and inequality. Violence is now among the five principal causes of death in several countries in the area. The annual homicide rate for Latin America and the Caribbean is among the highest in the world, with 25 homicides per 100,000 people compared to Africa's 22 and the United States' 5.5.[6]

In Central America, Haiti, Jamaica, and major cities in Brazil, gangs and criminal violence are a security priority, with some gang-population estimates reaching into the hundreds of thousands. These gangs do not just pose a concern in Latin America. They have spread from Los Angeles and New York to northern Virginia and southern Florida. Members cross borders, moving drugs and money. This is an issue not just for our partners in the region but for North

Americans on our own soil. The costs associated with violence in the region are difficult to assess, but according to the Inter-American Development Bank, they were estimated as close to 15 percent of the gross domestic product across this part of the world in 2005. This inhibits efforts to alleviate the underlying conditions of poverty and inequality. As stated earlier, we are fortunate as a hemisphere to have as neighbors democracies that virtually all share similar values with us. Unfortunately, poverty, inequality, and security challenges all contribute to a growing, frustrated expectation from the people for dramatic change.[7]

In some countries agents of change have successfully campaigned on themes of radical change, with promises of achieving sweeping results through unorthodox and unproven economic and political policies. These neopopulist governments do not share our views and are bent toward policies solely focused on allowing them to retain power and are economically unsound.

Regional Momentum

There is regional momentum to develop solutions to the challenges faced by the Americas. The defense ministers of thirty-four American nations met in October 2006 to examine the changing threat environment, both internal and external to the hemisphere. These ministers agreed that regional challenges need cooperative solutions and that the collaboration of virtually every nation is essential. They produced a consensus document that describes the region's commitment to combating the proliferation of weapons of mass destruction and that firmly condemns all forms of terrorism, drug trafficking, and transnational crime. The document also identifies the need to strengthen cooperative mechanisms to counter these threats. This event reinforced the importance of partnering and highlighted the need for cooperative solutions for problems such as poverty, gangs, money laundering, human smuggling, counter drug activities, and regional violence.[8]

U.S. Southern Command, through military-to-military engagements that emphasize human rights, supports partner nations' efforts to build their capacities to protect their own sovereign territories. Given our close linkages, this increased capacity and stability will also provide a first line of defense for the United States. Over time, these capabilities will ensure our partner nations have the means to control their borders and protect their citizens, while also deepening the roots of good governance. We also envision our partners being able to work together in a collective environment to be able to counter emerging and adapting threats.

Cooperative Security Measures

Terrorism, drug trafficking, and transnational crime are clear threats to states based on democracy and the rule of law. These transnational threats are complex in nature, operating not only within states but between states with no regard for civil society.

I would like to introduce a new term to our security lexicon: cooperative security measures (CSMs). Unlike confidence- and security-building measures (CSBMs), which are means to build confidence and security between two belligerents or potentially unfriendly states, cooperative security measures are established between states to build a security relationship in a specific area that does not go so far as to constitute an alliance or a treaty relationship.

The purpose of CSMs is to pursue and document effective bilateral and multilateral cooperative measures that will have an impact on these transnational threats. This is a broad-based cooperative approach to security to specifically address these growing threats. There are many facets to combating these threats to civilization. More effective cooperation among security and law enforcement organizations and agencies within a state ranging from border controls, customs, immigration, identification systems, internal security, intelligence, and investigative intelligence will certainly have an impact on these transnational threats.

Likewise the same sort of cooperation between states will oppose these threats more effectively. These cooperative measures are real and specific and diverse, crossing many different areas of political, military, law enforcement, and civil authority.

It would be very useful to document these cooperative security measures where we believe them to be, or potentially to be, effective. If documented, the cooperative security measures could serve as examples of "best practices" or proven effective measures helping to make the case for other nations to join in this effort, not only in Latin America and the Caribbean, but in other regions as well. The activities of the Joint Interagency Task Force–South, the Proliferation Security Initiative, the Container Security Initiative, and the Global Maritime Security Initiative are all examples of cooperative security measures.

Globally, the United States has been very vocal about the priorities of countering transnational terrorists. Many nations around the globe, even though they are very sympathetic to this call, are pressed on many sides with corruption, transnational crime, and illicit trafficking. The cooperative security/law enforcement skill sets that address transnational crime that are critical capacities for many of our partner nations are the same skill sets needed to counter transnational terrorists. By building cooperative security capacities in the region we directly address the most urgent security needs of our partner nations in the region while at the same time addressing the U.S. priorities of countering transnational terrorists in the Western Hemisphere.

Joint Interagency Task Force–South

Located in Key West, Florida, Joint Interagency Task Force–South (JIATF-South) is the nation's leading organization in addressing the challenges posed by transnational narco-terrorism and is a model for interagency and partner-nation cooperation. In a combined effort with the U.S. government interagency community and our partner nations, JIATF-South continues to disrupt record levels of cocaine bound for the United States and Europe. It conducts highly effective interagency operations by coordinating, integrating, and synchronizing scarce Department of Defense (DoD), interagency, allied, and partner-nation resources. Most of our partner nations do not have the resources to devote exclusively to interdiction, yet their willingness and governmental cooperation increase each year as the negative effects associated with the illegal drug trade spread and as our collective successes in attacking illicit drug trafficking increase throughout the region. The last three years alone resulted in cocaine disruptions of 219 metric tons (MTs) in 2004, 252 MTs in 2005, and 260 MTs in 2006, nearly a threefold increase in disruptions since 2000.[9]

Colombia

Colombia serves as a good example of a successful interagency effort on both ends of our relationship with one of our partner nations. Over the last decade, Colombia has achieved great success in its struggle for peace and security. Ten years ago, the headlines coming out of Colombia resembled the worst of those to come out of any war-torn country: beheadings, kidnappings, torture, and bombings occurred almost daily. Through its own interagency efforts and a steady stream of resources and support offered by the United States at Bogotá's request, Colombia has emerged from the brink of chaos. At great effort, Colombia has established government presence in all of its 1,098 municipalities, significantly deterring crime and terrorist incidents. This increased security presence, coupled with significant operational successes against the Revolutionary Armed Forces of Colombia (*Fuerzas Armadas Revolucionarias de Colombia*, or FARC), has contributed to the fastest sustained economic growth in a decade—over 5 percent annually for the past two years—and has encouraged a real sense of positive momentum for the entire country. Last year also marked the lowest homicide rate in two decades. These hard-fought successes, however, need continued U.S. support and steadfast effort from the Colombian government in order to fully win the peace. We are cautiously optimistic that Colombia is on the threshold of achieving its strategic objectives, and believe the Colombian government will benefit from U.S. support for at least the next two or three years.[10]

USSOUTHCOM Directorate of Interagency Partnering (J9)

USSOUTHCOM's experience working with interagency partners has evolved from successful past collaborations. In 2003, USSOUTHCOM established a joint interagency coordination group (JIACG), which facilitated participation of other agencies in USSOUTHCOM exercises, developed interagency information-sharing links, and synchronized planning efforts between USSOUTHCOM and other agencies. It also sought to improve USSOUTHCOM staff awareness of interagency activities in the region. USSOUTHCOM's Intelligence Directorate is manned by an increasing number of analysts from the intelligence and law enforcement communities. From increased staffing, strong collaboration has led to several major intelligence successes, most notably in support of the June 2007 arrests of four terrorist suspects in the plot to attack John F. Kennedy Airport. As previously mentioned, USSOUTHCOM's JIATF-South is a model of operational-level interagency and multinational cooperation.

The commander, USSOUTHCOM established the Interagency Partnering Directorate (J9) in February 2007. This ninth directorate was added to the traditional joint directorate structure and absorbed the JIACG to better integrate interagency personnel and initiatives into USSOUTHCOM day-to-day activities. The J9 mission is to identify opportunities for interagency and nongovernmental-organization (NGO) collaboration and capabilities to support that collaboration across

USSOUTHCOM. The directorate also expands opportunities for DoD to enable partner-agency strategic and operational planning to foster whole-of-government, long-term planning for the region. By establishing interagency partnering as an enduring characteristic of USSOUTHCOM, the J9 seeks to ensure that military activities are integrated with other instruments of national power.

Currently, the J9 is headed by a senior executive service member from the Department of Defense as the director, whose deputy is a senior foreign service officer from the State Department. The J9 has invited representatives from the U.S. Agency for International Development (USAID), the Department of Commerce, the Treasury Department, and the Department of Homeland Security. This will be in addition to a Federal Bureau of Investigation (FBI) special agent, an additional State Department foreign service officer, and a number of personnel with experience outside of DoD. About two-thirds of the staff are DoD civilians and military personnel from all branches—Air Force, Army, Marine Corps, and Navy.

The J9 is organized around the primary concepts of USSOUTHCOM's Command Strategy for 2016[11]—security, stability, and prosperity—with a secretariat and three deputy directorates: Interagency Integration, Security, and Stability and Prosperity. A key requirement for J9 personnel is familiarity with Washington interagency processes, roles, and responsibilities to help facilitate appropriate interagency participation in USSOUTHCOM efforts. The J9 currently maintains the USSOUTHCOM Washington office, which includes USSOUTHCOM's Congressional Affairs Office. The Washington office facilitates USSOUTHCOM's awareness of interagency events in the National Capital Region and represents the command's perspectives during high-level U.S. government deliberations.

USSOUTHCOM Interagency Partnering Directorate (J9)

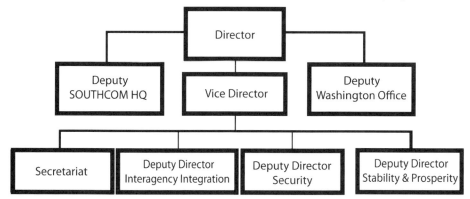

The J9 Directorate plans, coordinates, and executes an interagency consultation process that spotlights existing and emerging national security issues in Latin America and the Caribbean to support USSOUTHCOM staff and other interagency partners. The J9 convenes interagency meetings, in close coordination with the Office of the Secretary of Defense (OSD) and the Joint Staff, to learn about, exchange views on, and formulate ideas on critical cross-cutting issues that impact U.S. national security in the region. These meetings also generate recommendations for OSD and the Joint Staff that may be introduced to the formal National Security Council interagency decision-making process.

This interagency consultation process has two steps, consisting of interagency coordination groups followed by higher-level interagency partnering committees. Interagency coordination groups bring together action officer–level planners from relevant agencies and USSOUTHCOM staff to synchronize executions of U.S. government plans and activities, as well as to nominate issues for additional analysis. Interagency partnering committees are four-star executive-level forums for leaders from USSOUTHCOM and other agencies to review findings from interagency coordination groups or to explore other issues impacting the region. These meetings are convened at the direction of the commander, USSOUTHCOM, or at the request of our partner agencies.

The J9, in cooperation with other J-codes throughout USSOUTHCOM, has fostered collaboration with interagency partners across a variety of issues to ensure the success of the efforts. Working at the execution level with State and USAID, in coordination with OSD, J9 facilitates interagency cooperation in disaster-preparedness planning and response to catastrophic events, such as the summer 2007 earthquakes in Peru and hurricanes in Central America and the Caribbean. When the USNS *Comfort* deployed in 2007, J9 worked to expand governmental and nongovernmental-organization participation, which increased the capacity of this effort to support regional medical needs. J9 has convened meetings on the potential role of regional militaries in environmental security, assembling representatives from the U.S. interagency community and several NGOs. J9 also worked with the Department of Energy to support an energy exercise, with excellent interagency participation, including representatives from the State Department and USAID, among others. J9 also coordinates interagency participation in support of joint training and readiness exercises. This fosters more realistic exercise scenarios, allows military planners to anticipate needs and requirements from other agency partners, and improves understanding among counterparts regarding military roles and capabilities.

USSOUTHCOM's expanded interagency structure and functions provide significant opportunity for interagency coordination. The presence of other agency representatives, and the consultative process in place, are good mechanisms for sharing information and expertise. Our consultative interagency planning efforts are working to align the strategic- and operational-level planning processes among our various agencies.

With strong existing ties to the U.S. intelligence community, academia, and NGOs, and the evolution of interagency partnering through the JIACG, JIATF-South, and now the J9, USSOUTHCOM has accumulated, operationalized, and addressed many lessons learned.

Interagency representation at USSOUTHCOM is a critical enabler for improving U.S. unity of effort in Latin America and the Caribbean. Having adequate and consistent representation at the command, or formalized points of contact to departments and agencies, strongly enhances interagency support and collaboration. Additionally, the presence of interagency personnel improves DoD understanding and awareness of interagency capabilities and authorities, while improving deliberations on challenges in the region. In this respect, resource constraints often limit the ability of our interagency partners to assign personnel to USSOUTHCOM, especially with increasing requests from other regional combatant commands. We are working with our interagency partners to provide justification for additional personnel resources.

Lastly, there is growing promise regarding USSOUTHCOM's partnering with for-profit and nonprofit private-sector entities in implementation of a regional security strategy. The added capacity and specialized skills demonstrated by nongovernmental organizations in the 2007 USNS *Comfort* deployment to Latin America and the Caribbean is an excellent example of the benefits of such partnering. We are exploring ways to streamline coordination of such partnering, and develop deeper, more consistent relationships with private-sector partners. Working with other organizations that share our goals will maximize efficiencies and permit leveraging of limited resources to bring the greatest benefit to the people of the region.

Rethinking USSOUTHCOM

U.S. Southern Command is currently transitioning to a more integrated structure that expands its strong interagency perspective and capacity. We are rethinking the fundamental structure and approach of Southern Command in order to best meet the security challenges of the twenty-first century. This organization will have a dual-deputy structure with the chief of staff as the synchronizer across the staff and also responsible for strategic communication coordination. Directorates would be keyed to SOUTHCOM mission areas as opposed to traditional J-code structure. Additionally the staff would leverage the service components by pushing greater responsibilities to the components as appropriate.

We are carefully deliberating this new model in consultation with our interagency partners, to be phased in over three to four years. To succeed, the new model will require support from other U.S. government agencies; additional country liaison officers, including civilians; and support for public-private-partnership-coordination activity. We are moving in this direction now, but much work remains to be done.

Conclusion

The challenges in Latin America and the Caribbean are multiple and complex. Regional security challenges include crime, narco-terrorism, transnational terrorism, logistical support/fund-raising for Islamic radical groups, forgery, money laundering, narcotics trafficking, human trafficking, urban gangs, mass migration, natural disasters, and the rise of anti-American populist leaders. These security challenges are coupled with and complicated by conditions of poverty, social inequality, and corruption throughout the region.

As much as these challenges cannot be overcome by any one nation alone, neither can they be overcome by the military alone; they require a truly integrated interagency—and even private-sector—approach. The transnational and adaptive nature of these challenges requires unprecedented levels of cooperation across the full spectrum of governance not only within but among our partner nations in the region.

The challenge before us is to bring to bear the considerable experience across the various functions of the U.S. government, international organizations, nongovernmental organizations, and the private sector to facilitate and enable security, stability, and prosperity throughout Latin America and the Caribbean. This unified effort in cooperation with our partner nations will have the effect of consolidating and strengthening just democratic governance in the region.

Notes

1. ADM James G. Stavridis, "Sailing to a New Port" (commencement address, Naval War College, Newport, RI, 15 June 2007), pp. 8–9, available at http://www.southcom.mil/AppsSC/files/0UI0I1182279058.pdf.

2. Organization of American States, *Inter-American Democratic Charter*, AG/doc.8 (XXVIII-E/01), 6 September 2001, art. 1, available at http://www.oas.org/charter/docs/resolution1_en_p4.htm, quoted in Armed Services Committees, *The Posture Statement of Admiral James G. Stavridis, United States Navy, Commander, United States Southern Command, before the 110th Congress* [*Posture Statement*], 110th Cong., 1st sess., 21–22 March 2007, p. 5, available at http://www.southcom.mil/AppsSC/files/T100.pdf.

3. ADM James G. Stavridis, "Innovating in Southern Command" (address, AFCEA-USNI, 2 February 2007), p. 5, available at http://www.southcom.mil/AppsSC/files/0UI0I1170423096.doc.

4. *Posture Statement*, p. 6.

5. Ibid.

6. Ibid., p. 7.

7. Ibid.

8. Ibid., p. 34.

9. Ibid., p. 29.

10. Ibid., pp. 9–10.

11. United States Southern Command, *United States Southern Command Command Strategy 2016* (August 2007), available at http://www.southcom.mil/AppsSC/files/0UI0I1177092386.pdf.

Panel VII: Joint Interagency

Summary of Discussion

Deborah A. Bolton
State Department Advisor to
President, U.S. Naval War College

The panel's discussion of the status and direction of interagency cooperation, particularly in crises, was certainly consistent with the theme of the workshop. The fact that the three presentations described practical, actionable, and current initiatives for improved interagency cooperation and reform surprised and stimulated the participants. There was general agreement that while Iraq can be cited as an immediate inspiration for reform, the requirement preceded Iraq by decades and is expected to continue until addressed.

The presentations matched the sequence of the discussions, that is, starting with a proposed "whole-of-government" solution, continuing to the reform efforts of one key national security department, and concluding with a transformational interagency initiative at a combatant command. Much of the discussion was of a panelist's proposal to produce a more effective interagency (IA) through an empowered National Security Council (NSC) system, under focused presidential leadership and with congressional support for targeted reform of its oversight committee structure.

Acknowledging that the proposal did not require the level of post-9/11 reform, participants did question the receptivity of presidential aspirants and congressional leaders. The response confirmed that no unpopular, massive reform was in the works, but the proposal would require "changing processes and changing incentive structures to try to change behavior." Extensive missionary work with presidential campaign staffs and candidates, and with congressional offices, was under way. Campaign receptivity varied between those still seized with practical issues such as fund-raising and those whose follow-up communication indicated that serious planning was under way. When the proposal was described to the organizations as a nonpartisan, good-government idea, some campaign thinkers recognized that they will inherit "a mismatch between the nature of the problems they face and the machinery they have to try to grabble with them." Several participants focused on the need for engaged presidential leadership; while he or she has the authority to transform the NSC, would there be the commitment? Some discussion followed as to whether the frantic transition period would be the time to implement a change that was so dependent on the new president's attention. Most agreed that it would be and one suggested the tactic of linking the new framework to the Iraq denouement planning as a "small win" to demonstrate the effectiveness of new structure, but without condemning it to being Iraq-specific. Several participants confirmed that the Congress would be the most difficult customer for the new product. The response noted that the plan "doesn't take jurisdiction away as much as give additional oversight to the leadership" in the form of a select committee on national security. Although congressional committees are key power centers, even members admit the difficulty of managing security issues spanning several committees.

Discussion shifted to an initiative that emerged from a series of small steps to improve the State Department's ability to influence the IA, while improving its own performance. An early step was the State Department's "Project Horizon," which worked with the IA using scenario-based planning as a model for improved planning coordination, a tool increasingly adopted by some of the participating agencies. Another step was the Department of Defense's unprecedented invitation to State to help shape the Quadrennial Defense Review (QDR), leading to other opportunities to consult on products such as the secretary of defense's strategic guidance. The most recent step appears in the form of an October 2007 published progress report on the development of counterinsurgency (COIN) thinking and planning for the IA. One of the COIN process's goals is to develop a "vehicle through which we can use a trained diplomat in a high-threat environment." A problem with stability and reconstruction capacity in the IA is that the United States has no civilian tradition of colonial administration—nor is one sought. The needed skills and ability to operate in an extremely dangerous environment can be taught and accommodated in operational planning. One participant applauded this effort to engage the IA in COIN activities and scolded those who thought that State was the only one lagging on these issues. Another participant noted the interrelationship of development assistance both to the proposed COIN framework and to IA framework. A rejoinder pointed out that much of the required expanded capacity and improved capability belongs in a more muscular United States Agency for International Development (USAID) with improved planning ability.

A workshop participant raised the issue of the significance of the secretary of state wanting to resort to her discretionary authority to fill the newly established additional fifty slots at the Baghdad embassy. Respondents described the institutional difficulties the foreign service was having with its own "operational tempo" after five years of keeping an ever-expanding mission in Iraq staffed with the required nontraditional or rare skills in a semipermissive environment.

The third innovation topic introduced U.S. Southern Command's proposed reorganization that would create a civilian codeputy, with a military officer, to the commander in its wiring diagram and sparked curiosity. There seemed to be general agreement that the nature of the security threats and vulnerabilities in most combatant commands require solutions broader than the military, exquisitely coordinated. One question focused on how the Southern Command differed from U.S. Africa Command's proposed structure and why. The key point appeared to be that AFRICOM would have one deputy, a foreign service officer, and that the Title 10 military command chain would be addressed through a different device. This differs from Southern Command's choice of two codeputies, one civilian and one military. The explanation revealed that each U.S. Southern Command deputy position reflects complementary, but separate, sets of networks that need high-level, expert coordination. Clearly there will be close attention paid to the performance of both commands with their creative structures.

This discussion of significant, concrete change under way ensured that the workshop concluded on a positive note.

Concluding Remarks

Dr. Richmond M. Lloyd
William B. Ruger Chair of National Security Economics
U.S. Naval War College

Dr. Rich Lloyd

During this workshop we have explored setting future directions for defense strategy and forces. We explicitly considered security challenges and strategy; defense resources and risks; land, maritime, air, space, and special operations forces; and joint interagency efforts. Our primary focus has been to assess, evaluate, and recommend strategic and force choices for the future.

I want to thank all of you for the research you did in formulating your ideas and preparing your formal papers and for your thoughtful contributions throughout this workshop. Your papers and the strategic conversations we have had during each panel provide a very rich menu of ideas, insights, and pragmatic suggestions that will be of value as the nation reassesses its future defense strategy and supporting defense forces. We hope that your work here will also provide you with the building blocks for further dialogue, research, and future publications.

What's going to happen next? We will quickly produce a monograph that will include all of your papers and summaries of our discussions throughout the workshop. We expect to have the monograph online for the general public in mid-January 2008. (Our Web site is www.nwc.navy.mil/academics/courses/nsdm/rugerpapers.aspx.) Several thousand printed copies will be available in late February 2008. (Send requests for printed copies to the William B. Ruger Chair of National Security Economics at richmond.lloyd@nwc.navy.mil.) We plan to widely distribute the monograph throughout the national security community and the general public.

We will keep you informed of follow-on workshops and conferences that will be of professional interest to you and will benefit from your participation.

Again, thank you so very much for the extensive work you did in preparing for and participating in this workshop.

Participant Biographies

Rear Admiral Jacob L. Shuford, USN

Rear Admiral Jacob L. Shuford was commissioned in 1974 from the Naval Reserve Officer Training Corps program at the University of South Carolina. His initial assignment was to USS *Blakely* (FF 1072). In 1979, following a tour as Operations and Plans Officer for Commander, Naval Forces Korea, he was selected as an Olmsted Scholar and studied two years in France at the Paris Institute of Political Science. He also holds master's degrees in public administration (finance) from Harvard and in national security and strategic studies from the Naval War College, where he graduated with highest distinction.

After completing department head tours in USS *Deyo* (DD 989) and in USS *Mahan* (DDG 42), he commanded USS *Aries* (PHM 5). His first tour in Washington included assignments to the staff of the Chief of Naval Operations and to the Office of the Secretary of the Navy, as speechwriter, special assistant, and personal aide to the Secretary.

Rear Admiral Shuford returned to sea in 1992 to command USS *Rodney M. Davis* (FFG 60). He assumed command of USS *Gettysburg* (CG 64) in January 1998, deploying ten months later to Fifth and Sixth Fleet operating areas as Air Warfare Commander (AWC) for the USS *Enterprise* Strike Group. The ship was awarded the Battle Efficiency "E" for Cruiser Destroyer Group 12.

Returning to the Pentagon and the Navy Staff, he directed the Surface Combatant Force Level Study. Following this task, he was assigned to the Plans and Policy Division as chief of staff of the Navy's Roles and Missions Organization. He finished his most recent Pentagon tour as a division chief in J8—the Force Structure, Resources and Assessments Directorate of the Joint Staff—primarily in the theater air and missile defense mission area. His most recent Washington assignment was to the Office of Legislative Affairs as Director of Senate Liaison.

In October 2001 he assumed duties as Assistant Commander, Navy Personnel Command for Distribution. Rear Admiral Shuford assumed command of the *Abraham Lincoln* Carrier Strike Group in August 2003. He became the fifty-first President of the Naval War College on 12 August 2004.

Dr. Robert J. Art

Robert J. Art is Christian A. Herter Professor of International Relations at Brandeis University, where he teaches international relations and specializes in national security affairs and American foreign policy. He is also a research associate at the Olin Institute for Strategic Studies at Harvard University, a senior advisor at the Security Studies Program at the Massachusetts Institute of Technology, and director of MIT's Seminar XXI Program.

Professor Art received his B.A. from Columbia College in 1964 (summa cum laude) and his Ph.D. from Harvard University in 1968. He has received grants from the Center for International Affairs at Harvard University, the Council on Foreign Relations (International Affairs Fellow), the Guggenheim Foundation, the Ford Foundation, the United States Institute of Peace, and the

Century Foundation. In 2006, he received the Distinguished Scholar Award for Lifetime Achievement from the International Security Studies Section of the International Studies Association.

Professor Art is a former member of the Secretary of Defense's Long Range Planning Staff (1982) and a former Dean of the Graduate School of Arts and Sciences at Brandeis, and has consulted for the Central Intelligence Agency. He is a member of the editorial boards of the scholarly journals *International Security, Political Science Quarterly* and *Security Studies.* Since 1982, he has also co-edited Cornell University's "Series in Security Studies."

He has lectured at numerous American universities and research institutes and at the following U.S. military and foreign institutions: the U.S. Army War College, the U.S. National War College, West Point, the U.S. Air Force Academy, the U.S. Marine Command and Staff College, the U.S. Air Force Command and Staff College, the U.S. Air University, the U.S. Naval Postgraduate School, the U.S. Industrial College of the Armed Forces, the National War College (Beijing), the People's University (Beijing), the School of International Studies (Peking University), the Institute for War Studies (King's College, London), the Free University of Berlin, the Konrad Adenauer Institute (Berlin), the NATO School (Oberammergau), and the Führungsakademie (Hamburg).

He has published the following books: *The TFX Decision: McNamara and the Military* (1968); *A Grand Strategy for America* (2003)—a finalist for the Arthur B. Ross Award of the Council on Foreign Relations; *Reorganizing America's Defense* (1985)—contributor and co-editor, with Samuel P. Huntington and Vincent Davis; *U.S. Foreign Policy: the Search for a New Role* (1993)—contributor and co-editor with Seyom Brown; *The United States and Coercive Diplomacy* (2003)—contributor and co-editor with Patrick Cronin; *Democracy and Counterterrorism* (contributor and co-editor with Louise Richardson); and *America's Grand Strategy and World Politics* (forthcoming in 2008).

Deborah A. Bolton

Deborah Bolton is the Department of State Senior Advisor to the Naval War College in Newport, Rhode Island. She was appointed to the Senior Foreign Service rank of Counselor in 1999 and to the rank of Minister-Counselor in 2003.

Ms. Bolton was born and educated in Philadelphia, Pennsylvania. After graduating from St. Joseph's University in 1974 with a degree in International Relations, she entered the Foreign Service that year. She has held assignments in Latin America, Europe, Asia, and the Department of State.

Her early tours were to the American Embassies in Ecuador, Argentina, and Spain. In 1982 she began language training to serve as Chief of the Consular Section in Budapest, Hungary. In 1986 she became Country Officer for Uruguay and Paraguay at the Department. She remained in Washington as European Affairs Officer for the Ambassador-at-Large for Counterterrorism. In 1990 she became Chief of the Consular Section at the U.S. Interests Section in Havana, Cuba. Ms. Bolton spent the 1992–93 academic year at the U.S. Air Force War College at Maxwell Air Force Base in Alabama, earning a diploma in Security Studies. She returned to Washington in summer 1993 as Deputy Director for International Security and Peacekeeping Operations in the Bureau of

Political-Military Affairs. In August 1995 she began language training in Vietnamese. From January 1997 until July she served at the Embassy in Hanoi, Vietnam. In August 1997 she was assigned to open the U.S. Consulate General in Ho Chi Minh City where she was Acting Principal Officer until May 1998, then the Deputy until her May 1999 departure. In July 1999 she was Deputy Chief of Mission at the Embassy in Valletta, Malta. In September 2001 she became the Chief of Mission in Curaçao, Netherlands Antilles. From September 2004 until July 2007 she served as Political Advisor (POLAD) to the Commander, NORAD and U.S. Northern Command in Colorado Springs.

Ms. Bolton is the recipient of four Superior Honor Awards and one Meritorious Honor Award from the Department of State. From the Department of Defense she received the Chairman's Joint Distinguished Civilian Service medal and the Armed Forces Civilian Service medal. Her languages are Spanish, Hungarian, and Vietnamese. She is a member of the American Foreign Service Association and resides in Newport.

Rear Admiral William R. Burke, USN

Rear Admiral Burke, a native of Hornell, N.Y., graduated from the United States Naval Academy in 1978 with a Bachelor of Science in Systems Engineering. In 1985, he completed a Master's in Business Administration at Marymount University. In 1999, he earned a Master of Science in National Security Strategy at the National War College in Washington, D.C.

His first tour of duty was aboard USS Lafayette (SSBN 616) as a division officer. Subsequent assignments at sea included USS Key West (SSN 722) as the commissioning Weapons Officer, USS Omaha (SSN 692) as Navigator, and USS Cavalla (SSN 684) as Executive Officer. While on board Cavalla, he received the Admiral Chick Clarey Award for the 1992 Outstanding Navy Officer Afloat from the Honolulu Council of the Navy League.

Rear Admiral Burke served as Commanding Officer, USS Toledo (SSN 769) from September 1995 to June 1998. During his tour, Toledo completed Post Shakedown Availability, a Mediterranean deployment with the George Washington Battle Group, and earned the 1998 Battle Efficiency "E" Award.

He commanded Submarine Squadron 2 from July 2001 to July 2003.

Rear Admiral Burke's shore assignments included a tour in the Attack Submarine Division of the Staff of the Chief of Naval Operations and served on Capitol Hill as Assistant Deputy for House Liaison in the Navy Office of Legislative Affairs. He served on the Joint Staff as Chief of Training, Doctrine and Assessment Division and Assistant Deputy Director for Combating Terrorism (J34). He returned to the CNO staff in August 2003, serving in the Assessments Division (N81/N00X). His next tour was as the Executive Assistant to the Vice Chief of Naval Operations from June 2004 to July 2005. He recently served as Commander, Logistics Group Western Pacific/Commander, Task Force 73, headquartered in Singapore. He reported to his current assignment in September 2007.

Rear Admiral Burke wears the Defense Superior Service Medal, Legion of Merit (three awards), Meritorious Service Medals (three awards), the Navy Commendation Medal (four awards), and the Navy Achievement Medal (two awards).

Dr. Ashton B. Carter

Dr. Ashton B. Carter is Co-Director (with former Secretary of Defense William J. Perry) of the Preventive Defense Project, a research collaboration of Harvard and Stanford Universities. He is also chair of the International Relations, Security, and Science faculty at Harvard's John F. Kennedy School of Government.

Dr. Carter served as Assistant Secretary of Defense for International Security Policy during President Clinton's first term. His Pentagon responsibilities encompassed: countering weapons of mass destruction worldwide, oversight of the U.S. nuclear arsenal and missile defense programs, policy regarding the collapse of the former Soviet Union (including its nuclear weapons and other weapons of mass destruction), control over sensitive U.S. exports, and chairmanship of NATO's High Level Group. He directed military planning during the 1994 crisis over North Korea's nuclear weapons program; was instrumental in removing all nuclear weapons from the territories of Ukraine, Kazakstan, and Belarus; directed the establishment of defense and intelligence relationships with the countries of the former Soviet Union when the Cold War ended; and participated in the negotiations that led to the deployment of Russian troops as part of the Bosnia Peace Plan Implementation Force. Dr. Carter managed the multi-billion dollar Cooperative Threat Reduction (Nunn-Lugar) program to support elimination of nuclear, chemical, and biological weapons of the former Soviet Union, including the secret removal of 600 kilograms of highly enriched uranium from Kazakstan in the operation code-named Project Sapphire. Dr. Carter also directed the Nuclear Posture Review and oversaw the Department of Defense's (DOD's) Counterproliferation Initiative. He directed the reform of DOD's national security export controls. His arms control responsibilities included the agreement freezing North Korea's nuclear weapons program, the extension of the Nuclear Nonproliferation Treaty, the negotiation of the Comprehensive Test Ban Treaty, and matters involving the START II, ABM, CFE, and other arms control treaties.

Dr. Carter was twice awarded the Department of Defense Distinguished Service Medal, the highest award given by the Department. For his contributions to intelligence, he was awarded the Defense Intelligence Medal. In 1987 Carter was named one of Ten Outstanding Young Americans by the United States Jaycees. He received the American Physical Society's Forum Award for his contributions to physics and public policy.

A longtime member of the Defense Science Board and the Defense Policy Board, the principal advisory bodies to the Secretary of Defense, Dr. Carter continues to advise the U.S. government as a member of Secretary of State Condoleezza Rice's International Security Advisory Board, co-chair of the Senate Foreign Relations Committee's Policy Advisory Group, a consultant to the Defense Science Board, a member of the National Missile Defense White Team, and a member of the National Academy of Sciences Committee on International Security and Arms Control. In 1997 Dr. Carter co-chaired the Catastrophic Terrorism Study Group with former CIA Director John M. Deutch, which urged greater attention to terrorism. From 1998 to 2000, he was deputy to William J. Perry in the North Korea Policy Review and traveled with him to Pyongyang. In 2001–2002, he served on the National Academy of Sciences

Committee on Science and Technology for Countering Terrorism and advised on the creation of the Department of Homeland Security. He has testified frequently before the armed services, foreign relations, and homeland security committees of both houses of Congress.

In addition to his public service, Dr. Carter is currently a Senior Partner at Global Technology Partners and a member of the Board of Trustees of the MITRE Corporation, and the Advisory Boards of MIT's Lincoln Laboratories and the Draper Laboratory. He is a consultant to Goldman, Sachs and Mitretek Systems on international affairs and technology matters, and speaks frequently to business and policy audiences. Dr. Carter is also a member of the Aspen Strategy Group, the Council on Foreign Relations, the American Physical Society, the International Institute of Strategic Studies, and the National Committee on U.S.-China Relations. Dr. Carter was elected a Fellow of the American Academy of Arts and Sciences.

Dr. Carter's research focuses on the Preventive Defense Project, which designs and promotes security policies aimed at preventing the emergence of major new threats to the United States.

From 1990–1993, Dr. Carter was Director of the Center for Science and International Affairs at Harvard University's John F. Kennedy School of Government, and Chairman of the Editorial Board of International Security. Previously, he held positions at the Massachusetts Institute of Technology, the Congressional Office of Technology Assessment, and Rockefeller University.

Dr. Carter received bachelor's degrees in physics and in medieval history from Yale University, summa cum laude, Phi Beta Kappa. He received his doctorate in theoretical physics from Oxford University, where he was a Rhodes Scholar.

In addition to authoring numerous articles, scientific publications, government studies, and Congressional testimonies, Dr. Carter co-edited and co-authored eleven books, including *Keeping the Edge: Managing Defense for the Future* (2001), *Preventive Defense: A New Security Strategy for America* (1997), *Cooperative Denuclearization: From Pledges to Deeds* (1993), *A New Concept of Cooperative Security* (1992), *Beyond Spinoff: Military and Commercial Technologies in a Changing World* (1992), *Soviet Nuclear Fission: Control of the Nuclear Arsenal in a Disintegrating Soviet Union* (1991), *Managing Nuclear Operations* (1987), *Ballistic Missile Defense* (1984), and *Directed Energy Missile Defense in Space* (1984).

Information on Dr. Carter's current research is available at http://www.preventivedefenseproject.org.

Dean Cheng

Dean Cheng has been a senior analyst with Project Asia at the Center for Naval Analyses Corporation since 2001. He is a specialist on Chinese military issues, with a focus on Chinese military doctrine and Chinese space capabilities.

Prior to joining the Center for Naval Analyses, he was a senior analyst with Science Applications International Corporation (SAIC). From 1993–1995, he was an analyst with the U.S. Congress' Office of Technology Assessment, where he studied the Chinese defense industrial complex.

He has appeared frequently on CNN International, Voice of America, and National Public Radio to comment on Chinese space launches, and has been interviewed by the *Financial Times*, *Washington Post*, Phoenix TV (Hong Kong) and *South China Morning Post*, among others, regarding Chinese space and military activities.

He has written a number of papers and book chapters examining various aspects of Chinese security affairs, including Chinese military doctrine, the military and technological implications of the Chinese space program, and the dual-use nature of Chinese industrial and scientific infrastructure.

Recent publications include, "Space Power or *Taikong Quan*," *Spacepower: Foundational Precepts and Prospects,* "China's Space Program: A Historical Review," *Harnessing the Heavens: National Defense Through Space*, "The PLA and Joint Operations: Moving from Theory to Practice," in *Assessing the Threat*, ed. by Michael D. Swaine, Andrew N.D. Yang, et al., "Of Satellites and Stakeholders: China's ASAT Test," *Freeman Report*, "China's ASAT Test: Of Interceptors and Inkblots," *Space News*.

Lieutenant General David A. Deptula, USAF

Lt. Gen. David A. Deptula is the first Deputy Chief of Staff for Intelligence, Surveillance and Reconnaissance, Headquarters U.S. Air Force, Washington, D.C. He is responsible to the Secretary and Chief of Staff of the Air Force for policy formulation, planning, evaluation, oversight, and leadership of Air Force intelligence, surveillance and reconnaissance capabilities. As the Air Force's Senior Official of the Intelligence Community he is directly responsible to the Under Secretary of Defense for Intelligence.

General Deptula completed ROTC at the University of Virginia as a distinguished graduate in 1974, and remained to complete a master's degree in 1976. Earning his wings in 1977, he has flown more than 3,000 hours (400 in combat) to include multiple operational fighter command assignments. He has taken part in operations, planning, and joint warfighting at unit, major command, service headquarters and combatant command levels. He has served on two congressional commissions charged with outlining America's future defense posture—the Commission on Roles and Missions of the Armed Forces, and the National Defense Panel. Prior to assuming his current position, he served as Commander of the General George C. Kenney Warfighting Headquarters, and Vice Commander, Pacific Air Forces.

General Deptula has significant experience in combat and leadership in several major joint contingency operations. He was the principal attack planner for the Desert Storm coalition air campaign in 1991. He has twice been a Joint Task Force Commander—in 1998/1999 for Operation Northern Watch during a period of renewed Iraqi aggression where he flew 82 combat missions, and for Operation Deep Freeze, supporting forces in Antarctica. In 2001, the general served as Director of the Combined Air Operations Center for Operation Enduring Freedom, where he orchestrated air operations over Afghanistan during the period of decisive combat. In 2005, he was the Joint Force Air Component Commander for Operation Unified Assistance, the South Asia tsunami relief effort, and in 2006 he was the standing Joint Force Air Component Commander for Pacific Command.

General Deptula's major awards and decorations include the Defense Distinguished Service Medal, the Distinguished Service Medal with oak leaf cluster, the Defense Superior Service Medal with oak leaf cluster, the Legion of Merit, the Bronze Star Medal with oak leaf cluster, the Meritorious Service Medal with three oak leaf clusters, the Air Medal with four oak leaf clusters, the Aerial Achievement Medal, the Air Force Commendation Medal, and the Combat Readiness Medal with four oak leaf clusters.

E. Richard Diamond, Jr.

Dick Diamond is the Strategic Trends and Opportunities Analyst for Raytheon Integrated Defense Systems in Portsmouth, RI.

He came to Hughes Aircraft Company and then to Raytheon following a career in the U.S. Navy as a mostly overseas based cruiser-destroyer sailor, international negotiator, strategic planner and wargamer.

He is a graduate of the University of Dallas, Tulane University Graduate School and the U.S. Army Command and General Staff College. Dick attended Harvard's John F. Kennedy School of Government and Tuft's Fletcher School of Law and Diplomacy as a Federal Executive Fellow. He is currently an Adjunct Fellow of the Center for Strategic and International Studies (CSIS) in Washington, DC. In September 2006, he became a member of the London-based International Institute for Strategic Studies (IISS).

His commands at sea included USS KIRK (FF 1087) and USS BUNKER HILL (CG 52), both forward home ported in Yokosuka, Japan. During his numerous Washington, DC assignments, Dick founded the CNO's first Joint Operations and Doctrine Branch (OP-607), headed the Strategic Concepts Branch (OP-603) and initiated the Post Cold War strategic reviews, which produced the U.S. Navy's Future Vision Statements, "From the Sea" and "Forward From the Sea."

Although specializing now in alternative business futures, competitive assessments and national security trend analysis, Dick is continuing to build on more than twenty years of senior level wargaming and simulations management experience with the Joint Staff, Naval War College, NATO and various agencies of the Washington executive community. He recently acted as a principal author of the National Academies of Science Naval Studies Board's Sea Basing Study, the Commander THIRD Fleet Maritime Missile Defense Conops Study and helped to draft proposed legislative revisions for the Defense Acquisition Panel of "Beyond Goldwater-Nichols, Phase II" at CSIS. Current activities include traveling around the USA with the CNO New Maritime Strategy "Conversations with the Country" Briefing Team, helping to formulate the New Maritime Strategy and work on the NDIA Joint Integrated Air & Missile Defense Study.

Charles (Chuck) B. Dixon

Mr. Dixon is a Senior Managing Consultant with IBM Global Business Services. He is a member of the Navy Account Team focused on bringing solutions to the

Surface Warfare Enterprise. In support of IBM Public Sector efforts, Mr. Dixon brings his extensive experience in innovation and strategy, as well as maritime operations and strategy to IBM's Strategy and Change practice area.

Prior to joining IBM, Mr. Dixon served as a Naval Officer for over 27 years prior to retirement at the rank of Captain in 2006. During his Naval Career, Mr. Dixon served as nuclear trained surface warrior. His six sea tours included Command of the Guided Missile Frigate *HAWES* in Norfolk, Virginia and Command of the AEGIS Guided Missile Cruiser *COWPENS* in Yokosuka, Japan.

Mr. Dixon's shore assignments were in the Strategy and Policy arena. He served on the Navy Staff three times, as the Northeast Asia desk officer in N3/N5; as a staff member in support of the Chief of Naval Operations Executive Panel; and as the Deputy for Strategy and Policy in N3/N5. Outside Washington, Mr. Dixon was the first Assistant Chief of Staff for Operations, Plans and Policy when Commander, United States Naval Forces Southern Command was established in 2000.

A member of the United States Naval Academy class of 1979, Mr. Dixon earned a Bachelor of Science in Operations Analysis. He was selected as a 1995–1996 Federal Executive Fellow and assigned to The Fletcher School of Law and Diplomacy, Tufts University. During his fellowship he earned a Master of Arts degree in International Relations. Mr. Dixon served as a Chief of Naval Operations Fellow on the 2004–2005 Strategic Studies Group (SSG XXIV). In this role, he was one of nine hand-selected career officers conducting a ten-month study to develop innovative concepts relative to Navy's future role in combating terrorism and maintaining maritime security. Mr. Dixon and the group conducted extensive research in future trends, organizational change, and innovative solutions resulting in a comprehensive brief delivered to the Chief of Naval Operations, the Commandant of the Marine Corps, and the Commandant of the Coast Guard.

Dr. Peter Dombrowski

Dr. Peter Dombrowski is a professor of strategy at the Naval War College where he serves as the chair of the Strategic Research Department. Previous positions include director of the Naval War College Press, editor of the *Naval War College Review*, co-editor of *International Studies Quarterly*, Associate Professor of Political Science at Iowa State University and defense analyst at ANSER, Inc. He has also been affiliated with other research institutions including the East-West Center, The Brookings Institution, the Friedrich Ebert Foundation, and the Watson Institute for International Studies at Brown University among others. Dr. Dombrowski is the author of over thirty five articles, monographs, book chapters and government reports. He recently completed a book co-authored with Eugene Gholz, *Buying Military Transformation: Technological Innovation and the Defense Industry* (Columbia University Press, 2006). In 2005 he edited two volumes, *Guns and Butter: the Political Economy of the New International Security Environment* (Lynne Reinner, 2005) and *Naval Power in the Twenty-first Century: A Naval War College Review Reader* (Naval War College Press, 2005). Earlier books include *Policy Responses to the Globalization of American Banking* (University of Pittsburgh Press, 1996) and with Andrew Ross and Eugene

Gholz, Military Transformation and the Defense Industry After Next: The Defense Industrial Implications of Network-Centric Warfare (Naval War College Press, 2002). He received his B.A. from Williams College and an M.A. and Ph.D. from the University of Maryland. Awards include a Chancellor's Scholarship for Prospective Leaders from the Alexander von Humboldt Foundation in 1994 and the Navy Meritorious Civilian Service Medal in 2007 for his role in the development of the new Maritime Strategy.

Professor Roger H. Ducey

Roger H. Ducey teaches the Decision Making and Implementation and the Effective Command and Staff Officer curricula. Prior to his retirement from the Air Force in 2006, he taught in the National Security Decision Making and Joint Military Operations departments and served as the Senior Air Force Advisor to the Naval War College. He arrived in June 2002 from Grand Forks Air Force Base, North Dakota where he was the 319th Mission Support Group Commander.

He started his career as a missile launch officer, attended undergraduate pilot training, and spent the rest of his career flying KC-135A, R, R/T, and EC-135 aircraft. He served as operations officer and commander of the 99th Air Refueling Squadron, deputy commander, 19th Operations Group, and commanded deployments in support of Operations RESTORE HOPE, RESTORE DEMOCRACY, DELIBERATE FORCE, and DENY FLIGHT. Just before his arrival at the Naval War College he commanded the 319th Air Expeditionary Group (Provisional) deployed to Shaikh Isa Air Base, Bahrain in support of Operation ENDURING FREEDOM from October 2001 to March 2002. He served in various staff positions at Headquarters, Strategic Air Command and served as Deputy Chief, Aircrew Operations and Training Division, Headquarters, Air Mobility Command.

He holds a Bachelors of Business Administration Degree in International Finance from the University of Miami and Masters Degrees in Aviation Management from Embry-Riddle Aeronautical University and National Security and Strategic Studies from the U.S. Naval War College.

Dr. Thomas R. Fedyszyn

Dr. Thomas R. Fedyszyn is the course director for the strategy-oriented courses of the National Security Decision Making Department of the Naval War College. He joined the faculty after a 31-year Naval career, serving in six different cruisers and destroyers. His most recent military assignment was as the U.S. Naval Attaché to Russia. A former surface warrior, he commanded the USS Normandy (CG 60) and USS William V. Pratt (DDG 44). He served in numerous strategy, policy, and long-range planning billets for the Office of the Secretary of Defense and the Chief of Naval Operations and was a principal contributor to both the Lehman-era Maritime Strategy and NATO's New Strategic Concept following the Cold War. He received an M.A. and Ph.D. from the Johns Hopkins University in Political Science and was a member of the political science faculty at the U.S. Naval Academy. His most recent contributions have appeared in the *Providence Journal* and the U.S. Naval Institute *Proceedings*.

He specializes in NATO, naval strategy, and Russian security affairs. His most recent research interest is the Indian Navy.

Michèle Flournoy

Michèle Flournoy was appointed President of the Center for a New American Security (CNAS) in January 2007. Prior to co-founding CNAS, she was a Senior Adviser at the Center for Strategic and International Studies, where she worked on a broad range of defense policy and international security issues. Previously, she was a distinguished research professor at the Institute for National Strategic Studies at the National Defense University (NDU), where she founded and led the university's Quadrennial Defense Review (QDR) working group, which was chartered by the chairman of the Joint Chiefs of Staff to develop intellectual capital in preparation for the Department of Defense's 2001 QDR. Prior to joining NDU, she was dual-hatted as Principal Deputy Assistant Secretary of Defense for Strategy and Threat Reduction and Deputy Assistant Secretary of Defense for Strategy. In that capacity, she oversaw three policy offices in the Office of the Secretary of Defense: Strategy; Requirements, Plans, and Counterproliferation; and Russia, Ukraine, and Eurasian Affairs. Ms. Flournoy was awarded the Secretary of Defense Medal for Outstanding Public Service in 1996, the Department of Defense Medal for Distinguished Public Service in 1998, and the Chairman of the Joint Chiefs of Staff's Joint Distinguished Civilian Service Award in 2000. She is a member of the Aspen Strategy Group, the Council on Foreign Relations, the International Institute of Strategic Studies, and the Executive Board of Women in International Security. She is a former member of the Defense Policy Board and the Defense Science Board Task Force on Transformation. In addition to several edited volumes and reports, she has authored dozens of articles on international security issues. Ms. Flournoy holds a B.A. in social studies from Harvard University and an M.Litt. in international relations from Balliol College, Oxford University, where she was a Newton-Tatum scholar.

Dr. J. Michael Gilmore

Dr. Gilmore is the Assistant Director for National Security in the Congressional Budget Office (CBO). He is responsible for CBO's National Security Division, which performs analyses of major policy and program issues in national defense, international affairs, and veterans affairs. He holds a Ph.D. in nuclear engineering from the University of Wisconsin, Madison, Wisconsin and a B.Sc. in physics from the Massachusetts Institute of Technology.

Prior to joining CBO, Dr. Gilmore worked for 11 years in the Office of the Secretary of Defense, Program Analysis and Evaluation (OSD(PA&E)), first as an analyst responsible for missile defense and communications programs and ultimately as Deputy Director of OSD(PA&E) for General Purpose Programs.

Prior to his employment in the government, Dr. Gilmore was an analyst, and later manager for Electronic Systems Company activities in the McDonnell Douglas Washington Studies and Analysis Group. He also worked as an analyst at Falcon Associates, a defense consulting firm and as a scientist in the magnetic fusion energy program at the Lawrence Livermore National Laboratory.

Captain R. Robinson Harris, USN (Retired)

Captain Harris retired from the U.S. Navy in 1998 after 30 years of commissioned service. A Surface Warfare Officer, he served in a number of surface combatants and aircraft carriers. He first sea assignment was as Guided Missile Officer in USS ENTERPRISE (CVAN 65) in which he deployed to the Western Pacific. After attending Department Head school he was briefly assigned as Operations Officer in USS BRUMBY (FF 1044) and deployed to Northern Europe. Next he was assigned to USS SEMMES (DDG 18) as Operations Officer and deployed to the Mediterranean in the JOHN F. KENNEDY Battle Group. His next assignment was Material Officer and Special Assistant to the Commander, Cruiser Destroyer Group EIGHT (SARATOGA Battle Group) and again deployed to the Mediterranean. His next sea tour was Executive Officer of USS TATTNALL (DDG 19) in which he deployed to the Persian Gulf. His first command was one of the first TOMAHAWK Strike Destroyers, USS CONOLLY (DD 979), in which he deployed to the Mediterranean and Black Seas. His major command was DESTROYER SQUADRON 32 in which he deployed to UNITAS 32 and BALTOPS.

Captain Harris' shore assignments include: Assistant Professor, NROTC Unit, University of North Carolina, Chapel Hill; Long Range Planner, Chief of Naval Operations Executive Panel; Executive Assistant to the Assistant to the Chairman, Joint Chiefs of Staff; Director of Programs, SECNAV Office of Legislative Affairs; and, lastly, Executive Director, Chief of Naval Operations Executive Panel.

He was a key contributor to the development and author of the *Maritime Strategy* in the 1980s. He also developed and was the author of the CNO's strategy statement *Anytime, Anywhere* in 1997.

Since retiring from the Navy, Captain Harris has worked for Lockheed Martin where he currently serves as Director of Advanced Concepts for Lockheed Martin Maritime Systems and Sensors in Washington D.C. Since assuming his current position, he has led seminars, workshops, and wargames pertaining to the Navy's "3-1 Strategy," "1000 Ship Navy," "Global Fleet Stations," Riverine Warfare, and, most recently, The New Maritime Strategy. All these efforts have included leaders from the U.S. Navy, other military Services, academia, think tanks, and industry. Most recently he collaboratively worked with NAVSOUTH, USSOUTHCOM, the Center for Naval Analyses, State Department, the U.S. Coast Guard, OPNAV, the U.S. Marine Corps, and various Non-Governmental Organizations to develop the Global Maritime Partnership and Global Fleet Station concepts. He has met with the Flag Ship Commanding Officer and DESRON Commander who conducted Africa Operations for COMNAVEUR in 2006, in order to gain a set of lessons learned for possible application to the Global Fleet Station concept.

Captain Harris is a published author, having published 20 articles in the U.S. Naval Institute *Proceedings* and *Naval War College Review*. Also, he was the principal author of the Department of the Navy Posture Statements for the U.S. Congress in 1984, 1985, 1996, 1997, and 1998. He currently serves as an Adviser to the CNO Strategic Studies Group, and he is Chairman of the Board of Directors of the Baltimore Council on Foreign Affairs.

Captain Harris holds a bachelor's degree in history and political science from Pfeiffer University in North Carolina. He holds an MA degree in Political Science from the University of Georgia, and he completed his PhD studies in Policy Analysis at the University of North Carolina. He is a graduate of the Massachusetts Institute of Technology program for senior executives, SEMINAR 21; and the University of London Program in Arms Control. He was a CNO Fellow on the CNO Strategic Studies Group (SSG 12).

Dr. Thomas C. Hone

Professor Thomas C. Hone joined the faculty of the Naval War College in August 2006. He was an Assistant Director of the Office of Force Transformation in the Office of the Secretary of Defense (OSD) from the summer of 2003 to the summer of 2006. In 2001–2002, he was Principal Deputy Director of the Office of Program Analysis and Evaluation in OSD. He holds a PhD from the University of Wisconsin-Madison, and is a graduate of the Program Manager's Course of the Defense Acquisition University. He has taught at the Naval War College (1985–86) and at the Industrial College of the Armed Forces (1999–2001). He also served in the Partnership for Peace Program with the European Command in Germany, and was a special assistant to the Commander of the Naval Air Systems Command. He is the author or co-author of 5 books and over 30 articles. His awards include the Air Force Exceptional Civilian Service Award, the Navy Meritorious Civilian Service Medal, and the Department of Defense Exceptional Civilian Service Award.

Donna L. Hopkins

Donna Hopkins heads the Plans and Policy Team in the Office of Plans, Policy, and Analysis in the Bureau of Political and Military Affairs. She joined the Foreign Service in 1998, serving in Warsaw, Poland, the Bureau of European and Eurasian Affairs, and the Office of Weapons Removal and Abatement in Washington, D.C. before transferring in 2003 to the Civil Service. Ms. Hopkins and her team specialize in national security, defense, and interagency issues relating to foreign policy. She also serves as the PM Bureau's strategic planner, preparing and coordinating strategic and performance planning documents related to foreign policy, foreign assistance, and Congressional budget development and justification. She is the recipient of Superior and Meritorious Honor Awards from State, and was the peer-nominated Political Military Officer of the Year in 2006.

Having entered on active duty in the United States Navy in 1976, Ms. Hopkins became one of the first female naval officers to serve on ships at sea after the Combat Exclusion law was repealed in 1979. She qualified as a Surface Warfare Officer and served on three ships and an afloat group staff before transferring to the Naval Reserve in 1988. She was recalled to active duty during Operations Desert Shield/Desert Storm, Provide Promise, and Joint Endeavor. She has commanded six reserve units and holds the rank of Captain. In 1997, Ms. Hopkins earned a Masters Degree (with Highest Distinction) in National Security and Strategic Studies from the Naval War College in Newport, Rhode Island, and is a graduate of the first Advanced Joint Professional Military Education course conducted by the Joint Forces Staff College. She has been awarded the Defense

Superior Service Medal, Legion of Merit, Defense Meritorious Service Medal, three Navy Commendation Medals, and various unit and campaign medals.

Ms. Hopkins is married to John Hopkins, a retired naval officer and currently a senior information technology specialist with the Department of State. They have two grown children and reside in the District of Columbia.

Dr. Timothy D. Hoyt

Dr. Timothy D. Hoyt is a Professor of Strategy and Policy at the U.S. Naval War College, where he lectures on strategy, terrorism, counterinsurgency, military transformation, weapons of mass destruction, and contemporary conflict, and also teaches an elective course on South Asian security with Dr. Andrew Winner. He received his undergraduate degrees from Swarthmore College, and his Ph.D. in International Relations and Strategic Studies from The Johns Hopkins University's Paul H. Nitze School of Advanced International Studies in 1997. Previously, Professor Hoyt taught graduate courses on security in the developing world, South Asian security, technology and international security, and military strategy at Georgetown University's School of Foreign Service. He has served as an employee or consultant with the U.S. government and intelligence community, and is actively involved in Track Two diplomatic projects with India and Pakistan. In October 2003, he testified before two subcommittees of the House Committee on International Relations regarding terrorism in South and Southwest Asia. Dr. Hoyt's recent publications include chapters and articles on the war on terrorism in South Asia, security and conflict in the developing world, the limits of military force in the global war on terrorism, the evolution of Kashmir as a nuclear flashpoint, Pakistani nuclear doctrine and strategic thought, the U.S. maritime strategy, the impact of culture and ethnicity on Iraq's conventional military capabilities, and the impact of nuclear weapons on recent crises in South Asia. He is the author of Military Industries and Regional Defense Policy (Routledge, 2007), examining the role of military industry in the national security policies of India, Israel, and Iraq, and is beginning work on several book-length projects including an analysis of American military strategy in the 21st century (London: Polity Press, publications anticipated 2008) and a study of the strategy of the Irish Republican Army from 1913–2005. He is also the Assistant Editor of the Journal of Strategic Studies.

Captain Kevin C. Hutcheson, USN

A native of Horseheads, NY, Captain Hutcheson was commissioned in 1981 upon graduation from the University of Rochester through the NROTC program and was designated a Naval Aviator in 1983.

He has served five sea tours with units in the Atlantic and Pacific fleets and the Forward Deployed Naval Forces in Japan, and has participated in seven deployments to the Indian Ocean, Western Pacific, Mediterranean, and the Arabian Gulf. From 1999–2000 he was the Commanding Officer of Strike Fighter Squadron 27 an F/A-18 squadron in Atsugi, Japan forward deployed aboard USS Kitty Hawk. From 2004–2005 he was the operations officer for Carrier Strike Group SIX aboard USS John F. Kennedy.

Captain Hutcheson has accumulated over 3800 flight hours in the A-7E, and F/A-18C and has over 1000 carrier arrested landings.

Captain Hutcheson's shore assignments include duty at the Arms Control and Disarmament Agency where he was an action officer involved with the negotiation and implementation of the Convention on the Prohibition of Chemical Weapons and the Treaty on Open Skies. He was the deputy office director for the Office of Conventional Weapons, Bureau of Arms Control at the U.S. Department of State and routinely participated on the U.S. delegation to the Organization for Security and Cooperation in Europe (OSCE).

In 2006, Captain Hutcheson was assigned as the Deputy Foreign Policy Advisor and Interagency Liaison Officer to the Commander Combined Joint Task Force Horn of Africa located at Camp Lemonier, Djibouti. Subsequently, he was the Senior Liaison Officer for the Commander Combined Joint Task Force Horn of Africa to the Commander U.S. Central Command located at MacDill AFB, Tampa, Florida.

He holds a Bachelor of Science in Mechanical Engineering from the University of Rochester, a Masters of Arts in National Security and Strategic Studies from the Naval Command and Staff College, Newport, RI. In addition he was a Federal Executive Fellow at the Weatherhead Center for International Affairs at Harvard University in 2000–2001.

Captain Hutcheson is currently the Interagency Integration Division Chief in the Interagency Partnering Directorate (J9) at U.S. Southern Command located in Miami, Florida.

Dr. Bradford A. Lee

Bradford A. Lee is a Professor of Strategy at the Naval War College. Born in Charlottesville, Virginia, he received his B.A. from Yale University, where he played on a nationally ranked football team, pitched on the baseball team, and produced a senior thesis that was published as a book by Stanford University Press. He earned his Ph.D. as a Mellon Fellow at Cambridge University in the United Kingdom and then held a three-year post-doctoral fellowship in the prestigious Society of Fellows at Harvard University, during which time he did historical research on the Great Depression and World War II and language study in Chinese and Japanese.

Lee then served as a history professor for eight years at Harvard, winning the Levenson Memorial Prize as the best teacher among assistant and associate professors in the Faculty of Arts and Sciences. He taught a course on American–East Asian relations that went beyond the usual study of economic, diplomatic, and military interactions to explore the transmission and reception of ideas and images across the cultural divide of the Pacific; on average, one-quarter of all Harvard undergraduates took this course in their four years at the university. While at Harvard, Lee published studies on a broad array of subjects: military strategy, foreign policy, the domestic politics of national priorities, and macroeconomic theory and policy.

Lee joined the Naval War College faculty in 1987 and began to focus in a more specialized way on issues of military strategy. His most recent publications are a book of essays, *Strategic Logic and Political Rationality*, which he co-edited with Karl Walling and to which he contributed a piece on the recurring strategic problems that the United States has experienced in terminating its wars in a manner that produces durable political results; and a piece on "The Cold War as a Coalition Struggle" in Bruce Elleman and S.C. M. Paine, eds., *Naval Coalition Warfare*. He is currently at work on a long book entitled *On Winning Wars*.

Dr. Richmond M. Lloyd

Dr. Richmond M. Lloyd is a member of the Security, Strategy, and Forces faculty in the National Security Decision Making Department and holds the William B. Ruger Chair of National Security Economics. He is the chair for the U.S. Naval War College's Latin American Studies Group, which coordinates all college activities in Latin America. His research and teaching interests include strategy and force planning, national security and economics, defense and international economics, and logistics. He is coeditor of nine textbooks for the Naval War College on strategy and force planning, and is editor of the William B. Ruger Chair of National Security Economics Papers. He lectures on contemporary national defense topics at various sites throughout the United States and South America. He chaired the Naval War College's self-study efforts that led to congressional authorization for the college to award an M.A. degree in national security and strategic studies and to the accreditation of this degree. He received a Ph.D. in business administration and a B.S. in mechanical engineering from the University of Rochester, and an M.B.A. from the University of Chicago.

Colonel H.R. McMaster, USA

Colonel H.R. McMaster is Senior Research Associate at the International Institute for Strategic Studies in London and Special Assistant to Commander, MNF-I. He was commissioned as an officer in the United States Army upon graduation from the United States Military Academy in 1984. He holds a PhD in military history from the University of North Carolina at Chapel Hill.

Colonel McMaster has held a variety of command and staff positions in armored and cavalry units including command of a cavalry troop in the 1991 Persian Gulf War, command of a cavalry squadron in Schweinfurt Germany from 1999 to 2002, and command of the 3d Armored Cavalry Regiment at Fort Carson, Colorado and in Iraq from June 2004 to June 2006. From May 2003 to May 2004 he served as Director, Commander's Advisory Group at U.S. Central Command. Colonel McMaster's military education and training includes the Airborne and Ranger Schools, the Armor Officer Basic and Career Courses, the Cavalry Leader's Course, the Combined Armed Services Staff School, Command and General Staff College, and a U.S. Army War College fellowship at the Hoover Institution on War, Revolution, and Peace.

Colonel McMaster served as an assistant professor of history at the United States Military Academy from 1994 to 1996. He has published numerous articles on military history and national security affairs. His book, *Dereliction of Duty: Lyndon Johnson, Robert McNamara, the Joint Chiefs of Staff, and the Lies that Led to Vietnam*, was published in 1997. His monograph, "Crack in the

Foundation: Defense Transformation and the Underlying Assumption of Dominant Knowledge in Future War," was published in 2003.

Vice Admiral K. K. Nayyar, Indian Navy (Retired)

Admiral Nayyar, the former Vice Chief of the Indian Navy, has the rare distinction of having commanded both the Western and the Eastern Fleets of the Indian Navy. He also served as the Commander-in-Chief of the Southern Naval Command. He has also been closely connected with planning the growth of the modern Indian navy, having served as Director Naval Plans and Assistant Chief of Naval Staff Policy & Plans.

Post-retirement, Admiral Nayyar has been a member of the National Security Advisory Board and a Member of the Government Committee on Defence Expenditure. Currently he is the Chairman of the National Maritime Foundation and the Forum for Strategic and Security Studies, a New Dehli based think-tank dealing with national and international relations, the global security environment, Confidence Building Measures and defence economics. He is also a keen student of India's domestic political scene.

Admiral Nayyar is on the board of a number of corporations and has lectured extensively in India, the United States, Japan, the United Kingdom, Germany, Turkey, China, Iran, Nigeria, and the Asia-Pacific.

Ronald O'Rourke

Mr. O'Rourke is a Phi Beta Kappa graduate of the Johns Hopkins University, from which he received his B.A. in international studies, and a valedictorian graduate of the University's Paul Nitze School of Advanced International Studies, where he received his M.A. in the same field.

Since 1984, Mr. O'Rourke has worked as a naval analyst for the Congressional Research Service of the Library of Congress. He has written numerous reports for Congress on various issues relating to the Navy. He regularly briefs Members of Congress and Congressional staffers, and has testified before Congressional committees on several occasions.

In 1996, Mr. O'Rourke received a Distinguished Service Award from the Library of Congress for his service to Congress on naval issues.

Mr. O'Rourke is the author of several journal articles on naval issues, and is a past winner of the U.S. Naval Institute's Arleigh Burke essay contest. He has given presentations on Navy-related issues to a variety of audiences in government, industry and academia.

Dr. Mackubin Thomas Owens

Dr. Owens is Associate Dean of Academics for Electives and Directed Research and Professor of National Security Affairs at the U.S. Naval War College in Newport, Rhode Island, and editor-designate of the quarterly journal *Orbis*. He specializes in the planning of U.S. strategy and forces, especially naval and power projection forces; the political economy of national security; national security organization; strategic geography; and American civil-military relations. In addition to the core course on strategy and force planning, he teaches electives on The American Founding, Strategy and Policy of the American Civil War, The Statesmanship of Abraham Lincoln, Sea Power and Maritime Strategy, Strategy and Geography, and U.S. Civil-Military Relations. From 1990 to 1997, Dr. Owens was Editor-in-Chief of the quarterly defense journal *Strategic Review* and Adjunct Professor of International Relations at Boston University.

Dr. Owens is a senior fellow of the Foreign Policy Research Institute in Philadelphia, as well as a contributing editor to *National Review Online*. His articles have appeared in many publications, including *International Security, Orbis, Armed Forces Journal, National Review, The New York Times, The Los Angeles Times, The Christian Science Monitor,* the *Jerusalem Post,* and *The Wall Street Journal*. He currently is working on a book for the University Press of Kentucky tentatively entitled *Sword of Republican Empire: A History of US Civil-Military Relations*.

Before joining the faculty of the War College, Dr. Owens served as National Security Adviser to Senator Bob Kasten, Republican of Wisconsin, and Director of Legislative Affairs for the Nuclear Weapons Programs of the Department of Energy during the Reagan administration. Dr. Owens is also a Marine Corps veteran of Vietnam, where as an infantry platoon commander in 1968–1969, he was wounded twice and awarded the Silver Star medal. He retired from the Marine Corps Reserve as a Colonel in 1994.

Dr. Owens earned his Ph.D. in Politics from the University of Dallas, a Master of Arts in Economics from Oklahoma University, and his BA from the University of California at Santa Barbara. He has taught at the University of Rhode Island, the University of Dallas, Catholic University, Ashland University of Ohio, and the Marine Corps' School of Advanced Warfighting (SAW). He has been a Senior Visiting Fellow at the Center for Naval Analyses and a consultant to the Los Alamos National Laboratory; Plans Division, Headquarters Marine Corps; and J-5 Strategy, the Joint Staff.

Rear Admiral Frank Pandolfe, USN

Rear Admiral Frank Pandolfe graduated with distinction from the U.S. Naval Academy in 1980 and earned his Doctor of Philosophy in International Relations from the Fletcher School of Law and Diplomacy at Tufts University in 1987.

At sea, Rear Adm. Pandolfe served as Combat Information Center Officer and Auxiliaries Engineer in USS *David R. Ray* (DD 971); Operations Officer in USS *John Hancock* (DD 981); Assistant Surface Operations Officer on the staff of Commander, Carrier Group 6; and Executive Officer in USS *Hue City* (CG 66). Rear Adm. Pandolfe commanded USS *Mitscher* (DDG 57) from 1999–2001, earning three Battle Efficiency Awards, three U.S. Atlantic Fleet Golden Anchor Awards for Retention Excellence, the Chief of Naval Operations Environmental Protection Award, and the Naval Surface Force, U.S. Atlantic Fleet Self-Sufficiency Award. He commanded Destroyer Squadron 18 from March 2003–March 2004, operating as Sea Combat Commander for the *Enterprise* Carrier Strike Group, deploying to the Arabian Gulf in support of Operations *Iraqi Freedom* and *Enduring Freedom*.

Ashore, Rear Adm. Pandolfe served as an Action Officer in the Strategic Plans and Policy Directorate (J-5) of the Joint Staff, followed by a tour as

Military Aide and Advisor to the Vice President of the United States. He later headed the OPNAV Strategic Concepts Branch and served as Deputy Executive Assistant to the Chief of Naval Operations. From 2001–2003, Rear Adm. Pandolfe was Special Assistant to the Chief of Naval Operations, leading the *Sea Power 21* project. From July 2004–June 2005, he served as Executive Assistant to the Chief of Naval Operations.

Rear Adm. Pandolfe's first flag officer assignment was Deputy Director for Strategy and Policy, J-5, Joint Staff, Washington, D.C. In that role, he was responsible to the Chairman of the Joint Chiefs of Staff for the development and review of the National Military Strategy and policies related to Service and combatant command authorities and responsibilities.

Rear Adm. Pandolfe assumed command of *Theodore Roosevelt* Carrier Strike Group/Carrier Strike Group 2 on Sept. 14, 2007.

His personal awards include the Defense Superior Service Medal, Legion of Merit, Meritorious Service Medal, Joint Service Commendation Medal, Navy Commendation Medal, and Navy Achievement Medal.

Professor Gwyn Prins

Professor Gwyn Prins is the director of the LSE Mackinder Centre for the Study of Long Wave Events. At Cambridge he took a Double First and has an MA and PhD in History. He was first elected to a Fellowship in 1976 and was elected a Fellow of the Royal Historical Society in 1984. He joined LSE in 2000 successively as Professorial Research Fellow and then (2002–2007) took the first stint as the first Alliance Research Professor jointly at LSE and Columbia University, New York. Previously, for over twenty years he was a Fellow, Tutor and the Director of Studies in History at Emmanuel College, Cambridge. He was a University Lecturer in Politics.

Dr. Derek S. Reveron

Derek S. Reveron is an associate professor of National Security Affairs at the Naval War College in Newport Rhode Island. He received an M.A. in political science and a Ph.D. in public policy analysis from the University of Illinois at Chicago. He specializes in democratization, post-conflict reconstruction, and intelligence. He is the author of *Promoting Democracy in the Post-Soviet Region* (2002), the editor of America's *Viceroys: the Military and U.S. Foreign Policy* (2004), and numerous book chapters and articles that have appeared in *Orbis, Defense and Security Analysis, International Journal of Intelligence and Counterinsurgency, Low Intensity Conflict & Law Enforcement*, and the *National Review Online*. Additionally, he sits on the editorial board for the *Defense Intelligence Journal*. Before joining the Naval War College faculty, Dr. Reveron taught political science at the Joint Military Intelligence College, National Defense University, and the U.S. Naval Academy.

Commander Thomas C. Sass, USN

Commander Thomas C. Sass, USN reported to the Naval War College as the Special Operations Forces Chair in September 2007 after completing his tour as Commanding Officer SEAL Delivery Vehicle Team ONE in Pearl Harbor, Hawaii. He completed Basic Underwater SEAL Training in June 1988 with Class 151. He was subsequently assigned to SEAL Team THREE from 1988 to 1992 where he served as a SEAL Platoon Commander. Upon completion of the Basic Italian Language Course at the Defense Language Institute in 1993, he was assigned as an Exchange Officer with the Italian Naval Commando Unit in La Spezia, Italy. He returned to the Naval Special Warfare Center in 1995 for SEAL Delivery Vehicle School and follow-on assignment to SEAL Delivery Vehicle Task Unit Commander and Department Head on board the USS JAMES K. POLK (SSN 645). From August 1998 to December 2000, he served as an operations and plans officer on the Joint Staff in the Operations Directorate, Special Operations Division. In January 2001, he reported on board Naval Special Warfare Unit TWO, the maritime component command of Special Operations Command Europe, as the Executive Officer. From January 2002 to June 2003, he served as the Flag Aide to the Commander, United States Naval Forces Europe and Commander in Chief, Allied Forces South. Commander Sass earned a Masters of Public Administration degree from the John F. Kennedy School of Government at Harvard University in 1998. He completed his duties as the U.S. Navy Admiral Arthur S. Moreau Scholar while assigned to the Fletcher School of Law and Diplomacy at Tufts University from June 2003 to July 2005 where he earned a Masters of Law and Diplomacy and completed requirements for a PhD (ABD).

David A. Shlapak

David Shlapak is a Senior Policy Analyst with the RAND Corporation in Pittsburgh, PA.

He joined RAND at its Santa Monica, CA headquarters in 1982 as a research assistant, helping design and build the RAND Strategy Assessment System, an ambitious computer modeling and gaming tool developed for the Office of Net Assessment. After transferring to RAND's Washington, DC location in 1986, he worked on and led a wide array of studies on topics ranging from nuclear strategy and air campaign planning to protecting air bases from guerrilla and terrorist attacks.

Beginning in the late 1990s, Shlapak helped RAND Project AIR FORCE (PAF) establish a continuing stream of studies on the strategic challenges presented by the rise of China and has published on the military and strategic aspects of the China-Taiwan confrontation and the Sino-U.S. security relationship.

Shlapak moved to RAND's then-embryonic Pittsburgh office in 2001. He has recently led or been involved in several studies aimed at defining the nature of the "post–post–Cold War" security environment and scoping the demands it will make on the joint force. He is currently leading a RAND-funded project on the implications of a proliferated world for U.S. grand strategy.

Shlapak served as Associate Director of PAF's Strategy and Doctrine Program for five years starting in 2002 and was acting Program Director from October 2006 through January 2007. He is a graduate of Northwestern University and pursued graduate education at the UCLA. He and his wife, Belinda, a business systems analyst, share their 130-year-old rowhouse on Pittsburgh's North Side with seven cats.

Shlapak is author or co-author of numerous RAND publications, including *The United States and a Rising China: Strategic and Military Implications*; *The United States and Asia: Toward a New U.S. Strategy and Force Posture*; *Dire Strait?: Military Aspects of the China-Taiwan Confrontation and Options for U.S. Policy*; *A Global Access Strategy for the U.S. Air Force*; *U.S.-China Relations After Resolution of Taiwan's Status*; *Shaping the Future Air Force*; and *A New Division of Labor: Meeting America's Security Challenges Beyond Iraq*.

Dr. Richard Shultz

Professor Richard H. Shultz, Jr. is Professor of International Politics at The Fletcher School, Tufts University where he teaches graduate level courses in various aspects of international security. He is also the Director of The Fletcher School's International Security Studies Program. The program is dedicated to graduate level teaching and research on a broad range of conflict, defense, and strategic issues. Since 2003 he has directed the Armed Groups Project for the Washington-based National Strategy Information Center. The project seeks to understand the complex nature of armed groups and explore approaches for meeting these challenges. His recent books include *Insurgents, Terrorists, and Militias: The Warriors of Contemporary Combat* (Columbia University Press, 2006) and *The Secret War Against Hanoi: Kennedy and Johnson's Use of Spies, Saboteurs, and Covert Warriors in North Vietnam* (New York: Harper Collins, 1999, paperback 2000). He has a forthcoming monograph titled *Global Insurgency Strategy and the Salafi Jihad Movement* (Boulder, CO: Institute for National Security Studies U.S. Air Force Academy, 2008).

Professor Sean C. Sullivan

Sean C. Sullivan is an Assistant Professor of National Security Affairs at the United States Naval War College in Newport Rhode Island. He is assigned to the National Security Decision Making Department teaching the Policy Making and Process course. He is a subject matter expert on defense planning and the Department of Defense Formal Resource Allocation processes. Professor Sullivan coordinates all curriculum development on Defense Resource Allocation and is the author of numerous related articles, readings, and case studies on formal defense planning processes.

A retired naval officer, Sean Sullivan served in the United States Navy for twenty-three years. He served at sea in the Pacific for over fifteen years in various surface combatants, amphibious ships, and afloat staffs. He deployed five times to the Western Pacific and Arabian Gulf and once to the South Eastern Pacific Ocean.

Sean Sullivan holds a B.A. in Political Science from the University of Rochester and a M.A. in National Security and Strategic Studies from the Naval War College.

Dr. Geoffrey Till

Geoffrey Till is the Professor of Maritime Studies at the Joint Services Command and Staff College and a member of the Defence Studies Department, part of the War Studies Group of King's College London. He is the Director of the Corbett Centre for Maritime Policy Studies.

In addition to many articles and chapters on various aspects of maritime strategy and policy defence, he is the author of a number of books. His most recent are a major study *Seapower: A Guide for the 21st Century* for Frank Cass, published in 2004 [completed with the aid of a research grant from the British Academy] and *The Development of British Naval Thinking* published by Routledge in 2006. He has completed a major study of the impact of globalisation on naval development especially in the Asia-Pacific region. This will appear next year as an Adelphi paper for the International Institute for Strategic Studies, London. His works have been translated into 9 languages, and he regularly speaks at staff colleges and academic conferences around the world.

Professor Till has just completed a study of maritime security in Southeast Asia at the Rajaratnam School of International Studies at the Nanyang Technological University, Singapore, where he was a Senior Fellow. In 2008, he will be taking up the Kippenberger Visiting Chair at the University of Victoria, Wellington, New Zealand.

Dr. David Tucker

David Tucker is an Associate Professor in the Department of Defense Analysis and Co-Director of the Center on Terrorism and Irregular Warfare at the Naval Postgraduate School, Monterey, California. Before coming to the Postgraduate School, he served in the Office of the Assistant Secretary of Defense for Special Operations and Low-Intensity Conflict as the Deputy Director for Special Operations and as a Foreign Service Officer in Africa and Europe. He received his Ph.D. from the Claremont Graduate School and is a member of the Board of Visitors of the Marine Corps University and the Ashbrook Center, Ashland University. His most recent publications are *U.S. Special Operations Forces*, with Christopher Lamb (Columbia University Press, August 2007); *Confronting the Unconventional: Innovation and Transformation in Military Affairs* (Strategic Studies Institute, U.S. Army War College, October 2006).

Barry D. Watts

Mr. Barry D. Watts is a Senior Fellow at the Center for Strategic and Budgetary Assessments (CSBA), where he focuses on net assessment, airpower and the emergence of guided munitions, Air Force transformation, net assessment, and the military use of space.

Mr. Watts was the Pentagon's director for Program Analysis and Evaluation from May 2001 to June 2002. Prior to this 13-month stint advising Secretaries Rumsfeld and Wolfowitz on issues such as Crusader and transformation, Mr. Watts directed the Northrop Grumman Analysis Center. He also headed the Gulf War Air Power Survey's work on operations and effectiveness. Mr. Watts' USAF career included a combat tour in Southeast Asia with the 8th Tactical

Fighter Wing, subsequent F-4 assignments in Japan and Okinawa as an F-4 Wild Weasel aircraft commander, teaching philosophy and mathematical logic at the U.S. Air Force Academy, two tours in the office of the Director of Net Assessment where he worked on Korean and NATO–Warsaw Pact balance assessments, and a tour as a Soviet threat specialist (and later Red team chief) in the Air Staff's Project Checkmate.

Mr. Watts' published writings span such topics: as air-to-air combat tactics ("Fire, Movement, and Tactics," *Topgun Journal*, Winter 1979/80); measures of effectiveness (with James G. Roche, "Choosing Analytic Measures," *Journal of Strategic Studies*, June 1991); the effectiveness of Coalition air power in the 1991 Persian Gulf War (with Thomas Keaney, *Part II: Effects and Effectiveness*, Vol. II, *Gulf War Air Power Survey: Operations and Effects*, U.S. Government Printing Office, 1993); friction in war (*Clausewitzian Friction and Future War*, National Defense University Press, rev. ed. 2004, McNair Paper No. 68); military innovation during 1918–1939 (with Williamson Murray, "Military Innovation in Peacetime," Chapter 10 of *Military Innovation during the Interwar Years*, ed. Allan Millet and Williamson Murray, Cambridge University Press, 1996); military competition in near-earth space (*The Military Use of Space: A Diagnostic Assessment*, CSBA, February 2001); Air Force plans for anti-access/area-denial environments (with Andrew Krepinevich and Robert Work *Meeting the Anti-Access and Area-Denial Challenge*, CSBA, 2003); U.S. needs for long-range strike systems (*Long-Range Strike: Imperatives, Urgency and Options*, CSBA, 2005); and, the emergence of precision munitions since the 1940s (*Six Decades of Guided Munitions and Battle Networks: Progress and Prospects*, CSBA, 2007). He is currently working on the intellectual history of the Office of Net Assessment (ONA) since 1973, including a source book of seminal writings on diagnostic net assessment and ONA's view of the debate over revolutions in military affairs. In 2006 Mr. Watts also produced an assessment of military training and officer education for ONA. He is an adjunct professor in Georgetown University's security studies program, where he has taught a course on net assessment and strategic thinking.

Mr. Watts received an MA (philosophy) from the University of Pittsburgh and his BS (mathematics) from the U.S. Air Force Academy. He lives with his wife, the former Hope Algieri, in Bethesda, MD.

Dr. Cindy Williams

Cindy Williams is a Principal Research Scientist of the Security Studies Program at the Massachusetts Institute of Technology. Her work at MIT includes an examination of the processes by which the U.S. government plans for and allocates resources among the activities related to national security and international affairs and an examination of the transition to all-volunteer forces in the militaries of several European countries. Formerly she was an Assistant Director of the Congressional Budget Office, where she led the National Security Division in studies of budgetary and policy choices related to defense and international security. Dr. Williams has served as a director and in other capacities at the MITRE Corporation in Bedford, Massachusetts; as a member of the Senior Executive Service in the Office of the Secretary of Defense at the

Pentagon; and as a mathematician at RAND in Santa Monica, California. Her areas of specialization include the U.S. national security budget, military personnel policy, and command and control of military forces.

Dr. Williams holds a Ph.D. in mathematics from the University of California, Irvine. She has published in the areas of command and control and the defense budget. She is the editor of *Holding the Line: U.S. Defense Alternatives for the Early 21st Century* (MIT Press 2001) and *Filling the Ranks: Transforming the U.S. Military Personnel System* (MIT Press 2004) and is co-editor of *Service to Country: Personnel Policy and the Transformation of Western Militaries* (MIT Press 2007). She is an elected fellow of the National Academy of Public Administration and a member of the Naval Studies Board, the Council on Foreign Relations, and the International Institute of Strategic Studies. She serves on the advisory council of Women in International Security and on the editorial board of *International Security*.

Robert O. Work

Robert O. Work is the Vice President for Strategic Studies at the Center for Strategic and Budgetary Assessments (CSBA). He retired from the Marine Corps in September, 2001, after 27 years of active service. He served in a variety of command and staff positions. His last assignment was as Senior Aide and Military Assistant to the Honorable Richard J. Danzig, 71st Secretary of the Navy.

Mr. Work's areas of expertise include defense strategy, defense transformation, and maritime affairs. He has written several monographs on naval transformation, including papers on the Littoral Combat Ship, future fleet platform architectures, seabasing, and naval unmanned combat air systems. He has also prepared a series of reports on the future defense challenges, including the changing nature of undersea warfare; irregular warfare; power projection against regional nuclear powers; and power projection against future anti-access/area denial networks. He directs an extensive wargaming effort for the Office of Net Assessment, Office of the Secretary of Defense, which includes games that study near- to mid-term strategic challenges and future military regimes, as well as defense portfolio balancing options. He contributed to DoD studies on global basing and emerging military missions and provided support for the 2006 Quadrennial Defense Review.

Mr. Work has a Bachelor of Science in Biology from the University of Illinois; a Masters of Science in Systems Management from the University of Southern California; a Masters of Science in Space Operations from the Naval Postgraduate School; and a Masters in International Public Policy from the Johns Hopkins School of Advance International Studies. He is an Adjunct Professor at George Washington University, where he teaches defense analysis and roles and missions of the armed forces, and a visiting instructor at the National Defense University and Canadian Forces College.

GPO U.S. GOVERNMENT PRINTING OFFICE: 2008- 700-508